Communist China's Economic Growth and Foreign Trade

Communist China's Economic Growth and Foreign Trade

Implications for U.S. Policy

ALEXANDER ECKSTEIN

A VOLUME IN THE SERIES,
"THE UNITED STATES AND CHINA IN WORLD AFFAIRS"

PUBLISHED FOR THE COUNCIL ON FOREIGN RELATIONS BY

McGRAW-HILL BOOK COMPANY

New York · Toronto · London

COMMUNIST CHINA'S ECONOMIC GROWTH AND FOREIGN TRADE:
Implications for U.S. Policy

Copyright © 1966 by Council on Foreign Relations, Inc.
All Rights Reserved. Printed in the United States of America.
This book, or parts thereof, may not be reproduced in any form without permission of the Proprietor, Council on Foreign Relations, 58 East 68th Street, New York, N.Y. 10021
Library of Congress Catalog Card Number: 65-28588
23456789 VB 10987
18975

To Ruth and Bob

Foreword

This book is one in a series on The United States and China in World Affairs being published by the Council on Foreign Relations as part of a three-year program, begun in 1962 under a generous grant from the Ford Foundation. This program comprises studies and publications arranged by the Council to encourage more active and better informed public consideration of one of the most important areas of foreign policy with which the United States must deal.

The Council's program, which has been guided by a Steering Committee under the chairmanship of Allen W. Dulles, does not aspire to produce a single and simple set of conclusions. The phenomenon of China's role in the world, including the question of Taiwan, is far too complex for that. Each study in this series therefore constitutes a separate and self-contained inquiry written on the responsibility of its author, who has reached his own judgments and conclusions regarding the subject of his investigation and its implications for United States policy. The authors include persons with a variety of backgrounds in Chinese affairs and foreign policy. Some have had long personal experience in China. Others have studied China and Far Eastern problems during recent years or dealt with them as officials and administrators. They represent a variety of viewpoints, and each author has been able to consult from time to time with a group of individuals invited by the Council on Foreign Relations to meet with him.

Any discussion of United States relations with China must take into account developments on the mainland of China, what the Chinese Communists have been able to achieve, and their future prospects. The economy of the country is necessarily a major preoccupation of the government, for on its further development may depend the stability and permanence of the Communist regime and its ability to fulfill its foreign policy goals. The country's economic plans are also interrelated with its foreign trade, an important part of its external relations. All these questions bear on United States policy toward China—particularly on the existing embargo and trade controls.

There are many obstacles which hamper a full understanding of these matters. Often the interpretation of the economic situation in Communist China has been distorted by the wishful thinking of both those who are looking eagerly for signs of failure and those who are inclined to an optimistic view of what goes on there. There are also the obstacles which the Chinese Communists themselves erect to prevent free contacts between foreigners and Chinese and the controls they place on the flow to the outside world of information about developments on the mainland. Statistical information is often unavailable or slanted and unsatisfactory for analytical purposes. Despite these difficulties, much progress has been made in recent years in assembling, analyzing, and interpreting the available information. A continuing effort needs to be made to improve and expand the work that is being done in these directions.

The author of the present book, Dr. Alexander Eckstein, is one of the leading American scholars in the field of Communist China's economic development. Dr. Eckstein, who is professor of economics at the University of Michigan, is author of *The National Income of Communist China* and of numerous monographs and articles on related subjects. He is a member of the Joint Committee of the Social Science Research Council and the American Council of Learned Societies for the Study of Contemporary China and a former member of the Board of Directors of the Association of Asian Studies.

ROBERT BLUM,* Study Director
The United States and China in World Affairs

* The work on this volume was substantially completed and the Foreword written before Dr. Blum's untimely death. Professor Lucian Pye, Massachusetts Institute of Technology, succeeded Dr. Blum.

Preface

The idea for this book originated with Philip Mosely, who impressed upon me the need to revise and bring up to date my study of Sino-Soviet economic relations in *Moscow-Peking Axis*, published by the Council on Foreign Relations in 1957. I then set to work with the generous assistance of a grant to the Council by the Ralph E. Ogden Foundation. As I began to delve into the subject, it became apparent that an analysis of Sino-Soviet economic relations ought to be set in the broader context of Communist China's economic development and the role of foreign trade in that development. Professor Mosely was most sympathetic to this reorientation, and I want to acknowledge my intellectual and personal debt to him for his ever ready counsel and encouragement.

As my own approach to this topic crystallized, the Council initiated a new program of studies on the United States and China in World Affairs under the direction of Robert Blum. The new program then also sponsored the research and writing of this book. I am deeply indebted to Dr. Blum for his support, gentle prodding, and valuable comments and criticism. It is a tragedy indeed that his sudden death has not permitted him to see this project through to the publication stage.

I owe a special debt of gratitude to William Diebold, Jr., who has gone through the whole manuscript most carefully, pointed out a number of shortcomings, made most valuable comments, and in the final stages saw the manuscript through to the publication stage. David Albright was a most conscientious, careful, and hard-working editor who has done a great deal to improve the readability of this study. Helena Stalson was most helpful in checking on a number of technical points, testing the consistency of the data in the different tables, and thus significantly contributing to the betterment of the final draft.

During the 1963/64 academic year I was on leave from my duties at the University of Michigan, and that is when the largest share of the work on this book was completed. Because of the one- to two-year lag in the publication of most national statistics, data at that time were available only through 1962. As new data became available, I tried to bring the information up to date. Thus, most tables in the book now include series up through 1963. In some cases, however, the data for 1963 are preliminary. It is quite possible that by the time this book is published some of the statistics for 1963, and the occasional data concerning developments in 1964 and 1965, will be revised in the official statistical sources. Therefore, the most recent data should be treated with even greater caution than those for the period up through 1962. In the final stages of this study, I had an opportunity to visit Tokyo and Hong Kong and consult with China specialists in universities, government, and trading firms. I would like to express my appreciation to them for giving me so generously of their time and sharing their observations with me. They were kind enough to give me some information and data which though not classified are not readily available. Occasionally I drew on these sources without specifically citing them.

In completing this work, I was greatly aided by a study group under the chairmanship of August Maffry. Their searching questions and criticism contributed considerably to the improvement of the manuscript between the first and second drafts. The members of the group were: A. Doak Barnett, Robert Barnett, Joseph Berliner, Alexander D. Calhoun, Jerome B. Cohen, Arthur Dean, William Diebold, Jr., Arthur Dommen, Tillman Durdin, Samuel B. Griffith, A. M. Halpern, Edwin F. Jones, William W. Lockwood, Wilfred Malenbaum, Richard Moorsteen, Judd Polk, Peter Schran, and Harry Schwartz. Edwin Jones, drawing on his great wealth of knowledge about the Chinese economy, was particularly helpful on a number of specific points of fact. The members of the group, of course, bear no responsibility for statements in the book.

I also profited greatly from the comments of Abram Bergson, Morris Bornstein, Cheng Chu-yuan, Chao Kang, Gregory Grossman, Simon Kuznets, and Robert Stern, who read different chapters or parts of the book. As always, my discussions with Professor Ishikawa Shigeru concerning problems of mainland China's economic development proved most helpful, and I want hereby to thank him for giving me so generously of his time on the occasion of my visit to Tokyo.

I also wish to acknowledge with thanks the research assistance of Fred Surls and Robert Thorpe, who rendered yeoman's service in collecting some of the basic data, checking calculations, and doing a variety of other chores. Through her editorial assistance, Mrs. Grace Beardsley made a significant contribution to stylistic improvements. Last but not least, let me acknowledge the invaluable help of Mrs. Ruth Drilling Pashman and Miss Adrienne Sullivan in typing, collating, and generally keeping things moving.

ALEXANDER ECKSTEIN

Ann Arbor
June 1965

Contents

Tables

Figures

CHAPTER ONE

An Analytical Framework

Fifteen years of Communist rule in China have produced a united, totalitarian state on the mainland. It is a state led by an elite with a compelling urge to develop China into a major industrial and military power in the shortest possible time. To this end, it has pushed for rapid industrialization, particularly the growth of heavy industry, at the expense of agriculture. Its relentless pursuit of this objective has led to a more or less cyclical pattern of economic growth, characterized by spurts and halts, and is in large part responsible for the prolonged and acute economic crisis of the early 1960s.

The sharpening of Sino-Soviet differences during the crisis and the general slowdown in the pace of economic advance which resulted from the crisis suggest the need to re-assess the character of Communist China's economic development and its relationship to the nation's foreign policy. In a sense, the problem before us is twofold: What effect, if any, did or may economic development have upon the policy of the Chinese Communists, and what new threats or opportunities face U.S. and Soviet policy makers as a result? Theoretically, economic development of an underdeveloped Soviet-type economy such as China's could shape the character and effectiveness of the country's foreign policy in at least three ways: through its effect on the country's potential to wage war, through its effect on the country's capacity to expand international economic

1

relations, and through the possible appeal of its development model to other underdeveloped areas.

The Power Aspect of Communist China's Economic Development

It would be fair to say that the postwar drive for the economic development of underdeveloped areas has been fed mainly by strong and virulent nationalism and by a striving for higher standards of living. It would seem that the more dictatorial and totalitarian the auspices under which development takes place, the greater is the accent on nationalism and power at the expense of people's standards of living. This tendency is pronounced in Communist China, where policy makers, more or less uninhibited by the exercise of consumer sovereignty, have tried to impose their own preferences as between present and future consumption. However, as the Soviet example suggests, it is difficult if not impossible to deprive the consumer indefinitely of the fruits of industrialization, even in totalitarian states. Sooner or later, at more advanced stages of industrialization, the functional requirements of the system, operating through the effects of incentives upon labor productivity and a variety of much more subtle social transformations and influences, seem to demand significant concessions to the consumer sector. In the Soviet Union, where the collectivization debacle and World War II intervened, this process took about 35 years. It is, of course, impossible to forecast how long it might take in Communist China.

Mainland China's development—at least up to 1959—was particularly notable in the iron and steel, electric power, coal, cement, chemical, and engineering industries, *i.e.*, the branches most intimately linked with military potential. Simultaneously, the railway network was extended to encompass heretofore untouched areas, particularly in West China. These new trunk and feeder lines brought the different parts of the subcontinent much closer to each other. Moreover, they facilitated political control and economic interchange and established one of the essential preconditions for speedy economic and military mobilization.

Thus, after 10 years of Communist rule, China had developed an industrial base which far outstripped that of India and was catching up with that of Japan in some sectors. From a power standpoint, this growing industrial capacity was reinforced by the country's vast population. Despite the economic reverses of the early sixties, therefore, China is rapidly emerging as a major power in Asia, although in world terms it still remains a second-rate power.

At the same time, the food crisis of the early 1960s served to dramatize the fact that China's rising industrial strength may be undermined by stagnation in agriculture. If the regime continues to show enough flexibility to correct its mistakes in agricultural policy, of course, the setback in agriculture may turn out to be temporary. On the other hand, if the food crisis should assume chronic proportions, the regime in desperation may be driven to pursue an adventurist foreign policy. Thus, the propensity for aggression may rise at a time when capability is diminished.

From the long-run perspective, China may be expected to present both the United States and the Soviet Union with a most pressing foreign policy problem. The reason may lie precisely in the fact that China's industrial base, if we assume there is no agricultural breakdown, will be large enough to enable her to pursue a bold, aggressive, and expansionist foreign policy, but too small to assure her high output, income, and consumption per capita.

The Foreign Aid and Trade Aspect

A country may have a number of weapons at its disposal for the pursuit of its foreign policy. Some of these more or less clearly involve economic factors. Thus, as industrialization contributes to growing military prowess, it raises a government's capacity to use threats as one of the instruments of its foreign policy. Similarly, foreign economic relations can be used as prime weapons for political friendship or warfare.

International economic and political relations may be linked through four alternate or mutually complementary channels: exports, imports, foreign aid extended, and foreign aid received. In the case of Communist China each of these is of importance insofar as it affects her dependence on other countries, or vice versa. Foreign aid received constituted an important element in Sino-Soviet relations, while foreign aid extended is of considerable importance in China's relations with some Communist countries as well as with some underdeveloped neutralist countries. On the other hand, China's exports and imports are spread over a much wider range of countries than her foreign aid programs, and the effects in different areas vary widely.

Each of these elements in China's international economic relations will be analyzed in considerable detail in this study. Therefore, at this stage only an attempt to define the problems and the issues to be investigated will be made.

As far as foreign trade is concerned, one of the outstanding characteristics of the past has been the intimacy of relations between China and other Communist countries, most particularly the Soviet Union. This relationship was a function of close ideological and political bonds, reinforced by Western embargoes and controls on trade with China. Because of these controls, the Soviet Union and its European satellites became China's sole suppliers of military hardware, of many types of machinery, and of a whole range of other capital goods. This situation unquestionably placed China in a position of economic dependence vis-à-vis Russia.

Economic dependence was reinforced by the large-scale foreign aid which China received from the Soviet Union between 1950 and 1955. One of the most interesting and crucial questions about this aid is whether it ceased upon Soviet or Chinese initiative. That is, should one view Chinese repayments of Soviet credits, repayments which began in 1955, as a symptom of Russian niggardliness or of a Chinese urge to emancipate themselves from the Soviets? Did the aid to China impose such a burden on the Soviet economy that it amounted to a substitution of Chinese for Russian economic growth and thereby lead to resentment and irritation on the part of the Soviet leadership? Or did the Soviets possibly deny the Chinese aid for political reasons? Did the Chinese Communist leadership feel that China's rapid industrial expansion in the early fifties—an expansion made possible largely by Soviet aid—had placed the economy in such a strong position that it could stand on its own two feet? Or, on the contrary, has large-scale Soviet aid to India and other neutrals, at a time when China was receiving no new credits and was required to amortize her debts to the Soviet Union, evoked Chinese resentment?

In any case, while all the available evidence suggests that the Western embargoes and trade controls had at most a marginal effect upon China's economic development, they unquestionably pushed the Soviet Union and China closer together. Whether this involuntary aspect of their intimacy has been a divisive or cohesive factor in the Sino-Soviet alliance is another problem which will be explored in the later chapters of this book.

The trade control issue looms particularly large in China's relations with Japan. A considerable body of Japanese opinion sees in China a coveted export market and a valuable source of raw materials for its industries. Apart from their economic merits, to be investigated later, China trade controls have loomed large as a political issue in Japan—an issue that the Chinese Communists have tried to use as a means of obtaining *de facto* recognition and as a wedge for manipulating internal political forces in Japan. When their efforts to overthrow the Kishi government were frustrated in early 1958, they mounted a major trade offensive in Southeast Asia to try to drive Japan out of the markets of these countries. The offensive could not be sustained, however, because China was unable to meet the export commitments it had made. In effect, this failure meant that the economy of mainland China had not yet reached a stage of development where the Chinese could at short notice and with impunity conduct economic warfare on such a large scale.

Particularly since 1955, China has actively pursued trade relations with a number of underdeveloped countries in Asia, Africa, and Latin America. In many of these cases, the motivation seems to have been at least as much political as economic or commercial. In part, such trade may be designed to present an image abroad of a rapidly industrializing and expanding China which can become a supplier not only of textiles, fountain pens, and bicycles but of capital goods as well—a China able to compete with Russia for economic and political influence.

Similar motives are reflected in China's program of aid to uncommitted, underdeveloped countries. In addition, the Chinese use foreign aid to increase their influence in some Communist countries or to assure themselves a dominant position in certain areas. North Korea and North Vietnam could be cited as examples of the latter, while Albania and to a lesser extent Cuba could serve as illustrations of the former.

The Appeal of the Chinese Communist Development Model

Rapid industrialization not only augments a country's military potential and widens its latitude in using economic inducements in the conduct of its foreign relations but also enhances the appeal of its development strategy in other underdeveloped areas. While China's agricultural crisis of the early 1960s is likely to tarnish its appeal as a development model, this setback may be at least partly counterbalanced by conscious attempts to picture China as a dynamic force successfully building a power-oriented industrial base. The spirit of frugality and sacrifice coupled with high rates of saving and investment, the large allocations of investment to heavy industry, and the emphasis on catching up rapidly with the West are all elements of the strategy which have a strong potential appeal in newly emerging nation-states.

Of course, the same elements are more or less present in the Soviet case. Therefore, the success of Communist China's specific appeal will first of all depend upon her ability to sustain a rapid rate of industrialization over an extended period. On the other hand, geographic and cultural proximity may favor the Chinese in some instances (*e.g.*, Japan). In addition, China's stage of development, the recent vintage of her efforts at deliberate industrialization, and her experience of foreign domination over a long period bring her closer than Russia to many of the uncommitted countries of the underdeveloped world. The extent to which she can in fact exploit these potential advantages over Russia depends, of course, upon the success of her development strategy at home, the changing character of her relations with the Soviet Union, and her posture, policy, and tactics in these underdeveloped countries.

Of the three aspects of China's economic development cited above—the power effect, the trade effect, and the model effect—this study will focus largely on the second. First, the character and pattern of China's economic development since 1949 will be analyzed. Next, the role of imports in the expansion of industrial capacity will be explored. Then the impact of domestic economic development upon rising export capacity will be traced. The expansion of exports has served two general ends: the financing of imports to provide the essential wherewithal for industrialization and the use of trade for political purposes. Both these elements will be examined. Finally, the policy implications for the United States of these interrelated domestic and foreign economic activities, including the power and model effects, will be appraised.

CHAPTER TWO

Preconditions and Strategy for Economic Development in Communist China

The economic policies and performance of the People's Republic will be appraised in this and the next chapter against the background of China's economic heritage. Necessarily, this heritage circumscribed the direction and the speed at which the mainland economy could travel under Communist auspices. At the same time, the character of actual economic performance, its spurts and halts, affected Communist China's foreign policy capabilities in all of the three ways spelled out in Chapter 1: through its effect on the country's military capabilities; its effect on the volume, direction, and commodity composition of foreign trade; and its possible appeal to other countries as a development model for imitation.

Clearly, rapid economic development with particular emphasis on the growth of heavy industry and uninterrupted by slow-downs or crises could provide the underpinning for the gradual rise of a large and well-equipped defense establishment. On the other hand, agricultural difficulties and a subsequent crisis in food supply would not only curtail the pace of industrialization and thus reduce military supply capabilities but could also weaken the morale of the party cadres, the army, and the population at large. Achievement of a rapid pace of development would be accompanied by at least some foreign trade expansion, because of both rising import demand and increased export capacity. It could also augment China's ability to extend foreign aid. Therefore, rapid economic development would enhance the country's capacity to use international economic relations as an instrument of foreign policy. Naturally, an economic decline leading to a contraction in foreign trade would have the opposite effect.

Bearing these considerations in mind, Chinese planners concentrated on expanding as rapidly as possible the country's capacity to produce capital goods and military matériel. To attain this goal, they fashioned instruments to institutionalize a high rate of involuntary saving and channel the savings into selected lines of investment.[1] To this end and to mobilize and allocate resources quickly and with maximum flexibility, all segments of the economy had to be brought under the firm and direct control of the planners. Agrarian transformation; nationalization of banking, transport, industry, and trade; centralization of fiscal administration; rationing; price and wage control; and a variety of other regulations were all designed to achieve this objective. The extent to which the planners' design could be implemented and the objectives in fact attained will be examined below.

The Inherited Economy

Upon their conquest of the Chinese mainland, the Communists inherited what were essentially three different economies: the economy of traditional China still holding sway over most of the mainland; the more or less modernized, urbanized, and commercialized economy of the treaty ports; and the comparatively advanced and rapidly industrializing economy of Manchuria.

The traditional sector, largely rural, bore the earmarks of a backward and stagnant economy caught in a vicious circle of poverty. Both the capacity and the inducement to save and invest were lacking. The high population pressure upon arable land resources, compounded by prevailing inheritance practices and a lack of non-farm employment opportunities, led to a continuous fragmentation and pulverization of land holdings. This situation was aggravated by inequalities in farm size; 60 per cent of the farms averaged less than 3 acres.

The high-density farm population could be maintained only

by intensive land use, based on double-cropping of vast areas and age-old soil conservation and irrigation practices. The crop yields were high. They actually exceeded the levels attained in Meiji Japan, though they lagged appreciably behind those attained in Japan today. This fact suggests that crop production in China has been pushed about as far as traditional practices and methods will permit and that, as in Japan, large improvements in farm output can be attained only through the introduction of new technology and improved practices.

While yields per acre were relatively high, yields per man were quite low. Because of the high density of the farm population, limited alternatives for outside employment, and small size of farms, underemployment in agriculture was widespread. Traditionally, all these factors combined have kept the Chinese peasant at the bare margin of subsistence. Because of this very closeness to the margin, most peasants were unable to save enough to provide a cushion for meeting extraordinary expenditures necessitated by natural disasters or ceremonial obligations, such as weddings or burials. Such expenditures were for the most part covered by borrowing at high interest rates. These rates were justified by the high risks which the lender incurred; however, they greatly increased the peasants' burden and frequently led to land sales or sales of surface rights in land to repay the loans. Thus, a vicious spiral was created. At one end, the peasant resorted to credit for financing consumption rather than production, and at the other, the landlord, trader, and native lender accumulated capital but channeled it into consumption credit or land purchases and speculation. In effect, the process of capital accumulation—which rested on collection of land rent and interest, land speculation, and trade—was made possible by squeezing the peasant's narrow margin. In turn, to keep the peasant alive, at least some of the funds had to be channeled back to him in the form of consumer credit and land purchase.[2] As a result, the net saving and investment of China's traditional farm economy was negligible.

This narrow, circular-flow pattern greatly hampered the participation of the rural economy in the commercial sector and favored the persistence of a self-sufficient household way of life.

Inadequate and costly transport also was one of the key factors limiting the scope of the market. Because of the scanty railroad network, a large share of trade was carried by primitive modes of transport. These appear cheap per day but are expensive per mile.[3] Yet the pattern of rural self-sufficiency was not nearly as complete as has frequently been supposed. Agricultural families probably purchased more than one-quarter of the goods they consumed. The bulk of the farm products marketed was exchanged within the same county, and only an estimated 8 per cent was shipped to distant urban markets.

Consequently, China exhibited a highly cellular marketing pattern with wide interregional scarcity and price differentials. Frequent local famines were a reflection of this high degree of fragmentation. All these problems were greatly aggravated by civil strife and the lack of administrative unity.

At the risk of oversimplification, one can view the treaty ports as essentially creatures of and vehicles for the penetration of Western commerce into 19th-century China. In this sense, they were but a symptom of the general expansion of the world economy into hitherto isolated areas. As was the case with so many other countries, foreign trade served as the highway over which many of the disequilibrating forces and tendencies were introduced into the stagnant and underdeveloped economy of traditional China. While in several countries, of which Japan is perhaps the outstanding example, the challenge posed by the new forces served as a stimulus to economic change and growth, in China it led only to an abortive "take-off" during the period of the "self-strengthening" movement. The dynamic response was long delayed, and when it came, it was clothed in the robes of Communist totalitarianism.

In the meantime, economic growth in the treaty ports sector itself was quite rapid. The rise in foreign trade led to an expansion of shipping, banking, warehousing, and public and other services. The flowering of these branches of the economy then further stimulated foreign trade. Subsequently, after the Treaty of Shimonoseki (1895) opened the way for the building and operation of foreign-owned factories in the treaty ports, modern industry developed. During this period, cotton textile imports increased appreciably with the decrease in costs of overseas transport and the low-cost production of factory-made cotton yarn in India. These increased imports undermined the position of rural handicrafts, particularly the hand-spinning of yarn, and created a market for manufactured textile products. In turn, the growing demand for manufactured textiles provided the impetus for the development of a cotton textile industry within China, an industry which, as in many other economies, took the lead in the process of industrialization. The emergence of this cotton textile industry was followed by the rise of other consumer goods industries—flour mills, cigarette and match factories, and others—which developed as a by-product of foreign trade. At the same time, power plants and light engineering works, as well as railroads, were built to service these new industries.

This entire commercial and industrial complex remained confined largely to the periphery of the Chinese economy; it was linked to the traditional sector through domestic trade. In effect, the links between these two economic sectors may not have been much firmer than those which are typical for two distinct economies engaged in foreign trade. As a result, the treaty ports sector was never fused with but was simply grafted on to the traditional economy of "earthbound China."

A favorable population-resource balance, combined with Japanese skill in organization and management, led, between 1931 and 1943, to rapid industrial growth and development of the Manchurian economy. Compared with China proper, Manchuria had many of the features of an undeveloped frontier rather than an overcrowded and underdeveloped area. It was sparsely populated and, relative to China, richly endowed with forest, land, and mineral resources. With this combination of favorable resources and institutional conditions, industry grew rapidly under the stimulus of Japanese capital imports, entrepreneurship, and comprehensive planning for economic development.

Between the early 1930s and 1943, pig iron production doubled, the output of coal rose two and a half times, power capacity quadrupled, and cement production multiplied fivefold.[4] At the end of this period, Manchuria, with only about one-tenth of the mainland area, had one-third of mainland railway mileage, 40 per cent of its coal production, close to 70 per cent of its power capacity, more than 70 per cent of its cement, 85 per cent of its pig iron, and more than 90 per cent of its steel production. The pattern of Manchurian economic development presented a sharp contrast to that which had evolved in the treaty ports sector. Manchuria had emerged as a heavy-industry base, modest in relation to the country's size and population but nevertheless of substantial proportions, while the treaty ports remained the center of the light consumer goods industries.

These three economies, although more or less linked through trade, had developed separately and had definite political and institutional barriers between them—a situation which hampered economic integration and fusion. The breaking down of these barriers devolved upon the Communists, who were determined to harness the resources of each part in order to organize what, in effect, became a new economic entity. Of course their task was greatly facilitated by the termination of civil conflict and by the administrative unification of the country.

At the time of the Chinese Communist takeover in 1949, all three segments of the mainland economy were badly disrupted under the impact of prolonged civil war and Soviet dismantling of industrial plants in Manchuria. The most urgent problems facing the new regime were to restore agricultural production and to rehabilitate industrial plants and transport. At the same time, the institutional framework had to be restructured to bring every sector of the economy under the control of the planning authorities. With these preparatory tasks out of the way, the regime apparently felt ready to launch its First Five Year Plan.[5]

It is clear that although there were significant local variations, the broad outlines of the envisaged development pattern more or less followed the Soviet example, at least until 1957. This fact, however, raises the question of whether the preconditions for development were similar in China and in Russia. Specifically, by 1952 what state of development had mainland China's economy attained as compared to that of the Soviet economy on the eve of its First Five Year Plan in 1928? What advantages, if any, did the Chinese Communists enjoy as compared to their Soviet counterparts of 1928, and under what disadvantages did they labor? It is to an exploration of these questions that we now turn.

The Preconditions

In terms of a number of major indicators, mainland China of 1952 was comparable to Meiji Japan and to contemporary India —perhaps somewhat ahead of the former and slightly behind the latter, but she lagged considerably behind the Japan of the early 1950s and the Soviet Union on the eve of its First Five Year Plan.[6] To assess the preconditions for a Soviet-type development in mainland China, these findings need to be investigated further.

CHINA'S RESOURCES. The Chinese mainland population was officially estimated at about 540 million in 1949 and almost 650 million in 1957.[7] These figures would suggest that the population was growing at an average annual rate of 2.2 per cent and that an additional 14-15 million mouths had to be fed each year. In general, it is a young population with a high proportion of children, so the ratio of consumers to producers is comparatively high. Although urban population was increasing rapidly as of 1957, only 14 per cent of the people lived in cities.[8]

The mainland Chinese are settled over a land area that is slightly larger than the United States (about 3.7 million square miles as compared to 3.6 million for the United States, including Alaska and Hawaii) and much smaller than the U.S.S.R. The problem of population pressure is aggravated by the fact that 66 per cent of China's land area consists of plateaus and mountain ranges, 9 per cent of hills, 15 per cent of river basins, and only 10 per cent of alluvial plains. Moreover, rainfall in vast areas of the country is low. It ranges from 0 to 6 or 7 inches in the arid northwest and from 7 to 10 inches in the semi-arid western section of North China. Because of mountainous terrain and low rainfall, much of the land is unsuitable for agriculture. As a result, in 1957 less than 12 per cent of the total land area of

Communist China was under cultivation. Even according to the most optimistic official estimates no more than 20 per cent seems cultivable.[9]

These data, then, strongly suggest that in relation to her population China's farmland resources are severely limited. Historically, this limitation has been partially overcome in southern China by double-cropping and irrigation. Through intensive methods of cultivation, careful husbandry, and large-scale use of manure, the Chinese peasant attained relatively high unit yields with his pre-modern technology. Nevertheless, current crop yields in China are one-third to one-half below contemporary Japanese levels. The latter, however, are based on the intensive application of chemical fertilizer and other practices drawing on advances in the agricultural sciences. Therefore, if China's farm production is to be increased, much greater reliance than heretofore will have to be placed on modern methods of farm husbandry.

Mainland China seems much better endowed with energy than with agricultural resources—particularly in respect to coal and water power. Estimated potential coal reserves have been revised upward as the result of better and more comprehensive geological exploration. Figures on such reserves are necessarily elusive, yet there is no doubt that new deposits have been uncovered. Almost every province in Communist China has some amount of coal. However, before 1949, almost 84 per cent of these reserves were estimated to be in the northern part of the country. China's coal seems to be of fairly high quality with 77 per cent bituminous, 19 per cent anthracite, and 4 per cent lignite.[10] Communist China also possesses vast water power resources.

Of course, in the case of both coal and water power, converting reserves to actual production requires considerable investment in mining, in power-generating facilities, and in the development of transport and electric-power distribution. What this fact suggests is that the prime limitation upon energy output in China is not reserves but their accessibility on the one hand and the availability of capital on the other.

This conclusion is less applicable to petroleum. Formerly

thought to be poor in this resource, China, as the result of most energetic exploration, has uncovered new oil fields and identified new potential reserves. Nevertheless, her oil-producing potential is considerably less than that for coal or water power. It would seem that presently operating fields combined with known reserves would be more than sufficient to satisfy domestic requirements of the near future if adequate refining capacity, technology for the production of high-quality fuels, and transport for the distribution of petroleum and petroleum products were available. Thus, for the time being, while China's consumption of oil products is still comparatively low, reserves should be adequate to meet her domestic crude oil requirements.

Mainland China's energy resources, therefore, apparently present no obstacle to the country's industrial development. Of course, because of the backward state of the economy, these resources have been only partially tapped. The demand for energy is modest due to the comparatively low level of industrialization, which at the same time limits the capacity to expand the output of the energy-producing branches. As a result, China's developed energy supply in 1959 was about one-eighth that of the United States and slightly more than one-fourth that of the U.S.S.R. On a per capita basis, this gap is even larger. For the same year, China's per capita output was only a little more than 3 per cent of that in the United States and less than 10 per cent of that in the Soviet Union.[11]

Generally, mineral resources too are adequate for industrial expansion on the mainland. Thus, China is well endowed with iron ore and has large deposits of manganese and tungsten and lesser reserves of other non-ferrous metals.

OTHER CONDITIONING FACTORS.   While there are broad similarities in the conception and direction of Chinese and Soviet development policies, there are considerable differences in implementation. These are a function of: (1) differences in the resources of Russia and China, (2) differences in the origins and histories of the two Communist parties, (3) the circumstances under which the two regimes came to power, and (4) the existence of a crystallized Communist development model from which China could draw certain lessons concerning measures and policies to emulate as well as to avoid and upon which she could lean for economic support, at least for a while.

Both countries are vast in size with a diversity of natural resources and large internal markets. On the basis of presently available evidence, Russia would seem to be significantly better endowed with mineral resources, particularly oil, but this difference may stem partly from the fact that mainland China is not as well explored geologically as the Soviet Union. Unquestionably, however, the most important characteristic that distinguishes one country from the other is population dynamics. The population of China around 1952 was almost four times that of Russia around 1928. At the same time, her population pressure per acre of cultivated land was almost tenfold that of Russia. This fact, however, had through a process of age-long adaptation induced the Chinese to cultivate the land much more intensively than the Russians did so that they obtained much higher yields per acre. The per capita availability of domestically produced farm staples, therefore, may be a more adequate measure of the man-land ratios in the two countries and of their relative stages of agricultural development. According to the data in Table 2-1, Russia by this measure too was significantly ahead of China; it had two to three times as much domestically produced foodstuffs and cotton available per capita.

As a result, the Chinese worked with a much thinner agricultural and food supply margin. Therefore, poor harvests limited and conditioned the pace of economic advance much more decisively in China than in Russia. For instance, Russian grain exports between the two world wars reached their peak in 1931, the poorest grain-harvest year for the whole period.[12] The fact that the Soviet regime weathered the squeeze thus imposed on agriculture is proof not only of its brutality but also of the economy's capacity to absorb such a shock. In contrast, as will be described later, a corresponding decline in Chinese agricultural output during and after the Great Leap forced a drastic curtailment of agricultural exports. Perhaps the most eloquent demonstration of the differences in resources is provided by the fact that while the Soviet collectivization drive of the First Five Year Plan period (1928-32) was at least as destructive for Russian agriculture as communization was for Chinese farming, industrial expansion proceeded rapidly in the Soviet Union with only a brief interruption but was brought to a standstill in China.[13]

The difference in the stage of development of the two countries before planning began is even more striking if one compares the data for industrial production per capita (see Table 2-1). On this basis, China's output of steel, oil, timber, and flour was less than 10 per cent of Soviet production. It was less than 25 per cent for pig iron, chemical fertilizers, and sugar; less than 50 per cent for coal, electric power, cement, paper, and cotton cloth; and less than 70 per cent for cotton yarns, cigarettes, and salt. On an aggregate basis, however, the level of Chinese output exceeded the Soviet level in a number of industries. Electric-power generation, coal, cement, cotton textiles, and salt were perhaps the most important.

Many factors account for this sharp difference in per capita industrial output. Although Soviet industrial technology in 1928 was backward in comparison with Western Europe, it was more advanced than that of China in 1952. Moreover, the Soviet Union possessed a much larger reservoir of skilled technical and professional manpower on the eve of its forced-draft industrialization than China could rely on at the later date.[14] This advantage was reinforced by the fact that Soviet facilities in general, technical, and professional education at all levels were quantitatively and qualitatively much more highly developed.[15] Last but not least, the capital investment per industrial worker (*i.e.*, the capital-labor ratio) must have been considerably higher in Russia than in China.

On the other hand, it would be fair to say that China, like other underdeveloped countries, also "enjoyed" certain "advantages of backwardness."[16] Like Russia before, China could borrow technology from abroad and thus dispense with the long and expensive process of research and development. Since the technological gap between the industrially most advanced countries and mainland China was much greater in the early 1950s

T A B L E 2 - 1. Total and Per Capita Output of Selected Products in Communist China (1952) and U.S.S.R. (1927/28)

Commodity	Units	Total Output		Units	Output Per Capita		Chinese Output in 1952 as a Ratio of Russian Output in 1927/28	
		China 1952	U.S.S.R. 1927/28		China 1952	U.S.S.R. 1927/28 [a]	Total	Per Capita
Electric Power	billion kwh	7.3	5.0	kwh	12.76	34.08	144.9	37.4
Coal	1,000 MT	63,528.0	35,500.0	kg	111.65	241.50	179.0	46.2
Petroleum, crude	"	436.0	11,470.0	"	0.77	78.03	3.8	1.0
Steel ingots	"	1,349.0	4,250.0	"	2.37	28.91	31.7	8.2
Pig iron	"	1,878.0	3,282.0	"	3.30	22.33	57.2	14.8
Ammonium sulfate	"	7.0	12.8	"	0.01	0.09	54.7	13.3
Sulfuric acid	"	190.0	210.5	"	0.33	1.43	90.3	23.3
Soda ash	"	192.0	217.0	"	0.34	1.48	88.5	22.9
Caustic soda	"	79.0	58.6	"	0.14	0.40	134.8	35.6
Cement	"	2,860.0	1,850.0	"	5.03	12.59	154.6	40.0
Timber	million cubic meters	11.2	36.0	cubic meters	0.02	0.24	31.1	7.9
Cotton cloth	million meters	4,158.0	2,678.0	meters	7.31	18.22	155.3	40.1
Cotton yarn	1,000 MT	673.2	329.3	kg	1.18	2.24	204.4	52.8
Paper	"	372.0	284.5	"	0.65	1.94	130.8	33.9
Sugar, refined	"	451.0	575.4	"	0.79	3.91	78.4	20.3
Salt	"	4,945.0	2,336.0	"	8.69	15.89	211.7	54.7
Flour	"	2,990.0	24,000.0	"	5.26	163.27	12.5	3.2
Soap	"	117.0	360.0	"	0.21	2.45	32.5	8.4
Cigarettes	billion	132.5	49.0	number	232.86	333.33	270.4	69.8
Grains	million MT	138.1	73.2	kg	242.71	497.96	188.7	48.7
Potatoes	"	65.3	43.0	"	114.76	292.51	151.9	39.2
Meat	"	6.7	4.7	"	11.78	31.97	142.5	37.0
Eggs	billion	14.5	10.3	number	25.48	70.07	140.8	36.3
Cotton	1,000 MT	1,305.0	720.4	kg	2.29	4.90	181.1	46.9

Commodity	Units	Total Output		Units	Output Per Capita		Chinese Output in 1952 as a Ratio of Russian Output in 1927/28	
		China 1952	U.S.S.R. 1927/28		China 1952	U.S.S.R. 1927/28 [a]	Total	Per Capita
Locomotives	number	20	479	n.a.	n.a.	n.a.	4.2	n.a.
Railroad freight cars	"	5,792	7,870	"	"	"	73.6	"
Railroad passenger cars	"	6	387	"	"	"	1.6	"
Trucks and buses	"	—	670	"	"	"	0	"
Tractors	1,000 hp capacity	—	27.0	"	"	"	0	"
Diesel engines	1,000 hp	18.0	38.9	"	"	"	46.3	"
Steam and gas turbines	1,000 kw	—	35.7	"	"	"	0	"
Water turbines	1,000 kw capacity	7.0	12.0	"	"	"	58.3	"
Electric motors (d.c.)	"	639.0	258.6	"	"	"	247.1	"
Power generating equipment		—	75.0	"	"	"	0	"

[a] Based on population census of December 17, 1926.

Note: − stands for "none."
n.a. stands for "not applicable."

Sources:

China

Industrial production—Chao Kang, The Rate and Pattern of Industrial Production in Communist China (Ann Arbor: University of Michigan Press, 1965), Table C-1.

Agricultural production—State Statistical Bureau, Ten Great Years, Statistics of the Economic and Cultural Achievements of the People's Republic of China. (Peking: Foreign Languages Press, 1960), p. 119; Alexander Eckstein, The National Income of Communist China (New York: Free Press of Glencoe, 1961), Table A-2, pp. 94-96.

Population—"Population Statistics of Our Country, 1949-56," T'ung-chi Kung-tso [Statistical Work], no. 11, June 14, 1957, pp. 24-25.

U.S.S.R.

Industrial production—Warren G. Nutter, The Growth of Industrial Production in the Soviet Union (Princeton University Press: 1962).

Agricultural production—Naum Jasny, The Socialized Agriculture of the USSR (Stanford University Press, 1949); D. G. Johnson and A. Kahan, "Soviet Agriculture, Structure and Growth," in U.S. Congress, Joint Economic Committee, Comparison of the U.S. and Soviet Economies (Washington, D.C.: GPO, 1959), pt. 1, pp. 201-237.

Population—Frank Lorimer, Population of the Soviet Union, 1946.II.A.3 (Geneva: League of Nations, 1946).

than between these countries and Russia in the 1920s, China could theoretically make an even greater technological leap. The actual leap was limited by the availability of capital and of technical and professional manpower, but this obstacle was at least partially overcome by Soviet credits and technical assistance, about which more will be said later.

The advantages of backwardness were also more pronounced in the Chinese case because the mainland was a late comer not only to industrialization in general but also to its specifically socialist variant. This fact meant that China could borrow not only technology from the Soviet Union but institutions and policies as well. The Soviet Union presented a clear model of industrialization on the socialist pattern—a model which had undergone a number of tests, trials, and tribulations, from which the Chinese Communists could draw valuable lessons about policies to pursue and to avoid. To realize the importance of this "model effect" over and above the "technological effect," one need only recall the confusion, uncertainty, and groping of the Bolshevik leaders in the first years of their rule while they tried to crystallize a new economic order.

Marxism—whatever its validity or shortcomings as a critique of the capitalist system—was never intended as a blueprint for the socialist order. Marxist writings contained a number of vague hints, scattered suggestions, and programmatic pronouncements, but none of these, either separately or in combination, could serve as a basis for rational policy making. Lenin explicitly recognized this fact when he stated:

We have knowledge of Socialism, but as for knowledge of organization on a scale of millions, knowledge of the organization and distribution of commodities—that we have not. This the old Bolshevik leaders did not teach us. . . . Nothing has been written about this yet in Bolshevik textbooks, and there is nothing in Menshevik textbooks either.[17]

In fact, in the early years of the Bolshevik revolution, ideology often presented an obstacle to the formulation of economic policy. For instance, ideology and the traditions of the movement assigned an important role to the revolutionary zeal of the trade unions. Unions were expected to place maximal demands upon management. In light of this tradition, it took some time to make trade unions essentially agents of the state dedicated to raising labor productivity, rather than representatives of the workers pitted against the management of nationalized enterprises.

Similar problems arose in the field of wage policy. Following ideological precepts, a number of Bolshevik leaders favored an egalitarian wage structure. They did not understand that wage differentials have extremely important incentive functions even in a socialist system. That is, they did not grasp the relationship between wage differentials, the relative attractiveness of various occupations, and labor productivity.

Perhaps one of the most interesting illustrations of confusion in policy making comes from the area of monetary policy. The notion that money can and should be dispensed with and that an ideal Communist society is one based on barter was quite prevalent at the inception of the U.S.S.R. This attitude helped to undermine the remnants of resistance to inflationary methods of financing and thereby contributed to galloping inflation.[18]

By the time the Chinese Communists came to power in 1949, this whole phase of Soviet development was long past. The Soviet system had become institutionalized, and a number of policies which had been pursued were accorded ideological sanction and thereby canonized. The Chinese leadership could thus adopt many features and institutions of this system more or less ready-made and save itself costly and time-consuming groping.

In addition, the Chinese Communists had many opportunities to test their theories and policies prior to their capture of power in 1949. After late 1927, when the first Chinese Soviets were organized, the Communists at all times controlled and actually governed some parts of China. This situation was formalized in 1931 when a number of local Soviets, particularly in Hunan and Kiangsi provinces, joined to proclaim a "Chinese Soviet Republic." The Chinese Communists had to evacuate these areas in 1934, and they transferred their territorial base to Northwest China where they set up a Shensi-Kansu-Ninghsia Soviet government with Yenan as its capital.[19] It was from this base that Communist forces extended their control over other areas, particularly after 1945. Thus, because the civil war preceded rather than followed the capture of power, the Chinese Communist leadership—unlike its Soviet counterpart of 1917—had ample opportunity to gain governmental experience, particularly at the local level. As a result, the Chinese came to power much better prepared for building a new order, with a much clearer concept of what was to be done and how, than their Bolshevik colleagues at the time of the October revolution.

These intangible factors, however, were not China's only advantages. The new regime was able to lean on its "big brother" both politically and economically, as is concretely demonstrated by Soviet economic, military, and technical assistance, about which more will be said later. But this advantage was at least in part counterbalanced by embargoes and controls that non-Communist countries imposed on their trade with China.

The Strategy

In light of these preconditions and the relative advantages and disadvantages they entailed, how did the new regime proceed? What kind of economic development strategy did it adopt to accomplish its objectives?

From the outset, Chinese Communist development strategy was guided by the pursuit of total power over the economy. Therefore, the economic control levers had to be captured and shaped into prime instruments for resource mobilization and allocation to attain the central objective of maximizing the rate of industrial growth. The implementation of this strategy can be divided into four overlapping phases: rehabilitation from war devastation and plan preparation (1949-55), long-term planning for rapid industrialization (1955-57), the "Great Leap Forward" (1958-60), and the "agriculture first" program (1961 to the present).

In general, the decade and a half since the Chinese Communist advent to power has been a period of violent upheaval, disorganization, and change, during which long-term and systematic planning has been most difficult. Marked harvest fluctuations, the Korean War, rapid deterioration in Sino-Soviet relations since 1959, and a host of specific planning and policy errors have introduced many unforeseen and unforeseeable elements, so at times the tactical requirements of the moment have overshadowed the postulates of the longer-term strategy.

REHABILITATION AND PLAN PREPARATION. As of 1949, first priority had to be accorded to restoring productive capacity in agriculture and industry and to re-establishing transportation and trade channels. However, even at this early stage the regime did not lose sight of the need for (a) an institutional transformation designed to make all segments of the economy quickly and directly responsive to government policies and (b) the establishment of the technical and organizational basis for long-term planning.

The early economic objectives of the Chinese Communist regime were defined by Mao Tse-tung in 1950.[20] He proposed to bring about, in approximately three years, a "fundamental turn for the better" in the torn and disrupted economy of the mainland. This objective involved (a) capturing the "commanding heights" and thus extending and consolidating the state's control over the economy; (b) attaining fiscal and financial stability; (c) restoring the country's productive apparatus and output to pre-1949 peak levels; and (d) laying the groundwork for long-range planning.

In broad terms, all these goals were attained by the end of 1952. This comparatively rapid recovery represents an undeniable achievement, but it must be appraised against the background of certain favorable factors uniquely operative during the 1949-52 period.

The Communists, upon gaining control over the Chinese mainland in 1949, inherited an economy in which productive capacity had been appreciably curtailed by the Sino-Japanese War and later by Russian occupation and civil war. Manufacturing capacity had been particularly impaired in Manchuria, where the Russians in 1945 had dismantled and carried off more than half the capital stock in industry.[21] Industrial capacity in China proper had shrunk, though to a much lesser extent, owing to depreciation and obsolescence and to the flight of some of the movable facilities to Hong Kong and Taiwan. The situation was aggravated by a constant shortage of raw materials throughout 1949. This shortage was felt particularly in Shanghai, where many industries depended upon imported materials now cut off by the Nationalist blockade of the port. At the same time, the disruption of internal trade and transport multiplied domestic supply difficulties. Industrial output was further curtailed by a gradual demoralization of labor because of both hyperinflation and a breakdown of plant discipline after the Communist conquest of large cities. Urban labor tended to interpret the Communist victory as a signal for asserting its rights and placing its accumulated grievances and demands before industrial management. Several months elapsed before the new authorities were in a position fully to consolidate their control over the trade unions and disabuse them of their "misconceptions."

All these factors combined to reduce industrial production to 56 per cent of its pre-1949 peak.[22] According to the official index, the output of investment goods had dropped to 30 per cent of peak, while that of consumer goods had fallen only to 70 per cent. The much sharper curtailment in the heavy industries was primarily a reflection of the marked contraction in Manchuria's manufacturing capacity.

The rural sector of the economy was, on the whole, much less affected by the vicissitudes of the civil conflict than the industrial sector. Actually, civil war brought more disorganization and disruption to the countryside than it did devastation. Owing to the great importance of the subsistence sector in the rural economy, agriculture could much more easily fall back on its own resources than industry could. As a result, food production was only about 20-25 per cent below the pre-1949 peak.[23] Unfavorable weather, particularly floods, rather than civil war was the most important factor accounting for the decline. According to Chinese Communist sources, in 1949 mainland China had its worst flood since 1931; 120 million *mows* of land—constituting about 8 per cent of the total cultivated area—were affected.[24] Of course, it must be borne in mind that under more stable conditions the same weather would undoubtedly have created less havoc.

Recovery, plan preparation, and political stability all required a comprehensive attack upon fiscal and financial instability. This effort involved an initial curtailment (in early 1950) of government expenditure and a reorganization of the tax system based on increased rates of urban taxation. At the same time, fiscal management was greatly centralized through the transfer of many local government functions to the central government. After the outbreak of the Korean War, central government outlays began to increase once more, but most of this rise was covered by regular income or extraordinary levies and campaigns. The latter served as a means both of raising revenue and of mopping up liquid purchasing power.

In the face of continuing inflation, the regime decided to guarantee purchasing power in certain types of transactions. Accordingly, it began to express wage and salary payments, bank deposits, and some government expenditures and bond issues in terms of commodity basket values. These, called wage, parity deposit, and victory bond units respectively, were designed to discourage the flight from money into goods and to foster the accumulation of savings and bank deposits.[25]

In accordance with the series of stabilization moves of January-April 1950, the People's Bank began to pursue a tight, deflationary credit policy. As a result of this and other anti-inflationary devices, the Bank finally succeeded in curbing speculation and black market credit and in controlling the interest rate. Thus, monthly interest rates for loans to Shanghai traders rose from 24-30 per cent in June 1949 to a peak of 70-80 per cent in December and then declined continuously to 18 per cent in April 1950 and to 3 per cent a year later.[26]

The success of the whole stabilization effort depended upon the government's ability to guarantee the supply of consumers' necessities and the faith of the public in such a guarantee. This fact was clearly recognized by the Chinese Communists, as the following statement by a manager of the Bank of China illustrates:

The reserve for the issuance of *Jen Min Pi* [People's Currency] is not gold, but the supplies under the control of the government in the liberated areas. . . . The reserve is not kept in the vaults of the bank but is being continuously dumped on the market through the government-run trading companies. The duty of these companies is to stabilize the commodity prices, prevent sudden rises or declines, regulate supply and demand, and prevent speculative activities.[27]

However, the state trading mechanism could perform the function assigned to it only if a greatly increased volume of goods entered distributive channels. In turn, expanded volume necessitated not only a recovery in agricultural and industrial production but also restoration of the badly disrupted transport network. For this reason, rehabilitation and expansion of transport was one of the regime's high-priority targets. Therefore, in 1950 and 1951 a large proportion of government investment was devoted to railroad reconstruction. While in October 1949 less than half of China's total railway mileage was in operation, by mid-1951 all lines were restored, and their intensity of use greatly stepped up. At the same time, new railroad construction was vigorously pushed. The 320-mile Chunking-Chengtu railway—the roadbed for which had been prepared by the Nationalist government before the war—was completed in 1952. This railway greatly increased the Szechwan rice basin's accessibility for East and North China.

LONG-TERM PLANNING. Although economic rehabilitation was more or less completed by 1953, the country was far from ready for long-term national planning. For example, a national statistical bureau had been established only in the autumn of 1952.[28] The data collection network was inadequate, some areas were not yet statistically encompassed, and methods of definition, collection, and tabulation were not uniform. Moreover, business accounting was fragmentary, inconsistent, and unreliable, particularly in the private sector.

In one sense, the new regime began to lay the foundations for long-range planning as soon as it came to power. Yet it would be fair to say that the central preoccupation in the earlier years was with short-term, emergency measures to arrest inflation, mobilize resources for the Korean War, and restore production generally. With the termination of the Korean conflict, the emphasis shifted more and more in the direction of plan preparation. Although preliminary and quite fragmentary targets for the First Five Year Plan were announced in 1953, and although the plan was officially launched as of that year, a great deal of circumstantial evidence suggests that long-term planning was not initiated until mid-1955. It was at that time that detailed plan data and targets were announced.

By mid-1955 a nation-wide statistical system was established. Concurrently, all public enterprises were drawn within the purview of a more or less uniform business accounting system, which was then extended in modified form to large-scale private enterprises. These combined measures facilitated planning on the one hand and the control of plan performance on the other. It is probable that from January 1953 to mid-1955 mainland China's economy was operating on the basis of annual plans within the framework of some long-range targets, which were, however, projections rather than specific Five Year Plan stipulations. These years must have been a period of testing and experimentation in planning, for the Chinese Communists lacked a trained corps of planners, administrators, economists, accountants, statisticians, and the like.

Another factor that must have delayed effective long-term planning was the prolonged negotiations with the Russians concerning deliveries of equipment and capital goods. Agreement was reached only in 1953. As soon as negotiations were concluded, the Russians began shipping complete plants, and these constituted the backbone of China's industrialization.

All available indications suggest that the Chinese economy was operating on the basis of systematic, more or less comprehensive, and long-term planning for only two and a half to three years, between 1955 and 1957. While a Second Five Year Plan apparently was formulated and its preliminary targets were announced by Chou En-lai in late 1956,[29] it seems to have been stillborn and swallowed by the Great Leap Forward.

THE GREAT LEAP FORWARD. Despite eight years of rapid industrial growth accompanied by relatively nonviolent collectivization, Chinese Communist policy makers approached the end of their First Five Year Plan with some serious unresolved problems on their hands.

The First Five Year Plan, both in its conception and execution, bore all the earmarks of a Stalinist strategy of economic development with local adaptations. High rates of saving and investment institutionalized through agricultural collectivization; heavy emphasis on the development of those industries producing raw materials and investment goods; reliance on large-scale and capital-intensive technology in industry; and relative neglect of investment in agriculture, in consumer goods industries, and in social overhead represent the principal features of this Stalinist prescription.[30] It is a pattern of economic development which is bound to produce rapid industrial expansion at the expense of agriculture, *i.e.*, at the expense of agricultural productivity and of rural standards of living.

The most intractable issue confronting Chinese planners was agricultural stagnation. Farm production had grown only slowly, possibly just enough to keep pace with population growth. Harvests were subject to sharp annual fluctuations in response to changing weather conditions. A poor harvest would lead inevitably to domestic food shortages, which would be reflected either in rising prices or in tighter rations. This situation could, of course, have been alleviated by imports of food, but such imports would have cut down the purchases of capital goods needed for industrial expansion. In the absence of these imports, food shortages were bound to interfere with the provisioning of an expanding urban population and labor force. Thus, while urban population grew by about 30 per cent between 1952 and 1957 (at the same time that rural population increased by only 9 per cent), total government collections of grain remained more or less stationary. This statement applies even more forcefully to grain collections net of resales to the countryside.[31]

Under Chinese conditions, agricultural stagnation and poor harvests not only affected food supply but also had an almost immediate and direct impact on industrial production.[32] Inasmuch as the bulk of mainland China's exports had been agricultural, low farm production curtailed export capabilities and thereby reduced the country's capacity to import capital goods for industrialization. At the same time, it cut into the supplies of raw materials available to the domestic textile and food-processing industries. Unless agricultural output could be raised, therefore, the rate of growth in industrial capacity would be limited, and much of the existing plant would be forced to operate below capacity owing to shortages of agricultural raw materials. Thus, agriculture was clearly becoming the critical bottleneck in the future development of industry.

These various pressures on the agricultural sector were further accentuated by the reversal in China's trade balance after 1955. From a net import surplus she moved to a net export surplus position. This additional burden on the Chinese economy was imposed by a marked reduction and then cessation of Soviet credits and by the Chinese obligation to begin repaying the accumulated debt.

The competition for resources needed in both agricultural and industrial development and the necessity of making a choice in priorities confronted the Chinese Communist leadership with a series of disconcerting dilemmas, of which it was becoming ever more conscious in the latter half of 1957.[33] From the regime's point of view, it was unthinkable to divert investment resources, heretofore channeled into industry, to agricultural development and bring about a consequent decline in the rate of industrial growth. On the contrary, the objective was to maintain and possibly even accelerate the rate of industrial expansion at the same time that the vise of agricultural stagnation was broken. In other words, the leadership was groping for a method, a formula, a development strategy which would permit and foster the *simultaneous* development of agriculture and industry.[34]

All these problems converged in the course of 1957. This convergence may be attributed in part to a succession of two mediocre harvests in 1956 and 1957 and in part to strains, shortages, and bottlenecks created by a sudden and marked increase in the level of investment and a quickening in the pace of collectivization between 1955 and 1956.[35]

Against this background, a new development strategy was evolved during 1958. In the reluctance to divert investment resources from industry to agriculture, the new strategy still resembled the Soviet model. In other respects and in implementation, however, it represented a sharp departure from both the Soviet model and its specifically Chinese variant embodied in the First Five Year Plan.

At its core, the new strategy involved mass mobilization of

underemployed rural labor on a scale not attempted before, even in China. This additional labor was to be used largely at the local level for three purposes: (1) to work on labor-intensive investment projects, such as irrigation, flood control, and land reclamation; (2) to raise unit yields in agriculture through closer planting, more careful weeding, and the like; and (3) to expand small-scale industry rapidly. All these things were to be accomplished without a rise in rural consumption. There was at least an implicit assumption that: (a) this surplus labor had heretofore been consuming without contributing to output; (b) it would be employed in local productive tasks so that no transport costs need be incurred; and (c) such employment would lead to no increases in worker consumption.

Of course, none of these measures was entirely new. Mass labor projects are based on an ancient tradition in China and have only been perfected and modernized by the Communist regime. However, rural labor mobilization before 1958 was much less comprehensive and systematic than during the Great Leap Forward (1958-60).

The same can be said for the development of small-scale industry, which traditionally has been a subsidiary occupation for the Chinese farm population but confined mostly to the weaving of cloth and other handicrafts. Within the context of the new strategy, Chinese Communist planners viewed small-scale industry as one of the means for increasing the over-all rate of industrial growth. In effect, they decided upon the simultaneous development of two distinct industrial sectors: a modern, large-scale, capital-intensive sector and a more or less traditional, small-scale, labor-intensive sector. In pursuing this policy of technological dualism—or "walking on two legs," as it was officially termed in Chinese Communist writings and pronouncements—the planners promoted the expansion of small-scale industry in branches such as iron and steel, machine shops, fertilizer production, power generation, and coal extraction as well as in the more traditional textile and food processing industries.[36]

The strategy of dualism was not to be confined to technology, however. On the contrary, it seems that it was extended to include the notion of rapid development of a national economy containing two almost separate economic structures loosely linked through interregional and rural-urban trade. According to this concept, the bulk of the modern sector's final product would be channeled into either new plant construction or exports. The exports, in turn, would be used to finance imports of investment goods. Therefore, in one way or another, most of the modern sector's product would be saved (not consumed) and used for its own continued expansion and growth. Moreover, the flow of goods from the modern to the rural sector would be kept to a minimum. In this way, the rural sector's growth would likewise be based largely on its own output and investment.

Small-scale industry would be developed by using simple, locally manufactured equipment, local labor, and local raw materials. The output of these industries would then be used to satisfy rural demands for manufactured consumer goods, for tools, agricultural machinery, and other requisites of farm production. The rural sector would thus be pushed into involuntary and partial autarky—partial in the sense that it would not import from the modern sector but would be expected to provide a large, unrequited export surplus to it. The transfer would take place through agricultural taxation and/or through compulsory sales of farm products at below-market prices. In other words, the rural sector would need to save enough of its current income to finance its own development and also to contribute to the growth of the modern sector. Carried to its ultimate conclusion, this strategy would have entailed a conversion of the modern sector into an "input-input" economy and would have left only the rural sector performing the functions of an "input-output" system.

The strategy's success depended upon several crucial factors: whether underemployed labor could, in fact, be mobilized; whether this mobilization could be accomplished without curtailing farm production on the one hand and raising rural consumption on the other; and whether construction projects, such as earthen dams and canals, built almost exclusively by raw labor working without equipment could cope with major floods or droughts. Available evidence suggests that the Chinese Communist leadership genuinely believed that these problems of implementation could be resolved through institutional reform and a basic restructuring of the attitudes of cadres and the peasantry at large.

It became clear by early 1958 that the agricultural collectives (which were officially referred to as agricultural producers' co-operatives of the advanced type, and of which there were about 740,000 with an average membership of 160-200 households in the spring of 1958) were too small and too numerous to administer and control vast mass-labor projects. Communes, representing an amalgamation of almost 30 collectives and having an average membership of about 4,330 households, were much better suited to this purpose. Here was one of the principal reasons for their introduction.[37]

The Chinese Communist policy makers understood that to insure success of the program they had to couple better control and administration with adequate incentives. However, reliance on material incentives was precluded by the very character of the strategy. The strategy was based on the hope that the creation of capital projects—through investment of labor alone—would lead to increases in farm production which would then be converted into rising industrial investment and urban consumption. But such a goal could not be accomplished unless rural consumption was kept in check, for increased consumption would dissipate the increment in farm output. In the face of this situation, the leadership seems to have convinced itself that psychic income could replace increases in real income if the attitudes of rural cadres and of the peasantry could be changed.

The attitude of the party leadership was epitomized by the key 1958 slogan "politics takes command." Beginning in late 1957, all major speeches had this as their underlying theme. One gets the impression that policy makers had adopted the principle of "where there is a will, there is a way."[38] It would seem that the interplay of political, organizational, and economic developments between 1955 and 1957 had convinced the party that during this period it had overestimated difficulties and underestimated the possible impact of "ideological remolding" on the economy.

In a sense, what the Chinese Communist policy makers were saying was that economic development is ultimately a function of organization and attitudes as molded by ideology. There is no doubt that these variables condition economic development profoundly and can *within certain ranges* compensate for the lack of physical resources and capital and for backward technology. However, in late 1957 and in 1958 the Chinese Communist leadership talked and acted as if resource constraints were completely irrelevant. In assuming this posture, the party was apparently strongly influenced by its perception of the lessons to be drawn from the collectivization, the "hundred flowers," and the "rectification" campaigns.

Before mid-1955, the official approach to collectivization was cautious and gradualist. There is considerable evidence, however, of a debate within party councils in 1955 as to whether to maintain this go-slow approach or to accelerate the pace. When Mao decisively sided with those favoring the latter course, the die was cast, and collectivization was completed within a year and a half.[39] Viewed from the vantage point of 1957, collectivization was surprisingly successful. Contrary to expectations, it encountered no active resistance from the peasantry and was carried out relatively smoothly, without, at the time, the dire consequences which had been associated with collectivization in the Soviet Union. (The reasons for this difference will be examined later.) Such an experience, no doubt, greatly emboldened many elements of the leadership and the party as a whole. It led them to conclude that they had overestimated peasant resistance to change and that they had given too much weight to the counsel of the technicians and the experts who constantly called attention to the constraints, obstacles, and difficulties. As a result, the expert was downgraded, and a spirit of boldness was encouraged.[40]

The consequences of the "hundred flowers" campaign also lent support to the downgrading of the expert. During this campaign the hostility and ideological unreliability of the intellectuals and the professional groups became apparent. The party then embarked upon an all-out "rectification" campaign, which stressed the need for greater reliance on the "masses" and on politically tested elements even if these were technically less competent.

All these tendencies were greatly reinforced by the decentralization of economic management in late 1957. At this time, authority over a number of industrial and commercial enterprises was transferred to the provincial or local governments. Monetary and banking controls were decentralized. The power of the State Statistical Bureau was weakened, and many statistical organs were placed under local party jurisdiction. Last but not least, a number of economic planning functions were placed under local party control.[41] All these measures were designed to "release local initiative" and stimulate "economic development from below" through reliance on the "mass line." (The "mass line" envisaged the release of the "spontaneous initiative of the masses" and the mass mobilization of labor and of the total energies of the people as a whole.)

It is within this framework that the ambitious targets of the Great Leap were formulated and that maximum pressure was exerted on the cadres to fulfill and overfulfill them. The notion that nothing was impossible, the subordination of economic administration to local party control, and the general downgrading of the expert removed all the independent checks previously built into the system of economic planning and management. Thus, as I will show below, the door was opened wide to the type of self-generated delusions about accomplishments in agriculture and industry witnessed in 1958 and to the attendant consequences flowing therefrom.

The particular features of the Greap Leap—mass mobilization of labor, "walking on two legs," decentralization of economic management, and the communes—were unique to China. In the Soviet Union, there had been no attempts at mass mobilization on such a scale. There had, of course, been numerous shifts and reorganizations in economic management from the onset of the planning era. These shifts represented a continuing quest for the best decision-making unit—*i.e.*, the unit with the maximum centralization compatible with flexibility and efficient plant management and the minimum compatible with the central authority's full control over resource allocation. Decentralization, however, had never been carried as far as it was in China during 1958. That is, the principal locus of economic decision-making had never been placed as far down as the commune or the local party unit.

In seeking an explanation for this move and for the apparent belief that a "mass line" led and managed by local party cadres using largely their own judgment and initiative could succeed, one must perhaps reach back into the history of the Chinese Communist party. Although such a statement cannot be explicitly documented, it is quite possible that the Chinese Communist leadership in choosing this strategy was strongly influenced by its experiences during the long civil war from 1927 to 1949. On many occasions in these years, small Communist bands were isolated and had to shift for themselves with a minimum of or no contact with the party center. The leaders of these groups had to be given wide latitude, and they in turn had to use maximum initiative and judgment. Acting frequently without benefit of detailed party directives, they had to second-guess party policy and strategy as of that moment. By late 1957, the Chinese Communist policy makers may have concluded that if this approach led to success in fighting the civil war, then in peacetime giving local cadres a similar latitude in handling the local economy should work that much better.

In general, Chinese Communist writings and many major policy speeches suggest that Mao and his closest associates viewed the process of economic development as a series of military campaigns. These leaders, after all, had spent a major part of their lives in guerrilla warfare, and it no doubt left its mark on their modes of thought. In their eyes, economic development seems to have entailed a conquest of successive obstacles and fixed positions. Therefore, in formulating economic objectives or policies they naturally looked for ingredients and inputs which are essential to military success and exhibited little understanding or appreciation of the requirements for economic growth.

THE "AGRICULTURE FIRST" STRATEGY. As I will show in the next chapter, a profound economic crisis was brought about both by the policies of the Great Leap and by a succession of three years of bad weather. As the leadership became fully conscious of the depth of this crisis, it finally closed the books on the Great Leap and the development strategy associated with it. At the same time, it soberly reassessed the situation and enunciated a new economic policy at the Ninth Plenary Session of the Eighth Central Committee in January 1961—that is, when the food supply crisis was at its worst.[42] This policy shift crystallized further during the course of 1961, until it was articulated in a more nearly final form by Chou En-lai in his report at the National People's Congress in the spring of 1962.[43] While one of the objectives postulated during the Great Leap was to overtake Britain in a short span of years, the current policy phase is characterized by sobriety and caution. The earlier vision has now been reformulated as the "building of an independent, comprehensive, and modern national economic system *within a not too long historical period.*"[44] This much more gradualist approach to economic development is based on "agriculture as the foundation and industry as the leading factor."[45] It is combined with an industrial policy centered on "readjustment, consolidation, filling out, and raising standards." What do all these formulations of policy mean in concrete operational terms?

Fundamentally, the policy is one of "balanced" growth in the sense that it recognizes the close interdependence of agricultural and industrial development in a more or less closed agrarian economy. Chinese Communist planners have been aware of this interdependence all along. In the past, however, they accorded highest priority to industrial development and relied on short-term expedients to produce the complementary inputs from agriculture —with the adverse consequences pointed up in the next chapter. Under the impact of the crisis, the planners were finally prepared to accord agriculture, instead of industry, highest priority.

The policy is also one of "balanced" growth in the sense that it recognizes the interdependence of consumption and investment. Heretofore, priority had been accorded to investment, so consumption had been sharply curtailed. High rates of investment, in turn, had required high rates of taxation and forced saving. These latter measures, however, led to strong counterincentive effects upon producers, particularly in agriculture.

Thus, the new policy entails a far-reaching reversal of priorities. On the one hand, it involves a reduction in saving and investment and a corresponding rise in personal consumption.[46]

On the other hand, it means a change in the pattern of investment. A higher share than before is allotted to agriculture and consumer goods industries, and a correspondingly lower share goes into producer goods industries.

The focus of the new policy is agricultural recovery and development. To this end, greater inputs are channeled into agricultural production, and farm incentives are improved through a reduction in taxes and a reduction in the crop collection burden in general. Consumer goods industries are officially accorded higher priority than producer goods branches so that they will be better able to satisfy the demand for their products, particularly from the farm population.

In this new phase, moreover, industrial development is handled more selectively. Earlier, practically all efforts were concentrated upon the development of heavy industry, with particular emphasis on those branches which could produce investment goods for the further expansion of this sector. The emphasis has shifted to those producer goods branches that support agricultural development, notably the chemical fertilizer industry. Three additional considerations govern current industrial development policy: (1) reducing China's dependence on imports of strategic materials, (2) curtailing the dependence of consumer goods industries on agricultural raw materials so as to protect them from the consequences of sharp annual harvest fluctuations, and (3) encouraging the expansion of certain highly specialized industries which did not keep pace with over-all expansion during the Great Leap and which, like agriculture, created serious bottlenecks. The close attention paid to the continuous growth of the petroleum industry provides the outstanding example of the first; the encouragement given to the development of synthetic fibers production is an illustration of the second; and official moves to foster further expansion in certain branches of mining and in the production of special steels are instances of the third.

Finally, when industry is depressed and operates below capacity, there tends to be a marked shift in emphasis from quantity to quality in production. Thus, as output was reduced, the high-cost and inefficient plants were closed, and greater attention was paid to plant maintenance, to the general rationalization of plant operations, and to the improvement of management. As an integral part of this policy, the standing of the expert, the technician, and the manager was once more upgraded.

What the actual implementation of the new policies involves seems to be somewhat ambiguous, particularly with respect to heavy industry. The very notion of "agriculture as the foundation and industry as the leading factor" lends itself to several widely differing interpretations. In part, this ambiguity is apparently intended to cover the retreat from the Great Leap. It makes it easier to argue that the present policy is not such a sharp change in direction after all. On the other hand, the vagueness of the formulation could serve as a basis for a future shift in strategy if and when, from the planners' standpoint, the present policy outlives its usefulness.

CHAPTER THREE

The Pattern of
Economic Performance

In the preceding chapter, the broad phases of Communist China's economic development were sketched out, with primary emphasis on the policy shifts accompanying each phase. Four phases were identified: recovery and rehabilitation, long-term planning, the Great Leap, and the economic crisis. The first was a period in which dominant stress was placed on establishing economic order and stability. During the second, an ambitious development program more or less patterned on the Soviet model was launched. The third witnessed a bold attempt to break out of the vise of economic stagnation once and for all. During the most recent phase, the order of planning priorities was reversed under the pressure of economic crisis so that the importance of agricultural development was upgraded while industrial development policy was more selective. Against this background, the present chapter will examine the actual performance of the economy since 1949: its successes and failures, its strengths and weaknesses.

The Pattern of Investment

The development strategies of the First Five Year Plan and of the Great Leap were clearly reflected in the allocation of total national output and in the pattern of investment. As the data in Table 3-1 illustrate, the rate of investment was quite high for such a low-income, underdeveloped country.[1] It was not far below that for the Soviet Union at the beginning of its plan era, despite the fact that per capita income in Russia was by that time significantly higher than in mainland China today. The burden thus imposed on the average Chinese household is increased if we add defense expenditures to investment. Primarily because of the Korean War, such expenditures were relatively much more important in China than in the Soviet Union at a comparable stage.[2]

TABLE 3-1. Pattern of Resource Use
in Communist China, 1952–57

(in per cent)

Outlay Category	1952			1955		1957	
	E [a]	*H* [b]	*L-Y* [c]	*H* [b]	*L-Y* [c]	*H* [b]	*L-Y* [c]
Household consumption	70	75	75	73	68	70	68
Gross investment	19	14	15	16	22	20	22
Investment in fixed capital	10	10	6	14	11	16	16
Inventory changes	9	4	9	2	11	4	6
Defense	6	6 } 10		7 } 10		5 } 10	
Government consumption excluding defense	5	5 }		4 }		5 }	
Gross national product	100	100	100	100	100	100	100

Note: Minor inconsistencies result from rounding.

Sources: [a] Based on gross domestic product at market prices as estimated by Alexander Eckstein in *The National Income of Communist China* (New York: Free Press of Glencoe, 1961); all figures are rounded.

[b] Based on gross national product at market prices as estimated by William W. Hollister in *China's Gross National Product and Social Accounts, 1950–1957* (Glencoe, Ill.: Free Press, 1958).

[c] Based on net domestic expenditure by end use in 1952 prices as estimated by T. C. Liu and K. C. Yeh in *The Economy of the Chinese Mainland: National Income and Economic Development, 1933–1959* (Princeton University Press, 1965).

In many ways, the categories listed in Table 3-1 are so aggregate that they can shed relatively little light on the government's allocation policy and strategy. These emerge much more clearly from the pattern of investment shown in Table 3-2. Here the most striking feature is the large and growing share of investment allotted to heavy industry. This share rose from less than 30 per

TABLE 3-2. Pattern of Fixed Capital Investment in Communist China, 1952–60 [a]

	1952	1953	1954	1955	1956	1957	1958	1959[b]	1960[b,c]
Total Investment (in millions of yuan)	4,360	8,000	9,070	9,300	14,800	13,830	26,700	26,700	32,500
Sectoral Distribution of Investment (in per cent)									
Heavy industry	29.5	29.2	34.9	40.5	39.7	44.4	56.6	n.a.	n.a.
Light industry	9.3	6.2	7.4	5.7	6.4	7.9	8.2	n.a.	n.a.
Construction	2.1	3.5	3.9	3.5	4.4	3.3	1.0	n.a.	n.a.
Geological prospecting	1.6	2.4	3.2	2.7	2.7	2.2	1.7	n.a.	n.a.
Agriculture, forestry, water conservation, and meteorology	13.8	9.7	4.6	6.7	8.0	8.6	9.9	8.9	12.0
Transport, post, and telecommunications	17.5	13.4	16.5	19.0	17.7	15.0	12.7	18.5	20.9
Trade	2.8	3.4	4.3	3.7	5.1	2.7	2.1	1.4	1.3
Culture, education, and scientific research	6.4	6.8	7.8	7.5	6.3	6.7	6.7	2.5	3.5
Public health and welfare	1.3	1.9	1.7	1.1	0.7	0.9	0.4	n.a.	n.a.
Urban public utilities	3.9	3.1	2.6	2.4	2.4	2.8	2.2	n.a.	2.8
Other	11.8	18.4	13.4	8.4	6.2	5.5	2.9	n.a.	1.2

[a] These are official data which theoretically refer to total investment and thus encompass all of public (*i.e.*, both within- and outside-plan) and private investment. In fact, private investments, which were still fairly important prior to 1955, are probably not accounted for.

[b] Not comparable with earlier years since it includes only within-plan investments.

[c] Planned rather than realized.

Note: n.a. stands for "not available."

Sources: State Statistical Bureau, *Ten Great Years, Statistics of the Economic and Cultural Achievements of the People's Republic of China* (Peking: Foreign Languages Press, 1960), pp. 57–60; Li Fu-ch'un, "Report on the Draft Plan for the National Economy for 1960," *Jen-min Jih-pao* [*People's Daily*], March 31, 1960.

cent in 1952 and 1953 to almost 60 per cent in 1958. Light industry's share declined from 9 per cent in 1952 to 6 per cent in 1955; thereafter it rose to 8 per cent. For the period as a whole, about 85 per cent of industrial investment was channeled into heavy industry. As a consequence, while in the early 1950s the net output of producer and consumer goods was about the same, by the end of the decade that of consumer goods had declined in relative importance. It amounted to only one-third of the total industrial product.[3]

In contrast to heavy industry, agriculture received the smallest share of investment relative to its size. (This statement would be true even if the agricultural investment figures in Table 3-2 were adjusted to take account of self-investments by producer units in farming.) Thus, the sector which generated almost half of the national product had only about one-eighth of the investment resources at its disposal in 1952. Furthermore, this proportion had decreased drastically by 1954. Thereafter, it rose slowly but more or less continuously, yet it never recovered its earlier share. These observations, of course, are not intended to suggest that the pattern of investment allocation in an underdeveloped country should be governed by the prevailing composition of its national product. Were one to apply such a formula, economic development—in its very essence involving far-reaching changes in the structure of the underdeveloped economy—could easily be stifled. Nevertheless, as all the Soviet-type economies have amply demonstrated, the neglect of agricultural investment requirements is sooner or later bound to cause serious disruption of the development process. Such disruption is precisely what has occurred in Communist China, as we will have further occasion to observe below.

Table 3-2 points to the continuing and underlying sense of priorities which governed the character of investment policy and at the same time reveals some short-run adjustments to changing conditions. The continuity is clear from the fact that there is no drastic reordering of priorities during this period. Perhaps the only exception lies in the areas of health, welfare, education, and culture, which were apparently downgraded during the Great Leap.

Available evidence suggests that while the rise in industrial investment occurring after 1958 was planned, the increasing share devoted to transport was unintended. It was brought about largely by a series of *ad hoc* adjustments dictated by transport bottlenecks which had caused the accumulation of industrial equipment, raw materials, and finished products on railway sidings. The 1958 transport crisis, however, was itself a product of the new Great Leap strategy. The decentralization of economic management inaugurated in late 1957 and the great pressure for the development of small-scale and local industry meant that the volume of goods in transit at any one time increased markedly, as the fact that freight turnover rose by about 40 per cent in one year indicates.[4]

Another significant change in the investment pattern in response to circumstances is evident in agriculture. The 1960 plan, for example, called for increased allotments in this sector. It is more than likely that the actual allocations for 1960, 1961, and 1962—for which there are unfortunately no data—were even larger than those planned for 1960 because of the agricultural crisis which hit the Chinese mainland in 1959.

Economic Growth, Stagnation, and Structural Change

Under the impact of the economic policies analyzed in the preceding chapter and reflected in the distribution of capital and other inputs among the different sectors, mainland China's economy grew at an extremely rapid rate up to 1960. It then declined precipitously in 1961 but began to show signs of recovery in late 1962. This recovery continued through 1963 and 1964. These trends will be analyzed in greater detail below.

The pace of this advance and retreat can be best illustrated by the following estimates of gross domestic product (in billions of yuan at 1952 prices):[5]

1952	75.5	1957	103.5
1953	79.8	1958	(119.0)
1954	84.1	1959	(127.0)
1955	89.2		
1956	99.9	1962	(110.0)

These estimates are based on comparatively reliable data for at least some sectors during 1952-57. However, the quality of statistics deteriorated so badly that the 1958 and 1959 estimates are necessarily tentative. Since the Chinese Communists ceased publishing practically all statistics in 1960, it is not possible to make even semi-reliable estimates for subsequent years. The 1962 figure, therefore, is conjectural. The figure for agriculture is derived from the index for food crop production in Table 3-8 on the assumption that total farm product and food crops moved in the same direction and at the same rate. The figure for the non-agricultural sector is based on the assumption that by 1962 this sector had recovered to about the 1958 level but was still well below the peak attained in 1959 and 1960. This assumption, in turn, is based on official and semi-official statements of a qualitative (non-quantitative) character in the *People's Daily* and in a number of mainland journal articles as well as refugee and travelers' reports.

The above estimates indicate that the average annual growth rate during the period of the First Five Year Plan was about 6.5 per cent but for the 1952-59 period as a whole was almost 8 per cent. Up to 1955, the growth rate averaged 5-6 per cent; then it doubled in 1956 as a result of a good 1955 harvest and a marked increase in fixed-capital investment in 1956. This rapid expansion led to inflationary pressure, capacity bottlenecks in industry, and shortages of raw materials. These then forced a reduction in the growth rate. The tempo picked up again in 1958, when the Great Leap was launched, only to be slowed down once more later. GNP probably reached its peak in 1960 and then declined by perhaps as much as one-third within a year.

The rates of increase indicated for the expansionary phase placed China among the rapidly growing economies of the postwar world. She thus belongs in the same category as the Soviet Union, Germany, France, and Italy. Only postwar Japan's performance is clearly more impressive. These other economies, however, did not experience a sharp economic crisis but continued to expand, although in most cases the pace dropped off somewhat. From the vantage point of 1962 or 1964, therefore, China's comparative performance appears much less favorable.

Such rapid growth, followed by stagnation, was necessarily accompanied by marked structural changes in China's economy, as Table 3-3 shows. Thus, during the expansionary phase, agricul-

T A B L E   3 - 3 .   Communist China's Net Domestic Product by Industrial Origin, 1952–59

(in per cent)

Sector	1952	1955	1957	1959
Agriculture	47.9	44.7	40.0	29.9
Industry				
Large-scale	11.5	15.7	20.4	26.2
Small-scale	6.6	6.1	5.5	5.1
Construction	2.5	3.5	4.7	6.7
Transport				
Modern	2.9	3.7	3.9	4.2
Traditional	3.7	2.8	2.5	2.5
Trade	13.5	12.5	11.8	12.7
Government administration	4.6	4.8	5.2	5.1
Other	6.7	6.2	5.8	7.6
Total	100.0	100.0	100.0	100.0

Note: Minor inconsistencies result from rounding.

Sources: For the estimate of agricultural product, see note 5 in this chapter. Other sectors are based on T. C. Liu and K. C. Yeh, *The Economy of the Chinese Mainland: National Income and Economic Development, 1933–1959* (Princeton University Press, 1965), Table 8, p. 66.

ture's share of the national product consistently declined. The decline was particularly marked in 1959, when the setback in agriculture already was being felt but when the nonagricultural sectors were still expanding at a fast pace. On the other hand, modern, large-scale industry gained strikingly in importance—so much so that by 1959 its share of the national product almost equaled that of agriculture. Except for construction, which doubled its share of the national product, the relative position of other nonfarm sectors did not change much. Government administration gained slightly; small-scale industry and transport, on the other hand, declined somewhat. The proportion of the output derived from trade remained more or less the same.

Industrial Development

As was noted previously, industrial development in mainland China was unusually rapid during the first decade of Communist rule, *i.e.*, from 1949 to 1959. Industry expanded much faster than agriculture, and within industry, the investment goods branches grew more rapidly than those producing consumer goods. The priorities were reflected not only in the pattern of investment, shown in Table 3-2, but also in the fact that the inputs of capital, labor, and raw materials allotted to the favored sectors were actually available to them in the planned quantities or more if needed. Therefore, despite the fact that output targets for producer goods tended to be much more ambitious than those for consumer goods, the former targets were usually met or exceeded while the latter quite commonly were not.

Industrial production in mainland China grew at an average annual rate of 14-19 per cent between 1952 and 1957, the period for which the data are most reliable. (See Table 3-4.) The rates

T A B L E 3 - 4 . Average Annual Rate of Growth
of Factory Production in Communist China

(in per cent)

Period	Chao Index	Liu-Yeh Index
1949–57	20.5	n.a.
1952–57	14.4	19.4
1949–58	22.4	n.a.
1952–58	18.2	19.7
1949–59	23.7	n.a.
1952–59	20.6	21.1

Note: n.a. stands for "not available."

Sources: Chao Kang, *The Rate and Pattern of Industrial Growth in Communist China* (Ann Arbor: University of Michigan Press, 1965), Table 21, p. 92; T. C. Liu and K. C. Yeh, *The Economy of the Chinese Mainland: National Income and Economic Development, 1933–1959* (Princeton University Press, 1965), Table 8, p. 66.

of industrial expansion between 1949 and 1952 were even more rapid, but this period was one of recovery from abnormally low output levels amidst a great deal of unused or underused plant. During 1958-59, growth rates were once more above the Five Year Plan average as a result of the forced-draft industrialization program of the Great Leap. The data for these two years are much less reliable, however, so the indices are subject to much larger margins of error than those for the preceding years.

In the postwar period, the Chinese Communist record of industrial expansion has been approximated or exceeded only by Pakistan and Japan.[6] Pakistan, of course, initiated its industrial growth practically from scratch, *i.e.*, from an industrial base even smaller in relation to national product than China's. The fact that China, too, started its industrialization drive from a small base naturally was one factor which made for rapid advances in percentage terms. This factor, however, could hardly be the sole or even principal explanation for China's rapid advance. India began its development program from a slightly larger industrial base than China's, yet the rate of industrial growth there has averaged only 5-6 per cent.[7] On the other hand, the output of Japan, which already had a sizable industrial base, grew even more rapidly than that of China.

As a result of China's speedy industrial development, factory output almost doubled between 1952 and 1957 and nearly quadrupled between 1952 and 1959. As was indicated above, however, much greater weight can be attached to the 1957 than to the 1959 output level. Even the figures for physical production of individual products during 1958 and 1959 are of dubious reliability. Official coal production figures, for instance, indicate that output more than doubled between 1957 and 1958. The reality of such production is open to serious question. Considerable evidence indicates that during the Great Leap, quantity was substituted for quality in order to meet ambitious production targets. In a number of cases, this substitution seems to have been carried so far that the comparability of 1952-57 output with that for 1958 and 1959 is seriously impaired. An analysis based on the 1952-57 record alone, in other words, is more reliable than one based on 1949-59 or 1952-59 figures.

One striking feature of the industrial production record in China is the marked annual fluctuations in growth rates. In the early years, expansion was rapid as the existing plant was rehabilitated and as its capacity was exploited more fully. These relatively easy gains seem to have tapered off appreciably by 1954, when the rate of increase dropped to half that of the preceding year. There was another marked drop in 1955. It is interesting to note that output in the heavy industries continued to expand at a fairly rapid rate through 1955 but that the absolute level of production in the textile, paper, and timber industries actually declined. This decline was probably due largely to the fact that mediocre harvests in 1953 and 1954 caused considerable shortages of raw materials in 1955. Such shortages particularly affected the cotton textile industry. The overcutting of forests during the Korean War also had an adverse effect on timber and paper manufactures.

After the good harvest in 1955, investment was stepped-up considerably in 1956, plant capacity was increased, certain shortages of raw materials were alleviated, and the economy was pushed hard all along the line. As a result, the rate of growth greatly accelerated in 1956. However, this rapid growth and the dramatic rise in investment (60 per cent during 1956) produced acute inflationary pressures, supply bottlenecks, and serious shortages of consumer goods, so the rate of investment was curtailed in 1957. This curtailment, combined with another mediocre harvest in 1956, led to a considerable decrease in the rate of industrial expansion during 1957. With the launching of the Great Leap in 1958, a good harvest that year, and another significant rise in the rate of investment, industrial output increased rapidly once again—although probably not as rapidly as shown by either the official or the Chao indices.

Thus, there seems to be something akin to cyclical fluctuations in the rates of Communist China's industrial growth between 1949 and 1959. This phenomenon is clearly recognized in official statements and writings and is referred to as "saddle-shaped," "U-shaped," or "wave-like" development.[8] These statements indicate that periods of rapid expansion necessarily lead to periods of consolidation, during which marked imbalances and supply bottlenecks in the production process are alleviated and greater emphasis is placed on the quality rather than the quantity of production. Another factor clearly bearing upon these fluctuations is harvest fluctuations. A careful and detailed analysis of the character, shape, and background of this most interesting phenomenon, however, would be beyond our scope here. Nevertheless, it is a subject of sufficient theoretical and practical importance to deserve detailed study.

In the process of rapid development, individual industries grew at unequal rates. Their comparative rates reflected in large part the planners' sense of priorities. As the data in Table 3-5 show, expansion was fastest in electric-power generation, petroleum extraction, metallurgy, engineering, and chemicals. In these branches, growth was well above the all-industry average. They were the sectors which were most underdeveloped in relation to the technical requirements of modern industrialization and most directly related to military capability. In contrast, the consumer goods industries—food processing, textiles, and miscel-

T A B L E 3 - 5 . Average Annual Rate of Increase
in Production, by Industry, in Communist China

(in per cent)

Industry	1949–57	1952–57
Electricity	20.6	21.6
Coal	19.1	14.6
Petroleum	36.5	27.3
Ferrous metal	53.8	28.7
Nonferrous metal	46.5	29.9
Machine building	40.3	22.1
Chemical	43.1	25.7
Building materials	30.0	19.3
Timber	18.5	14.8
Textile	13.8	6.5
Paper	28.8	17.1
Food	14.1	9.3
Miscellaneous consumer goods	15.0	11.8

Source: Chao Kang, *The Rate and Pattern of Industrial Growth in Communist China* (Ann Arbor: University of Michigan Press, 1965), Table 24, p. 97.

laneous consumer goods—grew much more slowly, although at a rate well ahead of the pace of population growth. But this rate of increase in output does not necessarily mean that the per capita supply of these products available to the population rose similarly or rose at all, particularly since mainland China's total exports grew more rapidly than her manufacture of consumer goods and since these goods constituted an increasing share of the exports.

The pace of industrial advance, which carried the Chinese economy forward for 10 years, began to falter in 1960. Unfortunately, reliable and precise information on trends in industrial production, investment, and employment is not available for recent years. Therefore, it is not possible to measure rates of industrial change since 1960. Nevertheless, from official statements and from refugee and travelers' reports, it is possible to fathom the direction of movement even if one cannot quantify its extent.

On this basis, it is clear that the decline was at first confined to the food-processing and textile industries, which had to cut back production because of shortages of raw materials (*e.g.,* cotton and tobacco) resulting from the agricultural crisis. It would seem that in 1960 the level of investment was still increasing, although the rate in relation to national product probably declined. The situation changed greatly, however, when the Great Leap was officially abandoned and the level of investment was curtailed in 1961. A marked drop in production occurred in most, if not all, branches of industry—in consumer goods industries because of continuing shortages of agricultural raw materials and in investment goods industries because of reduced demand engendered by investment cutbacks. The decrease in investment was, in turn, also related to the agricultural crisis in the sense that a contracting farm sector could not support a level of saving sufficient to finance investment at 1958 or 1959 levels. Furthermore, the decline in the investment goods branches was accelerated by the exodus of Soviet technicians in the fall of 1960, a development which delayed the completion of a number of plants.

The curtailment of industrial production led to the closing down of a number of factories and thus produced significant pockets of urban unemployment. These became particularly pronounced in 1961. The result of this stagnation was a loss of much of the ground that industry had gained during the Great Leap. On the basis of qualitative indications, it would seem that the output of a number of industrial products fell back to 1958 and in quite a few cases even to 1957 levels. Steel illustrates this point quite well. In 1958, production (excluding the output of the backyard furnaces) was officially placed at 8 million tons.[9] By 1960, it may have risen to about 15 million. Estimates for 1963, even after a certain measure of recovery from the low point reached in 1961, ranged between 8 and 10 million tons.[10] Thus, the steel industry was operating well below capacity. The quantitative decline, it should be noted, was to some extent offset by improvements in the quality of output and by the mills' growing ability to manufacture a wider variety of finished products. Similar developments are evident in other industries. In the case of coal, for instance, the drop in production to well below the 1960 level has been counterbalanced, at least in part, by the closing down of the small and most inefficient mines and by a rise in the thermal value of unit output.

The only exceptions to the general industrial decline were crude oil extraction, chemicals, and agricultural machinery, all of which continued to expand throughout the crisis years. Security considerations probably played a major role in the expansion of the petroleum industry. As Table 4-5 shows, China has in the past been quite dependent on petroleum imports, which came almost exclusively from the Soviet Union. With the deterioration of Sino-Soviet relations, the Chinese have been most anxious to emancipate themselves from this dependence as soon as possible. The expansion of chemicals and agricultural machinery, on the other hand, is closely tied in with the "agriculture first" policy. According to some estimates, total production of chemical fertilizer was above two million tons in 1962 and not much below three million tons in 1963, as compared with less than one million tons in 1957.[11]

In line with the "agriculture first" policy, there has been a growing emphasis during the 1960s on developing the manufacture of synthetic fibers in an attempt to render the country's textile industry gradually less dependent on agricultural raw materials.[12] The strategy also seems to be supported by reallocations of industrial production—particularly electric power—to agriculture. Although total power generation is depressed as a result of the sharp reduction in industry's consumption of electricity, this very lack of demand in urban areas has released some of the output for use in agriculture.

As one looks at China's economy and its industrial establishment from the vantage point of the mid-1960s, there is no question that the country, despite its setback in the early 1960s, has become an important industrial power by Asian standards, although not yet by world standards. Under the impact of the marked advance in the 1950s, the gap between Communist China and the rest of the world in aggregate industrial production was beginning to narrow. Where China should be ranked on a world scale of industrial power, however, raises some difficult and to some extent insoluble problems. Should this rank be determined on the basis of total production or output per capita? Clearly, the latter criterion is more relevant from the standpoint of living standards. From the viewpoint of military or political power, though, the issue is much less clear. The answer really depends upon the extent to which total output is a substitute for per capita output and the weight that one can or should assign to sheer population size.

There is no doubt that China's influence in world politics is augmented by the magnitude of her population. It provides China with a moral claim for representation and participation in world power councils. At the same time it inculcates fear and respect based on fear among her neighbors, particularly since this vast population appears to be under firm control and led by a dynamic and ambitious regime.

On the other hand, a rapid rate of population growth when superimposed on an already large population mass can constitute a serious drag on industrialization in several ways. First of all, it forces a race between the rates of population growth and of increase in food supply. Consequently, it constantly threatens an already precarious food supply balance and can lead to periodic breakdowns and economic crises. As a matter of fact, the dilemmas posed by population and food supply are possibly the most decisive and at the same time least predictable for the future course of China's industrialization. At worst the population problem can undermine the very stability of the regime, and at best it will tend to slow down the rate of industrial expansion.

However, if we assume that the population-food supply dilemma is successfully resolved, China by virtue of sheer size will be in a position to develop and maintain quite a large industrial establishment, even if her rate of industrial expansion is slower than it was in the fifties. Therefore, within a relatively short span of time, Communist China's aggregate industrial establishment may be capable of supporting sizable and increasingly modern military forces that will permit the regime to pursue its foreign policy aims quite effectively. At the same time, it will necessarily take much longer for this industrial sector to grow to a point where rising total industrial product is translated into significant increases in per capita availability and consumption of manufactures. Thus, one may anticipate for some decades to come a rather paradoxical situation. China will remain quite backward as gauged by its per capita product and yet be an industrial power of some consequence, constituting a major force in world affairs and a foreign policy problem of prime importance to the United States.

Examining the data in Table 3-6 with these hypotheses in mind, we find that China by the late 1950s was undoubtedly among the first 10 industrial powers of the world, although in terms of per capita output it lagged far behind. For purposes of this comparison I have selected the year 1957. Had one based the comparison on 1959 or 1960, the years of peak industrial production for China, her world rank might have been somewhat higher than that shown in Table 3-6. On the other hand, if one had used 1964 as the year for comparison, China would probably have fared worse. After 1960 the output of other industrial countries continued to rise, while that of China declined.

As one might expect, mainland China's industrial rank is higher for some types of industry than it is for others. Thus, China is near the top in the manufacture of cotton yarn, which is closely associated with population size, but she is quite low with

TABLE 3-6. Production of Certain Industrial Products in Selected Countries in 1957

Item	Units	China	Japan	India	Soviet Union	Canada	United Kingdom	German Federal Republic	France	Italy	United States	China's World Rank
Coal	million MT	124.2	52.2	44.2	328.5	9.9	227.2	134.4	56.8	1.0	467.6	5
Metallurgical coke	"	5.0	5.9	2.6	48.6	3.5	20.8	45.3	12.6	3.7	68.9	9
Crude petroleum	"	1.5	0.3	0.4	98.3	24.6	0.1	3.9	1.4	1.3	353.6	24
Electric power	billion kwh	19.3	81.3	13.7	209.7	91.0	105.6	91.7	57.4	42.7	716.3	12
Pig iron	million MT	5.9	7.1	1.9	37.0	3.6	14.5	18.5	12.0	2.2	73.4	7
Crude steel	"	5.3	12.6	1.7	51.2	4.6	22.0	24.5	14.1	6.8	102.2	9
Cement	"	6.9	15.2	5.7	28.9	5.6	12.1	18.8	12.7	11.9	52.6	8
Paper (excluding newsprint)	1,000 MT	913.0	1,483.0	174.0	1,749.0	769.0	1,761.0	1,861.0	1,251.0	724.0	11,906.0	8
Newsprint	"	122.0	555.0	15.0	377.0	5,771.0	663.0	270.0	427.0	181.0	1,630.0	13
Cotton yarn	million meters	844.0	517.0	807.0	1,015.0	68.0	330.0	418.0	313.0	173.0	1,700[a]	3

[a] The exact figure is 1,645.6 million meters and refers to 1958. The 1957 figure is not available since cotton yarn production is given for census years only.

Sources: United Nations, Statistical Yearbook, 1961 (New York: Author, 1962); Chao Kang, The Rate and Pattern of Industrial Growth in Communist China (Ann Arbor, University of Michigan Press, 1965), Table C-1, pp. 120-132.

respect to oil extraction since the country is not well endowed with petroleum resources. As a coal producer she ranks quite high, and before the onset of economic stagnation she also was forging rapidly ahead in iron and steel, metallurgical coke, cement, and electric power. In the process, China has left India far behind, but with the exception of coal and cotton textiles, she still lags significantly behind Japan and the larger countries in Western Europe. Of course, Communist China nowhere approaches the Soviet Union (again with the exception of coal and cotton yarn) and even less the United States.

Agriculture and Food Supply

Mistaken policies combined with unfavorable weather led to the agricultural crisis in China. While all the blame was officially placed on nature, it is clear even from the regime's own pronouncements that the prolonged neglect of agriculture was bound to have had an effect sooner or later even if the weather had been favorable. This neglect was reflected in inadequate investment, unfavorable production incentives, perpetual reorganization and disorganization of agrarian institutions, and a host of specific planning errors. To understand the dimensions and the impact of this crisis, it is necessary to examine its background in greater detail.

Chinese agriculture traditionally has performed three major economic functions: supplied food to the population at large, provided raw materials for the food-producing and textile industries, and served as the principal bulwark of the country's exports. Before 1949, it should be noted, China was largely self-sufficient in performing the first two functions, though a net importer of grains and cotton during most years.

As in all underdeveloped areas which are subject to acute population pressure, agricultural production is intensive and is concentrated upon crops which have a high-energy yield. Livestock production has only subsidiary importance. No more than 20 per cent of China's farm output is derived from this branch of agriculture.[13] Since the bulk of the population lives close to the margin of subsistence, meats and other livestock products are a luxury in the domestic consumption basket, but they are of major significance in the list of exports.

The farm products of prime importance are rice, wheat, soybeans, and cotton. Rice is the food staple of South China, and wheat that of the north. Soybeans are a main source of fats and protein and the principal export crop. Cotton is the most important industrial raw material of agricultural origin. One should add that in the south, sweet potatoes represent an inferior substitute for rice, while millet and kaoling are frequently consumed in the place of wheat in the north. In light of these customary substitutions, there is some justification in treating all four food crops as a group.

TRENDS IN FARM PRODUCTION. As was pointed out earlier, once the new regime restored order and communications, agricultural production recovered rapidly. It reached its more or less normal level by 1952. Favorable weather conditions greatly assisted recovery, particularly in 1952. Official figures would indicate that food crop production increased by 19-20 per cent between 1952 and 1957. At the same time, population expanded by about 11 per cent. On this basis, the per capita availability of foodstuffs seems to have grown by 8 per cent, *i.e.*, at an average annual rate of about 1.5 per cent a year.[14]

At first glance, these figures seem to reflect quite a respectable rate of growth in food supply for the period of the First Five Year Plan. In reality, the picture was less favorable. Even the official data show that the rise in food crop production per capita was confined to the years before 1955. Production remained more or less stationary between 1955 and 1957. More significantly, however, the basic statistics for crop production are of dubious reliability. They seem to contain a strong upward bias as a result of the improvements in crop reporting and the broadening coverage of agricultural statistics between 1952 and 1957—most particularly between 1952 and the completion of the collectivization process in 1955-56. For example, a Chinese Communist source indicates that after collectivization it was found that about five million acres of cultivated land had not been reported previously and that these were then included as newly reclaimed land.[15] While it is impossible to estimate the degree of overstatement resulting therefrom, it is clear that the rise in the per capita output of food between 1952 and 1957 was significantly less than 8 per cent. As a matter of fact, for the country as a whole food production per capita may not have increased at all, or if so then imperceptibly.

At the same time, the export share of food crops and soybeans remained fairly stable, so no significant change in per capita availability could be expected on this account. Yet Chinese mainland periodicals and newspapers were replete with reports of food shortages and tight rations, particularly in urban areas. This situation is not too surprising if we correlate what we know about trends in total food production and procurement and trends in total and urban population.

As I indicated earlier, government purchase and taxation of food crops and soybeans seem to have remained more or less the same, while urban population was rapidly rising. This fact would suggest an ever tightening food supply in the cities. Such a conclusion is borne out by the increasingly stricter rationing regulations between 1952 and 1957 and by official statistics concerning levels of per capita food consumption in urban and rural areas.[16] It is further confirmed by reports concerning continuing difficulties in collecting the grain from the countryside. Therefore, it would seem that government agricultural policies not only failed in the field of production but also in the field of distribution. That is, collectivization, which was designed primarily to fortify official control over farm produce and its disposal, apparently did not increase farm collections. Moreover, it probably had a negative effect on farm production. As a result, contrary to the planners' scale of preferences, farm consumption may have risen, while urban consumption declined. Production may thus have been sacrificed for control, but control itself did not increase significantly despite collectivization and the attendant institutional changes.[17]

As far as other farm products are concerned, the production of oilseeds barely rose between 1952 and 1957. This fact affected the supply of vegetable oils, which are important in the Chinese diet. No comprehensive statistics are published on meat and other livestock production. However, the statistics on livestock numbers indicate a slow rise in the cattle population and marked annual fluctuations in the hog population but no clear trend. On the other hand, the sheep and goat population rose considerably.[18] All indications thus point to a decline in the per capita supply of pork and beef for most years and some improvement in the availability of mutton.

The effect of slow growth or stagnation in agriculture on consumer goods industries is most clearly illustrated by the experience in cotton growing. During most of the interwar and early postwar years, China was a net importer of raw cotton for its textile industry. The new regime was determined to reverse this trend and make the country self-sufficient in cotton. Therefore, cotton acreage was extended rapidly during the first few years. Eventually, however, expansion began seriously to eat into grain acreage. Because there were no significant increases in grain yields and because the population was pressing upon the available food supply, the cotton area had to be cut back. Then when a good grain harvest was anticipated for 1955, cotton acreage was expanded again. Owing to these fluctuations in acreage and weather conditions, cotton production fluctuated as well. This fluctuation, in turn, led to periodic shortages of raw materials for the cotton textile industry, so in some years it had to operate significantly below capacity.

It was against this background that the regime approached the Second Five Year Plan, the Great Leap Forward, and the year 1958. As was noted earlier, the leadership became convinced that an all-out effort based on comprehensive mobilization of labor could break the agricultural bottleneck. It felt that crop yields could be significantly raised by closer planting, deep plowing, more careful weeding, and ambitious soil and water conservation projects. With the downgrading of the technician and the statistician and with the decentralization of economic management in late 1957, this program was to be carried out under local party leadership and based on local initiative.

As a result of their optimism that far-reaching progress could be made in a short time if "politics was permitted to take full command" and the "mass line" was followed, the policy makers fixed agricultural production targets quite high to begin with. In addition, they introduced "the system of planning with two accounts." [19] Beginning in 1958, two sets of targets were to be used. A first set of targets, binding upon subordinate organs, would be formulated at each administrative level. Next, the subordinate organs would be asked how much they thought they could accomplish above and beyond the targets passed down to them. This second set of targets they would then pass down to the next level below. Thus, each administrative and planning level would operate with two sets of plans, one set for which it would be held responsible by the organ immediately above it and a higher set which it would consider binding upon the organs subordinate to it.

These conditions, combined with maximum pressure on the party cadres to fulfill and overfulfill the plans, set the stage for the fantastic claims made for agricultural production in 1958. As 1958 progressed, moreover, the targets themselves were raised with each report of fulfillment or overfulfillment. Under the double system of planning, a percentage change in targets at the top led to a more than proportionate rise at the bottom. The result was a mutually reinforcing mechanism for producing high claims. In retrospect, therefore, it is not too surprising that the annual communiqué of the State Statistical Bureau concerning economic development in 1958 claimed that the production of food crops and cotton nearly doubled in one year, *i.e.*, increased from 195 and 1.64 million tons respectively in 1957 to 375 and 3.35 million tons in 1958.[20] Thus, the targets of the 12-year program for agricultural development enunciated in 1956 were allegedly attained by 1958.[21] Proceeding from this quite high base, the Central Committee went ahead and set extremely ambitious targets for 1959 as well—for example, 525 millions tons for food crops (an increase of 40 per cent) and 5 million tons for cotton (an increase of 50 per cent).[22]

These production claims were made despite marked food shortages in 1958 and 1959. Such difficulties were blamed on transport bottlenecks, supposedly brought about by the unprecedented harvest, and on strains in collecting and distributing the vast output. This set of circumstances raises some extremely important questions about the character and motivations of the Chinese Communist leadership and the quality of its economic planning and management. Did the leadership accept the claims more or less at face value, or was it aware of the true situation but published the claims for their internal and external propaganda value, as proof of the correctness of the "general line," as a vindication of government policy, and as a means of spurring on the cadres and the peasantry to continuing effort? Without access to the Chinese Politburo's minutes, we have no way of knowing. Yet there are many indications that as of the end of 1958 the leadership may have become a captive of its own claims, and there are several reasons which might explain how such a thing could have happened.

As to external evidence, the planners, after the 1958 harvest, withdrew some acreage previously under cultivation. This step was coupled with the assertion that high unit yields made it pointless to keep marginal land in cultivation when it could be better used for pasture. Such a move may indeed have been rational from the standpoint of optimal land use in a period of relative agricultural abundance but not amidst acute scarcity.

Assuming that the reason given for the acreage reduction can be taken at its face value, how can one account for the apparent belief that such high yields had in fact been attained? It must be borne in mind that 1958 was unquestionably a favorable weather year during which a good crop was undoubtedly produced. Although the actual level of production is as yet unknown, it probably rose 10-15 per cent as compared to the 1957 level. Moreover, under carefully controlled and experimental conditions, unusually high grain and cotton yields had been produced. A good many of the yield figures reported in 1958 were within the ranges of yield which had been obtained from these experimental plots. This fact enhanced the plausibility of the figures. With the position of the State Statistical Bureau seriously weakened and the local statistical organs subordinated to local party control, the planners and policy makers at the top had apparently lost their only more or less independent and reliable channel for determining actual trends in farm production. Thus, they had to depend on qualitative indications on the one hand and inaccurate or padded quantitative information on the other.

The bubble of self-delusion finally burst in the late summer of 1959 when, in the face of the approaching harvest and continuing food shortages, it became abundantly clear that the 1958 figures and the 1959 targets were completely unrealistic. Both the claims and the targets were revised accordingly.[23] At a later date, these adjusted targets were then said to have been fulfilled. Table 3-7 may serve to clarify the situation as of 1959.

T A B L E 3 - 7 . Planned and Reported Food Crop and Cotton
Production in Communist China, 1957–59

(in millions of metric tons)

	1957	1958		1959		
	Reported Production [a]	Original Claim [b]	Revised Claim [c]	Original Target [d]	Revised Target [e]	Reported Production [e]
Food crops	185.00	375.00	250.00	525.00	275.00	270.05
Cotton	1.64	3.35	2.10	5.00	2.31	2.41

Sources: [a] State Statistical Bureau, *Ten Great Years, Statistics of the Economic and Cultural Achievements of the People's Republic of China* (Peking: Foreign Languages Press, 1960), p. 119.

[b] State Statistical Bureau, "Communique on the Development of the National Economy in 1958," *Jin-min Jih-pao [People's Daily]*, April 15, 1959.

[c] State Statistical Bureau, "Communique Concerning Adjustments in the Agricultural Production Statistics of 1958," in same, August 27, 1959.

[d] "Communique of the Sixth Plenary Session of the Eighth Central Committee of the Chinese Communist Party," in same, December 18, 1958.

[e] "Press Communique on the Progress of China's National Economy in 1959," in same, January 22, 1960.

The table would indicate that food crop production increased by about 35 per cent in 1958 and by another 8 per cent in 1959. However, the accuracy of these data is open to serious question, for they are clearly inconsistent with other verifiable elements in the total situation.

The increased food production should have been reflected in significantly higher food consumption per capita, in a large expansion of exports of food crops, or in rising stocks. Yet even in 1958 the Chinese press constantly reported food shortages, and these reports became much more urgent in 1959. Admittedly, money incomes, and with them effective demand for consumer goods, rose under the impact of rising investment and a rapidly growing nonagricultural labor force. With a 35 per cent increase in food production, however, it should have been easy to absorb this growing money income without undue inflationary pressure, particularly in view of continued food rationing. One might also have expected some increase in the food rations or some relaxation in rationing regulations. Neither took place. At the same time, there was only a modest increase in exports of food crops. A large-scale diversion of stocks is the only remaining explanation. Yet this hypothesis raises more questions than it resolves. There is no indication that mainland China's storage and warehousing facilities could have accommodated about 40 million tons of grain. Neither is there any evidence of an ambitious program of warehouse construction. One must wonder, consequently, where this grain could have been stored. Furthermore, if so much food had been stored in 1958, and more added in 1959, there should have been ample stocks to cope with the officially admitted farm production shortages in 1960 and 1961 and the resultant food crisis.

While one must, therefore, reject the official claims for 1958 and 1959 agricultural production, there are unfortunately no data presently available upon which reliable estimates could be constructed. It is doubtful whether the mainland authorities themselves have such data at their disposal. Several official statements contain hints that they believe Chinese food crop production increased by about 10-12 per cent in 1958.[24] This estimate seems reasonable in light of the quite favorable weather conditions of that year. As far as 1959 is concerned, production declined rather than increased. The weather was worse in 1958, and the acreage sown to food crops was reduced. To increase output, yields per acre would have to have been raised considerably, a most unlikely event in a poor weather year.[25]

After releasing the annual communique for 1959 plan fulfillment in January 1960, the State Statistical Bureau stopped publishing annual production results. Consequently, for later years we do not even have official production claims. However, it has been admitted officially that production declined after 1958. Some statements hint that it dropped to 1957 or even to 1955 levels.[26] Thus, the last more or less reliable set of mainland agricultural statistics is for 1957. Most of our subsequent information is based on qualitative and circumstantial evidence of the kind adduced above. In Table 3-8, these indications are translated into quantitative terms.

TABLE 3-8. Total and Per Capita Food Crop Production Trends in Communist China, 1957–63

Year	Index of Food Crop Production	Index of Population Growth			Index of Per Capita Availability of Domestically Produced Food Crop		
		Based on an Annual Growth Rate of:			Based on the Assumed Rate of Population Growth of:		
		1.5%	*2.0%*	*2.5%*	*1.5%*	*2.0%*	*2.5%*
1957	100	100.0	100.0	100.0	100.0	100.0	100.0
1958	115	101.5	102.0	102.5	112.9	112.3	111.8
1959	91	103.0	104.0	105.1	87.9	87.9	86.2
1960	86	104.6	106.1	107.7	82.4	81.2	80.0
1961	90	106.1	108.2	110.4	84.8	83.2	81.5
1962	96	107.7	110.4	113.1	89.1	86.9	84.8
1963	97	109.3	112.6	115.9	88.7	86.1	83.7

Source: The food crop production index was calculated by the author on the basis of output data published in *Current Scene*, v. 2, no. 27, January 15, 1964.

The data on the production of food crops are based on a systematic marshaling of available evidence on individual crop acreages, yields, weather conditions, rations, and food utilization patterns by the U.S. Department of Agriculture. In view of the large statistical gaps, however, they naturally are subject to considerable margins of error. The estimated year-by-year level of production in this series depends upon what figure one accepts for 1957 output. Official Chinese Communist reports place 1957 production at 185 million tons, but in the opinion of some observers the 1957 output of food crops could have been no higher and probably was lower than that in the bumper harvest year of 1955. On this basis, they estimate 1957 output at 170-175 million tons. For our purposes, the figure for any one year is less important than the indication of trends over the period as a whole.

Total agricultural production probably recovered much less rapidly than food crop production, particularly in value terms. Between 1957 and 1963, the output of food crops deteriorated significantly in qualitative terms because of a relative shift from rice and wheat to miscellaneous grains and sweet potatoes. Moreover, livestock production declined much more sharply than crop production. By 1963 it may have recovered to only about 75 per cent of its 1957 level. Industrial crops also fared less well than grains. Vegetable production, on the other hand, came back rapidly. But this quick recovery did not counterbalance the decline in other products. All in all, then, the total value of the agricultural product by 1963 may have reached no more than 90 per cent of the 1957 level.

Data on population are perhaps just as scarce and unreliable as those for farm production. If one accepts the official figures, population must have grown between 2 and 2.5 per cent a year between 1952 and 1958. In light of the depressed food situation after 1959 and of the nutritional deficiencies associated with it, the population certainly could not have grown at a rate higher than 2.5 per cent and probably expanded more slowly than that. In fact, it is highly probable that the rate fell somewhere between 1.5 and 2.5 per cent.

THE FOOD SUPPLY POSITION. The indices in Table 3-8 suggest that the production of food crops reached its low point in 1960 when the per capita availability of domestically produced grain declined by almost 20 per cent as compared to 1957. The same tendencies are visible in the area of food supply. All indications point to 1960/61 as the most critical year. Since then, the food supply situation has improved more rapidly than that of farm output. Grain imports made the most significant contribution to this narrowing of the deficit. Lower seed requirements resulting from a reduction in the acreage sown to food crops also helped, as did the higher average rates of grain extraction resulting from shifts in the composition of grain output in favor of sweet potatoes, for which there are no milling losses.[27]

In retrospect, it is clear that the acute food crisis of the early 1960s was brought about not only by a quantitative but also by a marked qualitative decline in the food supply. It was naturally aggravated by the fact that the average per capita caloric intake in China has traditionally been low—2,000-2,200 calories a day. Under such circumstances, a 10-20 per cent reduction can have deleterious effects. The qualitative deterioration was reflected in an increasing substitution of sweet potatoes for rice and of coarse grains for wheat. At the same time, the shortages of animal products, vegetables, and oil seeds became progressively more acute. Thus, it was the subsidiary and protective foods which were squeezed most. This qualitative deterioration assumes particular significance if we remember that such a decline was already in process well before 1957. During the period of the First Five Year Plan, for example, the average per capita consumption of pork, other meats, and eggs in Shanghai and Tientsin reportedly dropped.[28]

Reliable information on the dimensions of the food crisis is not available. What evidence we have is based mostly on reports of refugees in Hong Kong and of foreign visitors to China, some scattered reports in the Chinese press, and the incontrovertible fact that China has been importing grain from Canada, Australia, and, to a lesser extent, other countries.

As was noted above, available evidence would indicate that the food situation in mainland China reached its low point in the spring of 1961, just prior to that year's harvest. Food supplies shrank because of a further decline in food production in 1960, as compared with 1959. This decrease was occasioned not only by another poor harvest but also by the collectivization of hog raising and vegetable growing.

During the 1961/62 food consumption year, it would seem the level and quality of the Chinese diet definitely improved. The 1961 crop was apparently a little better. Grain imports were stepped up—about 5.8 million tons in 1961/62 as compared to 2.6 million tons in 1960/61. The reintroduction of private plots produced some recovery in livestock and vegetable production. This process of improvement seems to have been sustained since then as a result of reasonably good grain harvests in 1962, 1963, and 1964—apparently approaching or possibly even slightly exceeding the 1957 level, of continuing recovery in the production of vegetables, livestock, and other subsidiary foods, and of maintenance of high levels of grain imports.

As might be expected, the deteriorating food situation brought with it a rising incidence of nutritional diseases. These seem to have been most widespread in 1961. The effect upon the death rate of malnutrition and other health hazards occasioned by food shortage cannot be assessed in the absence of adequate data. The most that one can say is that while the food crisis has been serious, there have been no indications of mass famines. On the basis of information now available, but not available then, it is clear that the situation in the winter of 1960/61 was so serious that even military rations had to be cut. Partly on this account and partly because of the adverse situation soldiers saw all around them, adversity which affected their relatives and friends as well, army morale and discipline seem to have been undermined seriously. The situation also caused considerable demoralization among local party cadres and the local militia, and in some areas there were apparently peasant uprisings and almost complete disintegration of local administration and authority.[29]

INPUT TRENDS.   As was indicated in Table 3-2, the government's capital investment in agriculture, forestry, and soil and water conservation averaged around 9 per cent of total investment during the 1950s. It was above this figure in the first years of the decade, sank below 5 per cent in the mid-fifties, and then rose again in recent years as agriculture was accorded higher priority by the planners. In contrast, India—at roughly the same stage of development as China and with more or less the same proportion of its national product obtained from agriculture—devoted 32 per cent of its total investment to this sector during its First Five Year Plan and 20 per cent during the Second.[30] Even if we allow for certain self-investments in Chinese agriculture, this figure means that in relative terms India was investing almost twice as much in agricultural development as Communist China.

Since the opportunities for extending the area under cultivation are limited, agricultural investments in China have to be land-saving, *i.e.*, yield-increasing. Under mainland conditions, such investments involve primarily flood control and irrigation to reduce the size of annual harvest fluctuations and large-scale applications of chemical fertilizer to increase unit yields on the area sown. The regime paid considerable attention to the first but invested in these projects mostly labor and organizational resources rather than capital and materials such as iron, steel, and cement. This almost exclusive concentration on labor-intensive methods combined with a reluctance to supply the required quantities of capital and basic materials, poor project design, ineffective organization, and shifting and contradictory directives produced a whole host of technically deficient projects.

It has long been recognized that a significant increase in crop yields in China would require large-scale applications of chemical fertilizer. In this connection, it is interesting to note that Japan's average rice yields increased by about 20 per cent in the decade between 1880 and 1890. Similarly, the combined unit yield of six major crops rose by about 50 per cent in the four decades between 1880 and 1920.[31] A major part of this rise was accomplished through increasing applications of commercial fertilizer. By 1936, on a crop area about one-sixteenth that of mainland China, Japan applied 3.4 million tons of chemical fertilizer, as compared with about 200,000 tons used in China.[32] Before the war, the Chinese Agricultural Research Bureau conducted experiments which indicated that to raise unit crop yields by about 25 per cent, applications of 6.5 million tons of ammonium sulphate, 3.8 million tons of calcium super-phosphate, and 300,000 tons of potassium sulphate would be required. As of 1943-44, the ammonium sulphate capacity on the mainland was about 320,000 tons, practically all of it concentrated in Manchuria. Most of the output was exported to Japan before the war, but since the advent of the Communist regime, it has been retained in China.

Although the production and consumption of chemical fertilizer expanded quite rapidly after 1949, as the data in Table 3-9 indicate, they do not as yet come anywhere near the requirements postulated by prewar experiments. Fertilizer production is highly capital-intensive. Therefore, the expansion of domestic facilities for fertilizer production curtails the availability of capital for the investment goods and defense industries. Similarly, the import of fertilizer requires foreign exchange which might other-

T A B L E 3 - 9. Chemical Fertilizer Production and Supply in Communist China, 1949–63

(in thousands of metric tons)

Year	Production				Imports	Total Supply
	Ammonium Sulfate	Ammonium Nitrate	Super Phosphate	Total		
1949	27	—	—	27	n.a.	n.a.
1950	70	—	—	70	n.a.	n.a.
1951	129	5	—	134	n.a.	n.a.
1952	181	7	—	188	137	325
1953	226	23	—	249	366	615
1954	298	27	1	327	504	831
1955	332	n.a.	21	n.a.	923	n.a.
1956	523	n.a.	100	n.a.	1,083	n.a.
1957	631	120	120	871	1,313	2,184
1958	811	307	344	1,462	1,797	3,259
1959	1,000	333	444	1,777	1,500	3,277
1960	1,125	375	500	2,000	1,134	3,134
1961	814	271	362	1,447	1,172	2,619
1962	1,221	407	542	2,170	1,318	3,488
1963	1,640	547	729	2,916	n.a.	n.a.

Note: n.a. stands for "not available."

Sources: State Statistical Bureau, *Ten Great Years, Statistics of the Economic and Cultural Achievements of the People's Republic of China* (Peking: Foreign Languages Press, 1960), p. 86; Chao Kang, *The Rate and Pattern of Industrial Growth in Communist China* (Ann Arbor: University of Michigan Press, 1965), Table C-1, pp. 123 and 129; Asian Political Economic Association, *Chugoku seiji keizai soran* [*Abstract of China's Political Economy*] (Tokyo: Author, 1964), p. 521; J. C. Liu, "Communist China's Chemical Fertilizer Industry and Agricultural Development," unpublished manuscript.

wise be used for capital goods imports. Nevertheless, as Table 3-9 shows, circumstances forced planners to expand both fertilizer production and consumption appreciably. Such a trend continued even during the Great Leap and the economic crisis—so much so that the fertilizer industry was among the few industrial branches which continued to expand even after 1960. The production of chemical fertilizer in 1962 was estimated at around two million tons, and consumption at about three and a half million tons.[33]

This analysis suggests that it may be misleading to look only at fixed-capital investments in agriculture in trying to determine the relative position of agriculture on the planners' scale of preferences. A more appropriate measure would be based upon the total investment resources channeled into agriculture—including industrial resources such as electric power serving farm production, agricultural machinery, fertilizer, and investments designed to create the capacity to produce these. Yet such an assessment only strengthens the conclusion that until 1960 agriculture ranked low on the list of investment priorities. The bulk of the direct or indirect investments made were capital-cheap (with the notable exception of fertilizer)—so much so that the effectiveness and the productivity of many projects were seriously impaired.

Low investments alone, however, cannot explain the shortfalls in farm production. Resources invested were poorly used and therefore to a considerable extent wasted. Indeed, agricultural cadres often paid so little attention to the relationship between planting distance, depth of plowing, soil moisture, crop strain, and soil fertility that applications of chemical fertilizer were at times not only wasted but even counterproductive.

Similar difficulties plagued water conservation to an even greater extent. Thus, it was officially admitted that 40–60 per cent of the water in the large irrigation systems was lost through leakage.[34] This high seepage, coupled with inadequate drainage, caused waterlogging and sometimes serious alkalinization and salinization.[35] At the same time, the digging of extremely deep canals in the North China plain has tended to lower the water table to undesirable levels in some areas. A vast number of wells were dug, but more than half of these turned out to be either useless or so shallow as to become unproductive with only a small drop in the water table.[36] In some areas, artesian wells were used for irrigation, but artesian water often contains such high amounts of soluble salts that it is injurious to crops. As a matter of fact, some artesian water in Szechwan province proved saline enough to permit commercial production of the salt.[37] Last but not least, the fact that local cadres were under tremendous pressure to fulfill and overfulfill the extremely ambitious targets for water conservation encouraged the withdrawal of land from cultivation in some areas. For example, it was reported that irrigation canals under construction in the plains area of Honan province would reduce the cultivated area by about one-fifth to one-third.[38]

Technical deficiencies of these types characterized water conservation projects from the early 1950s on, but they became particularly pronounced during the Great Leap. The downgrading of the expert and the decentralization of economic management were felt perhaps more in this field than in any other. In the pursuit of the "mass line," projects were designed locally by the peasants according to the availability of local construction materials. The technical problems were solved by "letting all teachings contend"—that is, through free debate and practice.[39] Locally manufactured cement and steel were used; and wood, bamboo, tile, and other materials were substituted freely for steel, iron, and cement. There probably were as many "formulas" for concrete as there were construction sites. One such "formula" called for 70 per cent powder ground from old brick, 25 per cent lime, and 5 per cent gypsum; and a *hsien* in Ningsia was said to be making concrete with clay as the principal component.[40]

The zeal of the cadres and the pressure from above led to a misallocation of resources in many other ways as well. In the attempt to mobilize fully all the underemployed labor, even labor needed in farm production was caught up in the construction of irrigation canals, dams, and other water conservation projects. As a result, acute labor shortages developed in 1958 and 1959— to the point that in some places fields were overgrown because they were insufficiently weeded or were left uncultivated altogether.

LAND POLICIES. The difficulties produced by inadequate investment and technical deficiencies were greatly aggravated by the continual reorganization and disorganization in mainland China's agriculture after 1949. There were repeated policy shifts and changes in production priorities, all of which produced uncertainty among the peasantry and the party cadres and contributed to the disruption of farm production.

Chinese Communist land policy since 1949 can perhaps be divided into the following four phases: land reform (1949-52), mutual-aid teams (1953-mid-1955), collectives (mid-1955-1957), communes (1958-present). During each of these periods a particular form of land tenure and farm organization was predominant. But every phase was unstable and characterized by certain subphases; each of these represented seeds of change and the beginnings of the next phase. As a result, each form of land tenure had a rather short life.

During the first phase, the holdings of the landlords were expropriated, and the land was redistributed to the tenant cultivators and the landless workers. The average size of the resultant holdings was suboptimal from the standpoint both of production efficiency and of state control. From the regime's viewpoint, however, it was a tactically necessary stage designed to break the political and economic power of the landlords on the one hand and to gain the goodwill of the peasantry on the other. The power of the regime was not yet fully consolidated, so the support of the peasantry was still felt to be necessary.

As soon as land reform was completed, the peasantry was pushed, cajoled, and induced into progressively more advanced forms of producer cooperation. The method applied could be characterized as high-pressure gradualism based on a judicious combination of the carrot and the stick. The guiding principle of this program was to take the land from the peasants as soon as they obtained it in order to prevent them from consolidating their newly won gains.[41] Organization of mutual-aid teams served as one of the prime instruments for implementing this policy. At first, these were confined to so-called *ad hoc* mutual-aid teams, which were based on quite informal arrangements for pooling labor, particularly around harvest time. Gradually they were converted into three-season mutual-aid teams and finally into permanent ones.

In the permanent mutual-aid teams, the members maintained full control over their landholdings, which they continued to work as separate units. At the same time, they pooled their labor, the rewards of which were fixed in work-day units. Some of the teams had communal sinking funds which were used to finance the purchase of equipment and other products for the use of the team as a whole.

It was but a relatively short step from a permanent mutual-aid team to an "agricultural producers' cooperative of the less advanced type." In the latter, both land and labor were pooled. Land use was collectively determined, but the peasants retained their title and rights to the land. All these cooperatives had an accumulation fund to which a certain proportion of the annual return was allocated. After taxes in kind were paid and the allotment to this sinking fund was made, the rest of the net return was divided into a land share and a labor share. The land share was distributed according to the size of the landholding each peasant brought into the cooperative, while the labor share was divided on the basis of each member's labor input calculated in terms of work-day units.

After such cooperatives were organized, considerable pressure was gradually exerted to force them to reduce the land share. When the land share became zero and net return was divided only on the basis of labor inputs, the cooperative became one of the "more advanced" type. In this kind of collective, the peasants retained their title to the land but derived no income therefrom. They could theoretically withdraw from the collective and take their land or land of "equivalent quantity and quality" with them, but in practice it was rather difficult to exercise this right of withdrawal. At the same time, each member could retain a small plot of land for his own use—that is, to raise vegetables, fruit, or livestock.[42]

The whole process of transformation from private landholding to almost complete collectivization was compressed into the four years from 1953 through 1956. And it followed a three-year turmoil accompanying land reform. Thus, Chinese agriculture was in a state of constant instability between 1949 and 1956. Yet collectivization did not mark the end of the process. The introduction of the communes—at first slowly and cautiously at the end of 1957 and then at an unusually rapid pace in 1958—spelled further upheaval in the countryside.

The precise origin of the communes is rather obscure; but there is no question that they constituted an integral and essential element of the Great Leap. As was shown earlier, central to the Great Leap was the notion of the "mass line"—the release of the "spontaneous initiative of the masses," the mass mobilization of labor and of the total energies of the people as a whole. In the implementation of this strategy, economic management was decentralized, and the communes emerged as highly centralized instruments of local control and decision-making. Centralization at the top, in effect, was replaced by centralization at the bottom.

In keeping with the general character of the early phase of the Great Leap, the initial conception and direction of commune organization was quite radical. These larger units were formed by the amalgamation of a number of collectives (on the average about 30) into communes having an average membership of 4,000-5,000 households. Organization also entailed fusion of local governmental functions, including security and military, with agricultural and industrial activities so that in most cases the commune became coincident with the *hsiang*. Further, the commune was to handle local trade, finance, taxation, accounting, statistics, and planning—all, of course, under strong local party control. While from its inception the commune was subdivided into production brigades (roughly equivalent to the former collectives) and production teams (more or less corresponding to the producers' cooperatives of the less advanced type), in this early radical phase it was the center of economic decision-making and of resource allocation. It could shift labor from place to place, task to task, and village to village within its boundaries. It held broad control over land use and the planning of production. At the same time, it took over the last vestige of private landholding and of household farm production—the small private plots which the peasants had retained in the collectives.

A number of measures that were designed to collectivize and communize consumption, distribution, and social and family relations as well as production were also contemplated. Commune members were to be paid wages just like factory workers, although a part of the wages was to be in kind. Moreover, everyone was expected to work at least 28 days in the month.[43]

In essence, what seems to have been intended was a far-reaching and completely revolutionary change in the forms of agricultural production and in the pattern of rural life. The communes, in conception, did not differ too much from the "agrogorods" Nikita Khrushchev advocated at one time.[44] Both in a sense strove for the creation of agricultural cities in which the peasantry would be uprooted from the land and in effect proletarianized. Such measures, if successful, would not only greatly facilitate state control over the countryside but could lead (it was hoped) to a restructuring of peasant attitudes and thus render the peasants more amenable to the regime's objectives.

Not all the features of these early regulations for a model commune were implemented. The dismantling of villages, for instance, did not get far. Other measures were not carried out uniformly throughout the country. Nevertheless, many of the basic features of the communes that sprang up rapidly all over China did not depart much from the early model regulations.

The many difficulties encountered in instituting these radical changes during 1958 stemmed to a considerable extent from the incentive problem and from the shifting of resources (including labor) from place to place. Differentiated and incentive rewards were in this early phase more and more replaced by an egalitarian wage system based on "each according to his need." Such a system not only created a great deal of friction and tension but soon had a negative effect on labor productivity. The shifting of labor led to considerable disruption of agricultural production. By the end of 1958 and early 1959, therefore, the leadership was forced to begin its retreat from the early conception of the commune.

In December 1958, the party Central Committee adopted a series of resolutions designed to rationalize the communes, alleviate some of their most extreme features, and decentralize them.[45]

The effect of these changes was to transfer the locus of economic decision-making from the commune to the production brigade. These production brigades once more became the basic units for accounting, taxation, and income distribution.[46] As part of the reforms, the "free supply" system was de-emphasized, and the money wage payments geared to the quantity and quality of labor input were given greater weight.

With the deepening of the agricultural crisis in the course of 1960, schemes for the mobilization of labor were abandoned, and the construction and special production units which had proliferated during the Great Leap were discontinued. The commune was further decentralized so that the production team, with an average membership of about 40 households, gradually became the basic unit for resource allocation and economic decision-making. As part and parcel of this reversal, private garden plots were reintroduced, and peasants were permitted to raise livestock and vegetables on them.[47] By the end of 1961, therefore, the agrarian transformations of the Great Leap had run full circle. In many cases, even the communal mess halls were abandoned as the commune became largely a unit of local government. The forms of agricultural production, consumption, and distribution reverted, in essence, to those of the collectivization stage of 1955-56.[48]

Changes in the degree of centralization and in commune organization were clearly reflected also in farm savings policy. Thus, during the early radical phase when the commune center was the focus of resource allocation, quite a large share of annual output and income was channeled into the sinking fund. There were many reports that individual communes had set aside 50 per cent or more of their total income for this investment reserve.[49] Such a policy naturally aggravated the incentive problem, for so little commune income was left for distribution to members that the income of the farm households was drastically lowered. As the difficulties encountered by the communes multiplied and as the locus of decision-making shifted downward to the production brigade and then to the production team, the share diverted to the reserve fund was progressively lowered. The reversal went so far that during 1960, when the production team was assigned growing responsibilities, new regulations specified that no more than 5 per cent of the collectively earned income could be reserved for investment.[50]

This very experimentation and constant shifting of policy was bound to have a negative effect on incentives just because of the uncertainties engendered. In fact, the effect was perhaps even more adverse than that which a relatively unfavorable set of measures (unfavorable from the peasants' point of view) left unchanged for some time would have had.

The constant changes, of course, have not been confined to recent years but have characterized Chinese Communist agricultural policy since 1949. They are a reflection of the regime's continuous groping for an incentive system which would enable it to have its cake and eat it too—that is, a system which would permit the regime to extract the maximum surpluses from agriculture without interfering with farm production. The ideal situation, from the regime's standpoint, would involve stable consumption but rising production in agriculture.

The character of Chinese Communist land policy perhaps can best be brought out by comparing Soviet and Chinese experiences in agrarian transformation. Possibly the most critical difference between the two lies in the fact that in the Soviet Union land reform was "from below," while in Communist China it was carefully planned and engineered "from above." This fact profoundly affected the relations between the peasantry and the regime in the two settings.

In both cases, the redistribution of land was the first item on the agenda of the agrarian program. The Chinese Communists, however, came to power after a prolonged period of civil war, while in Russia revolution preceded civil war. Therefore, the Chinese were able to carry through their land reform program undisturbed by the clash of arms and in a systematic manner. But the Bolsheviks were plagued by acute problems of food supply during the period of "war communism" and, thus, had to resort to forced confiscation of grain and other agricultural produce. Such confiscations alienated the peasantry from the regime almost from the beginning and, moreover, turned out to be counterproductive from a procurement standpoint, for they created an atmosphere in which the peasants hid their grain, fed it to their livestock, or consumed it themselves rather than surrender it to the authorities. At the same time, Russian peasants reduced their plantings to meet only their own consumption needs.

In view of this situation, the Soviet regime found it necessary to beat a tactical retreat and to institute the New Economic Policy. One essential feature of NEP was heavy reliance upon market incentives as a means of expanding and procuring the marketable share of output. Such a policy, however, inevitably strengthened the economic and political power of the wealthiest peasants, the kulaks. Lenin explicitly recognized this fact: "We must not shut our eyes to the fact that the replacement of requisitioning by the tax in kind means that the kulak element under this system will grow far more than hitherto. It will grow in places where it could not grow before." [51]

The "scissors crisis" of the 1920s was but a reflection of the dilemma facing the Soviet regime during the NEP period.* The regime had committed itself to reliance upon market incentives, but it was reluctant to pay the price in terms of reduced savings and investments. Collectivization seemed the answer to this dilemma. In light of the power of the kulaks, though, collectivization was bound to meet with strong resistance, so if it was to be consummated rapidly, violent means would have to be employed.

Collectivization provided a short-run remedy for the situation, but in the long run it turned out to be the first link in a vicious circle which has plagued Russian planners throughout Soviet history. As I have indicated, one of the central purposes of collectivization was to create institutions which would bring about a high rate of saving in the economy. Because of the curtailment in farm output and in livestock numbers, however, the high rate of saving was imposed upon a shrunken farm product and income. As a result, not only were rural standards of living reduced, but

---

* "Scissors" is a term widely used in Russia and elsewhere to denote the relationship between the prices at which farmers sell their products and the prices at which they purchase industrial goods needed for agricultural production and household consumption. In essence, a "scissors crisis" arose because the peasantry was unwilling to sell grain in the quantities desired by the government at the prices being offered them.

peasant incentives, even in the collectives, were undermined. Thus, agricultural recovery was greatly impeded. At the same time, capital had to be diverted to replace the draft power of animals lost in the process of collectivization. The more these factors hampered agricultural recovery, of course, the greater the pressure on agriculture had to be.

Because the Chinese Communists came to power after a prolonged civil war, they had ample opportunity to prepare and even to carry out land reform in areas they controlled. They instituted varying types of land reform in Yenan. In the process, they were trying to see which measures would be best designed to carry out land reform most speedily and most effectively. They experimented with different kinds of land-reform tactics, tested the reforms' political appeal to the peasantry, and trained cadres in methods of land-reform implementation. They had further opportunities for experimentation when they conquered Manchuria between 1947 and 1949. After 1949, they could apply to the rest of the mainland the lessons they had learned.

The Chinese Communists' objective in carrying out land reform was political rather than economic, *i.e.*, to gain the goodwill of the peasantry and simultaneously to break the political and economic power of the landlord class. They viewed class struggle as an integral and necessary part of land reform. It constituted an essential prerequisite for extending and institutionalizing party control over the village and the countryside.[52] At the time land reform was consummated, therefore, the Chinese Communist position in the rural areas was markedly different from that of the Russian party in 1917-18. The former enjoyed more goodwill (however temporary it may have been) and exercised much more control than the latter.

The Chinese Communist policy makers, however, were exceedingly conscious of the Soviet collectivization debacle and most anxious to avoid a repetition of it.[53] This consideration was one of the prime reasons why they embarked upon varying forms of producer cooperation as soon as land reform was carried out. Because they did not want the peasants to consolidate their newly won gains, the policy makers deemed it imperative to begin taking the land away from the peasants before their economic position became so fortified that collectivization would have to be violent.[54] For the same reason, Communist leaders instituted a series of transitional forms of farm organization designed to facilitate the shift from private landholding to collectivization.

The only group in the countryside with both the capacity and the incentive to resist (the landlords) was broken, and many of its members were physically liquidated—particularly during the campaign against the "counterrevolutionaries" in 1951. No class of "rich peasants" (kulaks) was allowed to develop on a significant scale. The road to collectivization was subdivided into several steps, and these were so designed that the apparent distance from one to another was not too great. As a result of these tactics, China's road to collectivization was smoother than Russia's, and her agricultural procurement problems were less acute. Nevertheless, China's incentive problems turned out to be just as intractable as Russia's. As a matter of fact, the Chinese tactics had strong counterincentive effects, for peasants were careful not to produce too much or to accumulate too much livestock or too many tools lest they be classified as "rich peasants."

It is against this background that the Chinese Communists were seeking new means by which they could break out of the vise of agricultural stagnation. Having been relatively successful in their drive to collectivize, they were apparently emboldened to go beyond tested forms of agricultural and economic organization under socialism. They began to innovate (through communes, through decentralization, and through mass mobilization) and to depart from the Russian model. Their success in agrarian policy, however, lay in tactical adaptations of a tested model. From the vantage point of 1965, they appear to have failed when they embarked on radical innovation.

Thus, in trying to solve the agricultural and peasant problem, the Chinese Communists after 1957 fell into the same trap as their Soviet predecessors. The consequences were not quite the same, though. The drastic curtailment of crop and livestock production in Russia between 1928 and 1932 led only to a short halt in industrial growth, but the later contraction in China resulted in an industrial standstill after 1960. Except during World War II, when vast areas of European Russia were overrun by German armies, it is doubtful whether the Soviet economy ever experienced an industrial recession of comparable proportions. The Soviets, moreover, have never been forced to reverse their order of planning priorities as radically and as completely as the Chinese were forced to do in early 1962.[55]

The Recent Recovery

After 1960 the Chinese economy exhibited many of the classical symptoms of a deep economic depression, a phenomenon quite uncharacteristic of Soviet-type economies. Just as the Great Leap induced a sharp rise in urban employment and in migration to the cities, this depression contributed to the spread of urban unemployment. The swollen and partially unemployed city population, in turn, complicated the problem of urban food supply at a time of falling agricultural production. In coping with this situation, the regime apparently felt that the difficulties of urban food supply and of the collection burden in the countryside could be eased simultaneously by a more or less forced exodus to the villages. (This movement reached its peak in 1962.) The smaller urban population could then rely to a considerable extent upon grain imports for its supply of staples. As a result, the regime could avoid raising the agricultural tax and compulsory purchase quotas appreciably and thus maintain—at least for the time being—a more favorable incentive system for the farmer. Such measures, in effect, meant that China in some respects reverted to a prewar pattern of agricultural trade during the early 1960s. She once more became a net importer of grain and used these imports to relieve the burden imposed on internal transport and distribution.

Apparently, the 1960/61 consumption year marked the low point of the depression, while the 1962 harvest may have marked the beginnings of recovery. There is no question that there has been a significant improvement in the agricultural and food supply situation, and there have been increasing signs of a general economic recovery as well. As of 1964-65, indications pointed to the beginnings of a cumulative upturn. Whether this upturn will gain increasing momentum or be nipped in the bud will depend largely upon the quality of the harvest in the next few years and the character of government policies.

In this context, one needs to face the fundamental question of whether China's economic stagnation is a temporary, short-run phenomenon or a more chronic condition reflecting the existence of more durable and therefore less tractable variables. Here it is important to emphasize that the Chinese Communists mounted a program of economic development which carried them continuously forward with great momentum for "ten great years," 1949-59. The rapid rate of economic growth actually achieved in a sense provided its own self-justifying rationale and served as a vital sanction in spurring on the party, the cadres, and the people at large to increasing efforts and sacrifices. There were, of course, certain favorable factors uniquely operative in this period. During the first half of the decade, for example, economic expansion was based to a considerable extent on the rehabilitation of a war-devastated or -disrupted plant. As a result, relatively modest inputs could yield sizable increments in output. Other advantages were the availability of Soviet credits until 1957 and of Soviet technical assistance until mid-1960. On the other hand, certain uniquely unfavorable factors have been at work in recent years. Apart from a succession of three adverse weather years, the sudden withdrawal of Soviet technicians in 1960 and the near cessation of complete plant deliveries which followed contributed greatly to the sharp curtailment and disruption of industrial production.

Perhaps the most significant and possibly most lasting legacy of the Great Leap may lie in the damage it wrought in morale and in the organizational framework of the economy and the polity. The economic crisis must have destroyed the image of invincibility and infallibility in which the regime had so convincingly enveloped itself up to 1959-60. There is no question that the cadres were left confused and disillusioned and that the people's confidence in the leadership was shaken. At the same time, the institutional framework of the economy was weakened. Such a judgment applies particularly to agricultural organization, the pattern of land use, and the whole incentive structure in agriculture. Last but not least, statistical services were profoundly disorganized, and technical considerations were thrown to the wind.

These tendencies have, of course, been reversed since 1961-62. Beginning particularly with 1963, one can detect the return of an atmosphere of quiet self-confidence. At the same time, there are clear indications that the regime is acutely conscious of the need for caution. Nevertheless, strong temptations to embark on a bold course again as soon as agricultural conditions permit still persist. If the Chinese Communist leadership continues to pursue an "agriculture first" policy, if it can curb its ambitions for rapid industrialization, if it keeps the rate of investment at modest levels, and if it carefully nurtures a favorable incentive system in the countryside, the damage to the economy may gradually be repaired to the point where rapid industrialization would once more become feasible. While it is impossible to assess the amount of time required to accomplish this end, the Chinese Communist leadership appears to expect that the economy will have recovered sufficiently by the end of 1965 to permit the launching of a new Five Year Plan in 1966.

Conclusions

In this and the preceding chapter, the character of economic policy and performance in the 16 years of Chinese Communist rule was analyzed. The question is: What light does this analysis throw on the central problem of the present study, namely, the economy's capacity to support Communist China's foreign policy objectives? Most particularly, what has been the impact of economic policy and performance in terms of the power effect, the foreign trade effect, and the model effect?

We have seen that the Chinese Communists inherited a chaotic and badly disrupted economy which they welded together in a comparatively short time. Having rehabilitated this war-torn economy, they pushed ahead on a broad front of economic advance and achieved impressive gains, particularly in industrial growth. However, in its impatience and zeal to accelerate the rate of economic advance, the regime overreached itself. The

Great Leap was launched on a series of miscalculations, errors in plan design, and serious mistakes in plan implementation. As a result, the rate of growth was indeed accelerated in the short run, but at a high cost. The Great Leap produced far-reaching disorganization in agriculture—so much so that the economy as a whole was caught in the throes of a profound crisis. As will be shown in the next chapter, this setback cost the Chinese mainland economy approximately a decade of growth.

The depression reached its depth in 1961, but since 1962 the economy has been recovering gradually and without interruption. As a result, the regime's self-confidence, which seemed to have been shaken in the two to three years between 1960 and 1962, was restored.

What effect did these fluctuations have upon China's present economic power potential? In spite of the recent setbacks and just by virtue of its sheer size, China must be ranked among the 10 leading industrial powers in the world. There is an enormous gap between the size of her industrial establishment and that of the Soviet Union or the United States. On the other hand, the distance between her and Japan, Germany, France, Italy, or even the United Kingdom is much narrower in terms of total industrial production capacity, although not in terms of per capita product. This fact means that unless she suffers a political or economic breakdown as a result of foreign invasion or a chronic disequilibrium in the population-food supply balance, China has the economic capability to support a military establishment of such range and scope that she will be able to pursue her great power ambitions on the Asian continent and at the same time exercise considerable influence beyond it.

The mainland economic trends of the past 16 years naturally have affected the appeal of Communist China as a development model for other underdeveloped countries to emulate. This appeal was greatest during the first decade of Chinese Communist rule, when the economy was performing well and the country was rapidly industrializing. The Great Leap and its aftermath have tarnished the image of success, but not as much as one might expect. Increasing foreign aid commitments to underdeveloped countries, coupled with technical assistance and deliveries of industrial equipment, have to some extent at least obscured China's economic setback. Also, the almost total statistical blackout and the general lack of solid information concerning economic developments since 1960 have helped to veil the full dimensions of the recent crisis.

China's economic development has, of course, had a decisive impact on the character, scope, and extent of its international economic relations, as will be shown in the next three chapters. Economic expansion brought with it rapid increases in exports and imports. The geographic scope of these exchanges rapidly expanded to encompass more and more countries; simultaneously, trade levels with most of these rose as well. Such trade expansion, in turn, served as one of the principal vehicles for modernizing Chinese industry and for augmenting its production capacity. It also enabled China to use foreign trade pressures and inducements as one of the instruments for the implementation of its foreign policy objectives. However, as will be shown in greater detail in Chapter 6, the effectiveness of this particular foreign policy weapon was limited because of the relatively small volume of China's trade with any one non-Communist country. This limitation was accentuated when mainland trade began to shrink in 1960 under the impact of the economic crisis and its aftermath.

CHAPTER FOUR

Foreign Trade and the Economic Development of Mainland China

The traditional Chinese state, operating within a vast mainland economy, was largely inward-oriented. That is, its foreign trade was small in relation to its total domestic output of goods and services.[1] This trade was confined mainly to consumer goods and had a minimal effect on the character of domestic economic activity. While it did induce some innovations, these seem to have developed slowly and did not lead to far-reaching technical and social transformations of the type which took place later, *i.e.*, during the 19th and 20th centuries.[2]

Under the impact of Western pressure and initiative during the 18th century and later, the volume of foreign trade grew, its character changed, and its effect on domestic economic trends became much more significant. Imports opened the way to new goods, new and cheaper substitutes for existing goods, and to new methods of manufacture. As a result, by the late 19th century, factory yarn imported from abroad had displaced domestic handicraft spinning. Imported manufactures had partially replaced domestic output, but at the same time they had widened the market, raised the demand for cotton textiles, and thus created one of the preconditions for the growth of import-displacing industry at a later stage.[3] As a result, in the 20th century we witness the development of a sizable cotton textile industry in China and the gradual elimination of cotton textile imports. This transformation was based on the import of cotton textile machinery, the manufacture of which, in the face of clearly demonstrated home demand, was then also developed domestically as technical conditions permitted.

During the chaotic hundred years between the Opium War and the formation of the People's Republic of China, foreign trade grew significantly. In quantitative terms, to be sure, it remained a minor sector of the mainland economy. In qualitative terms, however, it assumed major importance—as a highway for introducing innovating influences in consumption and production and as a factor which widened the market. This qualitative role of foreign trade has been greatly enhanced in Communist China. Paradoxically, foreign trade has been performing this role despite the Chinese Communists' ideological and programmatic commitment to autarky in the long run.

The principal goal of Chinese Communist trade policy has been to facilitate and accelerate industrialization by increasing imports of required equipment and raw materials. Some raw materials are either not available domestically or available only in small quantities and in widely scattered locations. Moreover, China had no manufacturing facilities for many types of machinery and transport and little, if any, of the technical know-how needed to construct them. While it would probably be erroneous to say that the Chinese economy would not have grown without imports, growth would undoubtedly have been much slower and of a different character. Up to 1960, imports were largely producer goods, and their cessation would have forced cutbacks in investment and a drastic scaling down of the expansion program in heavy industry. The reduction in investment would necessarily have led to a decline in the rate of growth of the national product.* The economy, of course, might have gradually adjusted to such a cessation through a channeling of domestically available resources into the expansion of sectors not as dependent on imported technology, equipment, and raw materials, but such a reorientation would have run strongly counter to the planners' scale of preferences.

In tracing the interrelationships between trade and economic development, C. P. Kindleberger considers three alternative

---

* The quantitative dimensions of the cessation of imports will be explored in hypothetical form later in this chapter.

models: with foreign trade as the leading, the lagging, and the balancing sector.[4] The last of these models best fits Communist China. In this model, foreign trade plays no active role in defining economic objectives and in shaping the character of the development program. As this program is elaborated and translated into an economic plan, however, certain bottlenecks and inconsistencies become apparent, *e.g.*, the lack of certain types of raw materials, the lack of particular kinds of plant or equipment, the lack of some specific types of know-how. Faced with such deficiencies, the planners may be forced either to abandon certain projects or to fill the gap through imports. Total import requirements are then compiled on this basis and compared with export availabilities. The latter, of course, are adjusted to take account of credits and/or loan repayment obligations. The import requirements are then scaled down on the basis of planning priorities to coincide with these availabilities.[5]

Ultimately, in a large, underdeveloped, and densely populated country such as mainland China, both trade and economic growth may be considered a function of the state of food and agriculture. If the experience of the last decade and a half is at all indicative, it would seem that the agricultural output per capita largely determines the *rate of saving* in the economy. Thus, as the farm and nonfarm output per capita rose during the recovery period of the early 1950s, the rate of saving also rose. As the per capita farm product leveled off about 1953, however, so did the rate (not the level) of saving in relation to national income, despite the fact that nonagricultural output per capita continued to rise.

The planners' allocation of these savings to alternative lines of investment largely determines the rate and pattern of economic growth. One of the crucial policy decisions here is the share of investment assigned to agricultural as compared to industrial development. One could argue that in the Chinese case one of the principal reasons for agricultural stagnation even prior to 1959-60 was inadequate investment. As was shown in the last chapter, the reorganization of farm institutions and adverse incentives also played crucial roles in hampering agricultural development.

While per capita farm output and the rate of investment remained more or less stable, the volume of investment funds grew year by year. With rising investments and rapid industrial development, the demand for the import of machinery, transport equipment, and industrial raw materials increased as well, although not at the same rate. At the same time, as long as agricultural production expanded apace with population, the quantity of farm products available for export increased too. The expansion of exports, moreover, was facilitated by a gradual change in commodity composition from crude and unprocessed materials to manufactured products—mostly cotton textiles—which have a higher margin of value added per unit of raw material input.

The mutually reinforcing process of industrialization and expansion of foreign trade could proceed as long as farm output kept pace with population growth. With a sharp decline in agricultural production, however, a chain reaction set in. The per capita farm product dropped, the rate of saving declined, the rate of investment fell, and industrial production was curtailed. Consequently, the demand for imported capital goods and industrial raw materials decreased markedly, and agricultural imports rose sharply. In other words, imports changed in character and shrank partly because of the falloff in demand and partly because of the economy's greatly reduced capacity to provide exports with which to finance imports.

In the final analysis, the volume, direction, and commodity composition of Communist China's foreign trade are determined by the interplay of six closely related elements. These are domestic resources, the regime's commitment to industrialization, its commitment to growing military power, the course of domestic economic development, the state of Sino-Soviet relations, and the various controls restricting economic contacts with non-Communist countries.

The structure of import demand, for example, clearly reflected the regime's commitments and the inability to satisfy them just by relying on domestic plant and technology. This limitation explains why machinery and military matériel constituted a large portion of the imports. At the same time, the fact that these goods could not be obtained from the West but were available on credit from the Soviet Union and other Communist countries contributed greatly to the intimacy of Sino-Soviet economic relations. Such intimacy could continue unabated, even after the virtual cessation of Soviet credits in 1957, so long as China's import demand did not change markedly and her domestic resources and the course of her economic development could support the expansion of imports.

The harvest failures of 1959 and after, however, forced a shift in planning priorities and an accompanying shift in the composition of imports. Foods—particularly grain—displaced capital goods as the leading item on the import bill. The Soviet Union, faced with its own agricultural difficulties, was in no position to ship large quantities of grain to China. Several non-Communist countries, on the other hand, had large surpluses which were not subject to trade controls. Therefore, a change in the direction of trade inevitably followed from the change in commodity composition. This reorientation in direction would have been necessary regardless of the deterioration of Sino-Soviet relations, although the latter undoubtedly accelerated the process.

Trends in the Value of Communist China's Foreign Trade

In analyzing the foreign trade sector of the Chinese economy since 1949, one is faced with major difficulties. It is a sector about which the official authorities have been particularly secretive, so only the most aggregate data are available from Chinese sources. Fortunately, most of China's trading partners publish, in greater or lesser detail, foreign trade statistics which make it possible to reconstruct trends in the value, volume, direction, and composition of her foreign trade. This reconstruction naturally raises some problems. There are, first of all, certain margins of error inherent in converting data in different national currencies into dollars at the official rates of exchange. The problem is further complicated by the fact that other countries' imports are as a rule accounted for on a c.i.f. basis, that is, including costs of insurance and shipping. Since from China's vantage point these are exports which should be accounted for f.o.b. at the shipping point, the adjustment for the c.i.f. factor inevitably entails a certain margin of error. Finally, because commodity classifications of imports and exports differ in the national statistics of individual countries, the definition of common commodity categories involves aggregation or separation, and errors may result therefrom.

Nevertheless, it is unlikely that these errors are large enough to distort the results seriously. Moreover, some of the errors may be assumed to cancel each other out. At any rate, even though certain margins of error remain, the data thus derived are still better and much more detailed than the official statistics available. The principal reason is that Chinese Communist trade statistics contain a strong upward bias because of the overvaluation of the ruble in relation to the yuan—at least up to 1959 and possibly up to the revaluation of the ruble in 1960.[6]

In the Chinese statistics, trade with the Soviet Union and Eastern Europe was accounted for at an exchange rate of 1:1 (*i.e.*, one ruble to the yuan).* At the same time, trade with all non-Communist countries was based on an exchange rate of 2.36 yuan to the U.S. dollar. The official ruble-dollar exchange rate, however, was 4:1. Therefore, the ruble-yuan, the yuan-dollar, and ruble-dollar rates were clearly inconsistent. On the basis of the latter two, the ruble-yuan rate should have been about 1.7:1.0 (4.00:2.36) instead of 1:1. The impact of this foreign exchange distortion on the official trade figures perhaps can best be illustrated by the following hypothetical example:

Communist China's Trade Turnover	With Soviet Union and Eastern Europe	With Non-Communist World	Total Trade Turnover
(1) In original currencies	60 rubles	$40	—
(2) Converted into yuan at prevailing official exchange rates	60 yuan	95 yuan	155 yuan
(3) Row 2 converted into U.S. dollars at official yuan-dollar rates	$25	$40	$65
(4) Row 1 converted into U.S. dollars at prevailing official exchange rates	$15	$40	$55
(5) Row 4 converted into yuan at official yuan-dollar rates	35 yuan	95 yuan	130 yuan

* For the evidence and reasoning on which this statement is based, see Appendix C.

In this example, rows (2) and (3) are converted into yuan and dollars respectively on the basis of the official ruble-yuan rates, while rows (4) and (5) are based on the mutually consistent rates. As may be seen, the yuan figures in row (2) are above those in row (5); similarly, the dollar figures in row (3) are higher than those in row (4). For this reason, all foreign trade data in this chapter—whether stated in yuan or dollars—are based on the official yuan-dollar and ruble-dollar rates respectively unless otherwise indicated.

The value of Communist China's foreign trade grew rapidly and almost without interruption between 1950 and 1959. It is clear, therefore, that the fast pace of expansion in the economy as a whole was reflected in the international sector. Similarly, the general downturn in economic activity led to a sharp reduction in exports and imports after 1960.

China's exports and imports, as Table 4-1 shows, more than doubled between 1952 and 1959 but by 1962 fell back to the level of the early fifties. During the first few years—that is, through 1954—imports grew more rapidly than exports. This situation undoubtedly reflected the fact that China could draw on credits with which to finance imports beyond her capacity to pay with exports. Beginning with 1955, however, she started to amortize her debt to the Soviet Union, and therefore up to 1959 her exports expanded significantly faster than her imports. Even when her foreign trade began to contract in 1960, exports were less sharply curtailed than imports because of her repayment obligations. It is clear, therefore, that Soviet credits and then the necessity to repay them have played a significant role in determining the level and direction of China's foreign trade since the advent of the Communist regime.

The pace of Communist China's trade expansion may best be gauged by comparing it with movements in total world trade and in the trade of Japan, India, and some other countries. Through 1959 (see Table 4-2), her trade grew much more rapidly than total world trade, trade of all underdeveloped countries, or trade of all Asian countries as a group. Japan's exports, on the other hand, forged ahead at even a faster pace than China's did, but its imports lagged somewhat behind that rate. Japan's foreign trade

TABLE 4-1. Value and Direction of Communist China's Foreign Trade, 1952-63

(in millions of U.S. dollars)

Year	Soviet Union		Eastern Europe		Asian Communist Countries		Communist Countries Total	
	Exports	Imports	Exports	Imports	Exports	Imports	Exports	Imports
1952	416	554	(147)	(143)	(18)	(10)	581	707
1953	475	697	(183)	(199)	27	18	685	914
1954	578	759	(192)	(250)	45	30	815	1,039
1955	643	748	231	237	55	50	929	1,035
1956	764	733	237	264	65	60	1,066	1,057
1957	738	544	(249)	(284)	(90)	(55)	1,077	883
1958	881	634	294	410	(95)	(75)	1,270	1,119
1959	1,100	954	354	325	(135)	(80)	1,589	1,359
1960	848	817	316	340	(138)	(85)	1,302	1,242
1961	550	367	163	164	(187)	(144)	900	675
1962	516	233˙	147	78	(190)	(150)	853	461
1963	412	182	(154)	(89)	(200)	(155)	766	425

a Adjusted to take account of re-exports, which would have involved double counting.

b Data for 1963 are preliminary; for some countries, e.g., Cuba and Indonesia, they are incomplete. The world totals, therefore, include an allowance for these countries and are larger than the sum of the Communist and non-Communist world totals.

expansion, however, has continued up to the present, while the value of China's international transactions declined in the early 1960s and has been recovering only gradually.

Communist China's foreign trade performance, however, is somewhat less impressive when viewed from the vantage point of long-run historical perspective. Mainland Chinese trade attained its pre-Communist peak levels in 1928 and 1929. These earlier levels were then not surpassed on the import side until 1954 and on the export side until 1955 or 1956. Foreign trade continued to rise by about 60 per cent between 1954-56 and 1959. However, just as its growth was unusually rapid in the fifties, so was its decline precipitous after 1959. By 1962, imports had diminished by almost a half and had fallen below the 1928-29 level. Exports decreased somewhat less drastically. They dropped to just about (but not below) the prewar peak.[7]

Cuba		Non-Communist World				World Total			
		Unadjusted		Adjusted [a]		Unadjusted		Adjusted [a]	
Exports	Imports	Exports	Imports	Exports	Imports	Exports	Imports	Exports	Imports
—	—	348.4	272.0	290.3	183.4	929	979	871	890
—	—	413.5	285.3	353.5	193.3	1,099	1,200	1,039	1,107
—	1.2	352.6	285.8	304.2	219.8	1,165	1,326	1,119	1,260
—	0.4	467.6	314.9	415.8	285.5	1,397	1,350	1,345	1,321
—	—	606.0	429.6	546.0	408.2	1,672	1,487	1,612	1,465
—	—	598.6	527.7	537.3	508.3	1,676	1,411	1,615	1,391
—	3.6	725.3	767.0	641.4	742.4	1,995	1,890	1,911	1,865
—	0.1	664.4	669.9	632.0	651.4	2,253	2,029	2,221	2,011
9.6	32.1	732.4	655.5	698.4	636.8	2,044	1,930	2,010	1,912
83.3	91.5	615.0	663.3	588.0	647.4	1,598	1,430	1,571	1,414
97.0	89.0	676.2	602.7	647.1	589.3	1,626	1,153	1,597	1,139
n.a.	n.a.	753.1	709.5	712.3	698.6	1,740 [b]	1,282 [b]	1,699 [b]	1,271 [b]

Notes: Figures in parentheses are partially or wholly estimated by the author. For the methods on which these estimates are based, see Appendix B.
n.a. stands for "not available."
— stands for "none."

Sources: See Appendix B.

Direction of Trade

At this point, our primary concern is with an analysis of the broad geographic pattern of Communist China's foreign trade. We shall leave to the next two chapters a more detailed exploration of her economic relations with Communist countries and the non-Communist world respectively. As I noted earlier, this analysis rests on the foreign trade statistics of China's trading partners. Not all these data, however, are equally complete or reliable. The figures for the non-Communist world leave out a few small territories and principalities, but that fact should have no significant effect on the total. The Soviet data are comprehensive and detailed. On the other hand, it was not possible to obtain data for all the East European countries for one or two years. In such cases, I interpolated the missing elements by using the percentage

T A B L E 4 - 2 . Comparative Trends in the Foreign Trade
of Communist China, Other Selected Countries,
and the World, 1952–61

(in millions of U.S. dollars)

Area	Imports, c.i.f.			Exports, f.o.b.		
	1952	1959	1961	1952	1959	1961
World	86,500	120,700	140,200	80,000	115,200	133,400
Underdeveloped areas	24,300	27,300	30,700	20,900	25,800	27,600
India	1,696	1,986	2,246	1,299	1,304	1,386
Japan	2,028	3,599	5,810	1,273	3,456	4,236
Sterling Asia [a]	5,380	5,820	6,690	4,860	4,970	5,220
Other Asia [a]	2,720	2,600	3,320	1,940	2,250	2,280
Mainland China						
Unadjusted	979 [b]	2,029 [b]	1,430 [b]	929	2,253	1,598
Adjusted	890 [b]	2,011 [b]	1,414 [b]	871	2,221	1,571

[a] Excluding Japan and mainland China.

[b] Imports, f.o.b.

Sources: United Nations, *Statistical Yearbook, 1962* (New York: Author, 1963), Table 152, pp. 428–431, and Table 4–1 in this chapter.

share of trade for the preceding and succeeding years. The data situation was worse for the Asian Communist countries, *i.e.*, North Korea, North Vietnam, and Outer Mongolia. For these countries, the available information is most scanty and scattered, so the findings are subject to a considerable margin of error. Fortunately, trade with them constituted only a small portion of Communist China's total trade; therefore, this particular element of uncertainty need not seriously affect the reliability of the total figures.

It should also be noted that both the import and export figures for the Communist countries are f.o.b. at the border or shipping point. Most of the rest of the world, however, handles imports on a c.i.f. basis, *i.e.*, including the cost of freight and insurance up to the receiving point. For the sake of comparability, I have adjusted the latter to a f.o.b. basis as well.[8]

Except for the Communist countries of Asia, the margins of error resulting from these adjustments or interpolations are not likely to exceed 5-10 per cent. Therefore, they cannot alter the findings which emerge from an analysis of Tables 4-1 and 4-3. Thus, it is clear that China's trading pattern was radically altered by the advent of the Communist regime. Previously, the bulk of the country's foreign trade in the 20th century had been carried on with Great Britain, Japan, the United States, Hong Kong, France, and Germany. The order among these, however, had changed during the period. Trade with Eastern Europe had been negligible. Economic relations with Russia had been of considerable importance before World War I. About 11 per cent of China's exports went to her biggest neighbor, and 4 per cent of her imports came from there. But such trade dwindled to minor proportions in the interwar years.[9]

This pattern was sharply reversed after 1949 under the impact of Mao's "lean to one side" policy and free world embargoes on China trade. The first was an expression of a basic political commitment to an alliance between two Communist powers. This commitment was strongly reinforced in the economic realm by the second factor, which pushed the Chinese further into the arms of the Soviets. The direction of trade changed markedly again after 1960 because of the loosening of Sino-Soviet ties on the one hand and China's need for food imports from the West on the other.

The first sharp reorientation in China's trade took place in a relatively short period. It began as soon as the new regime came to power and was essentially completed by 1952. Within three years, trade with the Communist world rose from negligible proportions to a point where it absorbed nearly three-quarters of the total, and there was a correspondingly sharp decline in the relative standing of the non-Communist countries as a whole. As a result, while China's total trade rose by close to 20 per cent between 1950 and 1952, commercial interchange with the non-Communist countries fell by about one-half.

The speed with which this reorientation occurred is not surprising, for this was the period of the Korean War, when not only the United States but a host of other U.N. members im-

TABLE 4-3. Direction of Communist China's Foreign Trade, 1952–63, Adjusted

(in per cent)

	1952	1953	1954	1955	1956	1957	1958	1959	1960	1961	1962	1963
Imports												
Communist countries, Total	79.4	82.6	82.5	78.3	72.2	63.5	60.0	67.6	65.0	47.7	40.5	33.5
Soviet Union	62.2	63.0	60.2	56.6	50.0	39.1	34.0	47.4	42.7	25.9	20.5	14.3
Eastern Europe	(16.1)	(18.0)	(19.8)	17.9	18.0	(20.4)	22.0	16.2	17.8	11.6	6.8	(6.9)
Asian Communist countries	(1.1)	1.6	2.4	3.8	4.1	(4.0)	(4.0)	(4.0)	(4.4)	(10.2)	(13.2)	(12.2)
Cuba	—	—	0.1	negl.	—	—	0.2	negl.	1.7	6.5	7.8	
Non-Communist countries, Total	20.6	17.5	17.4	21.6	27.9	36.5	39.8	32.4	33.4	45.8	51.7	66.5
Exports												
Communist countries, Total	66.7	66.0	72.8	69.1	66.1	66.7	66.5	71.5	64.7	57.2	53.4	45.1
Soviet Union	47.8	45.8	51.7	47.8	47.4	45.7	46.1	49.5	42.2	34.9	32.3	24.2
Eastern Europe	(16.9)	(17.6)	(17.2)	17.2	14.7	(15.4)	15.4	15.9	15.7	10.4	9.2	(9.1)
Asian Communist countries	(2.1)	2.6	4.0	4.1	4.0	(5.6)	(5.0)	(6.1)	(6.9)	(11.9)	(11.9)	(11.8)
Cuba	—	—	—	—	—	—	—	—	0.5	5.3	6.1	
Non-Communist countries, Total	33.3	34.0	27.2	30.9	33.8	33.3	33.5	28.5	34.7	37.5	40.5	54.9

Notes: Figures in parentheses are partially or wholly estimated by the author. For the methods on which these estimates are based, see Appendix B.

— stands for "none."

negl. stands for "negligible."

Source: Table 4-1.

posed severe restrictions on their trade with China. At the same time, Communist China's "lean to one side" policy was implemented through the conclusion of a series of political and economic agreements with the Soviet Union in 1950. These laid the foundations for intimate economic ties between the two partners for some years to come.

In absolute terms, the non-Communist world's trade with China reached its low point in 1952 and then began to recover slowly after the Korean armistice. The pace of expansion, however, lagged behind the rapid growth of China's total trade, so in relative terms the process of displacement continued until 1954. As more and more countries relaxed their restrictions on trade with Communist China, total trade with the free world recovered to its former absolute level by 1957. In 1961-62, it began to regain its relative level as well. As a result, while Communist China's foreign trade declined by more than a third between 1959 and 1962, commercial interchange with non-Communist countries declined only about 4 per cent. By 1963 the downward trend in foreign trade was reversed under the impact of domestic recovery. This reversal was accompanied by a gradual rise in trade with the non-Communist world—so much so that it reached record levels in 1963.

A little more than half of China's trade in 1952 was with the Soviet Union, and almost a fifth was with Eastern Europe. Eastern Europe's share then fluctuated year by year without a consistent trend; however, after 1955 the importance of the Soviet Union declined somewhat as China's trade with the West expanded.

In value terms, on the other hand, the exchange of goods between China and the Soviet Union more than doubled between 1952 and 1959. Then it declined quite rapidly—so rapidly, in fact, that by 1963 it had shrunk to about one-fourth of the peak 1959 level. During the expansion phase, exports to the Soviet Union rose more rapidly than imports from it and then declined more slowly. Exports, for example, almost trebled between 1952 and 1959 and then declined by 1963 to about one-third of their peak level. Imports, however, less than doubled during the expansion phase and then dropped to one-fifth of their peak level. These contrasting tendencies reflect the fact that imports in the early

years were already relatively high because they were partly
financed by Soviet loans. Their further growth was slowed down
by the absence of additional long-term credits. In other words,
exports could at first lag behind imports, but as credits were
exhausted, exports had to be stepped up rapidly to take care of
both rising import requirements and loan repayments. Moreover,
the general economic contraction beginning in 1960 caused a
sharp curtailment in the demand for capital goods, which were
traditionally imported from the Soviet Union, while the drop
in food supply meant that highest priority had to be accorded to
food imports, which could not be obtained from the U.S.S.R.
The contraction was naturally reflected in reduced export
capacity as well, but the pressure of loan repayments induced
Chinese policy makers to exert every effort to avoid reductions
in shipments to the Soviet Union as much as possible.

Until the crisis-ridden years of the early 1960s, China's trade
with her Communist neighbors in Asia was small, although of
growing importance. Starting from practically nothing, it increased consistently year by year. By 1959-60, it amounted to 5-6
per cent of the total turnover. Then it apparently rose sharply
between 1960 and 1961 so that in the latter year for the first
time it exceeded China's trade with Eastern Europe.* Thus, total
trade turnover seems to have increased from less than $30 million
in 1952 to more than $300 million in 1962 and 1963. Not too
surprisingly, the trade series also show that each year China's
exports to these countries exceeded her imports from them. These
export surpluses were financed by Chinese loans and grants,
about which more will be said later.

The Regional Balance of Trade

Up through 1957 mainland China consistently maintained a trade
surplus with the non-Communist world as a whole. (See Table
4-4.) Exports to Europe exceeded imports through 1955. There
were small deficits in 1956 and 1957 and then much larger ones

---

* In view of the tentativeness of our data for China's trade with the Asian
Communist countries, these findings may need to be modified as more information becomes available.

until 1961. On the other hand, Asia as a whole purchased significantly more from China than vice versa in every year after 1952. This statement is particularly true for Hong Kong and, to a lesser extent, for Malaya-Singapore and Japan. Thus, in the early fifties Communist China accumulated considerable amounts of foreign exchange—especially sterling—in her trade with the West. Even afterward she continued to earn sterling in her Asian trade, but the surpluses were often canceled out by the deficits in her trade with the rest of the free world.

One of the most striking conclusions emerging from a detailed analysis of mainland trade with the non-Communist world (see Chapter 6) is the crucial and strategic importance of Hong Kong for China's economy. It is by far the most important and most secure source of foreign exchange earnings through trade, through remittances, and through a variety of other channels. The sterling earned there, for example, undoubtedly financed, at least in part, the grain imports from Canada and Australia.

China's trade balance with the Soviet Union and with the Communist countries as a whole followed just about an opposite course to that with the non-Communist world. Up through 1955, the mainland had deficits in its trade with both its senior partner and Eastern Europe. In subsequent years, the situation was reversed with respect to the Soviet Union but not with respect to the East European countries until 1959. The trade balance with the Asian Communist countries, however, was favorable throughout the period, and the combined surplus in China's trade with the Soviets and the Asian bloc after 1955 more than outweighed the deficits in trade with Eastern Europe. Hence, since 1956, China's deliveries to the Communist world as a whole have exceeded her purchases.

China could maintain an import surplus in trade with the Communist countries as long as she could draw upon Russian credits. Since she did not have to pay for all her imports from the Communist world with current exports, she could direct a larger portion of the latter to the non-Communist countries than she could have otherwise. Therefore, Soviet credits helped China, at least indirectly, in developing its export surplus with the free world.

Under the impact of all these different tendencies, Communist

TABLE 4-4. Communist China's Foreign Trade Balance, 1952–63

(in millions of U.S. dollars)

Year	Soviet Union	Eastern Europe	Asian Communist Countries	Communist Countries Total	Cuba	Non-Communist World Unadjusted	Non-Communist World Adjusted	World Total Unadjusted	World Total Adjusted
1952	−138	(+ 4)	(+ 8)	−126	—	+ 76	+107	− 50	− 19
1953	−222	(− 16)	+ 9	−229	—	+128	+160	−101	− 69
1954	−181	(− 58)	+15	−224	− 1	+ 67	+ 84	−159	−141
1955	−105	− 6	+ 5	−106	—	+153	+130	+ 46	+ 24
1956	+ 31	− 27	+ 5	+ 9	—	+176	+138	+185	+147
1957	+194	(− 35)	(+35)	+194	− 4	+ 71	+ 29	+265	+224
1958	+247	−116	(+20)	+151	—	− 42	−101	+105	+ 46
1959	+146	+ 29	(+55)	+230	—	− 6	− 19	+224	+210
1960	+ 31	− 24	(+53)	+ 60	− 22	+ 77	+ 62	+114	+ 98
1961	+183	− 1	(+43)	+225	− 8	− 48	− 59	+168	+158
1962	+283	+ 69	(+40)	+392	+ 8	+ 74	+ 58	+473	+458
1963	+230	(+ 65)	(+45)	+340	n.a.	+ 44	+ 14	+458	+428

Notes: Minor inconsistencies result from rounding.
Figures in parentheses are partially or wholly estimated by the author. For the methods on which these estimates are based, see Appendix B.
n.a. stands for "not available."
— stands for "none."

Source: Table 4-1.

China's aggregate trade balance was negative in the early 1950s but has been positive ever since. Even during the agricultural crisis of the early 1960s, surprisingly, she continued to export more than she imported. There are a number of indications which suggest that the Chinese Communists were determined to amortize their debt to the Soviet Union as rapidly as possible.* At the same time, the Chinese mounted a foreign aid program designed to assure the dominance of their influence in North Korea, North Vietnam, and Albania and the expansion of that influence into the underdeveloped and neutralist countries of Asia and Africa. The regime apparently assigned such a high priority to these political objectives that in 1962 it obtained a record export surplus in its trade with the Soviet Union and continued its foreign aid deliveries, although at a somewhat reduced level, even amidst the economic stagnation.

Commodity Composition of Communist China's Foreign Trade

Unfortunately, it is much more difficult to reconstruct the commodity composition than the direction of Communist China's foreign trade. This situation stems largely from the fact that most East European countries do not combine the country and commodity breakdowns of their trade even though they publish the two breakdowns separately. Moreover, in the case of the Communist countries of Asia, as I noted earlier, total trade and direction data, let alone commodity breakdowns, are scant. In contrast, the Soviet Union has published detailed foreign trade statistics, including commodity composition by country, for every year since 1955, and the U.S. Department of Commerce has compiled similar information year by year on trade between all non-Communist countries on the one hand and all Communist countries on the other.

We can account, therefore, for the commodity composition of about 80 per cent of Communist China's foreign trade (see

* These will be discussed further in the next chapter.

Tables 4-5 and 4-7). This percentage is sufficiently large to be fairly representative of total Chinese trade, the more so since the available data for Eastern Europe plus more general descriptive information suggest that the character of trade between Eastern Europe and China resembles that between the latter and the Soviet Union. While the weight of some specific subcategories would be different for Eastern Europe as a whole than for the Soviet Union, the relative importance of the principal commodity groups seems to be quite similar. Deliveries of machinery and equipment, for example, constituted 63 per cent of the Soviet export total in 1959 and 62 per cent in 1960. The corresponding proportions for Hungary, Poland, and Bulgaria combined (the only East European countries for which commodity breakdowns are available) were 58 and 64 per cent respectively. Since China's largest trading partners in Eastern Europe were Czechoslovakia and East Germany, the region's most industrialized countries, it is a fair presumption that capital goods figured more prominently in their exports to China. If these countries were included, therefore, it is probable that the percentages shown for this category in Table 4-5 would be somewhat higher.[10]

The changing commodity composition of Communist China's imports and exports, as shown in Tables 4-5 and 4-7, mirrors quite faithfully the regime's policies and the changing course of economic development which resulted partially therefrom. This observation is particularly true for imports because of their strategic role in the development process. The pace and character of domestic economic development determines the level and composition of import demand. In turn, import demand defines the value of exports needed to finance past and current imports. In such a system, planners tend to arrive at import demand first and then adjust it in the light of export capacity without paying much attention to efficiency and comparative costs.

IMPORTS. Communist China's imports prior to the economic crisis of the early 1960s were confined largely to capital goods, raw materials for industry, and arms. While there are no published data on purchases of military matériel and one cannot be absolutely certain that they are included in the trade statistics, there is at least a fair presumption that they are. It would seem that a substantial, although unknown, portion of Soviet credits to China went into the financing of military deliveries.[11] In fact, it is difficult to reconcile Soviet credit totals with the deficits China accumulated in her trade with the Soviet Union during the 1950s without assuming that military purchases are included in the statistics. The bulk of unspecified Soviet exports to China probably represents military deliveries.*

Machinery and equipment for both industry and transport constituted about one-third of China's total imports in the late 1950s. Perhaps the most significant aspect of such imports is the large-scale purchases of complete plants. The deliveries of complete plant installations were of prime importance from several points of view. First of all, such deliveries represent a rather special form of import, one based, figuratively speaking, on a "cradle to grave" proposition. That is, these plants are designed by the engineers of the exporting country (in this case the Soviet Union) according to the exporters' specifications, and the plant equipment is manufactured by that country. Then this equipment is installed by the exporting country's engineers and technicians, who come with the equipment and initially operate it. Although there are some precursors to this type of export, complete package deals are essentially novel. Second, there is probably no other country in which complete plant deliveries have assumed such importance as they did in China—in terms both of the volume of imports and of their role in the country's industrialization.

These complete plant projects constituted the very heart of the First Five Year Plan and of the Great Leap. Thus, complete plant imports grew continuously and rapidly—almost tenfold between 1952 and 1959–60. In 1961, however, they suddenly dropped to below even 1952 levels and have remained quite small since. This dramatic reversal within a single year is but another indication—perhaps the strongest and clearest at our disposal—that Chinese

---

* It must be borne in mind, however, that Soviet military deliveries could be hidden in several categories, not only in "other." For instance, if one sums up all the detailed subcategories under machinery and equipment, this sum differs from the total given for the category. The unspecified residual could, of course, be miscellaneous minor products and/or arms.

TABLE 4-5. Commodity Composition of Communist China's Imports, 1955–63 [a]

(in millions of U.S. dollars and in per cent)

	1955		1956		1957		1958	
	Value	%	Value	%	Value	%	Value	%
TOTAL IMPORTS	1,065.7	100.0	1,167.2	100.0	1,067.3	100.0	1,404.9	100.0
Foodstuffs, processed and unprocessed	22.8	2.1	22.5	1.9	24.5	2.3	33.5	2.4
Manufactured consumer goods	22.4	2.1	38.3	3.3	33.8	3.2	38.4	2.7
Drugs and cosmetics	10.7	1.0	10.1	0.9	13.0	1.2	12.4	0.9
Paper	12.7	1.2	18.4	1.6	10.7	1.0	5.1	0.4
Rubber and rubber products	26.4	2.5	48.9	4.2	78.5	7.4	92.0	6.5
Chemical products [b]	91.2	8.6	97.6	8.4	98.8	9.3	128.3	9.1
Fertilizer and insecticides	39.6	3.7	59.5	5.1	55.3	5.2	69.2	4.9
Building materials	1.3	0.1	1.1	0.1	1.0	0.1	0.8	0.1
Textile fibers	85.4	8.0	75.9	6.5	101.9	9.5	106.9	7.6
Metals, metal ores and concentrates	94.2	8.8	104.4	8.9	85.2	8.0	333.3	23.7
Petroleum and petroleum products	44.5	4.2	86.0	7.4	90.4	8.5	92.9	6.6
Machinery and equipment	243.3	22.8	346.2	29.7	337.4	31.6	387.7	27.6
Complete plants	141.5	13.3	217.2	18.6	209.0	19.6	166.2	11.8
Other	411.0	38.6	317.8	27.2	192.1	18.0	174.1	12.4

[a] Excludes Eastern Europe, Cuba, and Asian Communist countries, for which commodity breakdowns are not available.

[b] Excludes drugs, which are listed separately.

	1959		1960		1961		1962		1963	
	Value	%	Value	%	Value	%	Value	%	Value	%
TOTAL IMPORTS	1,624.7	100.0	1,486.1	100.0	1,015.1	100.0	829.2	100.0	906.7	100.0
Foodstuffs, processed and unprocessed	5.2	0.3	36.6	2.5	330.0	32.5	327.0	39.4	329.5	36.3
Manufactured consumer goods	38.6	2.4	22.5	1.5	20.9	2.1	25.5	3.1	27.1	3.0
Drugs and cosmetics	5.8	0.4	2.0	0.1	2.8	0.3	1.9	0.2	5.0	0.6
Paper	3.4	0.2	2.9	0.2	7.4	0.7	2.8	0.3	2.4	0.3
Rubber and rubber products	108.6	6.7	95.3	6.4	54.0	5.3	54.7	6.6	56.6	6.2
Chemical products b	126.7	7.8	82.6	5.6	56.8	5.6	56.6	6.8	97.7	10.8
Fertilizer and insecticides	43.7	2.7	30.8	2.1	29.4	2.9	27.1	3.3	47.0	5.2
Building materials	0.8	negl.	1.6	0.1	—	—	0.1	negl.	0.2	negl.
Textile fibers	91.7	5.6	134.9	9.1	101.6	10.0	78.7	9.5	136.9	15.1
Metals, metal ores and concentrates	247.5	15.2	268.3	18.1	78.6	7.7	61.6	7.4	62.8	6.9
Petroleum and petroleum products	117.7	7.2	113.1	7.6	120.7	11.9	80.5	9.7	60.7	6.7
Machinery and equipment	658.0	40.5	551.7	37.1	133.7	13.2	42.9	5.2	65.9	7.3
Complete plants	399.8	24.6	373.8	25.2	78.9	7.8	8.8	1.1	14.6	1.6
Other	220.7	13.6	174.6	11.7	108.6	10.7	96.9	11.7	61.9	6.8

Notes: The figures in this table differ from the data in Table 4–1 since it was not possible to adjust them to take account of re-exports.

negl. stands for "negligible."

— stands for "none."

Sources: Soviet Union—U.S.S.R., Ministry of Foreign Trade, *Vneshniaia Torgovlia SSSR za 1955–1959 Godi: Statisticheskii Sbornik* [*The Foreign Trade of the USSR for 1955–1959: A Statistical Compilation*] (Moscow: Vneshtorgizdat, 1961); *Vneshniaia Torgovlia SSSR za 1961 Godi: Statisticheskii Obzor* [*The Foreign Trade of the USSR for 1961: Statistical Handbook*] (Moscow: Vneshtorgizdat, 1962) and the volumes for 1962 and 1963 of this series of foreign trade handbooks

Non-Communist World—U.S. Mutual Defense Assistance Control Act Administrator, *Report to Congress* for various years.

Communist policy makers did not recognize until late in 1960 the depth and proportions of the economic crisis facing them. In other words, 1960 investment and foreign trade plans were still based on Great Leap assumptions, and it required the shock of a poor autumn harvest in 1960 and of a large balance-of-payments deficit to force cutbacks in domestic investment and in imports of capital goods.

The pace of industrial expansion in the 1950s was also reflected in the growth of raw material imports—namely, metals, metal ores and concentrates, rubber, petroleum, chemicals, and textile fibers. As a group, these commodities progressively displaced "other" imports in the course of the fifties. They rose, for example, from about one-third of the total in the early part of the decade to about one-half by the end of it. The close relationship between levels of economic activity on the mainland and raw material imports was underlined once again when the downturn of the sixties led to a decline in the relative weight of this category.

For most years from 1955 to 1963 metals and metal ores and concentrates were fairly important in mainland China's exports and imports. While China was a net exporter of these products during the period of the First Five Year Plan, the acceleration in industrial growth during the Great Leap increased raw material requirements in the metal processing industries so rapidly that imports for these industries had to be trebled and quadrupled, and the net export balance was converted to a sizable import surplus. With the collapse of the Great Leap, though, the situation reverted to one of export surplus.

Naturally, the metals exported and imported were of rather different types. China imported rolled steel, steel cables, pipes, nonferrous rolled products, and copper. She exported nonferrous metal ores, particularly tin and tungsten, as well as certain quantities of pig iron.[12] Paradoxically enough, China has been an exporter of pig iron ever since the 1930s, for her pig iron capacity and production have consistently outrun her steel-producing capacity and output. Before and during World War II, these exports flowed from Manchuria to Japan, but after 1950 the deliveries went mostly to Asiatic Russia.

Imports of petroleum, chemicals, and textile fibers were nearly equal in importance for most of the years. Each constituted roughly 5-10 per cent of the total. Since petroleum and its products are considered strategic goods, they fall under the purview of allied trade controls. As a result, all of China's imports of petroleum and petroleum products were drawn from the Soviet Union and Rumania, the overwhelming bulk from the Soviet Union. Purchases of these fuels expanded more or less at the same rate as total imports, so their import share was more or less constant, around 7-9 per cent, with one noteworthy exception. Total imports of virtually all categories except food declined sharply between 1960 and 1961, but purchases of petroleum products did not. As the figures in Table 4-6 show, however, this category of imports declined too by 1962.

It is clear from this table that imports of refined petroleum products reached their peak in 1961. The reason is not readily apparent, at least not from an economic point of view. With the decline in economic activity, one would have expected petroleum requirements to go down. As a matter of fact, one might *a priori* have expected imports of these products to decline even more rapidly than industrial or total output, for indications point to an expansion of domestic oil production throughout the crisis years. The explanation may lie in the military realm. As we now know, 1961 was the low point in the economic crisis, and a certain amount of political unrest developed. This unrest encouraged increasing infiltration by Nationalist troops and agents from Taiwan, as newspaper accounts at the time reported. Apparently either as a precautionary measure or as the result of a genuine fear of attack, the Chinese Communists instituted a large-scale buildup of troops and air power in Fukien. Such a buildup in and of itself must have raised fuel requirements. In addition, a war scare must have induced stockpiling of fuel over and above current requirements.

An analysis of Table 4–6 also reveals that while China traditionally imported large quantities of crude oil, such purchases ceased altogether in 1961. The reason for this sudden reversal is not clear either. One might hypothesize that the limited domestic facilities for refining combined with an expansion of domestic

TABLE 4-6. Soviet Exports of Petroleum and
Its Products to Communist China, 1955–63

(in thousands of metric tons)

	1955	1956	1957	1958	1959	1960	1961	1962	1963
Crude oil	378	397	380	672	636	568	—	—	—
Gasoline	639	641	573	640	1,256	1,055	1,325	765	455
Kerosene	264	240	373	333	380	386	512	488	476
Diesel fuel	233	377	380	663	557	707	841	378	333
Oils and greases	66	70	90	196	211	212	218	210	137

Note: — stands for "none."

Sources: U.S.S.R., Ministry of Foreign Trade, *Vneshniaia Torgovlia SSSR za 1956 Godi: Statisticheskii Obzor* [*The Foreign Trade of the USSR for 1956: Statistical Handbook*] (Moscow: Vneshtorgizdat, 1957) and the volumes for 1957, 1958, 1959, 1960, 1961, 1962, and 1963 of this series of foreign trade handbooks.

crude oil production made continued imports of petroleum in its crude state pointless.

As for chemicals, they are imported by China for three general purposes: use as industrial chemicals, requisites for agricultural production, and drugs destined for the consumer. The last is the least important; at no time have drugs constituted more than about 1 per cent of total imports. As a matter of fact, Chinese purchases of medicine from abroad dwindled quite rapidly after 1957, partly because of rising domestic production and partly because of an effort to conserve foreign exchange. Imports of chemical fertilizers and insecticides were of much greater importance than drugs. They made up roughly 4–5 per cent of the total imports through 1958 and then declined in both absolute and relative terms through 1962 but recovered again in 1963. The decrease occurred amidst increasing signs of preoccupation with problems of agricultural development and with the need to step up fertilizer applications. The seeming paradox is cleared up if one bears in mind that the crisis produced great pressure on foreign exchange resources and that the chemical industry, including fertilizer production, was one of the few at home which experienced continuing growth throughout the depression.

Imports of industrial chemicals, roughly equal in importance to those of fertilizer, reached their peak in 1959 and then declined as the general pace of industrial advance was slowed down and finally arrested. These imports include various acids used in manufacturing and dyeing, coloring, and tanning materials.

Until 1963 textile fibers, like chemicals, exhibited considerable stability in relative importance on the import bill. Like metals, however, they were both exported and imported. In 1955, 1956, and 1959 the exports exceeded the imports, but in other years the position was reversed. Under the impact of the agricultural crisis, domestic cotton production declined sharply in 1959. As a result, since 1960 China has had to step up its raw cotton imports—so much so that in 1963 these imports constituted 15 per cent of the import bill.

In general, Communist China exported wool, silk, hemp, jute, and ramie fiber and imported cotton, wool, and jute. Wool and jute, then, were traded both ways. In the case of jute, imports practically canceled out exports. Its two-way flow, therefore, probably must be explained more in political than in economic terms. There have been a number of occasions when China agreed to purchase certain products if such purchases were necessary to facilitate the conclusion of barter agreements. Then she has turned around and re-exported these as part of another barter deal. Jute provides an example of this type of transaction. The situation with respect to wool is rather different. Through 1958, China exported significantly more wool than she imported. After 1959, the reverse was true. The shrinking exports probably resulted from a decline in domestic wool production.

Throughout the whole period under consideration, China remained a net importer of cotton, her most important textile fiber. Despite Communist efforts to make China completely self-sufficient, the volume of cotton purchases in the 1950s was not significantly below that in the 1930s—an average of 60 as compared to 70 thousand tons.[13] With the considerable expansion in cotton textile production, however, the imported raw material constituted a significantly lower percentage of total raw cotton consumption than it did before the war.

There are two principal reasons for the failure to achieve self-sufficiency in raw cotton. In a country like China, which suffers from acute population pressure and a marked scarcity of cultivable land, there is always competition between food crops and industrial crops for land. In the early fifties, cotton acreage was expanded to the point that it cut into the area devoted to food crops. This situation then forced a readjustment. At prevailing levels of technology and with the limited cultivable land area, there are definite limits beyond which domestic cotton output cannot be raised. Moreover, China so far has not succeeded in growing high-quality, extra-long-staple cotton on a commercial scale.

The most dramatic reversal in Communist China's imports relates to foodstuffs. Traditionally, both before and after 1949, China has been a net exporter of agricultural products for human consumption. It was not unusual in pre-Communist days, however, for China to import cereals and sugar. The cereals were used particularly for distribution in the treaty ports. After the Communist advent to power, China became a net grain exporter. While she purchased some cereals in most years, these imports were small as compared to exports. Only in respect to sugar did she continue consistently to be in a deficit position. Thus, before 1961, foods constituted no more than 1–3 per cent of total imports. But as a result of the agricultural crisis and the ensuing large-scale grain imports, purchases of food rose tenfold in 1961, from about $37 million in 1960 to $330 million.[14] Similarly high levels of food imports had to be maintained in 1962 and 1963 at a time when exports were declining. The consequence was a marked pressure on foreign exchange resources.

This rise in cereal purchases occurred at the expense of all other categories of imports. The principal brunt of the displacement, as was noted above, was borne by machinery and equipment. The state of the economy and the low level of investment, however, meant that the drop in these particular imports probably did not present too serious a problem for the time being. The need for industrial and agricultural raw materials, particularly for textile fibers and chemical fertilizer, was of much greater urgency. But until 1963 purchases of these also had to be curtailed in order to finance grain imports. Reduced raw material availabilities, in turn, hampered the growth of the textile industry, which in recent years has been a major earner of foreign exchange. At the same time, raw material shortages also slowed the recovery of agricultural production, which is a prerequisite for the reduction of food imports. Thus, the grain purchases occasioned by the agricultural crisis in and of themselves undermined efforts to alleviate the crisis.

EXPORTS. Mainland China, following the typical pattern of an underdeveloped economy, traditionally exported agricultural products—mostly soybeans, oil cake, other oil seeds, livestock products, silk, tea, and tobacco—and nonferrous metals, pig iron, coal, and a wide miscellany of so-called "native products," *e.g.*, hair nets, carpets, and handicraft products of various kinds. This general export pattern has carried over to the Communist period but with some significant modifications.

Agricultural exports continued to be of major importance throughout the 1950s. However, as the figures in Table 4–7 illustrate, these exports did not increase much in absolute terms. From the early 1950s on, the relative weight of farm products on the export list diminished continuously, from about 70 per cent in 1952 to a low of about 20 per cent in 1961. Not surprisingly, the absolute level of farm exports fluctuated from year to year, partly in response to the quality of the harvest. For example, these exports increased in 1956 and 1959 after the good 1955 and 1958 harvests, and they decreased in 1957 in the wake of the preceding year's mediocre crop. Finally, the succession of poor harvests after 1959 led to a sharp decline in agricultural exports. They fell by more than one-half between 1960 and 1961. On the other hand, as agricultural recovery gained momentum, it was reflected in the volume of farm sales abroad. Consequently, agricultural exports increased by one-third between 1962 and 1963. However, they were still well below 1960 levels, absolutely and relatively.

In a sense, agriculture's loss was textiles' gain. From 1955 through 1963 the combined share of these two sectors was fairly stable. It fluctuated between 62 and 74 per cent. Thus, as farm exports were declining in relative importance, the share of textile

T A B L E 4 - 7 . Commodity Composition of Communist China's Exports, 1955–63 [a]

(in millions of U.S. dollars and in per cent)

	1955		1956		1957		1958	
	Value	%	Value	%	Value	%	Value	%
TOTAL EXPORTS	1,130.6	100.0	1,405.6	100.0	1,361.6	100.0	1,637.0	100.0
Soybeans, oilseeds, and products	196.2	17.4	195.7	13.9	145.3	10.7	127.9	7.8
Cereals	88.6	7.8	129.3	9.2	59.3	4.4	147.9	9.0
Livestock products								
Edible	140.9	12.5	138.0	9.8	115.1	8.5	178.8	10.9
Inedible	50.3	4.4	49.5	3.5	38.8	2.8	47.3	2.9
Fruits and vegetables	59.3	5.2	65.0	4.6	82.9	6.1	91.9	5.6
Tea	36.5	3.2	36.5	2.6	35.8	2.6	45.0	2.7
Tobacco	24.5	2.2	31.9	2.3	42.9	3.2	33.7	2.1
Textiles								
Raw materials	90.6	8.0	101.3	7.2	86.6	6.4	64.5	3.9
Fabrics	85.3	7.5	149.4	10.6	180.4	13.2	200.2	12.2
Clothing and footwear	18.6	1.6	37.9	2.7	66.9	4.9	153.5	9.4
Industrial fats and oils	10.3	0.9	39.2	2.8	32.6	2.4	32.2	2.0
Building materials	6.6	0.6	12.1	0.9	20.2	1.5	22.6	1.4
Chemical products	23.4	2.1	41.4	2.9	38.2	2.8	52.4	3.2
Metals, metal ores and concentrates	148.8	13.2	171.6	12.2	166.5	12.2	171.4	10.5
Non-metallic minerals	21.3	1.9	36.7	2.6	44.5	3.3	27.8	1.7
Machinery and equipment	11.8	1.0	11.7	0.8	9.2	0.7	11.4	0.7
Other	117.6	10.4	158.4	11.3	196.4	14.4	228.5	14.0

[a] Excludes Eastern Europe, Cuba, and Asian Communist countries, for which commodity breakdowns are not available.

	1959 Value	1959 %	1960 Value	1960 %	1961 Value	1961 %	1962 Value	1962 %	1963 Value	1963 %
TOTAL EXPORTS	1,793.7	100.0	1,614.8	100.0	1,195.2	100.0	1,208.9	100.0	1,234.9	100.0
Soybeans, oilseeds, and products	158.6	8.8	122.9	7.6	34.3	2.9	36.9	3.1	38.3	3.1
Cereals	176.5	9.8	129.5	8.0	28.7	2.4	39.9	3.3	58.8	4.8
Livestock products										
Edible	110.7	6.2	80.7	5.0	36.2	3.0	47.0	3.9	75.9	6.1
Inedible	48.3	2.7	50.0	3.1	28.2	2.4	23.5	1.9	40.2	3.3
Fruits and vegetables	83.9	4.7	69.6	4.3	41.2	3.4	48.2	4.0	60.3	4.9
Tea	41.2	2.3	35.0	2.2	22.9	1.9	20.5	1.7	20.0	1.6
Tobacco	31.6	1.8	13.9	0.9	4.5	0.4	1.5	0.1	2.1	0.2
Textiles										
Raw materials	127.4	7.1	101.4	6.3	56.2	4.7	41.6	3.4	52.8	4.3
Fabrics	269.2	15.0	305.7	18.9	272.9	22.8	263.0	21.8	252.2	20.4
Clothing and footwear	254.4	14.2	248.5	15.4	206.5	17.3	217.9	18.0	197.2	16.0
Industrial fats and oils	23.2	1.3	27.2	1.7	9.4	0.8	10.3	0.9	9.4	0.8
Building materials	12.7	0.7	13.1	0.8	13.4	1.1	14.8	1.2	23.2	1.9
Chemical products	34.3	1.9	32.2	2.0	23.5	2.0	25.5	2.1	31.7	2.6
Metals, metal ores and concentrates	161.7	9.0	154.5	9.6	130.5	10.9	112.5	9.3	70.8	5.7
Non-metallic minerals	19.1	1.1	18.2	1.1	10.8	0.9	19.0	1.6	17.0	1.4
Machinery and equipment	21.9	1.2	7.3	0.5	4.9	0.4	14.5	1.2	18.0	1.5
Other	219.0	12.2	205.1	12.7	271.1	22.7	272.3	22.5	267.0	21.0

Sources: See Table 4-5.

Note: This series combines data for Soviet imports f.o.b. at the Chinese border and data for non-Communist world imports c.i.f. It was not possible to adjust these data to take account of re-exports.

manufactures was rising from about 5 per cent in 1952 to about 40 per cent in 1960–63. The value of textile shipments, moreover, rose from $40 million in 1952 to a peak of $550 million in 1960. As a result, textiles displaced farm products as China's leading export. It is significant that even amidst the general decline in exports, textile deliveries were maintained at a high level—even after 1960 when shortages of raw materials forced a curtailment in mainland textile production. (These shortages resulted especially from a decline in cotton output.) One can safely conclude, therefore, that domestic textile consumption must have been curtailed so that Soviet loans could be repaid and that foreign exchange, so vitally needed for financing grain imports, could be earned.

The growing importance of textiles represents a marked departure from China's traditional export pattern. In effect, it epitomizes the end of a cycle in mainland economic history. Prior to massive Western contact, China was an exporter of textile handicrafts. At a later stage, in the 19th century, textile manufactures from abroad began to compete successfully in China's domestic markets, and they gradually displaced the handicraft production of yarn and then of cloth as well. As a result, textile imports grew rapidly, and China exported textile fibers, including raw cotton. A sizable market and a clearly demonstrated demand for textile manufactures encouraged the rise in the 20th century of a domestic industry, which involved both foreign and Chinese firms. As this industry expanded, its raw material requirements rose to the point where it became necessary to import rather than to export raw cotton. As the industry continued to grow, domestic production of cotton cloth gradually displaced imports in meeting the consumer demand for textiles. Finally, under the impact of accelerated industrialization under Communist auspices, China became a large net exporter of cotton textiles.

In addition to farm products and textiles, pig iron, tungsten, tin, and other nonferrous metals were of some importance in China's exports. They averaged about 10 per cent of the total in the period 1955–63. The remainder, a little more than 20 per cent of the total, was made up of a wide variety of miscellaneous products, among them manufactured consumer goods such as bicycles and fountain pens.

If we break down the agricultural export category somewhat, we note that not all groups of products behaved in the same way. Thus, certain raw materials of agricultural origin such as hides, skins, and hog bristles more or less maintained their relative positions. On the other hand, farm products for human consumption declined in importance throughout the period.

The movement of some of the more important categories of export products is examined in Table 4–8. It would seem that exports of tea, tobacco, and soybeans showed no marked trend between 1955 and 1960. Groundnuts, on the other hand, declined rather markedly, while rice seems to have exhibited an upward trend. The rising rice exports are particularly remarkable if one bears in mind that China imported an average of 500 thousand tons of rice before the war. This shift was part of a conscious policy of the regime and was made possible by the more or less forced substitution of sweet potatoes for rice. As a result, China became a leading shipper of rice and delivered a rising proportion of world exports. Another striking aspect of the table is the sharp fall in soybean exports because of the postwar decline in mainland soybean production.

The post-1960 data in this table serve to highlight once more the impact of the agricultural crisis, for virtually all agricultural exports, in contrast with earlier trends, dropped sharply. Thus, in 1961 China again became a net importer of rice, and the decline in exports of soybeans and other oilseeds was greatly accelerated.

The Role of Foreign Trade in Communist China's Economic Transformation

As was noted in Chapter 3, mainland China's economy has been undergoing profound structural changes in the last decade. The unusually rapid expansion in industrial capacity and in rates of industrial growth would have been inconceivable without the

TABLE 4-8. Mainland China and World Exports of Selected Farm Products, 1934–38 and 1955–61

(in thousands of metric tons and in per cent)

Product	1934–38	1955	1956	1957	1958	1959	1960	1961
Soybeans								
China	2,036	950	970	972	928	1,343	941	316
Per cent of world exports	89	32	32	28	27	28	18	8
Groundnuts								
China	137	347	376	250	95	71	28	2
Per cent of world exports	10	27	25	19	7	6	3	0.1
Rice								
Gross exports								
China	17	624	988	485	1,265	1,661	1,164	323
Per cent of world exports	0.2	11	15	8	19	25	17	5
Net exports	−687	466	902	374	1,253	1,661	1,135	−48
Tea								
China	41	35	38	44	46	44	38	36
Per cent of world exports	9	7	7	8	8	8	7	6
Tobacco								
China	15	32	45	54	51	44	23	10
Per cent of world exports	3	5	6	7	7	6	3	1

Sources: Food and Agriculture Organization of the United Nations, *Trade Yearbook* for 1958, 1959, 1960, 1961, 1962.

importation of manufacturing equipment, machinery, and installations of all types which could not be produced in China; new plant design; and new scientific and technical knowledge. This expansion was also facilitated by imports of industrial raw materials and semimanufactures.

The rapid industrial growth, however, was bought at the price of relative stagnation in agriculture. Such stagnation necessarily limited China's export capacity and therefore her ability to import. Before 1955, the pressures on agriculture were to some extent alleviated by allotments of foreign aid to China. Although Soviet aid almost ceased after 1955 and the Chinese began amortizing their debts to the Soviet Union, the export burden placed on agriculture did not rise, largely because mainland China's ability to export manufactured goods, especially textiles, increased considerably as her industrial capacity grew.

The close interrelationship between agricultural development, export capacity, and imports was forcefully brought home again by the poor harvests after 1959. It is now clear that because of these harvest failures China could not meet its export commitments in 1960, so if the Soviet Union had not been willing to make new financial arrangements to cover the deficit, mainland imports would have had to be curtailed drastically.[15]

The importance of foreign trade in the economic development of a country can be assessed in several ways. In the present study, first an aggregative indicator is derived by estimating the foreign trade share in national income for different years. Then the role of imports in capital formation and consumption is explored. Finally, imports and exports of leading items are compared with domestic output in order to appraise the role of foreign trade in structural terms.

The import and export ratios shown in Table 4–9 indicate that the role of foreign trade in national income in China was more comparable to that in the large countries such as the United States and the Soviet Union than that in Japan and the countries of Western Europe and Latin America.[16]

TABLE 4-9. The Export and Import Share in the National Product of Communist China, 1952-59

Year	Imports				Exports			
	in millions of U.S. dollars	in millions of yuan			in millions of U.S. dollars	in millions of yuan		
		converted at Y2.62:$1	converted at Y1.79:$1	converted at Y5.91:$1		converted at Y2.62:$1	converted at Y1.79:$1	converted at Y5.91:$1
	(1)	(2)	(3)	(4)	(5)	(6)	(7)	(8)
1952	890	2,332	1,593	5,260	871	2,282	1,559	5,148
1953	1,107	2,900	1,982	6,542	1,039	2,720	1,858	6,135
1954	1,260	3,301	2,255	7,447	1,119	2,932	2,003	6,613
1955	1,321	3,461	2,365	7,807	1,345	3,524	2,408	7,949
1956	1,465	3,838	2,622	8,658	1,612	4,223	2,885	9,527
1957	1,391	3,644	2,490	8,221	1,615	4,231	2,891	9,545
1958	1,865	4,886	3,338	11,022	1,911	5,007	3,421	11,294
1959	2,011	5,269	3,600	11,885	2,221	5,824	3,979	13,138

Year	GNP in billions of yuan	Import Share in GNP			Export Share in GNP		
		(2)/(9)	in per cent (3)/(9)	(4)/(9)	(6)/(9)	in per cent (7)/(9)	(8)/(9)
	(9)	(10)	(11)	(12)	(13)	(14)	(15)
1952	74.67	3.1	2.1	7.0	3.1	2.1	6.9
1953	78.99	3.7	2.5	8.3	3.4	2.4	7.8
1954	83.31	4.0	2.7	8.9	3.5	2.4	7.9
1955	88.43	3.9	2.7	8.8	4.0	2.7	9.0
1956	99.21	3.9	2.6	8.7	4.3	2.9	9.6
1957	102.67	3.5	2.4	8.0	4.1	2.8	9.3
1958	119.00	4.1	2.8	9.3	4.2	2.9	9.5
1959	126.60	4.2	2.8	9.4	4.6	3.1	10.4

Sources: Adjusted imports and exports in dollar terms come from Table 4–1; for the choice of conversion rates, see Appendix C.

GNP estimates are derived from T. C. Liu and K. C. Yeh, *The Economy of the Chinese Mainland: National Income and Development, 1933–1959* (Princeton University Press, 1965) with the following adjustments in their figures for agricultural product: The 1955 product was revised by applying the agricultural growth factor in William W. Hollister, *China's Gross National Product and Social Accounts, 1950–1957* (Glencoe, Ill.: Free Press, 1958) to the Liu-Yeh estimate for 1955, and then this revised figure was used to derive the 1956 and 1957 products by applying to it Liu-Yeh's improvement factors for 1955/56 and 1956/57. The 1958 and 1959 estimates were then obtained by applying to the 1957 figure the indices shown in Table 3–8.

Many students of economic development advance the proposition that import and export ratios are inversely correlated with the stage of development, *i.e.*, that low-income countries tend to be foreign-trade oriented and that the ratios for them generally will be significantly higher than those for high-income areas.[17] The data for China and India do not bear out this generalization, nor, for that matter, do those for the European countries. Comparison of the ratios of foreign trade and national incomes for a number of countries suggests that while these ratios tend to decline in the course of industrialization, the dominant variable at any one point in time does not seem to be per capita income but size—to be precise, size of GNP. As Simon Kuznets puts it:

Given the same trading propensities for various units composing the national product, and equal trading propensities for internal and external trade, *the larger country has a lower foreign trade proportion than the smaller country* because the distribution between internal and external trade can be much more favorable to the former than to the latter. In that sense the larger country, with a much larger internal market, does not depend as heavily on "the rest of the world" as the smaller country. . . . [italics added] [18]

Therefore, the ratios for the United States and mainland China are much closer than those for the United States and the United Kingdom on the one hand or for China and Burma on the other. It would be a serious error to construe these relatively low ratios as an indication or proof of the comparative unimportance of foreign trade for the Chinese economy. While it appears to be unimportant in a purely quantitative sense, it is of considerable significance from a qualitative and dynamic point of view. Imports constitute a vital highway for the inflow of innovating influences. They provide a stimulus for change and a sizable share of the wherewithal for growth. Therefore, these highly aggregate measures of the international sector's share in the national product are in many ways misleading.

While the ratios presented in Table 4–9 exhibit surprising stability, the dependence on foreign trade of a number of specific sectors and components was decreasing. At the same time some sectors—notably capital formation—were much more dependent on imports than the national product as a whole.

Estimation of the import component of capital formation raises a number of complicated data and conceptual problems. First of all, no reliable data on or estimates of China's total imports of machinery and equipment have been published. Table 4-5, for example, does not include such imports from Eastern Europe because no complete estimate of these could be found. Second, China exported some machinery and equipment, but our data on such exports are particularly fragmentary since many of these capital goods went to North Vietnam and North Korea. Third, in light of the ambiguity of Chinese Communist estimates of investment, no estimates at our disposal (including those derived by U.S. economists) can be considered true reflections of gross fixed-capital investment for the economy as a whole. Therefore, estimates of the equipment component in fixed-capital investment—which one would wish to compare with net machinery imports to measure trade dependence—are subject to sizable margins of error. Moreover, Chinese Communist statements concerning the share of fixed-capital investment devoted to equipment are so vague and general that one cannot use them with any degree of confidence. To obviate this particular problem, one might try to estimate the dependence of capital investment upon imports by comparing net equipment imports with domestic machinery production. This approach, however, presents difficulties of its own, for it cannot be automatically assumed that the total output of the machinery industry will be channeled into investment. An unknown part of it might certainly go into government consumption, particularly in the defense sector. Finally, these complications are further compounded by problems of pricing and foreign exchange. The bulk of China's imports of machinery and equipment has come from the Soviet Union. Although data on such exports are available from Russian trade returns, the trade returns are stated in rubles. The data for China's machinery output, on the other hand, are stated in yuan. At what rate of exchange should the ruble values be converted?

An estimate based on certain assumptions can nevertheless be made and used as indicative of the orders of magnitude involved. Such an estimate suggests that, depending on what exchange rate is used to convert our dollar figures for capital goods imports, about 15-20 or 35-50 per cent of the equipment component of investment was imported during the period of the First Five Year Plan.[19]

Even these ratios of capital goods imports are considerably misleading, however, for the import component of investment in the high-priority sectors was undoubtedly well above these averages. Another way of looking at this problem is to explore what the effect on economic growth would have been if there had been no imports of machinery and equipment at all. It could be argued that without capital goods imports the plants in which these were to be installed would not have been built and that investment would have been correspondingly curtailed. Then, investment during the period of the First Five Year Plan would have been reduced either by 15-20 per cent or by 35-50 per cent,[20] depending upon what exchange rate is used to convert the values of capital goods imports into yuan. Furthermore, under the assumptions on which these hypothetical calculations are based, the growth of the national product between 1953 and 1957 would have dropped from an average annual rate of about 6.5 per cent to about 3-5 per cent.[21]

The difficulty with this approach is that it both overstates and understates the impact of imports on investment and growth. It overstates the impact because it assumes that no projects dependent on imported equipment would be replaced by projects using domestically produced equipment. On the other hand, it understates the impact inasmuch as it measures only the direct effect of the cessation of imports and disregards the indirect effect. The latter consists primarily of the loss of innovating influences and learning opportunities. These are transmitted through the new technology embodied in the imported equipment and in the technical assistance frequently coupled with it. They need not be confined to the plants in which the imported equipment is installed; by example and through imitation they can and do spread to other factories and sectors.

Even if the cessation of imports had left the level of investment unaffected, it would have altered the investment pattern. Reliance on domestically-produced equipment would necessarily have forced the abandonment of many high-priority projects and their replacement by investments of lesser importance from the planners' point of view. To the extent that the construction of high-priority installations with only domestically available components would have been attempted, a significant reduction in quality and a rise in costs would have resulted. In either case, the cessation would have reduced the productivity of investments and thereby slowed down the rate of economic growth.

In contrast to investment, the role of imports in total personal consumption has been truly marginal except for 1961-63. During 1955-57, the only period for which we have some fairly good estimates of both total consumer imports and personal consumption, the contribution of the former to the latter was only about 0.5 per cent.[22] This fact does not mean that the import share of consumption had only minor importance in all cases. Important exceptions were medicine, sugar, and more recently grains. In general, however, China was a net exporter of consumer goods, at least up to 1960, and even in 1961 and 1962 her exports of textiles and all other consumer goods considerably exceeded her imports of food and other minor items.

Within large aggregates, such as investment and consumption, the dependence of specific sectors and products on imports naturally varied widely. This dependence ranged from complete or near complete in the case of rubber, for instance, to none in the case of a number of agricultural products. Between these extremes, but of crucial importance to economic development and to defense requirements, were the imports of machinery, petroleum and its products, some metals, chemical fertilizer, and pharmaceuticals. Of lesser importance, but far from negligible, were the imports of sugar, high-quality cotton, and special types of paper.

As the data in Table 4-10 illustrate, the import share for a number of goods, particularly machinery and metals, was declining in the 1950s. This trend seems to have continued through the Great Leap period. The decline is not too surprising if one bears in mind that in the late 1950s mainland plant capacity was growing rapidly as more and more of the new plants came into operation. For two types of commodities, dependence on im-

TABLE 4-10. The Import Share of Selected Goods
Available to Communist China, 1953–59

(in per cent)

Commodity Category	1953	1954	1955	1956	1957	1958	1959
Metal-cutting tools	35.8	40.8	29.1	24.1	n.a.	n.a.	n.a.
Forging-press equipment	31.6	27.7	26.9	28.1	n.a.	n.a.	n.a.
Rolled steel	36.4	28.8	24.7	14.2	n.a.	n.a.	n.a.
Nonferrous metals	38.2	34.2	11.9	8.2	n.a.	n.a.	n.a.
Chemical fertilizer [a]	59.5	60.6	72.3	63.4	60.1	55.1	43.5
Soda products	19.6	11.2	n.a.	0.7	n.a.	n.a.	n.a.
Raw cotton [a]	1.9	3.9	2.8	2.6	4.7	3.9	n.a.
Paper	n.a.	n.a.	0.8	1.3	n.a.	n.a.	n.a.
Sugar [a]	n.a.	2.6	11.4	11.5	6.7	10.6	n.a.
Pharmaceuticals	37.0	n.a.	10.5	n.a.	n.a.	n.a.	n.a.
Crude oil [a]	n.a.	n.a.	28.1	25.4	36.5	22.8	14.7
Gasoline [a]	n.a.	n.a.	n.a.	60.5	n.a.	n.a.	n.a.
Kerosene [a]	n.a.	n.a.	n.a.	55.4	n.a.	n.a.	n.a.
Diesel oil [a]	n.a.	n.a.	n.a.	51.4	n.a.	n.a.	n.a.

[a] Ratios derived from tonnage figures.

Note: n.a. stands for "not available."

Sources: T'ung-chi Kung-tso [Statistical Work], no. 13, July 14, 1957;
Jen-min Jih-pao [People's Daily], September 30, 1957; Chung-kuo
Nung-pao [Agricultural Journal of China], no. 17, September
1957; Yu. N. Kapelinski and others, Razvitie Ekonomiki Vneshnee-
konomicheskikh Sviazei Kitaiskoi Nardnoi Respublike [The
Development of the Economy and Foreign Economic Relations
of the Chinese People's Republic] (Moscow: Vneshtorgizdat,
1959); U.S.S.R., Ministry of Foreign Trade, Vneshniaia Torgovlia
SSSR za 1955–1959 Godi: Statisticheskii Sbornik [The Foreign
Trade of the USSR for 1955–1959: A Statistical Compilation]
(Moscow: Vneshtorgizdat, 1961); Chao Kang, The Rate and
Pattern of Industrial Growth in Communist China (Ann Arbor:
University of Michigan Press, 1965), Table C–1: Food and
Agriculture Organization of the United Nations, Trade Yearbook
for 1955, 1958, and 1961; Asian Political Economy Association,
Chugoku seiji keizai soran [Abstract of China's Political Econ-
omy] (Tokyo: Author, 1964), p. 521.

ports continued to remain high: petroleum products and chemical fertilizer. As was shown in Table 4-6, imports of crude petroleum ceased in 1961, but purchases of refined products rose. Since domestic production was increasing too, though we do not know by how much, it is difficult to determine whether dependence on imports rose, declined, or stayed more or less the same. Domestic fertilizer production rose rapidly enough to counterbalance falling imports—so much so that total supplies increased. As a result, the import share of total fertilizer consumption declined. Needless to say, the limitation on imports of both petroleum products and fertilizer is not absence of need but China's inability to finance higher levels of domestic consumption and her shortages of foreign exchange.

As was indicated earlier, the most striking reversal in the composition of China's foreign trade took place after 1960 when cereals displaced machinery as the country's leading import. How important a role did grain imports play in alleviating food shortages during these critical years? A precise estimate is difficult to make since neither production nor collection figures for these years are available. On the basis of the index presented in Table 3-8, the production of grains (exclusive of soybeans) can tentatively be estimated at 160, 165, and 181 million tons in 1960, 1961, and 1962 respectively. During these three consumption years (1960/61, 1961/62, and 1962/63), China imported 2.65, 5.80 and 5.46 million tons of grain.[23] On this basis, supplies from abroad amounted to less than 4 per cent of the total even in 1961/62 when grain imports were at a record high. However, inasmuch as food imports were destined principally for the cities and were designed to ease the pressure on state collections of grain, the latter might provide a more appropriate basis for gauging the importance of grain purchased from abroad. Unfortunately, information for collections is even scantier than that for production. In Chapter 2 (note 31), it was pointed out that collections net of farm resales and including soybeans averaged about 29 million tons during 1954/55-1956/57. If we exclude soybeans and allow for the decline in farm output, collections (net of farm resales) in the early 1960s may be estimated at 15-20 million tons. On this basis, grains imported during 1961/62 seem to have augmented domestic supplies available for distribution to the army and the urban population by about 30-40 per cent.

Examining the other side of the ledger, we see that no major category of exports was of the same relative importance to the Chinese economy as some of the imports just cited. That is, one cannot point to any exports which provided a decisive margin of difference either for consumption or investment as one can single out imports of machinery and certain raw materials. As we have already noted, the bulk of China's exports consisted of goods destined for consumption. Under the broadest possible definition of consumer goods, a maximum of 2 per cent would have been added to total personal consumption in 1955-57 if no consumer goods had been exported.[24] This observation is not to suggest that the effect would have been negligible but to highlight the fact that consumer standards for the country as a whole would not have been significantly improved even with the addition of these exports and the effect would not have been comparable to the impact of capital goods imports on industrialization.

This generalization can be tested by analyzing more specifically the export share of major consumer goods. The most important necessities of life in China are cereals (mostly rice in the south and wheat in the north) and clothing. How much improvement in levels of food consumption and in the availability of textiles could the retention of exported supplies have made? Rice was the only major food staple exported in appreciable quantities. Shipments of all other cereals combined, including wheat, were on the average no more than 200,000 tons.[25] As may be seen from Table 4-11, the highest export ratio for rice during the three years for which we have rather reliable data was 1.3 per cent. It probably was no higher in any preceding year and certainly did not rise in 1958. However, as may be seen from Table 4-8, net rice exports rose sharply in 1959—by about 30 per cent as compared to the preceding year and by more than 80 per cent in comparison with 1956. Thus, rice exports attained record levels at a time when the mainland produced either the

TABLE 4-11. Estimated Share of Communist China's
Exports of Selected Products in Relation
to Domestic Production, 1955–57

(in per cent)

Commodity Category	1955	1956	1957
Soybeans	10.4	9.5	9.7
Rice	0.8	1.3	0.6
All grains (including soybeans)			
(1) a	n.a.	0.6	0.3
(2) b	n.a.	4.7	n.a.
Groundnuts	11.8	11.3	9.7
Tea	35.0	37.0	44.0
Tobacco	10.7	11.3	13.1
Tung oil	27.0	35.0	34.0
Livestock products	7.8	7.7	6.0
Textile semimanufactures and finished goods	3.0	4.0	5.5

a Exports of soybeans, rice, and other grains combined in relation to total food crop production.

b Exports of soybeans, rice, and other grains combined in relation to grain collections net of farm resales.

Notes: All ratios were calculated by the author. Those for livestock products and textiles are based on export values and gross output values. Those for all other goods were derived from export and output data expressed in physical terms.
n.a. stands for "not available."

Sources: State Statistical Bureau, *Ten Great Years, Statistics of the Economic and Cultural Achievements of the People's Republic of China* (Peking: Foreign Languages Press, 1960), pp. 119, 124–125; Helen Yin and Y. C. Yin, *Economic Statistics of Mainland China, 1949–1957* (Cambridge: Harvard University Press, 1960), Table 9, p. 32; U.S. Department of Agriculture, *Trends and Developments in Communist China's World Trade in Farm Products, 1955–1960*, Foreign Agricultural Economic Report, no. 6 (Washington, D.C.: Author, September 1962), Table 12, p. 26.

poorest or next to poorest food crop of the whole Communist period.*

These figures suggest that except for 1959, when perhaps as much as 10 per cent of the rice crop was exported, rice shipments abroad did not absorb much more than 1 per cent of the harvest. Therefore, they could not have significantly improved the level of domestic food consumption in the country as a whole. At the same time, they undoubtedly would have eased the pressure on rice collections in some years and in some areas.

In the case of textiles, China exported an increasing share of its total output. In 1958 and 1959, output probably rose faster than deliveries abroad, but with the downturn in production during 1960 and 1961, export shares undoubtedly exceeded the 5 per cent estimated for 1957. Apparently the retention of textile exports during the period of the First Five Year Plan could have produced a modest rise in textile consumption per capita. On the other hand, the maintenance of high levels of exports despite reduced domestic output during the crisis years of the early 1960s was undoubtedly one of the prime factors contributing to the acute clothing shortage in Communist China.

In addition to these necessities, China exports a range of farm products which play a significant role in raising the quality and nutritional content of the Chinese diet. Among these are livestock products, soybeans and products, oil seeds, and vegetable oils. The export shares for these categories were appreciably higher than those for basic necessities, 6-8 per cent for livestock products and about 10 per cent for soybeans and groundnuts. There is no question that export deliveries contributed greatly to the monotony of the Chinese diet, significantly curtailed the content of fats and oils in it, and generally reduced its nutritional quality.

The highest export shares were in traditional lines of exports which are not essential consumer items. Tung oil is used primarily for industrial purposes, and there is no evidence to suggest that the sizable tea exports caused hardship or deprivation.

---

* It is fascinating to observe the coincidence with the year 1931 in Soviet economic history. As was indicated in Chapter 2 (note 12), 1931 was a year of record grain exports coupled with the poorest Russian harvest.

Conclusions

The contribution of foreign trade to mainland China's economic development was appraised in this chapter against the background of economic policies and performance analyzed previously. First the course of mainland China's total exports and imports was traced, then the shifts in geographic direction and commodity composition of this trade were investigated, and finally the interrelationships between foreign trade and domestic development were explored.

These explorations indicated that the fortunes of the foreign trade and domestic sectors of the Chinese economy are closely linked. Thus, during the "ten great years" of development (1949-59), when the whole economy grew rapidly, exports and imports rose virtually without interruption. As serious economic difficulties began to develop, they were reflected in a decline in foreign trade in 1960. As these difficulties assumed crisis proportions, they led to a sharp contraction in exports and imports between 1960 and 1962. The turning point came in 1963, when trade began to expand again, slowly and gradually, as China's economy began to improve. This modest recovery continued into 1964 and according to all presently available signs is proceeding in 1965.

Up to 1959 and 1960 mainland China's trade with all parts of the world followed the same general pattern. After that, however, there was a marked decline in trade with the Soviet Union and Eastern Europe, while trade with the Asian Communist countries increased. At the same time, trade with the non-Communist world more or less held its own and in recent years has even risen somewhat. As a result, a dramatic reorientation occurred in China's foreign trade after 1960. This reorientation is best illustrated by the shift in Chinese imports. In 1954 the Soviet and East European shares of China's imports were 60 and 20 per cent respectively, while in 1959 they were 47 and 16 per cent (see Table 4-3). But by 1963 China obtained only 14 per cent of her imports from the Soviet Union and another 7 per cent from

Eastern Europe. Similar, but somewhat less far-reaching, shifts took place on the export side.

The sharp decline in the importance of Russia and Eastern Europe as China's trading partners may be attributed principally to two kinds of factors—namely, deterioration in Sino-Soviet relations and changes in the commodity composition of China's imports imposed upon her by the agricultural crisis. This crisis forced a drastic curtailment of capital goods imports and most particularly a near cessation of complete plant imports, which were bought almost exclusively from the Soviet Union and Eastern Europe. For the same reasons, China had to start importing grain on a large scale at a time when the Soviets themselves were purchasing grain in the world markets. For these strictly economic reasons, one would have expected some reduction in the Soviet role in China's foreign trade. Growing political tensions between these two Communist neighbors naturally accelerated this tendency. The process was facilitated, of course, by the continuous easing of Western controls on China trade.

In conducting her foreign trade, China maintained a trade deficit with the Soviet Union and Eastern Europe through 1955— that is, as long as she could draw on Soviet credits to finance this excess of imports over exports. These credits, as will be shown in greater detail in the next chapter, dwindled in 1956 and 1957 and then virtually ceased. Since 1956, China's trade balance with the Soviet Union has been positive, with particularly large trade surpluses in 1958, 1962, 1963, and 1964. It is clear that China exerted every effort to maintain a large export surplus during these years as a means of amortizing her accumulated debt to the Soviet Union.

China's balance of trade with the non-Communist world followed just about the opposite course; that is, through 1957 China exported considerably more than she imported. In this way, she could accumulate sizable sterling reserves. These were later drawn upon to finance part of the trade deficits incurred during the crisis years.

How important was this trade for China's economy? In what way did it contribute to her development? Imports in all forms

provided the principal highway for the influx of modern technology, scientific knowledge, and innovating influences. More
tangibly, imports played a crucial role in new plant expansion,
particularly in industry. Complete plant deliveries and installations provided the backbone of industrial expansion during the
periods of the First Five Year Plan and the Great Leap. There is
no doubt that without capital goods imports the rate of economic growth, and especially the rate of industrial growth,
would have been markedly reduced. Moreover, the character
and quality of that growth would have had to be altered significantly, with less emphasis placed on the development of large-
scale and capital-intensive industries on the one hand and of
investment goods on the other.

Correspondingly, imports played a crucial role at a later
date in maintaining economic and political stability. After the
onset of the food crisis, grain imports significantly eased the
pressure on domestic distribution. More importantly, they played
a critical role in alleviating the consequences of the food shortage
which began to have a seriously debilitating effect on people's
health, their morale, and even their attitude toward the regime.

The situation was further aggravated by the fact that China
had to rely increasingly on textile exports to finance these essential imports of grain, cotton, and other vital raw materials.
However, domestic cotton production declined during the crisis,
and raw cotton imports could not be stepped up significantly
because of foreign exchange shortages. Therefore, textile production had to be curtailed because of raw material scarcities
at a time when textile exports had to be maintained. This combination of circumstances meant that the brunt of the reduction in
textile output had to be borne by the Chinese consumer.

This dependence on foreign trade to help maintain political
and economic stability and to develop industry suggests that the
outside world possesses at least some potential leverage over the
future course of Communist China's economy. The fate of that
economy will naturally be determined by factors that are largely
endemic to the system, such as the country's economic backwardness, the rate of its population growth, and the character

of its economic policies. Foreign trade, nevertheless, can smooth or seriously impede the path ahead. However, potential leverage can be translated into actual leverage only if all countries, or at least all major trading nations, agree on a common trade control policy vis-à-vis China. For instance, if all countries were to impose a total trade embargo and enforce it over a number of years, it could and probably would have a significant impact on the mainland economy. This possibility, of course, does not mean that such an embargo would be desirable or feasible.

CHAPTER FIVE

Economic Relations with Other Communist Countries

The ideological and political disputes between the Russian and Chinese Communists, disputes which became open after 1960, suggest the need for a thorough re-examination of the character of the Sino-Soviet alliance. Such an undertaking would entail a careful analysis of the relative strength of centrifugal and centripetal forces. A broad reappraisal of this sort, however, is beyond the scope of the present study. We shall look only at the economic aspects of the total problem.

Economic relations between China and the Soviet Union have been close since the founding of the People's Republic of China. Gradually these spilled over into a network of relations between China and other members of the bloc as well. Such economic contacts were comprehensive in scope and assumed a variety of forms. China imported goods and services, including complete plants, from the Soviet Union and Eastern Europe. These imports were financed partly by her own exports and partly by Soviet credits. China's exports to the Communist countries of Asia were financed by her imports from them and by her economic assistance to them. Thus, the salient elements in China's economic relations with the rest of the Communist world have been normal commercial intercourse and the conditions under which it has been carried on, Soviet credits to China, Chinese economic assistance to some of the Communist countries, Soviet technical assistance to China, and Chinese technical assistance to the Asian Communist countries.

What role did these relations play in shaping the alliance? May they have been a major factor in producing the tensions in the alliance, or did they tie the two partners together? Has politics really been a handmaiden of economics, or has economics been playing merely a passive role? In quite another vein, have the relations contributed to or detracted from Communist China's economic development? Have they, therefore, reinforced or weakened the impact of the "power effect," "the model effect," and "the trade effect" upon the conduct of Chinese Communist foreign policy?

Most studies of the Sino-Soviet alliance have tended to ascribe a major importance to the economic ingredient—although frequently from two opposing points of view. Some have emphasized that Soviet grants or loans to China have been quite limited and that Russian assistance to the economic development of mainland China must therefore be considered modest.[1] This situation, coupled with large-scale Soviet aid to other countries, has allegedly produced dissatisfaction and resentment on the part of the Chinese Communist leadership and has thereby served as a perpetual source of tension in the alliance.

On the other hand, in a most interesting and provocative paper, Professor Walter Galenson holds that Sino-Soviet economic relations have been quite disadvantageous to the Russians. For them, "Chinese trade meant a forced transfer of resources from growth to consumption, to the extent that they were not able in turn to reallocate their resources." [2] To an increasingly irksome extent, from the Russian point of view, Chinese growth was being substituted for Soviet growth. Thus, the apparent strains in the alliance stem not from Chinese dissatisfaction but from Soviet resentment at the economic burdens imposed by the relationship.

As I will attempt to show in this chapter, both conclusions are based on too narrow a reading of the evidence. The first interpretation concentrates exclusively on Soviet loans and grants and does not consider the flow of goods and services in all its forms.

The second devotes inadequate attention to the changing economic policies and production capacities of the Soviet Union over the last decade. Unquestionably, mainland China could not have achieved anywhere near the rates of industrial growth she actually attained without the capital goods, particularly complete plant installations, and technical assistance she received from the Soviet Union. This fact does not mean, however, that Chinese growth was substituted for Soviet growth. To support such a proposition, one would have to demonstrate that Soviet exports to China were either not paid for at all or not paid in full. This does not seem to have been the case, as will be shown at greater length below. One might also maintain that the relationship with China forced the Soviet Union to ship capital goods to its Communist neighbor and accept consumer goods in payment. As a result, so the argument runs, Soviet domestic investment had to be curtailed while personal consumption had to be raised. This view ignores the fact that the post-Stalin leadership consciously chose to grant concessions to the Soviet consumer for both political and economic reasons. Therefore, a significant component of Soviet economic growth during the last decade has been growth in per capita consumption and in the production of consumer goods. Imports of consumer goods from China may thus have facilitated the implementation of post-Stalin economic policy.

An appraisal of the economic aspects of the alliance must be based on an assessment of the relative costs and benefits of the relationship for each partner. The essential thesis developed here is that in light of the underdeveloped state of the Chinese economy and China's greater economic dependence on Russia, rather than vice versa, both the costs and the benefits of the relationship were far more significant for China than for Russia.[3] Such a pattern of dependence provided the Soviets with superior bargaining power in the economic sphere; however, there is no evidence to suggest that this power resulted in economic exploitation of the Chinese. Nor, would it seem, have the Soviets been able to use this economic bargaining power as a means of imposing their views on the Chinese. These conclusions do not necessarily imply, on the other hand, that China's economic dependence on the Soviet Union did not place certain constraints on Chinese ambitions and actions at specific times and in specific places.

Character of Economic Relations with Other Communist Countries

Formal economic relations between the Communist authorities in China and the rest of the Communist world were inaugurated with the signing of a barter agreement between the Northeast People's government and the U.S.S.R. in July 1949—that is, a few months before the official proclamation of the People's Republic of China. From these modest beginnings, ever closer and more intimate economic ties were gradually developed, at first with the Soviet Union and then with other Communist countries.

Economic relations between the Soviet Union and China were defined by a series of treaties signed in February 1950 at the end of Mao's visit to Moscow. The Soviet Union granted a credit of $300 million to be drawn upon in five equal installments. This loan, extended at an interest rate of 1 per cent, was to help finance the deliveries of complete plants and equipment. It was to be amortized over a 10-year period starting at the end of 1954.[4] The Russians also agreed to return free of charge the Changchun railway and the naval base of Port Arthur when a peace treaty with Japan was concluded, but not later than the end of 1952. China, however, contracted to repay the Soviet Union for expenses the latter incurred in restoring and constructing the naval installations after 1945. The status of Dairen was to be considered upon conclusion of a peace treaty with Japan. Significantly, no provision for a definite turnover date independent of a treaty with Japan was made.

About a month later, agreements for the organization of Sino-Soviet joint stock companies were reached. Five such companies were established in Communist China. Two of these, those for the Changchun railway and for the Dairen shipyards, were going enterprises before the Communist takeover; three others, those for air transport between China and the Soviet Union, for extraction of petroleum, and for mining of non-ferrous and rare metals in Sinkiang, were provided for by the agreements of February 14, 1950.[5] In the case of the first two companies, the Soviet contribution was represented by Japanese shares and holdings which had been expropriated by its occupation authorities in Manchuria. (This arrangement paralleled closely the pattern established in the East European satellites, where the Soviet share in joint-stock companies was based on expropriated German assets.) The situation was different with respect to the other three companies. They were based much more on a genuine partnership. The Soviet government provided the capital goods, such as planes, oil-drilling equipment, and mining equipment, and the Chinese furnished labor and materials for local construction.

These differences in the character of the enterprises were reflected in the manner in which they were liquidated. The Chinese Eastern railway was returned free of charge to the Chinese on January 1, 1953. The other companies, in contrast, were turned over only two years later, and the Chinese assumed an obligation for the Soviet share of investment. This obligation was to be paid off over a number of years.[6] Neither the total amount of compensation nor the size of the annual payments was announced.

Soon after the Soviets surrendered their shares in the joint-stock companies (January 1, 1955), they pulled out of Port Arthur and Dairen and left all naval and shipbuilding facilities to the Chinese free of charge. In this respect at least, the Soviets were generous, for the 1950 agreements provided for Chinese compensation for installations built after 1945, a provision the Russians apparently chose not to enforce. However, military stockpiles left in these two bases were to be paid for out of special loans advanced for this purpose.[7] With the abandonment of these bases in May 1955, all Soviet economic, political, and military positions in Manchuria were liquidated.

The basis for formal commercial relations between the two large Communist states was laid by a trade agreement concluded in April 1950.[8] Annual agreements and protocols since then have detailed the kinds and quantities of goods to be exchanged and the terms of exchange. Later in 1950, China entered into similar agreements with Czechoslovakia, North Korea, and East Germany. Agreements were made with Poland and Hungary in early 1951, with Bulgaria and Rumania in 1952, with Mongolia in 1953, and with Albania and North Vietnam in 1954.

All these were bilateral agreements which, in essence, provided for exchanges which had to be balanced annually. Of course, deficits could be financed by long-term credits, and surpluses could be accumulated as a means of repaying debts. The trade agreements did allow for the carryover of some small balances into the next year; however, these had to be liquidated in the first three months of the new year. The agreement with the Soviet Union limited such balances to six million rubles, and that with Czechoslovakia to two million.[9] If one of the trading partners exceeded these limits, it automatically incurred a short-term debt on which a 2 per cent rate of interest was charged.[10] While we have no precise information on this point, it would seem that the Soviets did not enforce these limits too strictly. Therefore, Communist China probably had some short-term commercial credits at its disposal to supplement its longer-term borrowing from the Soviet Union.

Mainland China's economic relations with all Communist countries have remained essentially bilateral rather than multilateral. There is some evidence that the Chinese resisted efforts at economic integration of the Communist world. Moreover, they never joined CMEA (the Council of Mutual Economic Assistance) but confined themselves to observer status until they withdrew altogether in early 1961. However, they did begin to negotiate long-term trade agreements with all East European countries in the late 1950s. These permitted long-range planning of foreign trade and integration of foreign trade with their national economic plans. But no such agreement was concluded between Russia and China, despite Soviet efforts to arrive at one.[11] On the contrary, the Chinese, particularly in 1958 and 1959, frequently changed import orders and specifications, asked for accelerated delivery schedules on short notice, expanded their trade volumes several times a year, and in many other ways introduced elements of unpredictability into Sino-Soviet economic relations. These practices placed considerable strains on some Soviet enterprises concerned with industrial production and foreign trade. Nevertheless, it would seem that while the Russians found this situation irksome, they tried to accommodate themselves to the demands of the Chinese.

The Chinese resisted measures toward economic integration because they perceived these as designed to maintain more or less of a status quo, to perpetuate the economic gap between themselves and the Russians. They were apparently reluctant to enter into long-term trade agreements with their leading economic partner because flexible quantities and mixes of imports could provide a cushion for poor harvests, planning errors, and other unanticipated short-term changes. Trade agreements fixed annual delivery quotas and terms in fairly specific ways, and longer-run trade agreements set at least the values of the trade turnover and the kinds of goods to be exchanged. In other words, they entailed a more or less fixed obligation which would have to be met even in the face of unforeseen contingencies such as a poor harvest. With obligations fixed in this way, the whole weight of unanticipated economic changes would have to be borne by the domestic economy. On the other hand, the shorter the term of trade agreements, the more easily could foreign trade serve as a shock absorber, as a vehicle to shift at least some of the burden of short-term adjustment to the trading partner. This fact was particularly apparent during the Korean War and the Great Leap. In contrast, it would seem that the Soviets were eager to plan their export commitments on a long-term basis in order to minimize inventory accumulation on the one hand and production or transport bottlenecks on the other. Here was a genuine case of divergent economic interests.

The harmony in Sino-Soviet economic relations was marred almost from the outset by other and perhaps even more important factors as well. One of these involved the financing of Russian deliveries connected with the Korean War. Although the evidence on the subject is contradictory, the Chinese apparently expected the Russians to supply military matériel for the war *gratis,* while the Soviets insisted that such matériel be financed by credits over and above the earlier 1950 loan and that these credits be repaid over a 10-year period.[12] Circumstantial evidence would suggest that disagreements also emerged when the Chinese were drafting their First Five Year Plan. The Chinese apparently wished to import much more equipment and many more complete plants and capital goods of all kinds than the Soviets were prepared to deliver. Possibly the Chinese hoped that these Soviet deliveries would be financed by additional credits over and above the 1950 loan, while the Russians refused to make any new loans. Agreement was finally reached after Li Fu-ch'un (then Vice Chairman of the Government Committee on Economics and Finance) stayed in Moscow for eight months, from August 1952 to May 1953, and after Chou En-lai visited the Russian capital twice, the first time in August 1952 and the second in March 1953 for Stalin's funeral. From the standpoint of Sino-Soviet relations, two aspects of this situation are noteworthy. First, the agreement was concluded only after prolonged negotiations and only after Stalin's death. Second, although the agreement was signed in May, the Chinese did not announce it until September, when Mao sent a letter to the Soviet government thanking it for undertaking to deliver 91 additional industrial plants.[13] These projects, to be completed by 1959, were to be delivered over and above the 50 installations agreed upon in 1950. The latter involved mostly rehabilitation of existing power, steel, and other plants in Manchuria, the equipment of which had been removed by Russian armies in 1945. The Soviets were in effect returning new equipment for the old they had taken away earlier, but the Chinese had to pay for it out of credits and current exports.

When Khrushchev and Bulganin visited Peking in October 1954, they agreed to export an additional 15 plants.[14] This commitment was then supplemented by another 55 units at the time of Mikoyan's visit in April 1956.[15] Thus, during the period of China's First Five Year Plan, the Soviets agreed to install a total of 211 complete plants. These were later merged or reduced to 166, with deliveries to be consummated by 1959. The Soviets also committed themselves to ship 125 more plants during the Second (1958–62) and Third (1963–67) Five Year Plans. By early 1959, then, the combined agreements provided for the installation of 291 "turnkey projects" at a total value of 13.1 billion rubles (about $3.3 billion at the official rate of exchange).[16]

As of June 1960, 130 complete plant projects with a total value of about 6 billion rubles were fully or partly completed and in operation.[17] To these should be added the 27 plants completed out of 64 under construction by East European countries. The total commitment in this case was 68.[18]

The last agreement for complete plant deliveries was concluded at the time of Chou En-lai's stay in Moscow for the 21st Congress of the Communist party of the Soviet Union in February 1959. As has been indicated elsewhere, complete plant exports to China reached their peak in 1959, declined somewhat in 1960, and dwindled rapidly afterward. This situation was in part a reflection of China's reduced demand for capital goods imports and in part a result of the withdrawal of Soviet technicians in 1960. (The assistance the technicians provided constituted an essential ingredient of such projects.) Therefore, the present status of the committed but as yet undelivered projects is not entirely clear. It is more than probable that the Chinese either canceled or suspended the orders for them.

If one collates the various elements of Sino-Soviet economic relations outlined above, it becomes clear that they varied during different periods. From the time of the official proclamation of the People's Republic to the death of Stalin, they were close but far from frictionless. The Soviets did extend a $300 million loan to the Chinese and entered into a number of other economic agreements, but disagreements over the financing of Korean War deliveries and the degree to which the Soviets would assist the Chinese in mounting their First Five Year Plan emerged. The latter problem was apparently resolved almost immediately upon Stalin's death, which marked the beginning of the second and perhaps happiest phase in Sino-Soviet economic relations.

During this period, running from early 1953 to the end of 1955, the Soviets advanced a second loan of $130 million, evacuated the naval bases of Port Arthur and Dairen, left naval stores and military stockpiles there which they sold to the Chinese on credit, and similarly sold on credit their shares in the joint-stock companies. Railroad links between China and the Soviet Union were significantly extended. Agreements for close scientific and technical collaboration between the two countries were concluded. These specifically provided for the exchange of patents, blueprints, and other technical documents free of charge except for the actual cost of reproduction.[19]

The 1956-60 period marked a third phase in Sino-Soviet economic relations. Soviet credits dwindled in 1956 and were completely exhausted in 1957. Yet, commercial intercourse between the two countries expanded rapidly. Deliveries of complete plants were stepped up markedly, and trade between the two countries attained its peak level. On the other hand, to the best of our knowledge the Soviet Union extended no new economic aid in credits or grants despite some indications that Mao requested it at the time of his visit to Moscow in the fall of 1957.

The sudden and unheralded withdrawal of Soviet technicians, beginning in July 1960, signaled a drastic turn in the economic ties of the two countries. Since then, these relations have been confined largely to shrinking trade which was partly supported by China's obligation to amortize its debt. Unless there is an improvement in Sino-Soviet relations in general and/or a marked improvement in mainland China's domestic economic position, trade between them may be expected to shrink further after 1965 when all Soviet credits will have been paid off.

Additional light has been thrown on the circumstances which led to the withdrawal of the Soviet technicians from China by Mikhail Suslov in a speech to the Central Committee of the Soviet party.[20] When the Chinese threw technical considerations to the wind during the Great Leap, the position of the expert was downgraded. The counsel of Soviet technicians was disregarded as well, and they were placed in an increasingly untenable position. Apparently the last straw from the Soviet point of view was the attempt of the Chinese Communists to convert the Russian technicians to their doctrinal position and in effect to use them as a fifth column in the Soviet Union.

Whatever the reasons for the withdrawal may be, it was executed in a manner calculated to inflict maximum damage upon

Chinese industry. The technicians left so precipitously in many cases that they had to leave projects under construction or in operation without an opportunity to brief their Chinese counterparts.

As one surveys Sino-Soviet economic relations between 1950 and 1963, several salient features stand out. The outstanding characteristic is the dominance of the Soviet Union and the Communist world as a whole in China's foreign trade until 1960. This trade took two forms: traditional exchange of goods and export of complete "turnkey projects" to China. Economic transactions were financed preponderantly out of current earnings, supplemented by Soviet credits. (More will be said about these later.) With minor exceptions, apparently at no time did any Communist country make any free grants to China. The exceptions were the exchange of scientific information mentioned above and some Soviet assistance to Chinese students at Soviet institutions.[21] There may also have been some military grants during the Korean War, but we cannot be certain.

The Role of Communist Countries in Communist China's Foreign Trade

Far-reaching dependence upon the Soviet Union has characterized China's economic relationship with her ally until recently. This dependence is apparent from the relative importance to the two countries of their mutual trade. As Tables 5-1 and 5-2 show, about 50 per cent of Communist China's trade was with the Soviet Union in the mid-fifties, while only about 20 per cent of Russian trade was with the mainland. Even in 1963, after a marked decline had taken place, about one-fifth of Chinese trade was still with the Soviets; on the other hand, less than 5 per cent of Russian trade was with China. Thus, while the Soviet Union to the present day remains China's most important trading partner, the reverse is no longer true. In 1955, 1956, and 1959, the People's Republic of China was Russia's leading trading partner, and it was in second place behind East Germany in 1957,

TABLE 5-1. Share of the Soviet Union and the East European Countries in Communist China's Foreign Trade, 1955–63 [a]

(in per cent)

Country	1955	1957	1959	1961	1962	1963
Soviet Union	52.00	42.60	48.50	30.70	27.40	20.00
Albania	0.05	0.22	0.08	0.73	1.97	(1.99)
Bulgaria	0.33	0.28	0.40	0.40	0.24	(0.21)
Czechoslovakia	4.43	4.93	4.61	2.54	1.37	1.85
East Germany	6.89	6.46	5.23	3.19	1.96	1.18
Hungary	2.45	2.02	1.98	1.54	0.84	0.78
Poland	2.63	2.73	2.34	1.58	1.38	1.21
Rumania	0.75	n.a.	1.40	0.97	0.46	0.94

[a] Calculations are based on adjusted totals for China's trade as given in Table 4-1.

Notes: Data in parentheses are the author's estimates.

  n.a. stands for "not available."

Sources: Tables 4–1, 4–3, and B–3; United Nations, *Yearbook of International Trade Statistics* for 1956, 1958, 1960, 1962, and 1963; U.S. Central Intelligence Agency, *Foreign Trade of the European Satellites, 1963,* Intelligence Report, (Washington, D.C.: Author, December 1964).

TABLE 5-2. Communist China's Share in the Foreign Trade of the Soviet Union and the East European Countries, 1955–63

(in per cent)

Country	1955	1957	1959	1961	1962	1963
Soviet Union	21.4	14.5	19.5	7.8	5.6	4.2
Albania	2.3	8.0	2.7	18.0	51.0	n.a.
Bulgaria	1.9	1.2	1.7	0.9	0.4	n.a.
Czechoslovakia	5.3	5.4	4.1	1.9	0.9	1.2
East Germany	7.1	5.7	5.4	2.1	1.4	0.7
Hungary	5.7	4.5	5.4	2.2	1.0	0.9
Poland	3.8	3.7	7.1	1.5	1.1	1.0
Rumania	0.2	n.a.	5.8	1.8	0.7	1.4

Note: n.a. stands for "not available."

Sources: See Table 5–1.

1958, and 1960. By 1962, however, China dropped to sixth place. She was displaced not only by East Germany but by practically all the other East European countries as well.

Almost the reverse holds true for Eastern Europe in one sense. For most countries and in most years, China occupied a somewhat more important place in their total trade than vice versa. Next to the Soviet Union, Communist China's largest trade turnover was with East Germany. Then came that with Czechoslovakia. However, with the decline in China's trade with the Communist countries in recent years, East Germany by 1961 had dropped to sixth place. The Soviet Union still remained first but was followed by Hong Kong, Australia, Canada, and the United Kingdom. Similarly, Czechoslovakia dropped from third to seventh place.[22]

TRENDS IN SINO-SOVIET TRADE. The volume and value of Sino-Soviet trade grew markedly during the 1950s as a result of the recovery and growth of both economies and a marked reorientation of the foreign trade of both countries. The value of total trade turnover increased about three and a half times. China's exports to the Soviet Union, however, expanded much more rapidly than her imports, principally because she maintained a sizable trade deficit during the first half of the decade but converted that to a surplus during the second half. The deficit was financed largely by Soviet loans, and the surplus was used to amortize the loans.

The availability of Soviet loans during the early part of the period facilitated and accelerated China's recovery from war devastation, contributed to plant rehabilitation, helped to ease the burden imposed on the Chinese economy by the Korean War, and served to finance part of the new investment designed to expand the plant and to increase plant capacity. Thus, Soviet loans enabled China to augment her domestic resources at a time when she most needed to do so. There is no question that longer-term loans with later starting dates for and longer periods of amortization could have considerably eased the burden which repayment imposed on the Chinese economy. Yet by the late fifties China was in a relatively more favorable economic position, for the great increase in her manufacturing and mining capacity had significantly enhanced her ability to export non-agricultural goods. In a sense, her readiness to extend foreign aid on an appreciable scale is an illustration of this fact even if one allows for the subordination of economic to political and prestige considerations. Moreover, it would be somewhat paradoxical for China to extend foreign aid to other countries while she continued to draw on Soviet credits or failed to amortize them. Such aid would really represent Soviet rather than Chinese foreign aid but would permit the Chinese to reap all the benefits therefrom.

It has been generally assumed that when the credits extended to China were exhausted, the Russians failed to renew them and that this action contributed to the heavy burden of repayment imposed upon the Chinese economy. However, one cannot completely rule out the possibility that the Chinese Communist leaders were eager to amortize these debts as quickly as possible to emancipate China from Soviet economic, and therefore political, dependence. Which of these two positions represents the more realistic assessment of the Sino-Soviet relationship is difficult to say. One can find documentation in Chinese or Soviet statements and writings to support either hypothesis. Yet, on balance, the evidence would perhaps support the former view more strongly.

There are a number of factors besides the availability of Soviet credits which shaped trends in Sino-Soviet trade. The most important of these were the quality of the harvest and the rates of investment in China. Thus, while China's exports to the Soviet Union increased almost without interruption until 1959 (see Table 5-5), her imports from there fluctuated much more markedly. Until 1954–55 (*i.e.,* until Soviet credits were almost exhausted), the growth of imports was closely associated with the trade deficit. Afterward, strenuous efforts must have been made to save on imports as a means of insuring a trade surplus. Nevertheless, imports did not significantly decline until 1957, which was a year of retrenchment and cutbacks in investment in China.[23] Under such conditions, the level of imports of investment goods could be held more or less constant while most of the other categories of imports were curtailed. With the resumption of rapid economic expansion during the Great Leap Forward in 1958 and 1959, however, imports rose rapidly once more and significantly surpassed the peak attained in 1954. Then they fell precipitously under the impact of the agricultural crisis.

COMMODITY COMPOSITION OF SINO-SOVIET TRADE. As was pointed out earlier, Sino-Soviet trade has been characterized by Chinese imports of capital goods, petroleum and petroleum products, and certain metals and exports of foodstuffs, soybeans, oilseeds and oilseed products, raw materials of agricultural origin (*e.g.*, hides and skins), nonferrous metals, and textile products. However, as may be seen from Tables 5-3 and 5-4, this pattern has been modified somewhat over the years.

The outstanding change in China's deliveries to the Soviet Union has been the continuous and rapid growth of textile products, particularly fabrics and finished manufactures. In value terms, these constituted almost two-thirds of all exports by the early 1960s. At the same time, the relative importance of unprocessed foodstuffs and industrial raw materials declined. For most of the period, more than 80 per cent of Chinese exports to Russia were either finished consumer goods or raw materials and semimanufactures for the production of consumer goods. Therefore, while Soviet exports were generally destined to augment, facilitate, and accelerate investment in China, China's exports were channeled into consumption in the Soviet Union.

On the side of Chinese imports, the most striking feature was the constantly rising importance of machinery and equipment—from about 10 per cent in 1950 to better than 60 per cent during the Great Leap years of 1959 and 1960. Particularly noteworthy in this connection was the growing share of complete plant installations in the import totals. The significance of the shipments of capital goods, not only from the Chinese but from the Russian point of view as well, may perhaps be gauged if one considers that in the late fifties China absorbed about half or more of Soviet exports of machinery to the Communist world as a whole.[24] As a recipient of complete plants, China was even more

T A B L E 5 - 3 . Commodity Composition of Communist China's Exports to the Soviet Union, 1955–63

(in per cent)

Commodity Category	1955	1956	1957	1958	1959	1960	1961	1962	1963
Soybeans, oilseeds, and products	19.9	16.4	12.6	9.4	9.1	6.2	0.2	—	—
Cereals	7.0	9.1	3.6	6.9	7.8	6.9	0.1	—	—
Livestock products									
Edible	11.6	9.1	5.9	9.4	4.5	2.4	0.5	—	0.6
Inedible	3.5	3.4	2.8	2.5	1.9	1.9	1.0	0.4	0.7
Fruits and vegetables	2.3	2.7	3.7	3.7	2.8	2.1	1.7	2.5	3.5
Tea	1.6	1.6	1.7	1.8	1.8	1.5	0.5	0.5	0.7
Tobacco	3.4	3.9	5.6	3.6	2.7	1.5	0.7	—	—
Textiles									
Raw materials	9.2	7.7	6.6	4.3	8.3	7.7	4.2	2.7	2.1
Fabrics	6.7	8.6	11.7	9.9	14.1	16.4	22.9	22.9	23.5
Clothing and footwear	2.5	4.5	8.3	16.2	22.0	27.8	35.2	39.1	42.4
Industrial fats and oils	0.7	1.0	1.0	1.0	0.8	0.5	0.3	0.5	0.2
Building materials	1.0	1.2	2.1	2.0	1.2	1.5	2.4	2.9	2.3
Chemical products	1.2	2.4	1.6	1.9	0.9	1.5	1.2	1.0	1.8
Metals, metal ores and concentrates	22.5	20.0	20.1	16.1	12.4	14.5	16.5	13.2	11.9
Non-metallic minerals	1.4	1.2	1.5	1.4	1.1	1.1	0.3	1.4	1.4
Machinery and equipment	1.6	1.2	0.9	0.5	1.1	0.1	0.1	1.7	1.7
Other	3.7	6.0	10.5	9.5	7.4	6.1	12.3	11.2	7.2
Total	100.0	100.0	100.0	100.0	100.0	100.0	100.0	100.0	100.0

Notes: Minor inconsistencies result from rounding.
— stands for "none."

Sources: The percentages were calculated by the author on the basis of ruble values given in U.S.S.R., Ministry of Foreign Trade, *Vneshniaia Torgovlia SSSR za 1955–59; Statisticheskii Sbornik* [*The Foreign Trade of the USSR for 1955–1959: A Statistical Compilation*] (Moscow Vneshtorgizdat, 1961); *Vneshniaia Torgovlia SSSR za 1961 Godi: Statisticheskii Obzor* [*The Foreign Trade of the USSR for 1961: Statistical Handbook*] (Moscow: Vneshtorgizdat, 1962) and the volume for 1963 of this series of foreign trade handbooks.

TABLE 5-4. Commodity Composition of Communist China's Imports from the Soviet Union, 1955–63

(in per cent)

Commodity Category	1955	1956	1957	1958	1959	1960	1961	1962	1963
Foodstuffs, processed and unprocessed	–	0.1	0.2	0.2	0.1	–	4.8	8.9	0.4
Manufactured consumer goods	0.6	0.7	1.1	1.1	0.6	0.5	0.8	4.2	6.1
Drugs and cosmetics	0.2	0.1	–	0.1	0.1	–	0.2	0.2	1.6
Paper	1.0	0.8	0.6	–	–	–	0.1	–	–
Rubber and rubber products	0.2	0.1	0.1	0.2	–	0.2	0.1	0.1	0.1
Chemical products	0.5	0.1	0.5	1.3	0.8	1.1	1.5	1.8	2.0
Fertilizers and insecticides	0.1	–	0.1	0.3	0.1	0.1	–	–	–
Building materials	0.2	0.2	0.2	0.1	0.1	0.2	–	–	0.1
Metals, metal ores and concentrates	12.0	10.9	7.8	12.5	6.0	8.7	11.3	14.6	18.1
Petroleum and petroleum products	5.9	11.7	16.6	14.6	12.3	13.8	32.9	34.5	33.3
Machinery and equipment	30.7	41.6	49.9	50.2	62.6	61.7	29.4	11.7	23.2
Complete plants	18.9	29.6	38.4	26.2	41.9	45.7	21.5	3.8	8.0
Other	48.7	33.7	23.0	19.7	17.4	13.8	18.9	23.9	15.1
Total	100.0	100.0	100.0	100.0	100.0	100.0	100.0	100.0	100.0

Notes: Minor inconsistencies result from rounding.
— stands for "none."

Sources: See Table 5-3.

dominant. More than two-thirds of Soviet deliveries of this type were channeled to her.[25]

The character and financing of these deliveries of complete plants have perhaps been subject to more misunderstanding than any other aspect of Sino-Soviet economic relations. This misunderstanding has arisen because (a) in Chinese and Soviet sources they are referred to as major "aid projects," (b) they are usually the subject of special agreements, and (c) the total value of the "aid projects" contracted for is frequently coupled with the announcement of new economic and/or political agreements. As a result, it has often been concluded that such deliveries represent

Soviet loans or grants-in-aid beyond those officially classified as such by Chinese and Soviet authorities.

Deliveries of complete plant installations do not represent aid in our sense of that term. In one respect, they are no more than a particular form of commercial export from the Soviet Union to China. It is true that deficits in the Chinese balance of payments resulting from these deliveries and other Soviet exports could be financed by long-term credits from the Soviet Union as long as these were available. However, such credits were exhausted by 1957, and the Chinese then had to pay for all the deliveries out of current earnings of foreign exchange.

On the other hand, it would be equally misleading not to recognize that deliveries of complete plant installations represent a most important form of development assistance. (Here the term "development assistance" is used in a special sense.) Foreign exchange expended to import capital goods in their traditional form will almost certainly yield lower rates of industrial growth in the underdeveloped country which receives the goods than the same outlay on complete plant installations will. This situation may be attributed to the fact that importation of separate components for plant construction and operation will probably produce higher costs and lower efficiency than will an integrated approach in which the design of the project, the building of the plant, the manufacture of the equipment, and the technical assistance in operating the plant are fully combined. Although the salaries and expenses of technicians are treated as a part of the costs of the project and thus are borne by the Chinese, the net gain to the Chinese economy is still considerable.[26]

In one respect, of course, such a situation does not prove much. It merely confirms the postulates of the classical theory of international trade; that is, that trade brings certain gains to each trading partner which would otherwise not accrue. However, the point to be made in the present context is that the gains to China exceed what might be characterized as "normal" gains from international trade. Moreover, the scale upon which this kind of project assistance was rendered would be hard to envisage without a close political tie between the two countries. After all, the so-called Soviet aid projects constituted the very heart of China's First Five Year Plan, and almost the same can be said for the industrial phase of the Great Leap. Practically all the basic plans for industrial expansion—for instance, the expansion of existing steel mills, the construction of new steel complexes, the building of new power plants, the development of railways, the installation of new chemical plants, oil refineries, etc.—were predicated upon these projects.

The political sensitivity of the projects was perhaps most clearly demonstrated during the early 1960s, for Soviet deliveries of complete plants dwindled under the impact of deteriorating Sino-Soviet relations. (See Table 5-4) In a sense, the whole program was undercut in 1960 by the sudden withdrawal of Soviet technicians, who apparently took the blueprints for plant installations back with them. Equipment on order and arriving from the Soviet Union could not be installed, so it began to pile up on railroad sidings, in warehouses, and in half-completed factories. In the face of this pile-up and the removal of technical assistance, continuing imports of complete plants became pointless. Moreover, as was indicated before, cutbacks in investment in China drastically curtailed the demand for such projects, so even if Soviet technicians had not been withdrawn, imports of complete plants would have been curtailed, although probably not as severely as they actually were. Soviet deliveries of complete plants reached their lowest point in 1962 when they were of almost negligible proportions. However, encouraged by gradual economic recovery in 1963, the Chinese placed new complete plant orders in Europe and Japan and at the same time slightly increased their plant purchases from the Soviet Union. It remains to be seen whether China, if and when her industrialization drive is resumed, will import these "turnkey projects" on a scale comparable with the past and from countries with which she has no close political alliances.

The Financing of Economic Relations

Communist China's economic relations with other Communist countries involve the flow of goods and services between herself and her Communist partners. From this fact stem two types of questions which are not always clearly distinguished. What goods and services are exchanged? How are the transactions financed? Let us turn to the second of these considerations and examine some of the special financing arrangements.

THE EXTENT OF SOVIET AID. The data concerning Soviet aid to China are rather obscure and in many ways inconsistent. The information that is available will be analyzed below in an attempt to interpret the evidence and reconcile the inconsistencies.

To the best of our knowledge, the Soviet Union has made no free grants to China since the advent of the Chinese Communist regime. According to official mainland announcements, however, sizable credits, totaling 5,294 million yuan, were extended over a period of eight years, *i.e.*, between 1950 and 1957. Of this total, 2,174 million yuan were lent between 1950 and 1952, while the remainder of 3,120 million was extended during the period of the First Five Year Plan.[27] At the same time, the annual rate of Soviet lending for 1952 to 1957 can be derived with a fair degree of precision from the official Chinese budget reports for these years.

A problem arises from the fact that these figures are much larger than the credits granted in the published loan agreements. The Sino-Soviet agreements of February 14, 1950, provide for credits of $300 million to be paid in five annual installments. In Soviet sources, the value of this loan is cited as 1,200 million rubles.[28] In October 1954 a second loan involving a long-term credit of 520 million rubles was announced.[29] The total of these loans, then, would be 1,720 million (old) rubles, or the equivalent of $430 million at the official rate of exchange. In contrast, the total given by the Chinese Minister of Finance would be equivalent to about 5,300 million or 8,960 million rubles, depending on what exchange rate is used to convert yuan into rubles.*

Two quite different attempts to resolve this problem have

---

* These figures are based on the assumption that Soviet credits were converted to yuan either at the "trade ruble" rate of 1:1 or at a mutually "consistent" rate of 1.7 old rubles to the yuan. For a discussion of the uncertainties surrounding these rates, see Appendix C.

been made. Professor C. M. Li bases his solution on what may be termed the "foreign exchange hypothesis." According to this view, the mutually "consistent" rate of exchange of about 1.7 old rubles to the yuan is inapplicable to these credits. Instead, an exchange rate of two yuan to the ruble would be appropriate.[30] On this basis, Soviet credits of 1,720 million rubles would be equivalent to roughly 3,440 million yuan; the difference between this amount and the official Chinese figure can be ascribed to the surrender (on credit) of the Soviet shares in the joint-stock companies and of the military stockpiles on the Port Arthur naval base. Professor F. H. Mah, on the other hand, accepts the Chinese loan figure, but he tries to show that the discrepancy arises from the fact that the $430 million (1,720 million rubles) credits constituted economic aid, while the rest represented military deliveries.[31]

On the basis of presently available evidence, it would seem that the "foreign exchange hypothesis" cannot be validated. It is quite clear now that the Soviet Union has advanced credits to China on several occasions besides the two announced.[32] Moreover, an analysis of the information which Russian sources give about Soviet loans to the Asian Communist countries suggests that credits totaling about 5,300 million rubles had been extended to China by the beginning of 1956.[33] Chinese drawings on Soviet loans to China were quite small between 1955 and 1957 (140 million yuan altogether). Since the ruble-yuan exchange rate effective in Sino-Soviet trade was apparently around 1:1, the expenditure figures of 5,154 million yuan (drawings up to and including 1955) and the loan figures of 5,300 million rubles would appear to be equivalents.[34]

If we assume that the Soviet Union did in fact extend a total credit of about 5,300 million rubles to China between 1950 and 1957, how were these funds used? Can Mah's hypothesis—that 1,720 million rubles of this total were economic aid and the rest were military aid—be validated? This question will be dealt with indirectly by comparing annual flows of Sino-Soviet trade and credit and by analyzing the circumstances under which the different credit agreements were concluded.

On the basis of the available data, it is not possible to

distinguish among the various economic loans for the period as a whole and much less for individual years. We know that these credits were used primarily for four purposes: to finance deliveries of complete plants and other capital goods, to finance shipments of military equipment and matériel both during and after the Korean War, to finance the purchase of the Soviet share of the four joint-stock companies turned over to the Chinese in 1954, and to finance the purchase of military stockpiles left in Port Arthur and Dairen when the Soviets left these bases in early 1955. However, an important distinction needs to be made between the first two and the last two types of credit. The former were used to finance shipments of new goods and services from the Soviet Union, while the latter served only as a means of transferring assets and inventories already located in China.

The first loan agreement for $300 million credits was concluded in February 1950, several months before the outbreak of the Korean War and almost a year before the Chinese intervened in it. Events, therefore, quickly rendered this early agreement obsolete, for the Korean War not only created new problems of military supply but also produced acute strains throughout Communist China. As a consequence, Russian deliveries of consumer goods and industrial raw materials as well as those of war matériel had to be stepped up. For this reason alone, if for no other, it would be difficult to draw a distinction between deficits incurred on military versus civilian account.

In retrospect and on the basis of available information, it would seem that a sizable share of Soviet credits was designed simply to finance Chinese trade deficits. These deficits resulted from the fact that the Chinese imported capital goods (particularly complete plant installations), industrial raw materials, military supplies, and other products in excess of their capacity to export.

With these qualifications in mind, let us nevertheless attempt to arrive at a crude estimate of the division of Soviet credits according to the purpose for which they were used. As Table 5-5 shows, China accumulated a deficit of 3,964 million rubles in her trade with the Soviet Union during the 1950s. At the same time, the Soviet Union extended an estimated total of 5,293 million rubles in credits to China. Assuming that none of the credits was used to cover deficits on service account (*e.g.*, technical assistance, expenditures by Chinese studying abroad, etc.), one could surmise that 1,330 million rubles (5,293 minus 3,964) were applied to the purchase of Soviet shares in the joint-stock companies and of the military stockpiles referred to above. To the extent that some credits may have been used to finance service expenditures, the estimated outlay for these shares and stockpiles would have to be reduced correspondingly.

Division of the trade credits between military and economic is necessarily even more speculative. One possible hypothesis is advanced by Mah; namely, that the 1950 and 1954 loans were the only economic credits advanced. In that case, one could surmise that of the total trade deficit incurred between 1950 and 1955, about 1,720 million rubles went to finance deliveries of investment and consumer goods and about 2,240 million rubles (3,964 minus 1,720) were absorbed by military matériel and defense equipment. The latter figure could then be viewed as one measure of Soviet military aid to its Chinese ally.[35]

The data in Table 5-5 also indicate that while credits exceeded the trade deficit during the fifties as a whole, during two years (1952 and 1953) the reverse seems to have been the case. Although the reason for this deviation is not clear, it is probable that for most years the actual deficit may have diverged from the planned deficit. Thus, in 1950 and 1951 there may have been some unexpended credits left which could then be used to finance deficits in 1952 and 1953.

Besides the 1950 and 1954 loans, the Soviets granted the Chinese either a new loan or a payment moratorium of 1,280 million old rubles ($320 million) in 1960 and an emergency sugar loan of 180 million old rubles ($45 million) in 1961. Both of these were to be paid off over four years. The payments on the first were to start in 1962, and those on the second in 1964.[36] Payments, of course, were to be made over and above the annual installments due according to the amortization schedules fixed before 1960.

The precise circumstances which led to the 1960 loan or

TABLE 5-5. Soviet Exports to, Imports from, and Credits to Communist China, 1950–63

(in millions of old rubles)

Year	Soviet Exports to China	Soviet Imports from China	Excess of Soviet Exports	Excess of Soviet Imports	Soviet Credits Used Annually [a]
1950	1,553	765	788		2,007
1951	1,914	1,325	589		
1952	2,217	1,665	552		167
1953	2,790	1,899	891		440
1954	3,037	2,313	724		884
1955	2,993	2,574	420		1,655
1956	2,932	3,057		125	117
1957	2,176	2,952		776	23
1958	2,536	3,525		989	—
1959	3,818	4,401		583	—
1960	3,270	3,390		120	(1,280) [b]
1961	1,470	2,200		730	180
1962	930	2,065		1,135	—
1963	749	1,651		902	—

[a] Data for 1950–57 were obtained from Chinese budget sources and were converted at the trade ruble rate of 1:1. Data for 1960 and 1961 were obtained from Soviet sources and are there expressed in rubles.

[b] This figure is in parentheses because it is uncertain whether it represents a new loan or merely a payment moratorium on the outstanding debt. For an explanation, see text.

Note: — stands for "none."

Sources: M. I. Sladkovskii, "The Development of the Soviet Union's Trade with the Chinese People's Republic," *Vneshniaia Torgovlia* [*Foreign Trade*], v. 29, no 10, October 1959, pp. 2–10; U.S.S.R., Ministry of Foreign Trade, *Vneshniaia Torgovlia SSSR za 1959 Godi: Statisticheskii Obzor* [*The Foreign Trade of the USSR for 1959: Statistical Handbook*] (Moscow: Vneshtorgizdat, 1960) and the volumes for 1961 and 1963 of this series of foreign trade handbooks; *Vneshniaia Torgovlia*, v. 41, no. 5, May 1961, p. 18; Helen Yin and Y. C. Yin, *Economic Statistics of Mainland China, 1949–1957* (Cambridge: Harvard University Press, 1960); Li Hsien-nien, "Report on 1954 Final Accounts and the 1955 Budget," *Jin-min Jih-pao* [*People's Daily*], July 10, 1955; and similar budget reports for 1956, 1957, and 1958 in *Hsin-hua Pan-yueh-k'an* [*New China Semimonthly*], no. 14, July 21, 1956, pp. 1–9; no. 14, July 25, 1957, pp. 16–28; and no. 5, March 10, 1958, pp. 3–12.

repayment moratorium are far from clear. In citing this transaction, Russian sources indicate that it was used for financing the 1960 deficit in China's trade with the Soviet Union. However, the Soviet foreign trade yearbooks show a small surplus in China's trade with Russia in 1960. It would therefore seem that this deficit may not have been a trade but a balance-of-payments deficit, probably incurred because the Chinese were unable to meet their 1960 loan repayment obligation to the Soviet Union.

If this supposition is correct, then one must ask why the 1960 installment of the loan repayment should have been as much as 1,280 million old rubles. This question, in turn, can lead to two alternative lines of speculation: (a) the Chinese had failed to meet their loan repayment obligations in the preceding years, and the Soviets demanded payment of all the accumulated arrears on the long-term credits extended between 1950 and 1957; (b) after 1957 (when long-term Soviet loans were exhausted) the Chinese had accumulated short-term debts which the Soviets then agreed to refinance and convert into a medium-term loan. In the first case, the subsequent transaction merely would represent a payment moratorium on a long-term debt and would not constitute a new loan over and above the credits which the Soviet Union extended to China between 1950 and 1957. In the second case, however, it would involve additional credits and would raise total Soviet lending to China. On the basis of presently available information, it is not possible to ascertain which of these two hypotheses is the correct one.

DEBT SERVICE. As was mentioned earlier, there is fairly complete though inconsistent information both from Soviet and Chinese sources about the totals of the loans extended and the annual rate at which these credits were drawn upon. In contrast, the terms of repayment are shrouded in considerable secrecy.

We know that the Soviets have made at least six long- or intermediate-term loans to Communist China. These include military loans of unknown value extended during the Korean War, two economic development loans of $300 million (1,200 million old rubles) and $130 million (520 million old rubles) granted in 1950 and 1954 respectively, two loans extended in 1954-55 for the purchase of the Russian share in the Sino-Soviet joint stock companies and of the Russian military stockpiles left in Port Arthur and Dairen, and finally a $45 million (180 million old rubles) sugar loan made in 1961. In addition, as has already been noted, in 1960 the Soviet Union either waived China's repayment obligation of $320 million (1,280 million old rubles) or granted a new loan for that amount.

Full details on the terms of repayment, however, were published only for the 1950 economic loan, the 1960 loan or repayment moratorium, and the 1961 sugar loan. The official reports of actual government expenditures for 1952–57, of course, contain data on total debt service and amortization. Although these totals include domestic debt service, this can be estimated within fairly narrow margins of error. In 1960, the Soviet Union agreed to a new repayment schedule on the credits still outstanding. But according to both Chinese and Soviet official statements, the new schedule was not followed, for the Chinese decided that they would accelerate the rate beginning in 1962.[37] Moreover, Chinese statements in the mid-1960s suggest that all Soviet credits will have been amortized by the end of 1965.[38]

According to published information, the interest charge on the 1950 loan would be 1 per cent. The loan itself was to be repaid starting on December 31, 1954, in 10 annual installments of equal amounts. Thus, it should have been fully amortized by the end of 1963. We do not know the interest rate or the period of repayment for any of the other loans extended up to the end of 1957. However, Soviet publications have occasionally mentioned loans to China (with no clearer identification) carrying a 2 per cent rate of interest.

On the basis of such partial information, it would seem that in the early 1950s Communist China's debt to the Soviet Union rose rapidly. It reached its peak in 1955 when the Soviets advanced a large credit to finance the transfer of their last assets to China. From then on, the debt gradually declined year by year. By the end of 1962, it had shrunk to one-third of its peak level, and as of December 1964 it was apparently less than $20 million.

In contrast to the Soviet loans to China, which had to be repaid in 10 years at an average interest rate of almost 2 per cent, the long-term credits of the International Bank for Reconstruction and Development normally run for 20–25 years at a 5–6 per cent rate of interest. If the same amount of credit were extended, the latter terms of repayment would yield lower annual obligations for debt service than the former. It would seem, then, that the Soviets traded lower interest rates for more rapid repayment and thereby considerably increased the burden of debt service imposed upon mainland China's economy. On the basis of our estimates, such debt charges and repayments may have absorbed about 10–40 per cent of China's export earnings in her trade with the Soviet Union. The ratio increased between 1956 and 1958, then fell by 1960 under the impact of the payments crisis, and finally rose to more than 40 per cent in 1962 and 1963. The weight of this burden became particularly onerous because of China's economic crisis after 1960, her shrinking exports, and her acute demand for food imports.

COMMUNIST CHINA'S ECONOMIC ASSISTANCE TO OTHER COMMUNIST COUNTRIES. Communist China officially launched its foreign aid program in 1953 with a large $200 million grant to North Korea which was to be drawn upon between 1954 and 1957.[39] There is considerable evidence, however, that during the Korean War, China extended several free grants to North Korea, none of which has been publicized. These have been estimated at about $75 million.

Up to the end of 1964, China had committed close to $2 billion in foreign aid (see Appendix E). Of this amount, perhaps more than $1 billion (exclusive of Korean War loans or grants) had been used. The bulk of China's actual aid outlays, as Tables 5-6 and E-2 indicate, went to other Communist countries—specifically, North Korea, North Vietnam, Mongolia, Albania, and Hungary. (Her actual expenditures for aid to Communist countries generally followed closely upon her commitments. In contrast, there was a sizable gap between her aid commitments to the non-Communist world and her actual outlays.)

One notable feature of China's aid to Communist countries is that about 60 per cent was in the form of grants and only 40 per cent in the form of credits. The credits were extended on generous terms. Several loans were interest-free, there were grace periods before repayment was to begin, and in some cases the periods of repayment were as long as 15 years. Except for North Vietnam, the pace and terms of China's economic assistance to these countries corresponded to the patterns set by the Soviets. That is, at first the Chinese largely followed the lead of the Soviets and then in more recent years began competing with them. In an attempt to outbid the Russians, the Chinese extended assistance to the small Communist countries on much more generous terms than those the Soviet Union granted to her.

T A B L E 5 - 6. Communist China's Estimated Expenditures for Economic Assistance to Other Communist Countries, 1953–64

(in millions of U.S. dollars)

Year	Total Aid to Communist Countries	Assistance to Individual Countries				
		Albania	Hungary	N. Korea	N. Vietnam	Mongolia
1953	25.00	—	—	25.00 a	—	—
1954	50.00	—	—	50.00	—	—
1955	104.00	4.00	—	50.00	50.00	—
1956	119.50	2.00	7.50	50.00	50.00	10.00
1957	139.00	4.00	25.00	50.00	50.00	10.00
1958	103.75	5.00	25.00	7.50	50.00	16.25
1959	94.00	19.00	—	8.75	50.00	16.25
1960	70.00	5.00	—	8.75	50.00	6.25
1961	107.00	42.00	—	26.25	22.50	16.25
1962	100.75	42.00	—	26.25	22.50	10.00
1963	99.75	41.00	—	26.25	22.50	10.00
1964	58.75	—	—	26.25	22.50	10.00

a This aid represents the last installment of China's grants during the Korean War.

Note: — stands for "none."

Sources: For sources and methods of calculation, see Appendix E.

Economic assistance to each Communist country has had its peculiar characteristics. Economic aid to Hungary, for example, was strictly an *ad hoc* measure within the context of a bloc-wide program for emergency relief after the 1956 rebellion. China contributed a free grant of $7.5 million in 1956 and extended a credit of $50 million in 1957. The latter was to be drawn upon over two years, and half of it was to be in convertible currency.[40] At the same time, the Soviet Union extended credits of $25 million and $190 million, and the other East European countries advanced $107 million. In addition, the Soviet Union canceled part of Hungary's outstanding debt and granted a payment moratorium on the rest. Here, then, was a case in which Chinese aid played a subsidiary rather than a major role.

China's aid to Hungary was directed toward certain short-run objectives, *i.e.*, the consolidation of the Kadar regime and the restoration of political and economic stability. However, it had no perceptible effect on either the direction or the commodity composition of Hungary's foreign trade. For example, in 1957, Hungary's trade with China was only one-fifth of its trade with the Soviet Union as compared to one-fourth in 1956 and one-third in 1955.

In contrast, Communist China has been intimately involved in the economic life of North Korea since a relatively early date and on a more or less continuous basis. Before the founding of the People's Republic of China and before the Korean War, North Korea was almost exclusively dependent upon the Soviet Union. In 1953, however, a clear pattern of rivalry began to emerge. At that time, China made a grant of $200 million, the Soviet Union provided a gift of $250 million, and the East European countries extended a credit of $265 million. In 1956 another Soviet grant of $75 million and a credit of $125 million followed. The Chinese countered with a small credit of $25 million in 1958 and a long-term loan of $105 million in 1960. The Soviets then canceled North Korea's debt of $190 million. As of 1961, therefore, the Soviets had managed to stay well ahead in the game. They had extended $500 million in grants and credits themselves, and Eastern Europe had thrown in another

$265 million. The Chinese in comparison had contributed only $330 million.

Most of China's economic aid to North Korea helped finance exports of capital goods (among them some complete plants), technical assistance, and raw materials. The 1958 loan specifically provided for the shipment of equipment for a power station, a textile mill, and two cement bag factories.[41] In more general terms, this aid permitted North Korea to maintain a deficit in her trade with China. In combination with other factors, it contributed to Korea's growing economic dependence on China. While data on Chinese-North Korean trade are scant, these show that the mainland's share in Korea's total trade rose from 9 per cent in 1955 to about 27 per cent in 1957, while that of the Soviet Union declined from about 80 to 57 per cent.[42]

The Communist country with the greatest economic dependence upon China has been North Vietnam. In 1955 and 1956 (the only years for which comparative data are available) China's trade turnover with Vietnam was, respectively, 31 times and 7 times the Soviet level. The same pattern holds with respect to economic aid. Chinese grants and credits between 1955 and 1961 amounted to $457 million as compared to Soviet and East European totals of $130 million and $145 million respectively. China's aid went to finance technical assistance; the export of complete "turnkey projects;" equipment for the rehabilitation of transport, industry, and irrigation works; raw materials for consumer goods industries; and various miscellaneous goods.

Unlike her involvement with North Vietnam and North Korea, China's close economic tie with Albania is of comparatively recent origin. Albania's international economic relations are a clear index to its stormy and changing political fortunes. Right after World War II, the country was both politically and economically a Yugoslav satellite. When the Soviets broke with Yugoslavia in 1948, Albania then became the recipient of Russian largesse. Its budget was subsidized every year through grants from the Soviet Union and from Eastern Europe; moreover, these grants enabled it to maintain a sizable trade deficit. Communist China did not enter the field until relatively late, that is, in 1955. At first she extended only small grants and credits. With the deterioration of Sino-Soviet relations and the growing *rapprochement* between Yugoslavia and Russia, however, relations between Albania and China became much closer. One indication of this new relationship was the great step-up in Chinese aid to Albania. The assistance program jumped from $25 million in 1959–60 to $125 million in 1961.

The shift from Soviet to Chinese economic tutelage was also reflected in Albania's trade. China's share in Albanian imports and exports remained of modest proportions through 1960; it rose from about 3 per cent in 1955 to 9 per cent in 1960. During the same period, the shares of both the Soviet Union and Eastern Europe fluctuated between 40 and 50 per cent. The sharp reversal came in 1961. China's share in Albanian imports jumped to 26 per cent, while the Soviet share declined to 28 per cent.

These growing imports, financed by the new Chinese loan, consisted of capital goods, agricultural machinery, grain, and "other commodities." The Chinese agreed, for example, to assist in the construction of 25 plants in the chemical, metallurgical, building materials, and light industries. Most surprisingly perhaps, they diverted to Albania 2.2 million bushels of wheat they had just bought from Canada. The new credits were also used to finance Chinese technical assistance in Albania. Mainland technicians arrived in large numbers to replace their Soviet counterparts who had been withdrawn.[43]

In contrast to Albania, where China's economic aid program filled the breach left by the Soviet withdrawal, mainland assistance to Mongolia does not seem to have shaken the Soviet hold on that country. This difference was due partly to the absence of vital political issues separating Mongolia from the Soviet Union and partly to Soviet readiness to counter Chinese economic competition. The clearest illustration of the latter point was provided in 1960. The Chinese offered a $50 million loan in May, but the Soviets topped that in September with a loan of $150 million. Previous Chinese grants and credits had amounted to $65 million as compared to a Soviet total of $325 million. Mongolia's foreign trade data confirm the image of Soviet economic primacy. Despite a significant growth in Mongolia's trade with China and a decline in its total turnover with the Soviet Union between 1955 and 1960, even in 1960 the volume of the latter exceeded that of the former by more than five times.

How much of a burden did this aid program impose on the Chinese economy? This question must be approached in a variety of ways to provide a full answer. Unfortunately, some of these approaches are ruled out by the lack of data. In the absence of detailed commodity breakdowns for China's trade with its aid recipients, it is extremely difficult to assess the actual economic cost of this program to the Chinese economy. Therefore, we have to resort to rather crude and aggregate measures of the burden.

It would seem that the total resource cost in terms of national income was quite negligible. Probably at no time did the aid program exceed 0.2–0.3 per cent of the national income. In the absence of a detailed breakdown of the commodity composition of the aid, its effect on household consumption and investment is difficut to assess. If we assume that all the aid shipments were consumer goods, total household consumption in the late 1950s probably could not have been reduced by more than 0.6 per cent. For the 1960s this percentage would have to be raised. If, on the other hand, all such deliveries were investment goods, fixed-capital formation might possibly have been curtailed by 2 per cent. The latter effect could be considered small but far from negligible for a country committed to rapid industrialization.

In one sense, these percentages overstate the burden, for aid shipments represented a mixture of raw materials, semimanufactures, consumer goods, and investment goods, with the precise composition varying from year to year. In another sense, however, the burden might be understated. If the load imposed by the aid fell particularly heavily on a strategic industry (that is, one upon which a number of other sectors depended), bottlenecks could have been created that would have resulted in more than proportionate reductions in output, consumption, or investment. Such a situation, however, is not likely to occur except in periods of planning failure and disorganization, such as 1958 and 1959. Under normal circumstances, goods shipped are probably produced in plants operating below capacity and using relatively more abundant raw materials. To the extent that such practices might have governed China's foreign aid program, its opportunity cost was minimized. In actuality, that cost was probably quite small.

If we assume that all the aid went to finance exports, such exports would have constituted about 10 per cent of China's total sales abroad in 1957, the year of highest aid outlays. This ratio is by no means insignificant. It must be re-emphasized, however, that it is undoubtedly an overestimate. Not all the aid went to finance the export of goods. Part of it was used to finance Chinese technical assistance and other services. This fact introduces another variable into the equation; namely, to what extent was the Chinese economy deprived of scarce technical and managerial talent through the export of technicians to aid-receiving countries? Unfortunately, this question cannot be answered on the basis of information presently available.

To round out this assessment, it is essential to compare the aid China extended to Communist countries with that it received from the Soviet Union. Total Soviet credits to China may be estimated at 5,480–8,960 million old rubles ($1,370–2,240 million). The actual amount is dependent upon (a) whether the 1960 loan is treated as a moratorium or as a new credit and (b) what rate of exchange is used to convert the 1950–57 credits from yuan into rubles. Of this estimated amount, about 3,300–4,580 million rubles ($825–1,145 million) were extended after the beginning of 1953 when China's own program got under way. By the end of 1962, China's total aid expenditures to other Communist countries (*i.e.*, assistance actually used) may be estimated at about $913 million. Hence, they were either somewhat below or somewhat above the value of the loans the Soviet Union had made to her since 1953, but they were still well below the total of all the loans the People's Republic had received since its birth. If we compare the aid China received and extended annually (see Tables 5–5 and 5–6), it becomes clear that up to and including 1955 she was a net importer of capital by a significant margin. Afterward, the situation was clearly reversed. If one also takes into account China's loan repayments in these years, net capital exports from the mainland become quite sizable.

Perhaps the most striking aspect of Communist China's aid program is that it apparently did not abate significantly amidst economic crisis and decline. In the year of most acute depression

(1961), China exhibited unusual aggressiveness in the foreign aid field by making a $157 million loan to North Vietnam and another of $125 million to Albania. The loan to Albania is particularly significant, for it was advanced while the Chinese were negotiating with the Soviets for balance-of-payments relief. Moreover, it involved shipments of grain to Albania, grain which China had purchased from Canada to relieve its own acute food shortage.

Benefits and Costs for Communist China of the Sino-Soviet Relationship

The analysis in the last and the present chapters shows that commodity imports and technical assistance from the Soviet Union made a decisive contribution to Communist China's industrialization during the past decade. The significance of the imports is heightened by the fact that China could not have obtained much in the way of machinery, equipment, and complete plant installations from any other source because of U.S. and allied trade embargoes. The same applies with possibly even greater force to Soviet technical assistance. Even without the embargoes and with a more favorable international climate, it is doubtful that China could have received, or indeed would have invited, technical assistance on such a scale and for such highly strategic capital projects as the development of electric power, atomic energy, and similar undertakings.

The scope of technical assistance perhaps can best be illuminated by the following quote from an authoritative Soviet source:

Soviet technical assistance takes a variety of forms: help to enterprises and establishments, scientific and technical institutes, assistance to Chinese specialists in the management of enterprises and establishments as well as in the training of technical cadres. Soviet organizations assume the obligation for rendering [technical] aid in the construction of enterprises. Soviet scientific designing and manufacturing enterprises render service to Chinese organizations in the Soviet Union by way of consultations, project design, laboratory analyses, etc. [Furthermore] Soviet organizations surrender their licenses and patents to Chinese organizations.[44]

Within the context of these arrangements, 10,800 Soviet and 1,500 East European specialists and technicians were sent to China between 1950 and 1960.[45] It has been estimated that at least 20 Soviet technicians were assigned to each of the complete plant projects. In some of the more important ones, the number rose to several hundred. For instance, more than 300 Soviet experts directed the reconstruction of the Anshan iron and steel complex in Manchuria. About 100 Soviet metallurgists and engineers were involved in the construction of the Wuhan steel complex, and about 500 Soviet specialists assisted in the development of the Sinkiang oil fields.[46] During the same period, about 8,000 Chinese engineers and skilled workers received training in Soviet enterprises, and more than 7,000 Chinese students attended Soviet educational institutions and scientific research institutes.[47]

In addition, Soviet institutes, establishments, and organizations transmitted to China a vast variety of technical blueprints and documents in accordance with a special Sino-Soviet agreement on scientific-technical cooperation, signed in October 1954.[48] Under this agreement, the Soviets also began the building in 1955 of an atomic reactor with a 7,000–10,000 kilowatt capacity and a 25 million volt cyclotron, and the Soviet Academy of Sciences sent a special, high-level delegation to China to help in the formulation of a 12-year plan for scientific development.[49]

Soviet sources explicitly indicate that the Chinese had to pay for all technical assistance except the blueprints, licenses, and technical documents just referred to. However, the economic importance of this technical assistance, regardless of whether or not it had to be paid for, cannot be overemphasized. Such assistance must have significantly accelerated the pace of technological progress in China. At the same time, it provided the small but essential margin of difference in know-how that determined whether Soviet deliveries of capital goods could be used effectively and efficiently.

I do not mean to suggest, of course, that imported capital goods were always used efficiently or that efficiency was automatically assured by the presence of Soviet technicians. One relevant variable here is the competence and quality of the Soviet scientists, engineers, technicians, and specialists sent to

China. Unfortunately, it is not possible to form a reliable judgment on this matter from presently available information. However, there is ample evidence that the withdrawal of Soviet technicians in mid-1960 and the tearing up of hundreds of agreements did lead to far-reaching disruption in China's industrial production.[50] This fact would suggest that whatever may have been the quality of the Russian technicians, their presence or absence made a significant difference.

The importance of the Soviet contribution to China's industrialization becomes even greater if one takes into account the credits which the Soviet Union advanced at a time when China most needed them. During the initial six-year period (1950–55), these credits financed more than a quarter of China's imports from the Soviet Union.* It should be noted, moreover, that the quite sizable loans extended to China between 1950 and 1952 came at a time when the Soviet Union was just completing its own recovery from war devastation and was extending no loans to any other country. On the contrary, it was receiving substantial unrequited imports as reparations from East Germany, Hungary, and Bulgaria and was forcing the other East European countries (*e.g.*, Poland) to sell their exports to Russia at prices well below the world level.

If we grant that there were these economic gains for China, we must then ask at what price they were purchased. It was pointed out earlier that China was economically much more dependent on the Soviet Union than vice versa. Was the Soviet superiority in economic bargaining power reflected in adverse trade terms for China?

Even if it could be shown that the trade terms were adverse, this would not constitute proof of Soviet exploitation of its bargaining power. The Soviet Union exported to China goods which were high on its planners' scale of preferences, while it imported from China commodities of comparatively low priority. The Chinese, on the other hand, exported articles which were relatively low on their planners' scale of preferences and imported those which were, from the Chinese point of view, high-priority items. This situation created a set of scarcity relations

---

* This figure is based on the assumption that about 1,330 million rubles of total credits went to finance the transfer of Soviet assets rather than imports.

that might have provided justification for the Russians to charge (in a bilateral context) prices higher than world prices for their capital goods exports to China and to pay prices lower than world prices for their consumer goods imports from China. As a matter of fact, one could argue that unless the Russians did in fact do so, they were in effect granting the Chinese a hidden subsidy. From a Chinese point of view, on the other hand, "overpricing" of imports (as compared to world prices) or "underpricing" of exports, whatever the reason, would represent the resource cost of a predominantly Soviet orientation in trade.

What in fact is the evidence concerning the terms of Sino-Soviet trade? Fortunately, we now have a careful and detailed study of this problem at our disposal.[51] It is based on a comparison of the unit values of Soviet exports to and imports from Communist China and non-Communist Europe during 1955–59.* To render the comparison meaningful, it was important to identify more or less homogeneous commodities and categories of commodities which the Soviet Union was exporting to and importing from both non-Communist Europe and China. About 20 per cent of total Soviet exports to China and about 40 per cent of total Soviet imports from China could be so identified. They constitute the sample for F. H. Mah's investigation of whether the Soviets "overpriced" their exports to China or whether they "underpriced" imports from China. Mah found that the Chinese paid on the average about 30 per cent more for their imports from the Soviet Union than did non-Communist Europe. On the other hand, there was no such clear-cut differential on the export side. In 1955 and 1956, the Soviets paid slightly more for their purchases from China than for those from Europe, while the reverse was true, again only to a small extent, in 1957, 1958, and 1959.

The central finding that emerges from this study, then, is that

---

* Unit values represent the price averages for a group of commodities which a country's trade returns list in a wider commodity category. For instance, the foreign trade statistics for steel may give the total quantity and value of steel exported or imported. These statistics, however, may encompass varying qualities, kinds, and shapes of steel. As a result, the unit values of two different transactions based on exactly the same set of prices and the same total quantities may differ if the quality composition of the two shipments differs.

trade with the Soviet Union involved a price disadvantage for China. Practically all this differential was due to Soviet "over-pricing" of its exports to mainland China as compared with its exports to non-Communist Europe. If the percentage differential found in the case of the sample were applied to all China's imports from the Soviet Union in 1955–59, China's "loss" would amount to about $940 million—about one-quarter of the value of her imports from Russia for these years.

What does this price differential mean? Can it be interpreted as price discrimination by the Soviets, the exercise of superior Soviet bargaining power to "exploit" the Chinese? Not at all.

The first question to be raised is whether there is indeed a price differential. Although Mah's findings definitely show one for the sample of goods studied, do the findings apply to all imports? Similar studies for other countries have amply demonstrated that findings such as these are extremely sensitive to the sample chosen. For example, the inclusion or exclusion of one commodity group can significantly alter the outcome. This fact is particularly important in the present case, for the import sample necessarily was confined to about 20 per cent of Soviet deliveries to China. Mah tried to protect himself on this score by experimenting with the sample; nevertheless, as he fully recognizes, the findings at best set up a presumption rather than a proof.

Further exploration of the possible reasons for such a price differential, however, tends to lend weight to the validity of the findings. All the calculations of unit values are based on official Soviet trade returns. We know, though, that most Communist countries, including China, define export and import prices f.o.b. at the port or borderpoint of arrival or departure. Since the bulk of Soviet exports to China move overland via the Trans-Siberian railroad, the prices of China's imports from Russia include the costs of long and expensive transport hauls. On the other hand, Soviet transport hauls to countries in Europe are much shorter; moreover, a large share of the goods is shipped by sea. Thus, the bulk of the price differential between Soviet exports to China and to Europe can be explained in terms of transport costs.

A similar comparison of Soviet imports from China and Soviet imports from Europe reinforces such an explanation. In this case, as was noted above, there is no clear-cut price differential. This fact is not surprising, for the overland transport distances for export goods moved from the point of manufacture in China to the Soviet border are much shorter than vice versa. As a result, the transport markup is significantly less than in the reverse case. Moreover, these distances do not differ markedly from those between European points of shipment and the Soviet border or port of arrival.

A price differential attributable to transportation costs would apply to all Soviet exports and imports and not just to Mah's sample, although the precise percentage markup for the total might well differ from that of the sample. Therefore, even if the Soviets had charged the Chinese the same factory prices they charged the Europeans, the former would have had to pay higher prices than the latter because of the transport factor.

If we assume that the transport markup explains the bulk but not all of the price differential, can the unexplained residual be attributed to superior Soviet bargaining power? Did the Soviets quote lower factory prices to non-Communist Europe than to China? If so, does that fact indicate exercise of superior bargaining power in Chinese markets or weakness of bargaining power in European markets? F. D. Holzman's studies of trade between the Communist countries of Europe suggest that the latter explanation seems more likely.[52] He compared their trade with each other and with non-Communist Europe, and he discovered what at first glance appeared to be intra-bloc price discrimination. Not only did the Russians seem to be discriminating against the East Europeans, but the East Europeans seemed to be discriminating against the Russians. However, this apparent discrimination may just mean that these countries as a group find themselves in poor competitive positions, both as buyers and sellers, in non-Communist markets. Such a situation could result from the lack of proper institutional facilities for trade in these markets, inadequate quality standards, or other reasons.

Finally, if we suppose that the Chinese, for whatever reasons, had to pay more for Soviet imports than Europe did, does this fact suggest that they could have done better by reorienting their foreign trade away from the Soviets? Not necessarily. Holzman's findings might be even more applicable to China than to the Soviet Union and Eastern Europe. That is, her competitive position in world markets might be even poorer than theirs. In the past, it probably would have been. To break or circumvent allied trade controls, she would have had to pay high, scarcity prices for imports of capital goods and raw materials from the non-Communist world. Of course, in many cases she could not have obtained these goods at any price. Similarly, she would have had great difficulty in placing many of her export products in West European or other non-Communist markets in sufficient quantities to finance the level of imports she maintained. In any case, she probably could have sold them only at bargain prices. Therefore, one could reasonably argue that during a period of rapid expansion in foreign trade a preponderantly non-Communist world orientation in commerce might have resulted in more adverse trade terms for China than she in fact experienced in her exchanges with the Soviet Union.

Benefits and Costs for the Soviet Union of the Sino-Soviet Relationship

As has been shown in this chapter, Communist China was the Soviet Union's leading trading partner during most of the past decade. The trade was based largely on an exchange of capital goods exports for consumer goods imports. Since the Soviet Union continued on a path of development oriented toward heavy industry, did this trade entail a sacrifice of Soviet growth for Chinese growth and produce an unintended transfer of resources from investment and growth to consumption as Professor Galenson believes?

The first question to be faced is what was the resource burden imposed upon the Soviet economy by the credits extended to China during 1950–55. As a percentage of both investment and GNP, the resources committed were truly negligible—an average of less than 0.4 and 0.1 per cent respectively for the six years. Even for 1955, the year during which Soviet lending to China reached its peak, the ratio is just a little more than 0.5 per cent for investment and more than 0.1 per cent for GNP [53]

Even if the aggregate resource burden was negligible, did not the shipment of a large amount of machinery to China markedly reduce the equipment available for investment in the Soviet Union and thus curtail the rate of investment and slow down the growth of reproducible fixed assets? In attempting to deal with this problem, let us first see what share of total equipment availabilities machinery exports constituted.

The estimates in Table 5-7 indicate that such exports were well below 2 per cent of Soviet machinery production or of the equipment component of investment in every year except 1959. (It should be noted that the Soviet Union was an importer of machinery, but such imports were so small that investment in new machinery and equipment can be used as a substitute for domestic machinery production with only a small margin of error resulting therefrom.) Even in 1959, when machinery exports to China attained their peak under the impact of the Great Leap, this ratio rose only to 2.5 per cent. It would seem unlikely, then, that these exports could have significantly affected capital goods availabilities within the Soviet Union. It is perfectly true, of course, that the Soviet Union was a net importer of capital goods from Western as well as Eastern Europe during all these years. However, this fact cannot be interpreted as proof that machinery exports to China reduced Soviet investment capabilities. The Soviets did not import the same kinds of equipment from Europe that they exported to China. Moreover, as various studies by the Economic Commission for Europe show, Eastern Europe needs a market in the Soviet Union for its engineering products and requires fuels and other industrial raw materials from the Soviets. Therefore, the sizable imports of equipment from Eastern Europe may be viewed as at least as much an accommodation to the needs and realities facing the economies of that region as an expression of a desire on the part of the Soviets to augment their own machinery supplies. [54]

In addition, not all the Soviet producer goods industries were operating at full capacity at all times. Therefore, in some periods and under some circumstances export orders for China may have

TABLE 5-7. The Share of Soviet Capital Goods Exports to Communist China in Relation to Machinery Output and to the Equipment Component of Investment in the Soviet Union, 1950–59

Year	Investment in New Soviet Machinery [a]	Equipment Component of Investment [b]	Machinery and Equipment Exports to China	Machinery Export Shares	
				(3)/(1)	(3)/(2)
	(in millions of old rubles)			(in per cent)	
	(1)	(2)	(3)	(4)	(5)
1950	46,300	32,700	171	0.37	0.52
1951	47,400	33,700	440	0.93	1.30
1952	41,400	35,200	620	1.49	1.76
1953	46,500	36,100	645	1.38	1.78
1954	55,800	44,400	790	1.41	1.53
1955	63,300	53,600	928	1.47	1.73
1956	70,400	66,300	1,231	1.75	1.85
1957	n.a.	73,600	1,090	n.a.	1.48
1958	n.a.	82,800	1,270	n.a.	1.53
1959	n.a.	94,900	2,370	n.a.	2.49

[a] As Moorsteen points out, imports of machinery during these years constituted a negligible proportion of total investment in machinery, so this series can be taken as a close approximation of domestic machinery production.

[b] Conceptually, the series in columns 1 and 2 are quite close; thus, the differences are due to different methods of estimation.

Note: n.a. stands for "not available."

Sources: Column 1—Richard Moorsteen, *Prices and Production of Machinery in the Soviet Union, 1928–1958* (Cambridge: Harvard University Press for the RAND Corporation, 1962), Table G–19, p. 453.

Column 2—U.S. Central Intelligence Agency, *A Comparison of Capital Investment in the U.S. and the U.S.S.R. 1950–1959,* (Washington, D.C.: Author, February 1961), Appendix B, Table 2.

Column 3—U.S.S.R., Ministry of Foreign Trade, *Vneshniaia Torgovlia SSSR za 1959 Godi: Statisticheskii Obzor [The Foreign Trade of the USSR for 1959: Statistical Handbook]* (Moscow: Vneshtorgizdat, 1960) and earlier volumes of this series of foreign trade handbooks.

been a boon to the Soviet machine-building industry, just as they were to an even greater extent to the same industry in Czechoslovakia.

It was stated above that an export share of 1.5–2.0 per cent for capital goods is not likely to affect domestic investment significantly. How can we be sure? How could we test whether or not this figure is significant? One way of approaching the problem might be to explore whether there has been any perceptible decline in the rates of growth of Soviet national income, investment, reproducible fixed assets, and industrial production during the past decade.

Recent studies by Abram Bergson, Richard Moorsteen, and Raymond Powell provide no evidence whatsoever that Soviet rates of investment and growth declined up to 1958. On the contrary, as the estimates in Table 5–8 demonstrate, these studies strongly suggest that the rates may have increased in the 1950s as compared with the prewar period. In terms of some indicators, there may even have been a rise in the late as compared with the early fifties, despite the stable or even growing export share of capital goods shown in Table 5–7. This finding seems to apply equally to the growth in national product, in industrial production, and, most importantly, in reproducible fixed capital.* Such a finding, of course, does not preclude the possibility that Soviet growth might have been even higher if capital goods had not been exported to China. Yet that possibility is not too probable for a number of reasons. The most general and most fundamental reason is that "the factor endowments of the Soviet Union are capable of producing virtually all essential commodities and the share of international trade in its national income is already so small as to render relatively unimportant—*from the point of view of the Soviet economy alone*—the principles on which it plans and conducts its foreign trade." [55]

We have thus far examined the question of whether the

---

* It is, of course, perfectly true that in the 1960s, as compared with the 1950s, we have witnessed a slowing down in Soviet growth rates, but this decline occurred at a time when machinery exports to China were drastically curtailed. Therefore, it cannot be ascribed to a deficiency in the capital goods available within the Soviet Union.

T A B L E 5 - 8. Economic Growth Indicators for the
Soviet Union, 1928–40 and 1950–58

I. *Average Annual Rates of Growth*
(in per cent)

	1928–40		1950–58	
	at 1937 prices	at 1950 prices	at 1937 prices	at 1950 prices
A. GNP at prevailing prices [a]	4.9	4.9	8.2	8.2
B. GNP at ruble factor cost [a]	5.5	5.4	7.6	7.6
C. NNP at ruble factor cost	4.2	n.a.	6.8	6.8
D. Final industrial product	9.8	8.4	10.2	10.5

II. *Investment in Fixed Capital*
(in per cent)

	1928–40				1950–58	
E. Average annual rate of growth in reproducible fixed capital at 1937 ruble factor cost	9.8				11.2	

	1950	1951	1952	1953	1954	1955
F. Gross investment in fixed capital as per cent of GNP in current rubles	17.1	18.0	17.3	18.8	20.5	20.2

III. *Per Capita Household Consumption*

	1928	1937	1950	1955	1958
G. Index at 1937 adjusted market prices	103	100	114	159	191

	1928–37	1950–58
H. Average annual rate of growth (in per cent)	—0.3	6.6

[a] These rates are for 1928–37 and 1950–55 respectively.

Note: n.a. stands for "not available."

Sources: A, B, and C—Simon Kuznets, "A Comparative Appraisal" in Abram Bergson and Simon Kuznets, eds., *Economic Trends in the Soviet Union* (Cambridge: Harvard University Press, 1963), Table VIII.1, p. 336.

D—Raymond P. Powell, "Industrial Production," in same, Table IV.1, p. 155.

E—Abram Bergson, "National Income," in same, Table I.2, p. 6.

F—Abram Bergson, *The Real National Income of Soviet Russia Since 1928*, (Cambridge: Harvard University Press, 1961), Table 82, p. 300.

G and H—Janet G. Chapman, "Consumption," in Bergson and Kuznets, cited, Table VI.1, p. 238.

capital goods exports of the Soviet Union retarded the country's economic growth. What about the reverse question? Did consumer goods imports from China represent an unintended bonus for the Soviet consumer and an involuntary reallocation of resources from the standpoint of the Soviet planner? Available evidence lends no support to this view. Bergson's and Janet Chapman's studies show that in the 1950s both domestic production and consumption of consumer goods rose rapidly in the Soviet Union. This rise is particularly striking in light of the fact that they declined during the prewar period of forced-draft industrialization. The change reflects the increase in Soviet wealth which permitted the raising of investment and consumption simultaneously for awhile (although not necessarily at the same rate). It also reflects the shift, at least to some extent, in the preferences of the Soviet planners. Within the last decade, Soviet policy makers have found it necessary to make a number of concessions to the consumer goods sector. Therefore, the increases in consumption were rooted in domestic Soviet realities rather than in the necessities imposed by trade with China.

In any case, imports of consumer goods from China constituted such a negligible share of Soviet consumption—only about 0.1–0.3 per cent between 1950 and 1958—that they could not have affected the outcome. At the same time, to the extent that they contributed to the qualitative improvement in consumption, they may have had some fairly significant incentive effects.[56] In that case, however, they were an intended, rather than unintended, bonus for the Soviet consumer.

The Balance of Benefits and Costs

From this analysis of the economic relationships of China and the Soviet Union during the past decade and a half, what conclusions can we draw about the character of this uneasy alliance? Have the Soviets been generous or niggardly in their assistance programs and commercial intercourse with China? Have the Chinese been unreasonable and impatient in their expectations and demands?

One way of approaching this problem might be to compare Soviet economic behavior toward China with that toward Eastern Europe. When the Soviets granted their first long-term credit of $300 million to China in 1950, they were still following an opposite policy in Eastern Europe. East Germany, Hungary, Rumania, and Bulgaria had to pay heavy war reparations, and Poland had to sell its coal to the Soviet Union at prices well below prevailing world levels. Moreover, the Soviets used joint-stock companies in Eastern Europe as one of the principal instruments for extracting an unrequited flow of resources from those countries. They took over going enterprises and simply appropriated half of their shares and earnings. To these enterprises, the Soviets contributed management but little capital. However, the situation was different in the case of China. The joint-stock companies did not play a major role in the country's economy and did not serve as exploitative devices. On the contrary, these were for the most part newly established enterprises in which the Soviets made new investments. Therefore, by the standards of their prevailing behavior in the early 1950s, the Soviets were quite generous to the Chinese. Their generosity appears even greater if we bear in mind that the Soviets were just completing their own process of recovery from war devastation.

Another factor which needs to be considered in the assessment is the financing of the Korean War. Unfortunately, the evidence on this subject is extremely sketchy. If, as it would appear, the Chinese accumulated a heavy debt to the Soviets during the Korean War, did this debt represent payment for all or only part of the deliveries? Did the Soviets extend some grants and some credits at the time? Is it possible that war material was delivered free but civilian goods for defense support were not? These questions cannot be answered on the basis of present information. Even if the Soviets charged for only part of the deliveries, however, a possible Chinese feeling that any charges at all represented a lack of generosity might seem well justified.

We can gauge Soviet generosity also by comparing Soviet aid policies toward Eastern Europe and toward underdeveloped countries of the non-Communist world with those toward China. Between January 1956 and July 1962, the Soviets extended large-scale economic assistance to the following countries: [57]

Communist Countries		*Non-Communist Countries*	
(in millions of U.S. dollars)			
East Germany	1,200	India	690
Bulgaria	570	Egypt	510
Hungary	380	Afghanistan	400
Poland	360	Indonesia	370

During this same period, new Soviet commitments to China probably amounted to no more than $45 million (180 million old rubles). But as we have already noted, before that (*i.e.*, 1950-1955) the Chinese obtained a total of about $1,325 million (5,300 million old rubles) in Soviet loans. Therefore, Soviet aid to China does not compare unfavorably with that to other countries. Nevertheless, on a per capita basis China's aid receipts from the Soviets would rank well below those of any of the other Communist countries.

An additional aspect of the situation is China's burden of repayment. The terms of Soviet credits to China, both as far as interest rates and periods of repayment are concerned, were similar to those the Soviets extended to other Communist countries. What is perhaps distinct about the Chinese experience is that while the Soviets have on various occasions canceled a part or all of the accumulated debts of Communist countries, there is no indication they have done so for the Chinese.

The terms of Soviet trade with China, on the other hand, appear to be quite equitable, if not generous. The Soviet Union provided China with a more or less guaranteed market for a wide variety of agricultural products and low-quality textiles. Seemingly, it paid world prices for these items of low priority from the point of view of planners. At the same time, Russia was prepared to deliver complete plants to China on a scale which made them the backbone of China's First Five Year Plan. The Soviets supplied technical assistance (most of which the Chinese paid for) of a wide-ranging character, and they went to considerable lengths to adjust to sudden and short-term changes in Chinese orders and specifications and in Chinese deliveries.

It would seem, therefore, that the total Russian contribution to Communist China's economic development could be considered quite generous by some standards and rather modest by others. Seen in this light, the frictions in the economic relations of Communist China and the Soviet Union were probably due to the markedly different positions from which the two partners approached these relations and the widely differing expectations they brought with them. Within the framework of the foreign economic policy which the Soviet Union pursued at least up to 1955, economic assistance to China must have appeared magnanimous. At the same time, this level of aid may have seemed much too small to the Chinese, particularly in view of their abiding urge to narrow the economic and military power gap between themselves and the rest of the world as rapidly as possible.

After 1955, however, the situation changed markedly. The Soviets began to mount a large-scale foreign aid program and at the same time sharply curtailed their economic assistance to China. The question is: Why did they do so, and how can one explain the fact that Mao's visit to Moscow in late 1957, on the eve of China's Second Five Year Plan, did not produce new Soviet credits?

Unless one assumes that the Chinese did not want further aid from the Russians, the Soviet Union's failure to extend economic assistance to China in the late 1950s must have been at least an irritant, if not one of the most important factors contributing to the tensions in Sino-Soviet relations. Moreover, there seems little doubt now that the abrupt withdrawal of Soviet technicians from China—however justified the action may have appeared to the Russians—greatly heightened the tensions. However, we still do not know the answer to one of the truly crucial questions. Why did Russian aid slow down after 1955 and virtually end in 1957?

CHAPTER SIX

Economic Relations with the Non-Communist World

China's trade with the non-Communist world has been conditioned by (a) China's import demand and export capacity (which, in turn, are a function of domestic economic trends), (b) trade control policies of Western countries, and (c) the state of Sino-Soviet relations. Trade controls placed a serious constraint on the expansion of Western trade with China, and the intimacy of Sino-Soviet economic relations placed a ceiling on China's possibilities and capacities for trade with the non-Communist world. With the relaxation of trade controls after 1955 and the deterioration of Sino-Soviet relations after 1960, there was a marked reorientation in China's commerce. However, this shift occurred at a time when China's total trade was stagnating under the impact of domestic crisis. As a result, the reorientation has thus far led only to small increases in the total value of commercial exchanges between China and the non-Communist world. The latter will have to await the renewal of an expansionary tide in China's domestic economic activity.

Within this general context, Communist China's policy on trade with the non-Communist world seems to be guided by two primary considerations: (a) to promote domestic growth and stability and (b) to serve foreign policy objectives ranging from attempts to buy goodwill to efforts to create strong relationships of economic and political dependency. While Communist China may try to pursue both objectives simultaneously in its trade with many countries, one or the other appears paramount in a number of cases.

China's trade with some countries is designed primarily to obtain vital supplies, *e.g.*, machinery, transport equipment, industrial raw materials, technical know-how, etc. With other countries, her principal interest seems to be to earn foreign exchange with which to pay for these supplies. In the case of a number of newly independent countries, non-economic objectives seem to carry great weight. Canada and Australia serve as the clearest examples of purely supplying countries, and Hong Kong and Malaya-Singapore are examples of countries which provide sizable sources of foreign exchange. On the other hand, trade with Western Europe is important from both points of view. Political motivation in foreign trade is most visible in the case of Africa. The close intertwining of economic and political considerations is perhaps best illustrated by trade with Japan.

In seeking sources of supply in the non-Communist world, China was severely hampered by strategic trade controls. Arrangements by NATO and its allies to control trade with the European Communist countries began to take shape in 1949. As they crystallized, three international control lists were formulated. The first was a total embargo list relating to arms, other implements of war, ammunition, and atomic energy materials. The second was a quantitative control list and included certain types of machine tools, raw materials, and equipment. The third, a watch or surveillance list, comprised a wide variety of commodities.[1]

After the outbreak of the Korean War, the United States embargoed all trade with Communist China. The rest of the NATO countries (except Iceland) together with Japan and others imposed controls of varying stringency. The NATO countries and Japan agreed on joint measures, but each country was free to enforce more drastic controls if it wished. The joint measures provided for a complete embargo on all items appearing on any one of the three lists referred to above and on an additional list of 200 items. These interdictions were greatly reinforced by financial, shipping, and bunkering controls.

In this way, restrictions on trade with China became much more stringent than those on commercial exchanges with other

Communist countries. As a result, during the period when the "China differential" was on the books, 1950–57, certain types of goods were transshipped from Western Europe to China via the Soviet Union or Eastern Europe. The effect of these differential controls, therefore, was simply to make the procurement of some special items (*e.g.*, certain types of machinery) a little more difficult and a little more expensive for the Chinese.

After the end of the Korean hostilities, many countries were increasingly reluctant to continue enforcing a China differential in trade controls. This attitude became particularly pronounced after 1954. At that time, the control lists applicable to trade with the European Communist countries were considerably shortened, and the China differential was thus widened. More and more countries began to make unilateral exceptions until the China differential was finally abandoned in 1957. In 1958 a new international control system was instituted. It was based on only two lists—an embargo list and a watch list—and was uniformly applicable to all Communist countries.[2] These changes in trade controls naturally affected the volume and commodity composition of trade between China and the non-Communist world.

Trends in China's Trade with the Non-Communist World

Before the advent of the Communist regime, the bulk of mainland China's trade, as we noted in the preceding chapter, was with non-Communist countries. This period was quite chaotic for the Chinese economy, disrupted as it was by war, civil war, and hyperinflation. Therefore, the country's export capacity was low, while its import needs were large (see Figure 6–1). As the Communists came to power, the United States and other Western countries sharply reduced their exports to China. On the other hand, as the regime consolidated its position between 1949 and 1950, both imports and exports rose. This process was reversed by the Korean War, during which China directed her trade sharply away from the non-Communist world and toward the

FIGURE 6-1A Mainland China's Exports to and Imports from the Non-Communist World, Unadjusted *

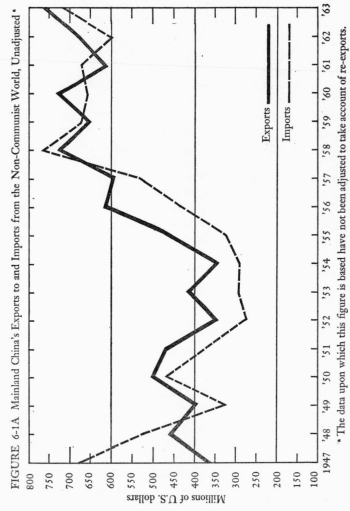

* The data upon which this figure is based have not been adjusted to take account of re-exports.

Sources: U.S. Mutual Defense Assistance Control Act Administrator, *Report to Congress* for various years; Table B-1 of the present volume.

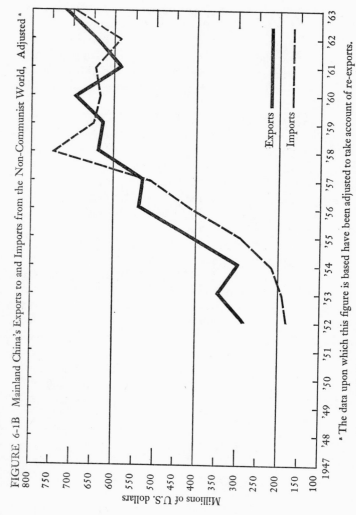

FIGURE 6-1B Mainland China's Exports to and Imports from the Non-Communist World, Adjusted [a]

Millions of U.S. dollars

Exports

Imports

[a] The data upon which this figure is based have been adjusted to take account of re-exports.

Sources: U.S. Mutual Defense Assistance Control Act Administrator, *Report to Congress* for various years; Table B-1 of the present volume.

Communist countries. Consequently, although her total trade grew, her commerce with non-Communist countries declined between 1950 and 1952. By 1954–55, the process of trade reorientation was completed. Trade with the non-Communist world had been recovering slowly since 1952, but the tempo picked up appreciably during the period from 1954–55 to 1959 as China's economy and commerce continued to grow at a time when a number of non-Communist countries were prepared to relax their trade controls.

In 1959, trade with the non-Communist world declined somewhat—largely because of the nature of China's import demands during the Great Leap. Complete plant deliveries from the Soviet Union increased more than twofold between 1958 and 1959. To pay for these, the Chinese had to curtail their exports to non-Communist destinations, particularly since the effects of the agricultural crisis were beginning to be felt. This curtailment, in turn, led to a reduction in imports.

In the early 1960s we witnessed another sharp turn in China's trade orientation—in the opposite direction from that which occurred during the Korean War. As was indicated in Chapter 4, this reorientation resulted in part from the deterioration of Sino-Soviet relations and in part from the crisis-induced changes in the character of China's import demand. Thus, the economic crisis affected China's trade with the non-Communist world much less than it did total trade.

As Figure 6–1 shows, China continuously maintained an export surplus vis-à-vis the non-Communist world between 1949 and 1957. After 1957, she had deficits in 1958, 1959, and 1961 and surpluses in 1960, 1962, and 1963. As a result, China was in a position to accumulate a total of about $550 million in foreign exchange—mostly sterling—through her trade with non-Communist countries up through 1957. From this figure must be deducted an allowance for shipping charges on China's imports, many of which were carried by foreign vessels. Thus, China may have accumulated a total of about $330 million in her trade with non-Communist countries between 1952 and 1957.[3] With the trade deficits of 1958 and 1959, these cumulative earnings may have declined to about $200 million by the end of the latter year. It is against this background that the Chinese Communists began to export silver in 1960. If one excludes silver from China's exports and allows for freight charges, the net cumulative earnings of foreign exchange through trade with the non-Communist world declined further, to an estimated $30 million by the end of 1962.

In assessing China's foreign-exchange position, we must of course take into account remittances by overseas Chinese. At most, these could have amounted to $50–100 million in any one year, and they were undoubtedly offset by a variety of miscellaneous obligations on the service account. Therefore, China's foreign-exchange reserves in the early 1960s must have been quite low indeed.

COMMODITY COMPOSITION.   More than half of mainland China's exports to the non-Communist world in the 1950s were agricultural products, *i.e.*, soybeans, cereals, livestock products, fruits and vegetables, tea, some textile fibers, and fats and oils for industrial use (see Table 6–1). However, in 1961, under the impact of declining farm output, agricultural exports had to be curtailed markedly. (As a result, their absolute as well as relative importance declined sharply between 1960 and 1961.) Over the years, exports of textile fabrics and to a lesser extent metals and metal ores, such as tin, some basic metals, and some iron and steel, increased significantly. Such exports, moreover, remained relatively high even when total deliveries abroad declined in the early 1960s.

Not too surprisingly, there were no marked differences in the composition of China's exports to the non-Communist world and the Soviet Union through 1960. After 1960, however, farm exports to the Soviet Union and Eastern Europe declined much faster than those to the non-Communist world. Correspondingly, textile exports to the Communist countries increased much more in relative importance than those to the rest of the world.

In contrast, throughout the period there were major differences in the composition of the imports which China obtained

T A B L E 6 - 1 . Commodity Composition of Communist
China's Exports to the Non-Communist World, 1952–63

(in per cent)

Commodity Category	1952	1954	1956	1958	1960	1961	1962	1963
Soybeans, oilseeds, and								
products	10.6	9.1	11.0	5.9	9.2	5.1	5.3	4.7
Cereals	11.5	12.6	9.4	11.5	9.2	4.4	5.8	7.2
Livestock products								
Edible	11.7	15.3	10.7	12.7	7.8	5.2	6.8	8.9
Inedible	—	5.6	3.7	3.4	4.4	3.5	3.1	4.6
Fruits and vegetables	14.5	10.3	7.0	7.8	6.7	4.9	5.1	5.6
Tea	—	4.3	3.7	3.9	2.9	3.1	2.6	2.1
Tobacco	—	0.4	0.3	0.3	0.2	0.1	0.2	0.2
Textiles								
Raw materials	—	6.6	6.7	3.6	4.7	5.2	4.0	5.4
Fabrics	7.1	6.0	13.0	15.0	21.7	22.8	20.9	18.9
Clothing and footwear	—	0.5	0.6	1.4	1.6	1.9	2.3	2.7
Industrial fats and oils	8.2	4.3	5.0	3.1	2.9	1.2	1.1	1.1
Building materials	—	—	0.4	0.6	—	—	—	1.6
Chemical products	1.8	2.8	3.6	4.8	2.5	2.6	3.0	2.9
Metals, metal ores and								
concentrates	0.5	0.2	2.9	3.9	4.1	6.1	6.4	2.6
Non-metallic minerals	0.8	1.8	4.2	2.1	1.1	1.5	1.7	1.4
Machinery and equipment	—	—	0.4	0.9	0.9	0.7	0.8	1.4
Other	33.2	20.2	17.6	19.2	20.0	31.6	31.0	28.9
Total	100.0	100.0	100.0	100.0	100.0	100.0	100.0	100.0

Notes: The percentages in this table are based on data which have not
    been adjusted to take account of re-exports.
    Minor inconsistencies result from rounding.
    — stands for "none."

Sources: U.S. Mutual Defense Assistance Control Act Administrator, *Re-
    port to Congress* for various years.

from the non-Communist world and the European Communist
countries. These differences were due to strategic trade controls
on the one hand and different resource endowments on the other.

    Generally speaking, imports from the Soviet Union were
much less diversified than those from non-Communist countries,
with machinery and equipment by far the leading category.
These goods plus arms, metals, and petroleum constituted the
bulk of Soviet deliveries. The non-Communist world, on the other
hand, supplied no arms, no petroleum products, and much less

machinery (see Table 6–2). The first two were totally embargoed, although some small shipments seem to have been delivered to China after 1960. Machinery was not embargoed but was subject to quantitative controls. The same was true with respect to metals and metal products. The amount of these goods exported to China, however, rose markedly between 1956 and 1958 and continued at a high level through 1960. It then declined as a result of the investment cutbacks in China and the curtailed import demand which these cutbacks engendered. The 1956–58

T A B L E 6 - 2 . Commodity Composition of Communist China's Imports from the Non-Communist World, 1952–63

(in per cent)

Commodity Category	1952	1954	1956	1958	1960	1961	1962	1963
Foodstuffs, processed and unprocessed	1.1	1.8	5.0	4.2	5.5	48.2	51.4	45.4
Manufactured consumer goods	—	4.0	7.6	4.0	2.8	2.8	2.6	2.2
Drugs and cosmetics	10.1	6.8	2.0	1.5	0.3	0.3	0.2	0.3
Paper	5.0	1.0	2.9	0.6	0.4	1.1	0.5	0.3
Rubber and rubber products	9.5	14.7	11.1	11.8	14.0	8.3	9.1	7.8
Chemical products	17.1	31.6	22.2	15.6	11.0	7.9	8.8	13.0
Fertilizers and insecticides	8.4	10.2	13.7	8.8	4.4	4.5	4.5	6.5
Textile fibers	40.3	18.2	17.5	13.9	20.2	15.7	13.2	18.9
Metals, metal ores and concentrates	2.1	2.9	5.7	32.9	29.5	5.7	4.6	4.1
Machinery and equipment	4.4	4.3	9.6	9.0	7.1	4.0	2.6	3.3
Other	10.4	14.6	16.4	6.4	9.2	6.0	6.9	4.7
Total	100.0	100.0	100.0	100.0	100.0	100.0	100.0	100.0

Notes: The percentages in this table are based on data which have not been adjusted to take account of re-exports.
Minor inconsistencies result from rounding.
— stands for "none."

Sources: See Table 6-1.

change is clearly traceable to the gradual dismantling of the "China differential" in the trade controls of European countries.

Security considerations also undoubtedly placed constraints upon China's demand for machinery from the non-Communist world. Since plants in many of the basic industries were militarily

TABLE 6-3. Direction of Communist China's Trade with
the Non-Communist World, 1952–63

(in millions of U.S. dollars and in per cent)

	1952					1954				
	Exports		Imports		Balance	Exports		Imports		Balance
Region	Value	%	Value	%	Value	Value	%	Value	%	Value
Europe	54.3	18.7	50.6	27.6	+ 3.7	94.3	31.0	89.5	40.7	+ 4.8
Near East and North Africa	6.7	2.3	8.9	4.9	− 2.2	11.5	3.8	12.0	5.5	− 0.5
Latin America	0.3	0.1	−	−	+ 0.3	−	−	2.6	1.2	− 2.6
Oceania	4.0	1.4	0.6	0.3	+ 3.4	4.4	1.4	3.2	1.5	+ 1.2
North America	24.3	8.4	−	−	+ 24.3	1.8	0.6	0.1	−	+ 1.7
Sub-Saharan Africa	0.2	0.1	−	−	+ 0.2	0.8	0.3	0.7	0.3	+ 0.1
East, Southeast, and South Asia	200.5	69.1	123.3	67.2	+ 77.2	191.4	63.0	111.7	50.8	+79.7
Hong Kong only	(87.2)	(30.0)	(2.4)	(1.3)	(+ 84.8)	(72.7)	(23.9)	(2.4)	(1.1)	(+70.3)
Total	290.3		183.4		+106.9	304.2		219.8		+84.4

of a sensitive character, it was natural for China to seek complete plants and other factory installations in Communist countries allied with her—particularly so if one remembers that a number of technicians and advisers came with the plants and worked in them for a while. It remains to be seen whether China will wish to import complete plants on a similar scale and under similar arrangements from non-Communist countries now that her economic relations with the Soviet bloc have been sharply curtailed.

For all these reasons combined, several product categories, such as rubber, textile fibers, and chemicals (including fertilizer), outranked machinery in China's imports from the non-Communist world. In the case of the first two, the non-Communist world was virtually the sole supplier. Rubber came largely from Ceylon, while Egypt and Pakistan provided most of the imported cotton.[4]

TRADE DIRECTION. Up to 1958–60, practically all of China's trade with the non-Communist world was concentrated in Asia and Europe (see Table 6–3). Initially, about two-thirds of the total was with Asia—a large part of it with Hong Kong. In 1955, however, China began to buy its imports in Europe and to have

1956						1958				
Exports		Imports		Balance		Exports		Imports		Balance
Value	%	Value	%	Value		Value	%	Value	%	Value
155.7	28.5	194.5	47.6	− 38.8		178.1	27.7	465.3	62.7	−287.2
29.8	5.4	26.3	6.4	+ 3.5		45.0	7.0	44.8	6.0	+ 0.2
1.0	0.2	1.6	0.4	− 0.6		1.8	0.3	8.9	1.2	− 7.1
5.1	0.9	10.5	2.6	− 5.4		8.8	1.4	29.9	4.0	− 21.1
5.7	1.0	2.5	0.6	+ 3.2		5.3	0.8	8.1	1.1	− 2.8
2.2	0.4	1.2	0.3	+ 1.0		13.7	2.1	10.1	1.4	+ 3.4
346.5	63.5	171.6	42.0	+174.9		388.7	60.6	175.3	23.6	+213.4
(121.7)	(22.3)	(2.4)	(0.6)	(+119.3)		(160.6)	(25.1)	(2.7)	(0.4)	(+157.9)
546.0		408.2		+137.8		641.4		742.4		−101.0

them shipped directly to Chinese ports instead of obtaining them through Hong Kong. As a result, while Hong Kong's role as a transshipment port for China's exports remained undiminished, its importance as a center for the procurement of imports declined drastically. Asia's role as a seller to China also declined—from more than 60 per cent of the non-Communist total in the early 1950s to about 20 per cent in 1961, 1962, and 1963. China's leading Asian suppliers were Japan, Ceylon, Indonesia, Malaya and Singapore, and Burma.

As the importance of Asia diminished, that of Europe grew correspondingly. China's leading trading partners in Europe were Germany and Britain. In the early 1950s, Switzerland was important, and in the early 1960s France began to loom large. In addition, Italy and the Benelux countries have from time to time carried on fairly large-scale trade with China.

The Middle East, Africa, and Latin America are of minor commercial importance to China, although trade with them has been expanding somewhat. While they supplied only about 5 per cent of China's imports from the non-Communist world in 1952, this share grew to around 13 per cent in 1962–63. A similar trend is observable on the export side. China's exports to these areas grew from 2 per cent in 1952 to about 10 per cent in 1962–63.

TABLE 6-3. (*Continued*)

Region	1960				
	Exports		Imports		Balance
	Value	%	Value	%	Value
Europe	248.4	35.6	378.3	59.4	−129.9
Near East and North Africa	39.5	5.7	55.1	8.7	− 15.6
Latin America	0.6	0.1	6.2	1.0	− 5.6
Oceania	10.8	1.5	30.0	4.7	− 19.2
North America	5.8	0.8	8.9	1.4	− 3.1
Sub-Saharan Africa	19.1	2.7	28.4	4.5	− 9.3
East, Southeast, and South Asia	374.2	53.6	129.9	20.4	+244.3
Hong Kong only	(173.5)	(24.8)	2.3	0.4	(+171.2)
Total	698.4		636.8		+ 61.6

Notes: The figures for total trade in this table have been adjusted to take account of re-exports, and those for exports have been adjusted to take account of the c.i.f. factor.

Data in parentheses are the author's esimates of Hong Kong's trade with Communist

Egypt was the only country of any identifiable importance throughout the period. In 1962, however, Argentina was an exporter of some importance to China.

As a rule, most of the major regions of the world were much less dependent on trade with China than vice versa. China's share in the exports of non-Communist Europe, for example, was well below 1 per cent for most years,[5] but Europe's share in China's imports fluctuated between 6 and 25 per cent.* This situation, of course, is not surprising. China is economically backward and thus accounts for only a small share of world exports or imports. Europe, on the other hand, is a major world trader. A similar contrast, however, is apparent in China's trade with non-Communist Asia. The mainland's share in that region's exports has fluctuated between 1 and 2 per cent in the last few years, while Asia's share in China's imports, even though consistently

---

* A significant portion of China's exports are routed through Hong Kong and then re-exported from there, while China's imports are brought in directly from the countries concerned. Therefore, the import percentage is a better indicator of the share of different regions in China's trade than the export percentage is.

	1962				1963			
Exports		Imports		Balance	Exports		Imports		Balance
Value	*%*	*Value*	*%*	*Value*	*Value*	*%*	*Value*	*%*	*Value*
175.5	27.1	148.7	25.2	+ 26.8	181.0	25.4	172.5	24.7	+ 8.5
44.8	6.9	32.1	5.4	+ 12.7	43.0	6.0	47.0	6.7	— 4.0
0.9	0.1	27.1	4.6	— 26.2	1.2	0.2	3.4	0.5	— 2.2
11.5	1.8	101.1	17.2	— 89.6	15.4	2.2	212.7	30.4	—197.3
4.2	0.6	137.0	23.2	—132.8	4.8	0.7	96.9	13.9	— 92.1
22.4	3.5	15.7	2.7	+ 6.7	21.0	2.9	41.4	5.9	— 20.4
387.8	59.9	127.6	21.7	+260.2	445.9	62.6	124.7	17.8	+321.2
(183.2)	(28.3)	1.5	0.3	(+181.7)	(219.4)	(30.8)	1.4	0.2	(+218.0)
647.1		589.3		+ 57.8	712.3		698.6		+ 13.7

China net of re-exports.
— stands for "none."

Source: Table B–1.

declining, has still been around 5–8 per cent. This unequal degree of dependence is also noticeable with respect to the Middle East and Africa, although to a lesser extent.

A number of factors account for these tendencies. Up through 1960, roughly 60–80 per cent of China's trade was with other Communist countries. Although China's trade shifted away from them after that time, the shift took place as total Chinese exports and imports were declining and those of other regions of the world were expanding.

China maintained a favorable balance of trade with the non-Communist world until 1958 and was thus in a position to accumulate foreign exchange. This favorable balance resulted largely from a consistent surplus in China's trade with non-Communist Asia, especially Hong Kong.

In trade with Europe, on the other hand, China accumulated surpluses in certain years and deficits in others. The unfavorable balances were particularly large in 1958 and 1959. They were so large, in fact, that they led to deficits in her trade with the non-Communist world as a whole.

China's trade with Canada and Australia after the mid-1950s, but particularly after 1960, was also characterized by sizable deficits. In contrast, China accumulated consistently favorable trade balances with Africa, although these were small. As one examines the trade balances in Table 6–3, it becomes clear that since 1961 the foreign-exchange earnings accruing from the export surpluses in Asia have in effect paid for the large-scale grain imports from Canada and Australia which are reflected in the trade deficits with North America and Oceania.

China's Principal Non-Communist Trading Partners

As Table 6–3 shows, China's most important non-Communist trading partners have been in Asia and Europe. Hong Kong, Japan, Indonesia, and Malaya and Singapore have been of particular importance in the former, and the United Kingdom, West Germany, and France in the latter. In addition, Canada and Australia have begun to loom large as exporters to China. The character of and prospects for commercial interchange between China and these countries are examined in greater detail below.

HONG KONG. Hong Kong plays a truly major role in mainland China's commercial relations with the non-Communist world. It is the most important single market for China's exports outside the Communist bloc, it is the principal source of China's foreign exchange, and it plays a most significant role as middleman between China and the rest of the world. Moreover, the colony's importance in all these roles seems to have been increasing in recent years. For example, mainland exports to the colony have been rising quite markedly (see Table 6–4).

According to estimates made in Hong Kong, China's total earnings of foreign exchange in the colony in 1962–63 may have ranged between U.S. $400 million and $600 million.[6] Export surpluses contributed about $180 million in 1962 and almost $220 million in 1963. Remittances by overseas Chinese have been placed at $100–110 million. To these amounts must be added allowances for food packages mailed from Hong Kong to the mainland and for earnings from water sales to the colony and a variety of other minor sources.

Hong Kong provides banking, insurance, and shipping facilities for the China trade, and it serves as a prime point of commercial contact between China and the West. Thirty-five non-Communist countries plus Cuba maintain professional consular staffs, trade commissioners, or both there. These, as well as many of the banks, shipping companies, insurance underwriters, merchants, and manufacturers, were formerly based in Shanghai. They have a highly specialized know-how of the mainland market and the institutional framework within which trade with Communist China must be carried on.

When the Chinese Communists came to power, they had to channel the bulk of their exports and imports through Hong Kong for a number of reasons. They did not have an adequate foreign-trade network and organization, and they lacked the facilities for foreign-trade financing. Moreover, up to early 1953 they could not get direct shipments or through bills of lading from Europe to China—partly because of the blockade imposed by the Nationalists. All cargo had to be shipped to Hong Kong and then forwarded to China under a separate bill of lading.[7] As the new regime became better established, however, it began to build up its own trade contacts and gradually placed less reliance on Hong Kong as far as imports were concerned.

These trends are clearly reflected in the data in Table 6–4. In 1950 more than half and in 1951 more than two-thirds of China's imports from the non-Communist world were obtained through Hong Kong; however, these imports declined sharply in 1952 and then dropped more or less continuously in later years. In contrast, China's exports to the colony grew markedly over the period as a whole. As a result, a sizable trade deficit was converted into an expanding surplus.

As was noted above, remittances from overseas Chinese to assist their families and friends on the mainland supplemented foreign-exchange earnings from trade. Such remittances have traditionally represented an important source of foreign exchange for the mainland economy. Unfortunately, there are no reliable estimates for these payments. The reasons for this situation are

TABLE 6-4. Trade Between Hong Kong and Communist China, 1950–63

Year	Hong Kong's Trade with China					
	Imports		Exports		Balance	
	Unadjusted	Adjusted	Unadjusted	Adjusted	Unadjusted	Adjusted
			(in millions of U.S. dollars)			
1950	150.1		255.7		+105.6	
1951	161.9		305.0		+143.1	
1952	145.3	(87.2)	91.0	(2.4)	− 54.3	(− 84.8)
1953	150.0	(90.0)	94.6	(2.4)	− 55.4	(− 87.6)
1954	121.1	(72.7)	68.4	(2.4)	− 52.7	(− 70.3)
1955	157.1	(105.3)	31.8	(2.4)	−125.3	(−102.9)
1956	181.7	(121.7)	23.8	(2.4)	−157.9	(−119.3)
1957	197.9	(136.6)	21.6	(2.2)	−176.3	(−134.4)
1958	244.5	(160.6)	27.3	(2.7)	−217.2	(−157.9)
1959	181.0	(148.6)	20.0	1.5	−161.0	(−147.1)
1960	207.5	(173.5)	21.0	2.3	−186.5	(−171.2)
1961	180.0	(153.0)	17.3	1.4	−162.7	(−151.6)
1962	212.3	(183.2)	14.9	1.5	−197.4	(−181.7)
1963	260.2	(219.4)	12.3	1.4	−247.9	(−218.0)

Note: Figures in parentheses are net of re-exports as estimated by the author. For the method of estimation, see Appendix B.

many. The largest portion of payments flows through the small native banks and exchange shops in Hong Kong. Some, however, are sent via Macao, and yet others are transmitted through a wide variety of channels. In some cases, such as that of the United States, the remittance of these funds is illegal, and this fact adds to the difficulties of estimation.

Moreover, remittances are subject to sharp annual fluctuations in response to changing economic conditions in Communist China. Perhaps a distinction should be made here between strictly family remittances and transmittal of funds for investment by overseas Chinese. Other things being constant, a deterioration of economic conditions tends to discourage the flow of investment funds. On the other hand, it seems to encourage the flow of strictly family remittances designed to alleviate declining standards of living.

Nationalization, income distribution, and land policies also seem to influence the volume of these remittances. For instance,

As Share of Total Hong Kong Trade				As Share of Total Chinese Trade			
Imports		Exports		Imports		Exports	
Unadjusted	Adjusted	Unadjusted	Adjusted	Unadjusted	Adjusted	Unadjusted	Adjusted
(in per cent)				(in per cent)			
22.5		38.9					
18.9		39.1					
21.9	(13.1)	17.9	(0.5)	9.3	(0.3)	15.6	(10.0)
22.1	(13.3)	19.7	(0.5)	7.9	(0.2)	13.7	(8.7)
20.1	(12.1)	16.1	(0.6)	5.2	(0.2)	10.4	(6.5)
24.1	(16.2)	7.1	(0.5)	2.4	(0.2)	11.2	(7.8)
22.7	(15.2)	4.2	(0.4)	1.6	(0.2)	10.9	(7.5)
21.9	(15.1)	4.1	(0.4)	1.5	(0.2)	11.8	(8.5)
30.4	(20.0)	5.2	(0.5)	1.4	(0.1)	12.3	(8.4)
20.9	(17.1)	3.5	(0.3)	1.0	0.1	8.0	(6.7)
22.0	(18.4)	1.7	(0.2)	1.1	0.1	10.2	(8.6)
17.2	14.6	2.5	0.2	1.2	0.1	11.3	(9.7)
18.4	15.7	1.9	0.2	1.3	0.1	13.1	(11.5)
20.1	16.9	1.4	0.2	1.0	0.1	15.0	(12.9)

Sources: Hong Kong, Department of Commerce and Industry, *Hong Kong Trade Bulletin;* Table 4-1 and Appendix B of the present volume.

indications point to a sharp fall in 1959. With the organization of the communes, remittances often found their way into communal accumulation funds, and even when they did not, fear that they would naturally discouraged the transmittal of funds.

In view of these various trends and considerations, remittances may have ranged between U.S. $10 million and $110 million annually. The flow probably was nearer the upper limit in the early 1950s and 1960s, and it probably reached its low point in 1959. Between 1952 and 1958, it may have averaged $50–60 million.[8]

To a considerable extent, the growth in China's exports to Hong Kong was due to a rapidly rising demand for consumer goods in the colony. This demand was occasioned in part by the large influx of people from the mainland. Thus, Hong Kong's population is estimated to have increased from 1,860,000 in 1949 to 3,592,000 in 1963. For most of the period under consideration, processed and unprocessed foods (including live animals for slaughter) constituted about 50 per cent of Hong Kong's imports from China. The bulk of these was for local consumption.

Textiles and clothing were the next in importance. They constituted only about 5 per cent of total imports in the early fifties, but that figure has risen to 25–30 per cent in recent years. Imported cotton yarn and cloth, however, were directly competitive with the colony's own textile industry. Unlike foodstuffs, therefore, textile products were for the most part re-exported.

The rest of Hong Kong's purchases from China were crude materials, mostly of agricultural origin. These were of major importance at first but have diminished in relative standing. They have been replaced largely by manufactured products. The latter include not only textiles but a wide miscellany of consumer goods, *e.g.*, clocks, fountain pens, and paper products. These are partly for local consumption and partly for re-export.

Most Hong Kong exports to China are not of local origin but are re-exports.[9] For instance, during 1958–63 sales to China of home-produced goods averaged just under 10 per cent of the total. For most years, chemicals (particularly dyeing and coloring materials) and medical and pharmaceutical products were by far the leading category of total exports. In some years, fertilizer shipments were of considerable importance. Special-quality textile fibers and manufactures, paper and paper products, metals, and professional and scientific instruments were also of some significance. However, it must be borne in mind that the volume shipped in any one of these commodity categories could not play a significant role in China's imports since total Hong Kong exports to the mainland were continuously below $30 million after 1955.

JAPAN. To China and Japan, the problem of their mutual economic relations is a subject of prime importance. China, as the largest and most populous country in Asia, represents actually or potentially a market of considerable proportions and a major source of raw materials for Japan. At the same time, Japan, as the most advanced and industrialized nation in the area, is in an excellent position to supply China with the necessary where-withal for industrialization—capital equipment, know-how, and possibly even credits.

Moreover, Japan has a long history of involvement with China. It has borrowed heavily from Chinese culture ever since the days of the T'ang dynasty.[10] Its defeat of China in 1895 opened the way to far-reaching political and economic incursions on the mainland. The Japanese established a vast network of enterprises in China proper and gained a strong foothold in Man-churia. By the 1930s, they dominated Manchuria and much of North China. This area of control was then extended to the whole coastal region during the wartime occupation.

Under such circumstances, Japan enjoyed a special and pri-vileged position with respect to China, and this position provided the basis for large-scale trade. On the eve of the Sino-Japanese War of 1937, about 11 per cent of Japan's imports came from the mainland of China, while 18 per cent of its exports were delivered there. In turn, about 14–16 per cent of China's (including Man-churia's) exports and imports went to or came from Japan. China exported mainly raw materials—soybeans, iron ore, coal, pig iron, salt—in exchange for textiles for China proper and capital goods for Manchuria.[11]

This legacy has profoundly conditioned Japanese attitudes on trade with China. As a result, the subject of trade with China has become a major political issue in the country. It is closely inter-woven with the broader and rather complex issues of Sino-Japanese relations in general. In essence, the pressures for closer trade relations stem from an amalgam of strictly commercial considerations—the search by business enterprises for markets and cheaper sources of raw materials—and much more subtle emo-tional and political influences. Among the latter are Japan's ad-miration for China's past and a profound sense of guilt for Japanese wartime behavior in China. In addition, the image of a strong, unified, and dynamic China attracts the Japanese intelli-gentsia and youth. Finally, various controls restricting the free flow of goods between China and Japan have symbolized to large segments of the Japanese public the continuing American presence. Many Japanese believe that these controls represent the principal obstacle to close, intimate, and wide-ranging economic relations and thus resent them.[12]

It would be beyond the scope of this study, however, to analyze the political and psychocultural aspects of the China trade issue in Japan. Instead, our primary concern here is with the economic aspects of the problem, *i.e.*, with the character of Japan's economic relations with China since 1950, the factors which have shaped the relationship, and the short- and medium-term prospects for Sino-Japanese trade.

Trends in Sino-Japanese trade. Since 1950 Sino-Japanese trade has been much less important for both countries than it was during the prewar period (see Table 6–5). One striking characteristic of this trade has been the much greater fluctuation in Japan's exports to China as compared with its imports from China. This difference is largely due to political barriers imposed by both sides. While both exports and imports declined between 1950 and 1952 under the impact of the Korean War, the fall in exports was the more drastic, for U.S. occupation authorities, who maintained ultimate control over Japanese affairs until 1952, virtually embargoed exports. Once the Korean armistice was signed, trade grew fairly rapidly. It recovered to its 1950 level by 1954. Then within a year imports doubled, and within two years exports trebled. The Chinese brought this expansion to a halt in 1958. In the spring of that year, they suddenly canceled their purchase orders from Japan in an abortive effort to topple the Kishi government and influence the outcome of the Japanese elections held later in the year. As a result, Japan's exports shrank to almost negligible proportions in 1959 and 1960. They picked up again, however, in 1961 when the deterioration of Sino-Soviet relations and the decline of Sino-Soviet trade caused China actively to seek alternative sources of imports.

Economic contacts between China and Japan have been growing rapidly in scope, scale, and depth since 1962. In 1963, for instance, more Japanese companies than ever before sent representatives to the Canton trade fair. In October of the same

TABLE 6-5. Sino-Japanese Trade, 1934–36 and 1950–63

Year	Japan's Trade with China			As Share of Total Japanese Trade		As Share of Total Chinese Trade	
	Exports	Imports a	Balance	Exports	Imports	Exports	Imports
	(in millions of U.S. dollars)			(in per cent)			
1934–36	170.0	102.0	+68.0	18.2	10.7	14.3 b	15.7 b
1950	19.6	39.3	−19.7	2.4	4.1	(2.2)	(5.4)
1951	5.8	21.6	−15.8	0.4	1.1	n.a.	n.a.
1952	0.6	14.9	−14.3	0.05	0.7	1.7	0.1
1953	4.5	29.7	−25.2	0.4	1.2	2.9	0.4
1954	19.1	40.8	−21.7	1.2	1.7	3.6	1.5
1955	28.5	80.8	−52.3	1.4	3.3	6.0	2.2
1956	67.3	83.6	−16.3	2.7	2.6	5.2	4.6
1957	60.5	80.5	−20.0	2.1	1.9	5.0	4.3
1958	50.6	54.4	− 3.8	1.8	1.8	2.8	2.7
1959	3.6	18.9	−15.3	1.0	0.5	0.9	0.2
1960	2.7	20.7	−18.0	0.1	0.5	1.0	0.1
1961	16.6	30.9	−14.3	0.07	0.5	2.0	1.2
1962	38.5	46.0	− 7.5	0.8	0.8	2.9	3.4
1963	62.4	74.6	−12.2	1.1	1.1	4.4	4.9

a These figures do not agree with those in Table B-1, for these data include the costs of insurance and freight while those in Table B-1 do not. As a result, the imports from China are comparable with total Japanese imports.

b These percentages are for 1935–36 only.

Notes: Figures in parentheses are estimates by the author.
  n.a. stands for "not available."

Sources: Warren Hunsberger, *Japan and the United States in World Trade* (New York: Harper and Row for the Council on Foreign Relations, 1964), Tables 5-1, 7-1, 7-2, and 7-5, pp. 106, 184–185, and 203; Y. K. Cheng, *Foreign Trade and Industrial Development of China, A Historical and Integrated Analysis Through 1948* (Washington, D. C.: University Press of Washington, 956), Table 16, p. 45; *Far Eastern Economic Review, 1965 Yearbook* (Hong Kong: Author, 1965); Table 4-1 in the present volume.

year, the Japanese organized an industrial exhibition in Peking, and this exhibition later moved to Shanghai. The Chinese put on three trade fairs in Japan in the course of 1964. In the fall of 1964 resident trade delegations were exchanged between Peking and

Tokyo. Yet another indication of closer relations was the conclusion of a tourist agreement. Under this agreement, Japan is to
send 3,600 tourists a year to China between 1964 and 1967. This
number is to be stepped up to possibly 6,000 in 1968 and 10,000
in 1969.

Under the impact of all this activity, Japan's exports to and
imports from China increased significantly. Total turnover rose
from $85 million in 1962 to $135 million in 1963 and to an estimated $300 million in 1964. While the increases up to 1963 repre-
sented merely a recovery to levels previously attained in 1956 and
1957, the rapid expansion of 1964 clearly carried Sino-Japanese
trade to a new postwar high.

There is ample evidence that both governments have been
encouraging closer economic relations within certain limits and
constraints, to be discussed below. Perhaps the most notable sign
of a changed atmosphere in Sino-Japanese economic relations was
the sale in 1963 of a large synthetic-textile plant to Communist
China by the Kurashiki Rayon Company.[13] This deal was of
considerable significance from several points of view. To begin
with, it represented the first Chinese purchase of a complete
plant from Japan. (It was followed, however, by another complete plant sale by the Nichibo Company in January 1965.) As
such, it was part and parcel of Communist China's new trade
policy, which seeks to fill the gap left by the exodus of Soviet
technicians and the cessation of complete plant deliveries by
the Soviet Union. Secondly, the Japanese for the first time
granted medium-term credit to Communist China. The terms of
the purchase included a down payment of 25 per cent and payment of the balance over a five-year period from the date of
shipment. The rate of interest on this credit was fixed at 6 per cent.

Two additional aspects of Japan's trade with China are particularly noteworthy. At no time since 1950 has China's share in
Japan's total exports exceeded 3 per cent. The figure for the
prewar period, in comparison, was 18 per cent. China's share of
Japanese imports was a little higher. It reached 4 per cent in
1950 and came close to this figure in 1955. For 4 out of the 14
years between 1950 and 1963, however, both the import and
export shares were below 1 per cent. As a result of the postwar

decline in trade, China slipped from its position as Japan's most important single export market before the war to 13th place in 1950 and 57th in 1960. From this low, she recovered to 29th place in 1962 and 11th place in 1964. As a supplier of Japan, China dropped in rank more gradually. She occupied 3rd place in 1934–36, 5th in 1950, and 32nd in 1960. Then she recovered to 23rd place in 1962 and 11th place in 1964. With the rapid expansion in trade between the two countries in 1963 and most particularly in 1964, China's import and export rank improved considerably.[14] Yet trade with China still constitutes significantly less than 3 per cent of Japan's total commerce.

Because of the greater volume of Japan's exports and imports, Sino-Japanese trade loomed larger in China's total trade than it did in Japan's. This difference in mutual trade dependence became more pronounced after 1960, for Japan's trade continued to expand while China's was contracting. In 1955–57, when the turnover in Sino-Japanese trade was the highest since 1950, about 5–6 per cent of mainland exports were destined for Japan, and about 2–5 per cent of imports were obtained from there. At the time, Japan was the leading non-Communist exporter to China and was outranked only by Hong Kong as an importer of Chinese products. If one includes Communist countries in the comparison, Japan's trade turnover with China was exceeded only by that of the Soviet Union, East Germany, and Czechoslovakia. In 1962, when China's trade with all Soviet bloc countries was declining while that with Japan was recovering from its 1959–60 low, Japan occupied 4th place in mainland exports and imports; in 1963 Japan had forged further ahead to 3rd place in both imports and exports.

Another striking feature of Sino-Japanese economic relations is the sharp reversal in the trade balance during the 1950s as compared with the 1930s. Before the war, there was a net flow of capital from Japan to the mainland to finance a surplus of Japanese exports to China. Since 1950, however, Japan has consistently maintained a sizable surplus of imports.

The reasons for the surplus of imports are not entirely clear. Up to 1957, Japan adhered much more faithfully to allied trade controls than the United Kingdom or other West European countries.[15] This policy seemingly had a double effect. First, the controls in and of themselves barred or restricted Japanese exports of certain categories of goods, notably various types of steel products and machinery. Second, the differential in controls encouraged the Chinese to continue their exports to Japan in order to build up trade surpluses and apply the foreign exchange they earned there to purchases in Europe, where many goods could be obtained more freely than in Japan. In possible support of this hypothesis, it is interesting to note that a trade balance was most nearly approximated in 1958, the year after Japan considerably relaxed its trade controls and brought them into line with those of other countries.

The effects of this relaxation were not permitted to work themselves out, however, for the Chinese imposed a virtual boycott on imports from Japan for purely political reasons. It would seem that this method of applying pressure was not confined to 1958 and 1959, although it was carried to greater lengths then. In other years as well, China's purchases from Japan were circumscribed not only by the aforementioned trade controls but by a conscious Chinese policy to limit imports from Japan. Such a policy was probably in part a retaliation for Japan's enforcement of trade controls and in part an attempt to use the lure of the Chinese market to bring about a relaxation of controls and possible recognition or just to increase the discontent of the Japanese people with their government's China policy.

The profound changes in general Sino-Japanese relations after 1950 and the structural transformations in the economies of the two countries were naturally reflected in some changes in the commodity composition of imports and exports. Actually, the composition of China's exports to Japan did not change much. Soybeans and products, salt, coal, pulses, oilseeds, and base metals continued to be significant in most years after 1950. Iron ore and pig iron shrank in importance as compared with the prewar period, while rice became one of China's major exports.[16]

The shifts were more pronounced in Chinese imports from Japan. The absolute and relative decline in textile purchases is particularly notable. Cotton textiles, for example, declined from about 30 per cent before the war to less than 10 per cent during the 1950s. Machinery and metals did not change a great deal in relative weight. There were two reasons for this fact. Manchuria had imported such products on a large scale during the 1930s, and Japan restricted such exports to China during the 1950s. In contrast, Chinese imports of chemical fertilizer and synthetic-textile fibers (*e.g.*, rayon yarn) gained in importance. For instance, a three-year agreement concluded in August 1964 provides for Chinese purchase of a million tons a year of urea and ammonium sulfate. The agreement came as a real boon to the Japanese fertilizer industry, which had been operating well below capacity.

Factors limiting Japan's trade with Communist China. A number of non-economic factors have hampered the development of trade between China and Japan. Among these have been the absence of diplomatic relations—though the absence of such ties has not proved a significant barrier to active trading between China and countries like Canada or Australia—allied controls on China trade, China's retaliatory controls on its exports, China's manipulation of trade levels and composition for political ends, and the unpredictability and instability of Sino-Japanese trade from year to year. In addition, various difficulties and frictions have been caused by the fact that private Japanese traders motivated by strictly commercial considerations, although operating within political constraints, have to deal with China's state trading companies, which may or may not be guided by the same considerations.

It would be a serious error, however, to attribute the narrow scope of Sino-Japanese trade to these barriers alone. Of perhaps even greater importance is the fact that up to 1961 about 65 per cent of China's trade was with other Communist countries. China exported to the Soviet Union and to Eastern Europe the same products which she had once exported to Japan and for which there is a continuing import demand in Japan. Thus, her capacity to export soybeans, oilseeds, other farm products, pig iron, and nonferrous metals to non-Communist countries was limited. Similarly, as long as she could freely obtain capital goods, complete plants, and technical assistance from the Soviet Union, she had no strong economic incentive to obtain them from Japan even if she could have done so.

A corresponding limitation has been Japan's dependence on trade with the United States. The United States has been by far Japan's leading trading partner. In recent years, its share of Japan's exports has been about 30 per cent, and its share of Japan's imports has been even larger. Moreover, for a number of commodities—particularly soybeans, hides and skins, coal, and nonferrous metals—China and the United States are potentially competitive sources of supply. At the same time, the United States absorbs 50 per cent or more of Japan's exports of a wide range of commodities. Such commodities and commodity categories constitute almost 60 per cent of total Japanese exports to the United States.[17] This marked export dependence accounts in part for the extreme sensitivity of Japanese political and business leaders to American public opinion, and concern about American reactions limits Japan's freedom to revise its trade controls vis-à-vis China and to shift its sources of supply from the United States to the mainland.

Japan's relations with Taiwan impose another constraint on commercial intercourse with Communist China. During most years since 1950, Taiwan has been a more important trading partner for Japan than has mainland China. While this situation did not seem to prevail in 1964, Taiwan still remained important.[18] Apart from political considerations, therefore, Taiwan is an economic factor which Japan might not wish to ignore, particularly since prospects for trade with China are at best uncertain. The interrelationship of Japan's trade with the "two Chinas" was brought home most forcefully after the Kurashiki Rayon Company deal was concluded. The Nationalist government threatened to break off economic and even diplomatic relations with Japan in retaliation for the "economic aid" this deal rendered to Communist China.

The most fundamental limitation to the growth in the volume of trade, however, is China's economic backwardness. The per capita level of her exports and imports, for example, is much lower than Japan's. Although Japan has a population of about one-seventh that of China, Japan's foreign trade in 1958 was about one and a half times that of the mainland, and in 1962–63 it was four times. (The size of the latter figure, of course, is in part due to the decline in foreign trade which resulted from China's agricultural crisis.) Under these circumstances, Sino-Japanese trade can grow as it is now doing until China has completed the reorientation of her trade away from the Soviet bloc, but further increases will depend upon the rate of growth of Chinese exports. That rate of growth, in turn, will depend primarily on the rate of expansion in agriculture, mining, and manufacturing.

Prospects for Sino-Japanese trade. Japan's long-range economic plan envisages a two-and-a-half-fold increase in foreign trade between 1959 and 1970—a little more for exports and a little less for imports.[19] Exports of machinery and transport equipment are expected to rise particularly rapidly. Deliveries of textiles and apparel are to grow more slowly, and their relative importance is expected to decline significantly. These projected changes in the commodity composition of Japan's exports are clearly congruent with Communist China's long-run demand for imports. With the structural changes in the mainland economy since 1949, the market for Japanese textiles has virtually disappeared. It has been replaced by a sizable market for machinery and chemicals, the future development of which hinges largely on the speed of economic recovery in Communist China.

The Japanese plan envisages exports to Communist countries that will amount to $480 million in 1970, or 5 per cent of the anticipated export totals. In other instances, a 5 per cent share for exports to China alone has been projected. If we assume that Communist China's GNP will grow for the rest of this decade at an average annual rate of 4–5 per cent and that the import ratio in 1970 will be the same as in the peak import year of 1959, China's purchases from abroad would be around $2.2–2.3 billion. Under these circumstances, China would have to be willing to buy about one-fifth to one-fourth of her total imports from Japan in order for Japan to sell 5 per cent of its exports to the mainland.

What about the outlook for China's exports and her ability to finance imports from Japan at this level? Were China to reorient her trade so markedly that she obtained a quarter or a fifth of her imports from Japan, her export orientation would have to follow suit. For her exports to Japan to approximate the $500 million level, China probably would have to step up her soybean, iron ore, and coal deliveries considerably. With Japanese equipment and technical assistance, mainland mines could probably raise their productivity appreciably, and exports of iron ore and coal could thus be expanded well beyond current levels or beyond those which were attained earlier. The same cannot be said for soybeans, the production of which has fallen below prewar levels. Increases in the production of this crop could be achieved only by raising yields, necessarily a slow process.

Another major factor which will affect the course of Sino-Japanese trade is the comparative costs of imports from China and from the United States. In general, the c.i.f. price for iron ore and coal from the United States has been higher, while that for soybeans has been lower.[20] However, Japanese consumers—like those in Hong Kong—have a strong taste preference for Chinese soybeans, so they are willing to pay a premium price for these. The price differential for ore and coal apparently is more than canceled out by the significantly higher quality of the American product. On the basis of a comparable iron and caloric content, iron ore and coal imports from the United States seem to be cheaper than those from the mainland.

Moreover, the Japanese iron and steel industry has become conditioned to the use of high-grade iron ore and coal. On the other hand, it wishes to develop the Chinese market and recognizes that it cannot do so unless Japan steps up purchases of mainland products. Against this background, the Chinese, after considerable delay and reluctance, have agreed in principle to accept Japanese technical assistance in the mining of iron ore, although the detailed arrangements still must be worked out. If this technical assistance is coupled with deliveries of mining equipment, both the productivity of China's iron mining industry and the quality of the iron ore could be raised considerably. Such improvements could, depending on the degree of success attained, remove one initial bottleneck to the further development of Sino-Japanese trade.

This trade, of course, could be developed even without a substantial expansion of Chinese exports if the Japanese extended medium- and long-term credits to China. Short-term commercial credits, in part guaranteed by the Japanese Export-Import Bank, were extended in 1963 and 1964. Furthermore, the synthetic-textile plant sales of 1963 and 1965, which were noted above, provided for a 25 per cent down payment on the sales values of $20 million and $26.5 million respectively, payment of the remainder over a five-year period from the time of shipment, and a 6 per cent rate of interest. Additional plant deals and medium-term credits have been held in abeyance because of the fear that they would have repercussions on Japan's relations with Taiwan. Therefore, political constraints have thus far placed severe limits on credit amounts and terms.

Yet the internal pressures in Japan are such that this barrier is likely to be broken sooner or later. In this connection, it is noteworthy that in the fall of 1964 Japan sold a urea plant to the Soviet Union on eight-year credit terms and that the United Kingdom sold another plant to the Russians on 15-year terms. Both these deals represent a departure from the prevailing practice of limiting the terms of credit to Communist countries to five years. Since the precedent has now been set, pressure from China and from Japanese commercial interests for the liberalization of credit may be expected to mount.

For all these reasons combined, a trebling in Japan's exports to and imports from China between 1964 and 1970 seems quite possible but perhaps not too probable. It is readily apparent that business enterprises in Japan, Hong Kong, and Western Europe are competing keenly for the China market. Products which Japan can furnish, China can also obtain elsewhere. Therefore, unless the Japanese can consistently underbid their competitors or unless both the Chinese and the Japanese decide to subordinate economic to political considerations, the possibilities for expansion will be limited. This evaluation naturally does not mean that trade is unlikely to increase substantially beyond current levels. Unless some major holocaust occurs, the Japanese economy may be expected to continue growing at a rapid rate through the 1960s. With this growth, one can anticipate expansion in the country's foreign trade. Unless new political and institutional barriers are erected, this general expansion in foreign trade should provide a favorable setting, on the Japanese side, for an increase in trade with China. Economic prospects on the mainland, however, are much more uncertain and much less clear. Therefore, the extent of China's economic recovery and progress during this decade will largely condition and limit the growth of trade between China and Japan.

SOUTH AND SOUTHEAST ASIA. South and Southeast Asia is another trading area with which China has maintained a sizable and consistent surplus of exports. She has thereby provided herself with an additional source of foreign exchange. The region's role in this respect is much less important than that of Hong Kong but more significant than that of Japan.

Despite its importance as a source of foreign exchange, South and Southeast Asia has played a modest role in China's total trade. As Table 6–6 shows, about 8–10 per cent of mainland exports went to this region, and an even smaller portion of her imports came from there. On the other hand, the area has been less dependent on trade with China than China has been on trade with it. Only about 1–3 per cent of the region's imports or exports came from or flowed to China. Even if we exclude India, Ceylon, and Pakistan and look at the situation in Southeast Asia alone, trade with China does not appear much more significant. There is no doubt that China's share in South and Southeast Asia's trade would be higher if we discounted intraregional trade in figuring total trade for the region, but our results would not be substantially different.

China has for the most part been importing raw materials from South and Southeast Asia and exporting foodstuffs and industrial products. The mainland has obtained almost all its rubber from this region—specifically, from Indonesia, Ceylon, and, to a much lesser extent, Malaya. In the early fifties and in some other years as well, she bought raw cotton and raw jute from Pakistan, copra from Indonesia, and rice from Burma. China paid for these primarily with cotton textiles, which make up a

TABLE 6-6. Communist China's Trade with South and
Southeast Asia, 1957–63 [a]

I. SOUTH AND SOUTHEAST ASIA

Year	Trade with China			As Share of Total South and Southeast Asian Trade		As Share of Total Chinese Trade	
	Exports	Imports	Balance	Exports	Imports	Exports	Imports
	(in millions of U.S. dollars)			(in per cent)		(in per cent)	
1957	122.5	126.1	− 3.6	2.1	1.8	7.8	8.8
1958	122.0	175.7	−53.3	2.2	2.9	9.2	6.5
1959	129.5	173.5	−44.0	2.2	2.8	7.8	6.4
1960	124.9	179.1	−54.2	2.0	2.5	8.9	6.5
1961	106.7	135.2	−28.5	1.8	1.8	8.6	7.5
1962	87.6	160.4	−72.8	1.5	2.1	10.0	7.7
1963	60.9	155.4	−94.5	n.a.	n.a.	9.1	4.8

II. SOUTHEAST ASIA

Year	Trade with China			As Share of Total Southeast Asian Trade		As Share of Total Chinese Trade	
	Exports	Imports	Balance	Exports	Imports	Exports	Imports
	(in millions of U.S. dollars)			(in per cent)		(in per cent)	
1957	64.0	90.7	−26.7	1.7	2.3	5.6	4.6
1958	87.5	122.5	−35.0	2.3	3.7	6.4	4.7
1959	94.7	129.0	−34.3	2.5	3.8	5.8	4.7
1960	73.0	142.8	−69.8	1.8	3.8	7.1	3.8
1961	78.9	121.5	−42.6	2.3	3.0	7.7	5.6
1962	57.6	146.0	−88.4	1.5	3.4	9.1	5.1
1963	26.9	122.3	−95.4	n.a.	n.a.	7.2	2.1

[a] Exclusive of Hong Kong.

Note: n.a. stands for "not available."

Sources: United Nations, *Yearbook of International Trade Statistics* for 1961 and 1962;
U.S. Mutual Defense Assistance Control Act Administrator, *Report to Congress*
for various years; Tables 4–1 and B–1 of the present volume.

major share of her exports to all the Southeast Asian countries, and in recent years with textile machinery and even some complete plants. (The latter went to Cambodia, Ceylon, and Indonesia.) In addition, exports of cement to Malaya and Singapore and Ceylon, paper and paper products to Burma, and transport equipment to Ceylon recently have gained some importance. Although industrial products occupied the leading place in China's exports to the region, rice shipments also played a significant role in most years. For example, trade with Ceylon between 1953 and 1960 was based on a barter of rice for rubber. After 1960 it was broadened to include other Chinese export products as well. China has also shipped rice to Malaya and Singapore and Indonesia in most years. In her trade with Malaya and Singapore, moreover, livestock products, oilseeds, vegetable oils, and other foods have been of considerable importance.[21]

The region, then, is economically important to China mainly as a supplier of industrial raw materials and as a source of foreign exchange. Moreover, its economic dependence on China is not great, although the Chinese market is important for individual commodities of some countries, such as Ceylonese rubber. For example, out of total rubber exports which averaged about 100,000 tons a year in the first half of the 1960s, Ceylon shipped an average of 31,000 tons a year to Communist China.[22]

A number of indications point to Chinese efforts to render at least some countries economically dependent on her. Foreign aid provides the clearest evidence. In this field, the Chinese devoted special attention to Southeast Asia. Through 1964, the Chinese had committed about $800 million in loans and grants to non-Communist countries, and close to half of this total was designated for countries in South and Southeast Asia: $84 million to Burma, $107 million to Indonesia, $50 million to Cambodia, $41 million to Ceylon, $43 million to Nepal, $60 million to Pakistan, and $4 million to Laos. Up to 1964, however, Cambodia had used only $35 million; Ceylon, $11 million; Indonesia, $27 million; Nepal, $6 million; and Burma, less than $5 million. The Pakistani loan was extended in late 1964, so drawing upon it could not begin until 1965. If we assume that outlays for 1964 loans to Ceylon and Indonesia also did not begin until 1965, then China's actual expenditures for the region as a whole through 1964 were only about one-fifth of her commitments.

Up to 1965, however, China had not been the largest or principal donor for any of the seven countries. Chinese aid was of most importance in Cambodia, yet even there it never amounted to more than about 20 per cent of the total.[23] But with the cessation of U.S. aid to Burma, Cambodia, and Indonesia, the situation is rapidly changing. Chinese aid may in the future play a major role in these countries.

One can only speculate about Chinese motives in this foreign aid program and in other efforts to penetrate Southeast Asia. There is no doubt that the region is rich in resources and thus represents a valuable prize. In 1955–63, it annually exported, on the average, about 1.7 million tons of rubber, 3.5 million tons of rice, 110 thousand tons of tin, and 20 million tons of crude oil and oil products.[24] Therefore, the integration of this region with the mainland economy would certainly solve China's acute fuels problem and could fully emancipate her from dependence on the Soviet Union for raw materials or on the West for grain.

It is far from obvious, however, that the best method of achieving such economic integration is territorial conquest. For the most part, China can now obtain the food and raw materials she needs through the normal processes of international trade. Furthermore, the incorporation of Southeast Asia into China would not necessarily give her readier access to these products. Outright confiscation or compulsory purchase at low prices would have counterincentive effects and, as the Chinese Communists' experience with their own peasantry has amply demonstrated, would almost certainly lead to declines in production. If the government wanted to assure the maintenance or expansion of food and raw materials output in the area, it would have to extend favorable price terms to the growers and to channel investment resources into the conquered region. Under such circumstances, the costs of raw materials might considerably exceed those at which the same products could be purchased through international trade channels. For these reasons, if for no other, it is highly doubtful that Communist China's policy vis-à-vis Southeast Asia stems primarily from economic considerations such as a quest for food and raw materials. In the case of Pakistan in particular, the political motivation for the 1964 loan of $60 million is relatively clear. It seems to be designed to widen the wedge between Pakistan and India on the one hand and Pakistan and the United States on the other.

NON-COMMUNIST EUROPE. Mainland China's trade with non-Communist Europe * increased more or less continuously after the Korean armistice and up to the onset of the agricultural crisis in the early 1960s. China's imports were highest in 1958, while her exports did not attain their peak until 1960. The process of trade expansion apparently gained momentum after 1955 as more and more European countries relaxed their controls on commerce with China.

Export and import trends. In general, imports from Europe grew much faster and declined more rapidly than exports to the area. Imports more than quadrupled between 1953 and 1958 but dropped to less than one-third of their peak level by 1962. It is apparent, therefore, that China's imports from Europe were closely correlated with levels of economic activity at home.

Periods of rapid economic expansion such as the Great Leap led to a marked rise in the demand for European imports. In 1958, for example, about one-quarter of China's purchases from abroad were obtained from there. As a result, China at that time imported more from non-Communist Europe than from Eastern Europe (excluding the Soviet Union). In effect, reorientation of her trade away from the Soviet Union and Eastern Europe and toward non-Communist Europe started on the import side before the acute deterioration in Sino-Soviet relations. This development was probably due to the fact that as China's demand for imports grew under the impact of the Great Leap, purchases from the

* In the following discussion, "non-Communist Europe" refers to the Scandinavian countries, the Common Market countries, Austria, Greece, Ireland, Portugal, Spain, Switzerland, Turkey, the United Kingdom, and Yugoslavia (see Appendix B).

Soviet Union had to be curbed so that export surpluses to be used for loan repayments could be accumulated.

The different trends in imports and exports naturally affected the balance of trade with Europe. At the beginning and the end of the period from 1952 to 1963, China maintained small trade surpluses (see Table 6–7).[25] These were years when the level of economic activity on the mainland was low. Between 1956 and 1960 and particularly during the three years of the Great Leap, however, China had sizable trade deficits.

It is apparent from the data in Table 6–7 that Europe played a larger role in China's exports and imports than vice versa. In all the years examined, China's share in European imports from overseas was 1 per cent or less, but Europe's share in Chinese imports (except for 1952) was more than 7 per cent and in some years as high as 20–25 per cent. Moreover, in the 1960s, it has been above 12 per cent. On the export side, at no time did more than 3 per cent of Europe's overseas sales go to China, while (except for 1952) 8–13 per cent of mainland deliveries went to Europe. Thus, Europe's dependence on China as a market or as a source of raw materials has been almost negligible, but Europe's place in China's foreign trade has been significant.

China's leading trading partners in non-Communist Europe have been West Germany and the United Kingdom. As markets for mainland products, these two countries outdistanced all others by a wide margin. The same is not true with respect to exports to China. Here Switzerland was of considerable importance until 1956–57, but then its position declined. France and Italy, on the other hand, gained in relative importance during the 1960s. As a matter of fact, in 1962–63 France assumed first place among European exporters to China and thus edged out Germany and the United Kingdom. In addition to these countries, The Netherlands has been of some importance—occupying third to fifth place—as an importer from the mainland, while Belgium-Luxembourg has played a similar role as an exporter.

Most of Europe's imports from China have been processed and unprocessed foodstuffs and raw materials of agricultural origin. These two categories together amounted to about 70–80 per cent of the continent's purchases during the 1950s. The single

TABLE 6-7. Non-Communist Europe's Trade with Communist China, 1952–63

Year	Europe's Trade with China (in millions of U.S. dollars)			As Share of Total European Trade (in per cent)		As Share of European Overseas Trade (in per cent)		As Share of Total Chinese Trade (in per cent)	
	Exports	Imports	Balance	Exports	Imports	Exports	Imports	Exports	Imports
1952	50.6	54.3	− 3.7	0.18	0.18	0.38	0.35	6.2	5.7
1953	100.8	121.3	− 20.5	0.36	0.41	0.75	0.79	11.7	9.1
1954	89.5	94.3	− 4.8	0.30	0.29	0.62	0.56	8.4	7.1
1955	111.2	124.5	+ 13.3	0.33	0.34	0.71	0.67	9.3	8.4
1956	194.5	155.7	+ 38.8	0.52	0.38	1.13	0.74	9.7	13.3
1957	236.3	141.0	+ 95.3	0.57	0.31	1.24	0.65	8.7	17.0
1958	465.3	178.1	+287.2	1.12	0.42	2.54	0.94	9.3	25.0
1959	413.6	216.7	+196.9	0.92	0.48	2.02	1.04	9.8	20.6
1960	378.3	248.4 [a]	+129.9	0.74	0.47	1.71	1.03	12.4	19.8
1961	177.9	196.6 [a]	− 18.7	0.32	0.34	0.81	0.81	12.5	12.6
1962	148.7	175.5 [a]	− 26.8	0.26	0.29	0.68	0.69	11.0	13.1
1963	172.5	181.0	− 8.5	0.27	0.27	0.75	0.66	10.7	13.6

[a] Includes sales of silver.

Sources: U.S. Mutual Defense Assistance Control Act Administrator, Report to Congress for various years; United Nations, Yearbook of International Trade Statistics for 1961 and 1963; Table 4-1 in the present volume.

most important item was eggs and egg products. This constituted nearly 15 per cent of total imports between 1955 and 1958. Soybeans, oilseeds, and meats followed in that order. Of the raw materials, which amounted to about one-third of the imports, cashmere, hog bristles, and feathers were of greatest importance.

In the early sixties, deliveries of foodstuffs, soybeans, and oilseeds from China to Europe declined markedly in both absolute and relative terms. Shipments of raw materials such as silk, wool, animal hair, etc., also fell but not so greatly. As a consequence, the importance of this group of commodities rose. The same thing happened to tin and some other nonferrous metals. Most significantly, China's exports to Europe during the period of crisis were held up by sizable sales of silver in 1960, 1961, and 1962.

While it is unclear whether all these silver sales were for monetary purposes, there is no doubt that the bulk of them were. Silver shipments, for example, appeared in the trade statistics only in 1960, 1961, and 1962, *i.e.*, the years when China had an acute balance-of-payments problem (engendered largely by her large-scale grain imports from Canada and Australia). In addition, there is abundant direct evidence of China's silver sales in the London market.[26]

During the three-year period, it seems that European imports of silver from China (in thousands of U.S. dollars) were:

	1960	1961	1962
United Kingdom	6,887	43,444	27,600
West Germany	1,623	6,577	10,100
France	5,625	911	2,800
Italy	—	2,149	2,700
Netherlands	—	—	2,500
Switzerland	—	453	1,400
Total	14,135	53,534	47,100

These totals, however, may not be fully representative, for there may have been some smaller sales to other European countries which were not reported. Nevertheless, it is unlikely that these would change the results substantially.

On the basis of these figures, then, it would seem that silver sales constituted about 6 per cent of Communist China's exports to Europe in 1960 but about 27 per cent in 1961 and 1962—indeed a substantial share of exports. Such evidence reinforces the conclusion that China financed its balance-of-payments deficits during this period in part by selling silver in Europe.

While for the most part Europe imports agricultural products from China, its leading exports to the mainland comprise chemical fertilizer, other chemicals, iron and steel products, machinery and transport equipment, and some textile products. For most of China's major European trading partners, fertilizers have been the most important export since the mid-fifties. Metal and metal products and capital goods were significant up to the sixties, but their importance then declined considerably because of the curtailment in China's investment demand. They were replaced by shipments of wheat, wheat flour, and barley from France and West Germany.

Recent developments and prospects. The year 1963, in retrospect, may mark a major turning point in Sino-European trade relations. It was characterized by a change in atmosphere which seemed to portend future trade expansion and by modest increases in exports and imports. The change in atmosphere was most clearly demonstrated by the visit in the spring of Lu Hsu-chang, the Vice-Minister for Foreign Trade, to the United Kingdom, Switzerland, and The Netherlands. Visits to Peking by unofficial trade delegations from several European countries and to Europe by representatives of Chinese trading corporations followed.

The pace was accelerated in 1964 with the French recognition of the People's Republic of China and the staging of several fairs and exhibitions in Peking. The British had three trade fairs there: an exhibition of scientific instruments in April, an exhibition of mining and construction equipment in June, and a large industrial fair in November. The French put on a similar exhibit in September, and the Swedes were planning one for 1965. In addition, some individual firms arranged exhibits in 1963 and 1964. A great deal of time and effort went into the organization of these fairs. For example, the British industrial exhibition in

November 1964 had the official backing of the British government, and the list of about 350 firms which participated reads like a who's who of British industry.[27]

These fairs, of course, provide an avenue for trade information, open up trade contacts, and spread technical knowledge. For instance, they save the Chinese the effort and expense of sending shopping delegations abroad and enable them to prepare and/or conclude trade deals on their home ground. Moreover, such fairs enable the Chinese to expose a vast number of engineers, technicians, and students in scientific and technical fields to advanced technology in a highly concentrated form. In this connection, it is interesting to note that the Chinese do not open these exhibitions to the general public but do see that a large number of specialists attend. An incidental benefit of the fairs is that the Chinese can usually obtain machinery, equipment, and scientific instruments at rockbottom prices when the exhibitions end, for the manufacturers are reluctant to incur the heavy costs of shipping them back home.

As a result of the deterioration in Sino-Soviet relations, economic recovery on the mainland, and the "atmospheric" changes just described, China's exports to and imports from Europe rose somewhat in 1963. Present indications point to a further increase in 1964. In light of the sharp reorientation in China's foreign trade, however, it is somewhat surprising that trade with Europe has not been recovering faster. The explanation for this situation lies primarily in (a) the slowness of China's general economic recovery up to 1962–63 (although the speed seems to have picked up in 1963–64), (b) the continuing requirement for grain imports from Australia and Canada (which constitute a major drain on foreign-exchange resources), and (c) the obligation to repay Soviet loans (which compels China to maintain a high level of exports to Russia). This last element will have disappeared by the end of 1965 when, as was noted in Chapter 4, the Soviet loans are expected to be fully amortized. Another factor has some bearing on the situation, though. So far, the reorientation in China's trade has led to more rapid recovery in commercial interchange with Japan than with non-Communist Europe. In other words, Japan and Europe are beginning to find themselves in competition for China's trade in general just as Australia and Canada are competing for its grain trade in particular.

Perhaps more important than the modest recovery in the volume of Sino-European trade is the change in its form. This change was dramatized by the sale of eight complete plants to China in 1963 and 1964.[28] Their total sales value is estimated at around $70 million, and they were to be delivered over a period of two or more years beginning in 1964 in some cases and in 1965 in others. China's purchases of these "turnkey" projects evoked a great deal of attention—partly because they were the first of the kind from non-Communist Europe and thus provide another clear indication of China's shift away from the Soviet bloc.

Another significant feature of these contracts is that they represent a means of extending credits and technical assistance. The contracts provide for down payments varying from 10–25 per cent, five-year credits for the balance, and interest rates of 5–6 per cent. In effect, then, the Chinese are obtaining medium-term credits of about $90 million from the non-Communist world (including the credit for the two complete plants obtained from Japan). If this rate of plant sales were to continue in future years, the annual credits would amount to about $40 million. The 1950 Soviet loan to China, in comparison, called for credits of $60 million annually.

China's imports of complete plants were largest in 1959 when their total value reached $600–650 million. All the deliveries came from the Soviet Union and Eastern Europe, and they accounted for about 40 per cent of these countries' total exports to China in that year.[29] By comparison, the recent contracts for complete plants from Europe seem small, both in absolute terms and in relation to total European sales to China. If one prorates these plant deliveries over three years and assumes that total imports from non-Communist Europe will remain constant at 1963 levels, the complete plant shipments would constitute only about 10 per cent of Chinese imports from Europe.

Such comparisons, however, are grossly misleading, for the circumstances under which complete plants were imported in 1958–60 are vastly different from those prevailing at present. China was then engaged in an extremely ambitious effort at rapid industrialization on a broad front. As we have seen, this effort was in part responsible for the collapse of the Great Leap and the economic crisis which followed. Complete plants were then part and parcel of a comprehensive investment program focused mainly on the development of producer goods industries. In contrast, the investment program of the 1960s is taking place during a period of economic recovery from a depression and is focused on selective development of certain industrial sectors.

This new phase of recovery and development seems to be characterized by rather different planning and investment priorities from those that prevailed during the Great Leap. It places major emphasis on the further expansion and development of (a) agriculture, (b) industries which can provide the necessary inputs for agricultural development (such as chemical fertilizer and insecticides), (c) oil extraction, oil refining, and petroleum by-products (to emancipate China from dependence on foreign oil), (d) the manufacture of synthetic fibers (to reduce the textile industry's dependence on the vagaries of the cotton harvest), (e) export industries such as mining, food processing, and textiles (all of which are also needed to serve the domestic market), and (f) water and overland transport (necessary for and complementary to the expansion of all sectors already mentioned).

These priorities and considerations appear to be reflected in Communist China's trade policy as it crystallized in 1963–64. For example, of the eight complete plants ordered from Europe, three were for the manufacture of fertilizer, two for the production of other chemicals, two for petroleum refining, and one for the manufacture of alcohol. The plants ordered from Japan, as we noted earlier, were for the manufacture of synthetic fibers.

In the 1960s, moreover, the Chinese Communists have assiduously attempted to raise their textile exports in order to increase the weight of manufactured products in their deliveries abroad. Their efforts, however, have been seriously constrained by shortages of domestically-produced cotton. Therefore, it might make good economic sense for them to import textile fibers—either natural or synthetic—and export semimanufactured and finished textile products. The extent to which they can and should do so will depend on the relative prices of the imported raw materials and the exported manufactures.

In light of prevailing circumstances, one might reasonably expect the Chinese to step up their imports from Europe and Japan of fertilizer; synthetic fibers; oil-refining, mining, and food-processing equipment; and certain types of textile machinery and transport equipment as well as complete plants for the manufacture of all these. The total value of the import demand will depend not only upon the course and pace of China's domestic development but on the evolution of Sino-Soviet relations. As far as complete plants are concerned, there may be a further limitation —Chinese reluctance to admit technicians in large numbers. In the case of the complete plants already ordered from The Netherlands, Italy, and Britain, for instance, it is not yet clear whether, when, how many, and under what terms plant technicians will be sent to China to help install the plants and operate them in their initial phases.

What levels of trade between China and Europe might one reasonably expect then? In trying to answer this question, one must keep in mind a number of points. In 1955, Europe's share in the exports of the non-Communist world to China was a little more than one-third. It then rose rapidly until it reached almost two-thirds by 1958–59. To understand this rapid growth, one must look more closely at the structure of mainland China's trade at that time. Between 1955 and 1959, China's total imports rose more than 50 per cent. At the same time, the share of the non-Communist world in these import totals also increased as more and more countries relaxed their controls on trade with China. The bulk of these increases, however, was concentrated in Europe and, until mid-1958, in Japan. China's imports from South and Southeast Asia grew much more slowly. These were largely raw materials, the demand for which was relatively inelastic. During 1958, Japan dropped out of the picture almost completely because of the nearly total embargo the Chinese Communists imposed on imports from Japan. Therefore, through 1960 Europe had an almost clear field for expanding its exports to China.

This state of affairs changed dramatically in 1961, when Europe's sales to the mainland fell by more than half despite an increase in total exports from the non-Communist world to China. The principal factor in the precipitous decline was China's acute need for grain, which she began to import from Australia and Canada. These imports forced her to divert to these Commonwealth countries resources of foreign exchange that might otherwise have been used for purchases in Europe. In a sense, Japan's return as a vigorous competitor for the China market in 1962 further aggravated the situation.

Against this background, what are the short- and intermediate-term outlooks? One possible way of approaching this problem is to use the assumptions spelled out on page 209 as a point of departure for a hypothetical projection. According to this projection, China's imports might increase from a low of $1.1 billion in 1962 to about $2.2 billion in 1970—that is, a level roughly equivalent to the 1959 peak values. The Communist world's share of these totals is particularly difficult to project, for there are so many imponderables involved. Different countries, for example, might pursue different policies vis-à-vis China. One can, perhaps, make two alternative assumptions: (a) that the import share of the Communist countries would be about one-half of the total, *i.e.*, roughly the same as the 1962–63 ratio, or (b) that it would decline to about 20 per cent of the total. Under the first assumption, in 1970 China's imports from the non-Communist world would be $1.1 billion, and under the second, $1.76 billion.

Adopting a fairly optimistic view, we might project $1.5 billion as the value of exports from the non-Communist world to China in 1970, a considerably higher level than any attained up to 1965. China's demand for imports from South and Southeast Asia, Africa, and Latin America will be governed largely by her requirements of raw materials for domestic growth. During the First Five Year Plan and the Great Leap periods, China's raw materials imports rose about half as fast as GNP. If we assume that GNP will grow at an average annual rate of 4–5 per cent and that the earlier relationship between GNP and imports of raw materials will prevail during the projected period of growth, we can hypothesize that between 1962 and 1970 China's import demand for raw materials will increase by about 20 per cent. In these terms, the exports of Africa, Latin America, and South and Southeast Asia to China would be around $200 million. If we also assume that by 1970 agricultural production per capita will surpass the 1957 level and that there be no further need for grain imports, China might then wish to buy about $1,300 million worth of other commodities from the rest of the non-Communist world. Under such circumstances, it should be possible for Europe's exports to China to exceed their previous peak level (nearly $500 million in 1958) by 1970. How fast the gap between the 1963 level of about $170 million and the 1958 peak level can in fact be closed will depend largely on when China's requirements for grain imports are curtailed, on how effectively Europe can compete with Japan, and on the fate of Sino-Soviet relations.

CANADA AND AUSTRALIA. China's trade with both Australia and Canada was of almost negligible proportions until the mid-fifties (see Appendix B). Even then, it was only of minor importance. These two countries, however, became major exporters to China in 1961. Since that time, about 20–25 per cent of mainland imports have been obtained from these two sources. In 1963, China's purchases from the two Commonwealth countries exceeded her imports from the Soviet Union and were well above those from Eastern Europe. They were also greater than mainland imports from Asia and Europe. The explanation of this dramatic change lies, of course, in China's agricultural crisis and in the demand for imported grain which that crisis produced.

Apparently, it was only in late 1960 or early 1961 that the Chinese Communist leadership faced up to the full dimensions of the agricultural crisis. It finally decided to commit itself to a grain-import policy, at least for several years. Thereafter the Chinese signed three-year contracts for large-scale shipments of grain from Canada and Australia and made additional purchases from Argentina, France, and other scattered sources.

As Table 6–8 shows, grain imports were highest during the

TABLE 6-8. Grain Exports to Communist China,
1960/61–1963/64 [a]

(in thousands of metric tons)

	1960/61	1961/62	1962/63	1963/64
Wheat				
Canada	780.8	1,967.7	1,677.7	1,004.8
Australia	1,113.0	1,953.0	2,058.6	2,543.1
Argentina	—	88.2	97.9	988.0
France	—	177.6	994.0	187.2
Mexico	—	—	—	450.0
Total	1,893.8	4,126.5	4,828.2	5,173.1
Wheat Flour [b]				
Australia	62.1	—	—	—
West Germany	10.3	387.2	119.8	—
France	—	81.8	—	34.6
Hong Kong	0.2	—	—	—
Japan	—	0.1	—	—
Total	72.6	469.1	119.8	34.6
Barley				
Argentina	—	—	—	31.1
Canada	359.1	504.0	23.6	271.8
Australia	208.7	137.4	—	18.7
France	26.8	287.6	—	127.6
Iraq	—	—	9.9	—
Syria	—	—	13.7	—
Total	594.6	929.0	47.2	449.2
Oats				
Argentina	—	—	—	27.5
Australia	65.3	47.4	26.9	100.1
Total	65.3	47.4	26.9	127.6
Maize				
Argentina	29.5	212.3	169.7	198.6
Cambodia	—	12.0	36.0	—
Federation of Rhodesia and Nyasaland	—	—	53.5	—
France	—	—	—	0.7
South Africa	—	—	153.3	—
Total	29.5	224.3	412.5	199.3
All Grains [c]				
Canada	1,139.9	2,471.7	1,701.3	1,276.6
Australia	1,449.1	2,137.8	2,085.5	2,661.9
Argentina	29.5	300.5	291.1	1,259.5
France	26.8	487.0	994.0	350.1
West Germany	10.3	387.2	119.8	—
Other	0.2	12.1	266.4	450.0
Total	2,655.8	5,796.3	5,458.1	5,998.1

[a] The data in this table are for years running from July to June.

[b] Wheat equivalent.

[c] Including sorghum and millets in 1962/63 and 1963/64.

Note: — stands for "none".

Sources: Food and Agriculture Organization of the United Nations, *World Grain Trade Statistics* for 1960/61, 1961/62, 1962/63, and 1963/64.

1961/62 and 1963/64 consumption years. Actually, the data for 1960/61 are not comparable with those for later years, for grain shipments only started in 1961. In other words, figures for 1960/61 refer only to half a year, while the later statistics refer to deliveries during a 12-month period. It is most interesting to note that grain imports were increased in 1963/64 at a time of apparent agricultural recovery on the mainland. This can be viewed as another indication that the Chinese Communist authorities were committed to maintaining food consumption levels both in urban and rural areas.

With the low levels of farm output in the early sixties, grain imports may have constituted about 3 per cent of total available supplies in 1961/62 and 1962/63. However, they were much more important in relation to the grain collected for non-farm consumption. In these terms, they contributed an estimated 30–40 per cent of total supplies.[30]

As a result of these grain purchases, China became an important customer of both Australia and Canada. She took about 7 and 2 per cent respectively of their total exports in 1961 and 4 and 2 per cent in 1962. It was in their grain trade, however, that she was really of significance. In 1961/62 and 1962/63 she absorbed about one-fifth of Canada's total exports of wheat and one-third to one-half of Australia's.

China thus emerged as Australia's fourth or fifth best customer. Only the United Kingdom, Japan, the United States, and in some years New Zealand outranked her. Moreover, she began to import increasing quantities of wool from Australia; in 1962–63 she was taking about 3 per cent of that country's huge wool production.[31] In this connection, it is interesting to note that Australia has been extending technical assistance to help modernize the spinning of wool and the manufacture of woolen textiles in China. The Australians are apparently quite eager to assist in the expansion of this industry in order to raise the demand for wool.[32]

Mainland China's large-scale purchases of grain naturally have affected trends in the world grain market. Mainland imports of wheat absorbed about 12 per cent of total world shipments in the three years from 1961/62 to 1963/64. The market and grain transport situation tightened greatly when the Soviets began large-scale purchases of grain in 1963. The complete change in the market outlook for grain did encourage acreage expansion in several countries, notably Canada.[33] Nevertheless, it also complicated China's task of procurement. Because of the heavy world demand in the last half of 1963, Canada and Australia were unable to supply all the grain China requested for delivery in 1964. Therefore, she had to seek grain from smaller suppliers.[34] The same circumstances placed a great pressure on shipping. According to some estimates, the Chinese may have had to pay $2–3 more a ton for shipping wheat in 1963/64 than they did in the preceding year.[35]

How long will China continue to be a major factor in the world grain market and thus a leading customer of Canada and Australia? All present indications certainly point to China's intentions to continue grain purchases. It is most improbable that these purchases will be continued once the agricultural product per capita recovers to 1957 levels. However, unless the current rate of agricultural progress is dramatically accelerated, such a recovery in per capita levels may be expected to take a number of years.

From the point of view of the Chinese Communists, there are strong incentives for curtailing grain purchases as soon as possible. Because of these purchases, China has had large deficits in her trade with Canada and Australia—about $220 million in 1962 and nearly $300 million in 1963 (see Table B-1). The deficits have been covered partly by sterling earned in trade with Hong Kong and Southeast Asia and partly by short-term loans. The Canadian grain contract of 1961 provided for a down payment of 25 per cent on shipment and payment of the balance within nine months. The new agreement signed in 1963 specifies the same down payment but extends an 18-month credit for the rest.[36] The Australians demand only 10 per cent in down payment and provide a 12-month credit for the balance.[37]

Whatever the terms of payment, there is no question that grain imports represent a major drain on foreign exchange. They thus curtail imports of complete plants, capital goods, and production requisites for agriculture (*e.g.,* fertilizer). They even slow down the development of agriculture—directly, by reducing the availability of production requisites, and indirectly, by competing with "agriculture-supporting" industries for resources of foreign exchange.

SUB-SAHARAN AFRICA. China's trade with the underdeveloped world and most particularly with sub-Saharan Africa is of relatively recent origin, is small, and is rapidly changing, almost from year to year and month to month. Therefore, generalizations are difficult to make and are in danger of becoming rapidly obsolete. Moreover, Africa is one case where it is difficult to disentangle ideological, diplomatic, and economic motivations in Communist China's policy.[38] There is no question that the different types of activities mutually reinforce each other. Perhaps one may be safe in hypothesizing, however, that Communist China's entrance onto the African stage was motivated largely by political considerations. In the 1960s, these must have been reinforced by intense Sino-Soviet rivalry for the soul, goodwill, and support of Africa. The Soviets, for example, stepped up their aid activity in Africa. Through 1962, China extended aid totaling $65 million to three African countries (see Table E-2), while the Soviet Union and Eastern Europe committed about $400 million to six countries. The latter was extended at about the same time and was to be used over roughly the same period as Chinese aid.[39] However, the Chinese countered in 1963–64 by placing another $22 million at the disposal of countries which had already received assistance from them and by adding almost $120 million to five new recipients.

Communist China had little contact with sub-Saharan Africa prior to 1957. As more of the former colonies became independent, however, the Chinese became active both diplomatically and commercially, gradually entered into trade agreements with these new countries, and extended economic aid to them. Despite this activity, trade has thus far been of quite modest proportions. African purchases from the Chinese increased from about $7 million in 1957 to more than $20 million in 1962–63 (see Table B–1), while sales rose from about $7 million in 1957 to $41 million in 1963. The fluctuation on the export side was due chiefly to large shipments from South Africa in 1959 and 1960. If it is excluded, then the region's sales to China expanded from $4 million in 1959 to $35 million in 1963. Imports are not affected, for South Africa did not purchase much from China.

It is interesting to note that China's trade with this area (excluding South Africa) continued to grow even after total mainland trade began to shrink under the impact of the agricultural crisis. As a result, sub-Saharan Africa's share in China's exports rose from less than 0.5 per cent to 1.0-1.5 per cent during this period. The import share rose correspondingly, from less than 0.3 to about 3.0 per cent. Even so, the trade was still not of appreciable importance. China's share in Africa's trade also remained quite small—less than 1 per cent.

During 1955–58, mainland trade was primarily with East Africa, Nigeria, French West Africa, and South Africa. By the early 1960s, the situation remained roughly the same, although the number of China's trading partners in both East and West Africa had increased significantly.

In 1959, Guinea was the first country to rebel against De Gaulle's plan for a continued French presence south of the Sahara. China donated 5,000 tons of rice to Guinea at that time. The following year China added another 10,000 tons of rice and concluded an agreement, during Sékou Touré's state visit to Peking in September 1960, to provide Guinea with a loan of about $25 million for economic and technical aid. Since then, Chinese agricultural experts have been sent to Guinea, and nine development projects have been agreed upon, although so far only a cigarette and match factory and experiments with a new tea plantation have been started.[40] Imports and exports, however, have been of modest proportions thus far.

A trade agreement was signed with Mali in February 1961, and in September of that year a loan of $20 million was extended. These financed, among other things, imports of machines to transplant rice.[41] Trade, however, is still quite small.

Formal commercial relations with Ghana were inaugurated with the signing of a trade agreement in August 1961 during Kwame Nkrumah's visit to Peking. At the same time, China granted a $20 million credit to be used for the purchase of arms factories, textile mills, and enamelware and ceramic factories.[42]

In 1962–63, Ghana's imports from China, a major portion of which were cotton fabrics, declined from $3.6 million to $2 million. Ghana's exports, largely confined to cocoa, also fell by about half, from $1.2 to $0.5 million.

Nigeria's trade relations with China have expanded steadily, but they have been confined almost exclusively to imports, mostly cotton textiles.[43] Total imports have fluctuated between $2.7 million and $6.0 million since 1957.

China's economic relations with East Africa have been dominated by cotton. In July 1958, China signed a barter agreement with the Sudan which enabled the Khartoum government to dispose of its cotton surplus. China's imports—mostly of raw cotton—grew from about $1.7 million in 1957 to a peak of $9.6 million in 1962, when a formal trade agreement was signed.[44] At the same time, China's shipments to the Sudan—mostly of cotton textiles—increased from $700 thousand to more than $4 million. China has also been buying cotton from Uganda. These imports rose from $5 million in 1960 to more than $11 million in 1963. In the latter year, the Chinese bought up 70,000 bales, more than one-fifth of Uganda's total cotton crop.[45]

In 1963, the Chinese extended a $20 million loan to Somalia. They coupled with it an outright gift of about $2 million. Thus, by the end of 1963 Communist China had concluded some sort of formal economic agreement with Ghana, Guinea, Mali, Somalia, and the Sudan and had extended economic aid to all of them except the Sudan. The aid involved a commitment of $85 million in interest-free loans, of which only about $6 million had actually been used through 1963 (see Table E–2). Although the credits are to be exhausted sometime between 1963 and 1967, repayment is not to start before 1970. Each debt is to be amortized in 10 equal installments.[46]

It is interesting to note that of the countries receiving aid, only Ghana carried on any appreciable trade with China. China's other leading trading partners in sub-Saharan Africa were the Sudan, Nigeria, Senegal, Uganda, the Federation of Rhodesia and Nyasaland, and South Africa, but she has concluded no formal aid or trade agreements with any of these except the Sudan. This situation may be attributed in part to the fact that the aid was extended relatively recently and not enough time has elapsed for its impact on trade to be felt.

Although political motivations may be strong in China's trade with Africa, there are also perfectly valid economic reasons for the trade. The region is a large importer of cloth and could provide a sizable potential market for mainland China's exports of cotton textiles if she can hold her own in quality and price competition. As time goes on, China might also be in a position to increase her exports of capital goods, although she might find it much more difficult to compete in this field. On the supply side, cotton is perhaps of greatest importance to China. It is unlikely that the mainland would become a major importer of coffee or cocoa, but it could become an importer of rubber. For the time being, though, China can obtain this item more cheaply from sources closer at hand. From time to time, the region also has been quite important as a shipper of grain to China. As the data in Table 6–8 show, China imported maize from South Africa and the Federation of Rhodesia and Nyasaland in 1962/63. Because of South Africa's racial policies, however, one can reasonably expect that the Chinese Communists will cease trading with it as soon as their situation with respect to grain supply becomes less tight.

In any case, China need not aim for a bilateral trade balance with Africa. She may consciously wish to build up an export surplus. Indeed, she has in most years maintained such a surplus. Some trade sources suggest that this surplus, particularly in the case of the former French colonies, has been a matter of policy and has been designed to earn foreign exchange with which to finance an import surplus with France. A greater export surplus in China's trade with Africa would enable China to step up her purchases in France, where she has difficulty finding a market for her exports.

NEAR EAST AND NORTH AFRICA. Communist China's trade relations with the Near East and North Africa were established earlier and are therefore much more extensive than those with sub-Saharan Africa. As a result, both the region's share in Communist China's exports and imports and China's share in its trade have been larger than they have been in the case of Africa. About 1–3 per cent of mainland exports have been destined for the Near East and North Africa, and about 1–4 per cent of her imports have been obtained from there.

Egypt has consistently been China's leading trading partner in the area on both the export and import sides. Through 1960 Egypt's exports substantially exceeded her imports from China. While Egyptian sales to the mainland increased from $24 million to $45 million between 1956 and 1960, its imports rose from $10 million to $24 million in 1958 and then declined to about $18 million in 1960. Since 1960, however, exports and imports have remained more or less balanced at a level of about $15–20 million. Raw cotton comprised the bulk of Egyptian exports to China, and it was the reduction in cotton shipments that accounted for the decline in Egypt's exports to China after 1960. China sold iron and steel semimanufactures, oilseeds and vegetable oils, tea, and tobacco to Egypt.[47]

China also carries on a fair amount of trade with Morocco, Iraq, and Syria, although much less than with Egypt. Morocco concluded its first formal trade agreement with China in 1957 and has consistently imported considerably more from the mainland than it has exported to it. Green tea, Morocco's national drink, has dominated imports, which in the early 1960s ranged between $6 million and $9 million. Exports, on the other hand, fluctuated between $4 million and $7 million; they consisted of phosphates used for fertilizer, cobalt ore, and trucks assembled in Morocco by a French firm.[48] A large chemical complex, financed by French and West German capital, was to begin producing 8 million tons of superphosphates and hyperphosphates in 1965. The Chinese reportedly have indicated an interest in purchasing a sizable portion of the output when it becomes available.[49]

Iraq, like Morocco, has had an unfavorable balance in its trade with China. During 1959–63, its exports ranged from $1.5 million to $4.5 million, and its imports from $3 to $12 million. Trade grew, however, right through the years of mainland depression. China has been a major customer for Iraq's principal export, dates. She purchased one-quarter of the country's total exports of this product in 1962/63. It is interesting that China was prepared to spend several million dollars on this luxury item even in the years when the economy was in the depth of a crisis. Dates are traditionally consumed at Chinese festivals. Apparently the regime considered the maintenance of supplies important for psychological and morale reasons. Mainland China has also purchased some grain from Iraq. For example, she bought about 10,000 tons of barley in 1962/63. Iraq's principal imports from China have been textile products, which have comprised about two-thirds of the country's total purchases.[50]

Syria, in contrast to Morocco and Iraq, consistently maintained an export surplus in her trade with the mainland. Exchanges between the two countries were largely confined to exports of raw cotton to China in return for iron and steel products and textiles.[51]

Communist China's foreign aid to the Near East and North Africa has been somewhat more modest than the $210 million program for sub-Saharan Africa. It has consisted of a small free grant of $5 million to Egypt in 1956 (used up by 1965), an interest-free loan of $13 million to Yemen in 1958, an interest-free loan of $50 million to Algeria and a loan of $16 million to Syria in 1963, and loans of $80 million to Egypt and almost $30 million to Yemen in 1964 (see Table E–2).

The first credit to Yemen went to finance the construction of the country's only modern highway, which linked the inland capital with a new port. At one time more than 800 Chinese laborers and technicians were engaged in this project. The road was officially opened to traffic on January 1, 1962, at which time most of the Chinese left. However, a limited number of technicians stayed to direct road maintenance and train Yemenis to succeed them.[52]

Algeria represents a clear-cut case of Sino-Soviet rivalry. In anticipation of Chou En-lai's African tour in early 1964, the Soviets extended a new $100 million loan to Algeria. The Chinese then countered with a $50 million loan. While the Soviet loan carried an interest rate (however low), the Chinese credits were interest-free and repayable over 20 years starting in 1970.[53] Though the Chinese loan was smaller, its terms were more generous. The Algerian credits are to be used partly for road construction across the Sahara to link Algeria's ports with the landlocked sub-Saharan states of Chad, Mali, Niger, and Upper Volta. The Chinese are to provide technical assistance for this construction work and therefore can apply the experience they gained in Yemen. Some of the loan is also to be used for the development of small-scale industries.[54]

In this region, Soviet economic influence is much more massive than Chinese with respect to both trade and aid. As of December 1963, for example, the Communist countries had extended a total of $1.4 billion in foreign aid to the area, only $85 million of which had come from China.[55] About half the total was Soviet aid to Egypt—in large part for the construction of the Aswan Dam. Even if one disregards Egypt, however, Soviet aid still dwarfs that of the Chinese.

LATIN AMERICA. Communist China's economic contacts with Latin America were quite limited until 1959. The trade turnover was even smaller than it was in the case of sub-Saharan Africa. If one excludes Cuba, the situation did not change markedly until 1962.

Latin American exports to China (excluding those from Cuba) fluctuated widely but did not exceed $9 million until 1962, when they suddenly jumped to $27 million. Practically all these exports came from Argentina and, in earlier years, from Mexico, Uruguay, and Brazil. Argentina exported mostly grain to China. Brazil's shipments were largely confined to raw cotton, and Uruguay's to wool.[56]

Latin American countries bought little from China. Imports, for example, were always below $2 million. As a result, China had an unfavorable balance of trade with this part of the world. This statement is true even if trade with Cuba is taken into account.

China entered into formal economic relations with Cuba in July 1960 by signing a trade and payment agreement and an agreement for scientific and technical cooperation. Under the first, China obligated itself to purchase one million tons of sugar from Cuba. The Cuban government was to buy Chinese exports of an equivalent value, but the kinds of exports were not specified. Under the second, China was to help Cuba in the training of its technical personnel. These agreements were followed later that year by a Chinese loan of 240 million rubles ($60 million), which was to be drawn upon between 1961 and 1965. The loan was to be used to finance exports of complete plants to Cuba and "other technical aid to help Cuba develop its economy," and it was interest-free.[57]

Soviet loans covering the same period totaled $327 million, and those of the East European countries $107 million. In other words, Cuba had at its disposal total annual credits of $98.8 million, of which $12 million came from Communist China and the rest from the Soviet bloc. During 1961 and 1962 the Communist countries provided additional aid to Cuba by buying sugar at prices well above the world market. This subsidy may have amounted to as much as $200 million, but in 1963 the world price rose well above that paid by the Communist countries. In 1964, the U.S.S.R. agreed to buy large quantities of sugar over five years at a price higher than it had paid before but still below the world price of that time. Whether this trade agreement proves to be a source of indirect aid depends on the future course of the world price.[58]

Before 1958, China's trade with Cuba was negligible. It assumed perceptible importance for the first time in 1958 when imports from Cuba rose to almost $4 million. They dropped temporarily in 1959, the year of the revolution, but have been growing rapidly since. By 1962, China's purchases were almost $90 million, and her sales more than $100 million. This exchange was based on imports of sugar, as was noted above, and exports of foodstuffs, soybeans, textiles, machinery, iron and steel products, and chemicals (listed in order of importance).

Communist China's Aid Program

By the end of 1964, China's aid commitments to underdeveloped countries in the non-Communist world amounted to almost $800 million; this figure constituted around 10–15 per cent of total commitments by all Communist countries.[59] On the basis of actual aid expenditures, rather than commitments, China's share would be even less. If one looks at the underdeveloped world as a whole, then, China was not a significant factor in the aid field. This fact is but a reflection of her limited economic and trade capabilities —limited as compared with those of the Soviet Union or the United States.

Much the same situation prevailed in the field of technical assistance. Out of about 10,000 experts and advisers from Communist countries posted around the globe in mid-1962, about 70 per cent were from the Soviet Union, 20 per cent from Eastern Europe, and only 10 per cent from Communist China.[60]

On the other hand, the Chinese aid program was much more concentrated than that of the Soviet Union. It was confined to 19 countries in the non-Communist world, while that of the Soviets covered about 30 countries. In areas where the Chinese were active, therefore, their aid constituted a significantly larger share than 10–15 per cent. However, in practically no case was China the leading donor even so.

As we have noted, in a number of countries economic aid has become an arena for intense rivalry and struggle for influence not only between China and the West but also between China and the Soviet Union. In this competition, the Chinese have tried to make a virtue out of necessity and to convert quantitative weakness into qualitative strength. While their aid has been much smaller than that which the Soviets have extended, it has been based on much more generous terms. A larger share of the aid, for example, has been in the form of outright grants. In addition, many more of the credits have been interest-free, have had longer grace periods before repayment starts, and have had longer periods of repayment. The Chinese have also insisted that their technical assistance personnel live at the same level as their counterparts in the countries receiving aid. In many cases, of course, this policy involves much less of a sacrifice for mainland Chinese than it would for Soviet or U.S. technicians. The Chinese, moreover, have attempted to impress upon receiving countries that their aid, in contrast to Soviet and U.S. aid, is free of strings. In 1964–65, they even issued more or less outright warnings to underdeveloped countries not to accept Russian aid lest they become too dependent on the Soviet Union. Self-reliance, they preached, is the best guarantee of national independence. Another theme they have stressed is that their greater technological backwardness makes their experience, conditions, and path of development more applicable to planning and development in nonindustrialized countries than those of the much more highly industrialized Soviet Union. As a result, they have argued, the kind of technical advice China renders and the types of goods and equipment she delivers can more easily be introduced into the countries concerned even if such advice and equipment are of inferior quality.[61]

At this writing, many of the Chinese aid programs are too recent in origin to permit a real appraisal of their strengths and weaknesses. Appraisal is also complicated by the fact that actual aid outlays have lagged badly behind commitments. In fact, through 1963 only $109 million had been used out of a total of about $800 million extended.

It would seem, nevertheless, that the Chinese foreign aid record is mixed. There have been some notable successes such as the roadbuilding project in Yemen and some failures resulting from delayed deliveries of equipment and materials. At the same time, some of the Chinese propaganda appeals with respect to aid seem to be falling on fertile ground in parts of Africa and Southeast Asia.

Communist China's Economic Relations with Industrialized vs. Underdeveloped Countries

Mainland China's trade with the non-Communist world, as has been indicated, expanded more or less continuously between 1952 and 1958. Exports more than doubled, while imports quadrupled. Not all areas, however, shared equally in this growth. Trade with the industrialized countries expanded much more rapidly than that with the underdeveloped areas. This difference was particularly notable in the case of imports. China's purchases from underdeveloped countries increased by one and a half times, but those from the industrialized parts of the world grew about ten-fold. Consequently, while in 1952 less than 30 per cent of China's imports came from the high-income countries, that share had risen to 75 per cent by 1958.

The clue to these trends must be sought in the character of mainland China's economic development. With the rapid pace of industrial advance in the late fifties, China's demand for iron and steel products, machinery, and chemicals rose rapidly. These were of course the types of products which could be supplied only by the already industrialized countries of the world. From the underdeveloped countries, on the other hand, China imported primarily industrial raw materials such as rubber and textile fibers (mostly raw cotton). However, the elasticity of demand for imported raw materials was rather low in China. That is, the requirements for imports of raw materials lagged behind the rise in national product, but the requirements for imports of machinery, metals, and chemicals kept pace with or even ran ahead of the growth in total output.

The composition of China's exports to underdeveloped and industrialized countries was less divergent. Foodstuffs and other agricultural products were important in both cases, although the demand for these rose somewhat more rapidly in the high-income countries. On the other hand, China's exports of textile fabrics, which have been expanding markedly, found their principal markets in the underdeveloped countries.

As the Chinese economy recovers from the crisis of the early 1960s and then expands, it is reasonable to assume that past trends in export composition will continue. That is, textile exports will continue to rise in importance, and because of the low quality of the fabrics, the principal markets for these will be found in the low-income countries. In that case, the industrialized parts of the world might decline in relative importance as a market for China's exports. However, these areas may be expected to remain the dominant source of mainland imports for some time to come.

In the short run, China may be expected to encounter some difficulties in finding markets for its cotton textiles. Since the country's debts to the Soviet Union will presumably have been paid in full by the end of 1965, exports to Russia are likely to be reduced. As a result, domestic consumption of textiles will probably be stepped up, and/or new markets will have to be found. This situation could lead to sharp competition between China and Japan in Southeast Asia and to greatly increased efforts to raise textile sales to Africa.

The level of China's textile exports will be limited not only by marketing possibilities but by total textile production. The latter in turn will be severely circumscribed by the availability of raw materials. In the face of this difficulty, China has considerably stepped up her imports of raw cotton in the 1960s. Were China to pursue this policy in the future, the way would be open for some barter arrangements with some underdeveloped countries (particularly in Africa), arrangements which would provide for a guaranteed supply of raw materials on the one hand and a market for finished textiles on the other.

From the standpoint of the industrialized countries, China may be expected to be a comparatively small market for some years to come. However, because it could in the future evolve into a major market if and when the Chinese economy is more developed, it presents an ever-present lure—just as it has for at least the last 100 years. Its latent potential is a continuing point of attraction for traders and governments and prompts an inordinate expenditure of effort to break into this market and widen its scope.

CHAPTER SEVEN

Policy Implications

Mainland China's economy, as this study has shown, has undergone rapid growth and considerable structural change since the advent of the Communist regime in 1949. In its early phases, this development was in part based upon rehabilitation of China's war-devastated production plant, but as the result of high rates of investment, this plant was greatly expanded. The momentum engendered by the policies and measures of the new regime carried the economy continuously forward between 1949 and 1960. Development, however, did not proceed at an even pace, either intertemporally or intersectorally. Although the economy expanded year by year, the rate of growth itself was marked by sharp fluctuations, largely because of harvest changes. At the same time, expansion was confined mainly to the industrial, urban, and commercialized sector of the economy, while agriculture more or less stagnated.

In the end, agricultural stagnation and a sudden radicalization of economic policy based on a highly unrealistic assessment of the economy's capabilities produced an acute crisis. Between 1960 and 1961, this crisis led not only to a slowing down in the pace of growth but to a far-reaching decline in absolute terms as well. Thus, the economy of the Chinese mainland entered the throes of a deep depression, from which it has been recovering only quite slowly. As a result, it may take about 10 years for Chinese agriculture to recover to its 1957 level of output per capita, and the peak national product levels of 1958–60 may not be attained until the late sixties. In short, it may turn out that the Great Leap will have cost the Chinese economy roughly a decade of growth.

This setback has undoubtedly reduced China's expansionist power and forced it to pursue a relatively cautious foreign and domestic policy, at least for the time being. However, it did not undermine the basic stability or viability of the Communist regime. There is no doubt that the economic crisis led to some unrest in the spring of 1961, and it also apparently jarred the self-confidence of the regime. But with the gradual economic recovery, the regime seems to have regained its earlier sense of self-assurance and a measure of dynamism. One could even argue that since the regime survived this ordeal, its faith in its indestructibility may have been reinforced. The fact that it could weather a profound agricultural and food crisis—even if that crisis was partially of its own making—and manage to avert a mass famine without any economic aid from the Soviet Union or anyone else must have been viewed by the leadership as a self-vindication. Moreover, the apparent fact that even at the depth of the crisis no organized opposition arose must have been interpreted both by the regime and by the people at large as an element of strength. Thus, there is no evidence to support the wishful, but nevertheless widely held, notion that the Chinese Communist regime was on the verge of collapse and that an inevitably "descending spiral" was about to drive it from the seat of power.

What are the implications of this conclusion for U.S. policy? If a regime hostile to us is on the verge of collapse, there is no point in dealing with it. On the contrary, a strong case can be made for ignoring and quarantining it lest contact in any form—commercial, cultural, or diplomatic—serve to strengthen it, possibly delay its demise, or even prevent its breakdown altogether. Indeed, if a hostile government is on the verge of collapse, why not apply maximum economic pressure to hasten its downfall? From this perspective, then, there is a rationale for tight trade controls and for other measures such as keeping Communist China out of the United Nations.

If, on the other hand, the "collapse" theory cannot be

validated by actual developments in Communist China, an entirely different range of policy implications emerges. Such a finding does not in and of itself argue for or against admission of Communist China into the United Nations or any other specific policy. But it does suggest a different policy posture for the United States—one that accepts Communist China as a body politic, a society, and an economy that seems to be here to stay for some time to come.

Communist China's Economic Development and International Capabilities

In the conduct of its foreign relations, Communist China can and does use military force, the threat of force, trade and aid, moral suasion, and propaganda appeals. Its ability to employ all these means, however, is in one way or another affected by the size of its national product, the structure of its economy, the state of its economic development, and the rate at which its economy is growing and being transformed from a backward and preponderantly agricultural economy into a modern, industrialized one. The relationships are most direct, of course, in the field of trade and aid. Yet they are also of major importance with respect to the country's military posture. On the other hand, they carry less decisive weight as far as propaganda capabilities are concerned.

In appraising the potency of economic instruments in the conduct of Chinese Communist foreign policy, it is important to start with a brief analysis of the present state of the mainland economy, its strengths and weaknesses, its accomplishments and its unresolved problems as brought out at greater length in the different chapters of this study.

Undoubtedly the most fundamental and intractable problem facing economic policy makers in China is that of population and food. On the basis of highly fragmentary and rather unreliable data, mainland China's population in 1964 was estimated to be about 730 million. This vast population is supposed to be growing at an average annual rate of 2 per cent or more. Thus, about 15 million people are added each year. Maintaining such a rapidly growing population just at the prevailing standards of living entails heroic efforts. It requires an average annual rate of growth in food supply of 2-3 per cent; it places a heavy demand on investment resources for housing, school construction, hospitals, and other educational, health, and welfare facilities.

This population has high birth rates and fairly high death rates—*i.e.*, it is a preponderantly young population with a high ratio of consumers to producers. These characteristics are conducive to high consumption and low saving. Furthermore, a sizable share of savings needs to be channeled into investment in social overhead rather than production facilities.

These relationships pose a series of dilemmas, which are common to all economies subject to acute population pressure. At the end of the First Five Year Plan period (1957), it seemed that China might be on the way to breaking out of this vicious circle of backwardness. Seen from the perspective of 1965, one can be much less certain of this.

There is no doubt that the Chinese Communist leadership is fully conscious of the problem and is trying to attack it from two directions simultaneously. As was shown in Chapters 2 and 3, it has in recent years accorded high priority to agricultural development. At the same time, it has embarked on a program of family planning, thus far largely confined to the urban areas.

Present indications are that this two-pronged attack has produced some recovery and progress. However, unless there is a miraculous boon in the form of unusually good harvests or foreign aid on a large scale, further economic growth and advance in China may be expected to be significantly slower than in the 1950s. Correspondingly, the Chinese Communist vision of becoming a top-ranking industrial nation may have to be postponed for a long time to come.

This prospect could be altered if Communist China were to gain access to foreign credits or grants. In this respect, China is in a unique situation, for it is perhaps the only underdeveloped country today that has no long-term credits or foreign aid to draw upon. On the contrary, since 1955 it has been a net exporter of capital. These capital exports have been used to amortize the Soviet loans and to finance Chinese foreign aid programs. It would seem that in contributing to rising Sino-Soviet tensions, the Chinese Communist leadership must have chosen to buy increasing self-reliance and freedom of action in foreign affairs at the price of economic development at home.

China's development prospects could also be altered markedly by changes in domestic policy. In recent years, the Chinese Communists have pursued a prudent and more or less conservative economic policy—easing the tax and collection pressure on the peasantry, trying to foster a generally more favorable incentive system for agriculture, keeping the savings burden down, and channeling a large share of investment to agriculture and agriculture-supporting industries. However, this policy yields a pattern of resource allocation which runs strongly counter to the ideological and programmatic commitments of the leadership. It tends to produce a lower rate of investment and a lower rate of industrial growth. Therefore, the current economic policies are in many ways distasteful to the regime—so much so that they become a continuing source of tension between what the leadership desires and hopes for and what it considers possible and necessary. This tension may in turn tempt the leadership to resort once more to bold measures to break out of the vise of backwardness. Such attempts could easily lead to another economic breakdown and crisis. Consequently, one of the most serious problems for the leadership is to curb its own sense of impatience.

According to some assessments, the very intractability of the population-food dilemma might drive the Chinese Communists into adventurism, particularly in Southeast Asia. The adherents of this view maintain that Communist China's current interest in Vietnam is at least partly motivated by a desire to gain access to the rice surpluses and the rich mineral resources of Southeast Asia. However, it is difficult to see what the economic gains of conquest would be. What could China obtain through conquest of this region that she cannot now get through the normal processes of international trade?

Implicit in this view is an assumption that the Chinese Communists could move in and confiscate the rice and other commodities. This region, however, depends on rice and mineral exports for essential imports. If Communist China conquered the region, she would have to assume responsibility for maintaining economic and political stability. This task would mean assuring a modicum of incentives to farmers to induce them at least to maintain, if not expand, production. Forced confiscation might yield some produce for a year or two but would unquestionably be counterproductive in the long run. The Chinese Communists have a great deal of difficulty with their own peasantry. It is hard to believe that they would expect to overcome these difficulties with a conquered peasantry.

For these reasons one probably has to look to historical, cultural, ideological, and strategic considerations rather than to economic motivations for the primary explanation for Communist China's interest in Southeast Asia.

THE ECONOMIC BASE FOR MILITARY POWER. In terms of total size, mainland China's economy definitely is among the 10 largest in the world. According to the data in Table 7-1, China in 1962 was outranked in total production by the United States by a ratio of nearly 14:1, by the Soviet Union by about 6:1, by Germany, Britain, France, and Japan by about 1.8–2.3:1, and by Italy barely at all.

Taken by themselves, however, these figures are misleading, for they overstate China's economic capabilities as compared to those of the more highly developed and more industrialized countries. Roughly 40 per cent of mainland China's national product never enters marketing channels, while in the United States the figure is only about 5 per cent. The other countries listed in Table 7-1 lie between these two extremes. Therefore, a sizable share of the goods and services produced in China are "frozen" within the household and cannot readily be mobilized or reallocated to alternative uses. *Pari passu* resources are "tied" to specific patterns of use which cannot easily be shifted into the military sector.

Bearing this fact in mind, we may perhaps better approach an analysis of relative capabilities by comparing the size of the

TABLE 7-1. The Gross National Product of
Communist China and Selected Countries

(in billions of U.S. dollars)

Country	1962 GNP (at 1961 prices)
United States	551.8
U.S.S.R.	256.3
Germany (Federal Republic)	96.2
United Kingdom	91.5
France	83.6
Japan	77.0
Italy	52.8
China [a]	
1957	40.0
1960	50.0
1962	42.0

[a] The estimates are for gross domestic products at 1952 prices; however, the figures would not be significantly altered even if they were stated in 1961 prices.

Sources: The 1957 estimate for China is based on the estimate of T. C. Liu and K. C. Yeh, *The Economy of the Chinese Mainland: National Income and Economic Development, 1933–1959* (Princeton University Press, 1965) as adjusted in Table D-1 and converted into dollars at the official rate of exchange. This method of conversion introduces a sizable margin of error; however, it is far from clear whether this leads to an overvaluation or undervaluation of China's product in comparison with that of other countries. The official exchange rate of 2.62 yuan to the dollar probably undervalues China's agricultural product and overvalues the output of the investment goods industries. The direction of the bias is less clear for the other sectors. Thus, it is not possible to determine—short of a detailed national income estimate weighted both in Chinese and U.S. prices—the extent of the bias for national product as a whole. The 1960 estimate is based on the 1959 Liu-Yeh figure as adjusted in Table D-1 and then rounded upward to allow for some assumed expansion between these two years. The 1962 figure is a guess based on qualitative indicators of economic trends between 1960 and 1962.

The data for other countries are much more reliable than those for China. They were taken from U.S. Congress, Joint Economic Committee, *Annual Economic Indicators for the U.S.S.R.*, 88th Congress, 2d sess. (Washington, D.C.: GPO, 1964), p. 96.

T A B L E 7 - 2 . Comparative Industrial Production of
Communist China and Selected Countries, 1962

(in billions of U.S. dollars)

Country	Industrial Product [a]
United States	180.2
U.S.S.R.	86.7
United Kingdom	39.3
Germany (Federal Republic)	32.8
France	21.3
Japan	18.4
Italy	15.0
China	
1957	8
1960	13
1962	10

[a] Value added in manufacturing, mining, and public utilities.

Sources: See Table 7-1.

industrial product of China with that of the other countries. This
measure encompasses only "modern" economic sectors which are
fully commercialized and monetized. Within industry, therefore,
factors can be more rapidly reallocated between branches in
response to changing needs. Moreover, military capability is more
directly related to industrial production than to any other branch
of the economy. Analyzing the data in Table 7–2, then, we find
that the conclusions emerging from Table 7–1 are indeed modified.
That is, the gap between China and the other countries is
significantly greater in terms of industrial product alone than it
is if gauged by national product as a whole.

While in terms of the foregoing indicators, China is outranked
by all the large industrial countries, her economy seems vast
indeed in relation to other underdeveloped areas—that is, all of
Asia (except Japan), Africa, and Latin America. The implications
of size are further underlined by the apparent fact that pre-World
War II Japan was capable of engaging in a major world conflict
and sustaining it more or less successfully for four-five years with
a total industrial product which probably was smaller than

Communist China's is today. Admittedly, Japan was even then much more advanced technologically and much more highly industrialized than China is now. Furthermore, prewar Japan had a much smaller population to care for than China does, so it could allocate a much larger share of its total industrial product to expanding the military and closely related sectors. Therefore, one certainly could not conclude from this comparison that what Japan was capable of doing then, China could do now. Nevertheless, the comparison does suggest that if China continues on her industrialization path, it may not be too long before her warmaking power may match that of Japan in the 1930s.

One of the most critical questions is whether population size should be treated as a source of weakness or strength. If one compares Communist China with her immediate continental neighbors, who are roughly at the same stage of development as she is, there is no doubt that population size represents an element of strength and power. If one compares Communist China with the United States and Russia, population size might represent an element of strength in the context of conventional warfare waged on the Asian continent. Within certain limits, sheer manpower might serve as a substitute for firepower. In a nuclear confrontation, however, it might have no effect at all, except in the macabre sense that a vast population has a somewhat better chance of leaving behind survivors.

Viewed in the above light, the economy—as underdeveloped as it is—is capable of providing Communist China with a military potential which can, and indeed has, significantly altered the power balance on the Asian continent despite the fact that it may not permit the Chinese to challenge the Soviet Union and the United States in other parts of the world.

TRADE AND AID AS INSTRUMENTS OF FOREIGN POLICY. While China's size alone—its land area, population, and economy—gives it a significant weight in international affairs, this very size combined with the country's relative backwardness has tended to reduce its participation in world trade and thereby to reduce the importance of international trade as an instrument of Chinese Communist foreign policy. A vast country necessarily will tend to be more self-sufficient and to rely principally on internal markets and sources of supply. For this reason, its exports and imports will tend to be small relative to the total flow of goods and services produced in the economy. At the same time, the absolute level of foreign trade, regardless of its share in the national product, will tend to be a function of the country's stage of development. Thus, of two countries with roughly the same size of population, the one with the higher per capita income will tend to have the larger trade volume. It is not surprising, therefore, that even in its peak trade year of 1959, Communist China ranked only 12th in world imports and 13th in world exports.[1] A number of smaller but highly developed countries outranked her. West Germany and the United Kingdom, with gross national products about twice as large as that of mainland China, carried on a volume of trade that was four to five times as large. Even a country as small as The Netherlands carried on a volume of foreign trade twice as large.

These discrepancies were greatly magnified in the 1960s by the sharp slump in China's foreign trade under the impact of the economic crisis. As a result, by 1962 China slipped to 18th place in world rank with respect to exports and 30th place with respect to imports. This slump further curtailed the effectiveness of trade as a tool of foreign policy.

Foreign trade can provide a country with maximum power leverage if that country serves as the market for a vast share of another country's exports without itself being too dependent on these or, alternatively, if that country becomes a major source of its trading partner's supplies of imports without being too dependent on this market. Short of these circumstances, however, economic power can still be translated into political power via foreign trade when a country serves as a major market for another's principal exports or as a leading source of vital raw materials for the other's industries. For example, various agreements for a guaranteed market or for preclusive purchase can be of significant aid to particular industries or economic interests. Such a situation can be used to gain influence and to exercise pressure—if need be by threatening a sudden trade rupture with its attendant dislocations.

In the Chinese case, as has been noted in preceding chapters, only for one country—namely, the Soviet Union—did mainland China constitute both a truly major market for exports and an important source of supply. Yet even in this instance, China's trade dependence on the Soviet Union during the 1950s was two to three times greater than vice versa. Moreover, the disparity in trade dependence increased in the 1960s, for China's share in Soviet foreign trade dropped to around 5 per cent while the Soviet Union's share in mainland commerce was still around 20 per cent. Before 1960, about 30–60 per cent of Russia's exports to China consisted of plant and transport equipment and machinery. The drastic curtailment in the purchase of these items in the 1960s might have led to some disruption in the Soviet machine-building industry. One cannot, for example, rule out the possibility that this curtailment of purchases may in the short run have placed a considerable burden of adjustment on individual factories producing for the China market. Nevertheless, the effect on the industry as a whole could not have been too serious, for by 1962–63 less than 1 per cent of its output was exported to China.

The only other area with a major trade orientation toward China has been Hong Kong. The latter obtains about 20 per cent of its imports from China, while the mainland now buys only a negligible share of its supplies from the colony. In and of itself, this situation gives the Chinese Communist regime limited leverage over Hong Kong, for the colony can find alternative sources of supply for its food and raw materials, although some inconvenience and possibly higher costs might be involved. Moreover, Hong Kong's dependence on Chinese supplies is counterbalanced by China's dependence on the colony as its principal source of foreign exchange. What this situation suggests is not that Communist China has no power or influence in Hong Kong but rather that its influence rests primarily on military and political —not economic—factors.

In addition, for several countries trade with mainland China has been of considerable importance to particular sectors rather than to the economy as a whole. Such, for instance, is the case with respect to grain exports from Canada and Australia. Both these countries had accumulated large grain surpluses, so Chinese purchases on a large scale offered definite relief to the farmers and traders of the two countries. The significance of these purchases can best be illustrated by the fact that since 1961 China has absorbed large shares of Australian and Canadian wheat exports. Although the Chinese are quite dependent on this grain, they have neutralized some of the effects of this dependence by fostering among the suppliers a spirit of competition for the China market. For example, they opened negotiations to buy a million tons of wheat from the French, who in 1964 were reported to have about two million tons of surplus wheat for export.[2]

The situation of the chemical fertilizer industry in Japan is analogous. It had been operating well below capacity, but its fortunes have undoubtedly been improved by a three-year fertilizer agreement concluded with China in 1964. According to this agreement, China will purchase a substantial share of Japan's total production of fertilizer and of its fertilizer exports.

Czechoslovakia's engineering industry was in a somewhat similar position. This industry is quite dependent on exports, and its products account for a large portion of the country's total export earnings. Up to 1960, about 15 per cent of Czech engineering exports were sold to China. Moreover, the 1961–65 Czech plan envisaged a sizable expansion of these exports to China. Therefore, the collapse of the China market, as the result of deteriorating Sino-Soviet relations and the curtailment of the demand for investment goods within the country, was a serious blow to this industry.[3] The sudden reduction in China's agricultural exports to Czechoslovakia, moreover, aggravated the already precarious food supply situation in the latter country.

If one grants that particular economic branches in some countries can become more or less dependent on trade with the mainland, how can China use such dependence as an instrument of foreign policy? The potentialities and the limitations of trade as such an instrument perhaps can best be illustrated in the Southeast Asian context—that is, a region of vital concern to China. The mainland relies upon this region for its supply of rubber, which is produced in China only on a limited scale. For many years, she has been bartering rice for rubber from Ceylon. In this way, China has been providing a guaranteed market for about 25–30 per cent of Ceylonese rubber exports. Rubber, in turn, contributed about 15–20 per cent of Ceylon's total export earnings.[4] China, therefore, constitutes a significant factor in Ceylon's rubber market. In the absence of other purchases, however, China's importance from the standpoint of Ceylon's total earnings of foreign exchange is quite limited. On the other side of the ledger, China supplied about 50 per cent of Ceylon's imports of rice as of 1963,[5] but Ceylon could obtain this rice elsewhere. Therefore, these exports to Ceylon do not provide China with strong bargaining power. They may more properly be viewed as a form of payment Ceylon was willing to accept in order to find an outlet for her rubber.

By far the most important of Ceylon's exports is tea, which China herself exports. Besides rice, other significant items among Ceylon's imports are wheat and wheat flour, petroleum and petroleum products, chemicals, textiles, and machinery. In the case of petroleum and products, China too is an importer. She exports most of the other items, but all these are available from other sources as well. Whether and in what quantities they will be purchased from the mainland will thus depend on relative cost considerations.

Other suppliers of rubber in the region are Indonesia, Malaysia, and to a lesser extent Cambodia. China could easily purchase all of Cambodia's rubber exports, but only at the cost of reducing her purchases from Ceylon. She could use the threat of such a shift as an instrument of foreign policy vis-à-vis both countries, but the threat could be effective in relation to both countries simultaneously only as long as it was not carried out. In the case of Indonesia, rubber contributes about 35–45 per cent of total exports. Were China to purchase all her imported rubber from Indonesia, she could not absorb more than 5 per cent of the country's total rubber crop.

Similarly, if China bought all her imports of petroleum and oil products solely from Indonesia, the purchases would constitute no more than one-fifth to one-fourth of the latter's total sales. The same general picture applies to Indonesia's other exports and imports. That is, China can buy only limited quantities of exports which are vital to Indonesia, while imports which

China can supply are usually obtainable elsewhere—frequently on better, or at least no worse, terms.

The situation is rather different with respect to Cambodia, a small country with a small total volume of exports and imports. If Communist China wished, she could supply Cambodia, and in recent years has increasingly done so, with its modest imports of foodstuffs, textiles, and iron and steel. Similarly, she could buy all of Cambodia's rubber, rice, and corn surpluses. The additional costs thus incurred would undoubtedly be modest and could be borne if the political returns seemed promising enough.

What are the implications of this analysis for China's ability to use trade as an instrument in the conduct of its foreign relations? It is evident from these cases that the moderate size of total mainland exports and imports makes it difficult for China to impose a pattern of economic dependence and thereby to gain dominance over a country through trade. From China's point of view, the primary function of trade is to facilitate the maintenance of economic stability and to foster economic development at home. If at the same time trade can open new channels of communication for the spread of propaganda and political influence, so much the better. In other words, imports must be purchased from countries which can provide them on the most favorable terms, and exports must be sold in such a way as to maximize earnings of foreign exchange.

Therefore, China cannot afford to use import orders or export supplies just to impose patterns of economic dependence. I do not mean that trade cannot be used as a weapon in special cases where the additional costs incurred might be modest—either because economic and foreign policy considerations happen to coincide or because the country concerned is small (*e.g.*, Cambodia). Occasionally, for example, China may engage in preclusive buying at prices higher than world market prices or sell in specific markets at prices lower than world market prices. To the extent that China uses the trade weapon in one place, however, her capability of using it in other places is correspondingly reduced.

For all these reasons combined, trade is best suited to perform a supporting rather than independent role in the Chinese Communists' pursuit of their foreign policy objectives. It is really of importance in two rather different contexts. In countries where China has already made heavy inroads through the use of a whole arsenal of weapons, trade may serve to reinforce and accelerate an ongoing trend. In highly industrialized countries, it can serve as a prime avenue for gaining a certain measure of influence by creating the illusion of enormous trading potentials even in the face of currently modest trading levels. The ever-present lure of a "market with hundreds of millions of customers" seems to be just as strong today as it was in the 19th century. China's sheer size and population magnetically attract traders who do not want to miss possible opportunities and do not want possible competitors to get there ahead of them. In making certain policy moves, therefore, trading countries may consider it opportune to take into account the possible reactions of the Chinese Communists. This statement would certainly apply to Japan and perhaps to a lesser extent to Canada, Australia, Britain, France, and some additional European countries. But in none of these cases is trade of such importance as to provide Communist China with enough political bargaining power to impose a sharp turn in the direction of foreign policy.

The same general conclusions hold true with respect to China's economic aid capabilities. As was shown in Chapter 6, China's aid program is quite modest as compared with those of the United States and the Soviet Union. To some extent, the Chinese Communists seem to have succeeded in "packaging" their relatively small program in such a way as to maximize the political returns from their investment. In some African countries, for example, the aid and the Chinese Communist technicians who came with it apparently went some way in buying goodwill and in counterbalancing Soviet influence. They may even have swayed a few votes on the question of the admission of Communist China to the United Nations. The Chinese aid program also has had a definite political impact in Southeast Asia, particularly in Cambodia and Burma. In both these cases, however, aid seems to have followed rather than led the way. That is, Chinese economic aid became important only after the governments concerned had made a political decision to pursue a more neutralist or pro-Chinese policy. Such decisions were then also reflected in the forced withdrawal of U.S. aid from these countries.

Chinese economic aid enjoys a near-monopoly position in only two countries, Albania and North Vietnam. In neither case was political dependence on China bought by economic dependence. Political dependence in the first case is based on a complex maze of political relationships involving Yugoslavia and the Soviet Union, and in the second case on the military conflict with South Vietnam and the United States and on geographic proximity to mainland China.

COMMUNIST CHINA AS A DEVELOPMENT MODEL. To the extent that China does not rely upon force or the threat thereof—whether military or economic in nature—ideological appeal plays a significant role in its foreign policy arsenal. An important ingredient of this ideological appeal is what may be termed the "development-model effect." Depending upon the actual course of economic development on the mainland, the way this reality is handled in Chinese Communist propaganda, and the way it is perceived by the countries toward which the propaganda is directed, the effect may be either positive or negative. Here we are concerned only with the first aspect of this problem—namely, what this model effect might be in the absence of any propaganda effort based on it.

During the first decade of its existence, the Chinese Communist regime succeeded in creating an image of a vigorous, dynamic, and rapidly growing economy with some singular accomplishments to its credit. First of all, the regime rapidly restored the war-devastated economy and brought the prolonged inflation and hyperinflation to a halt. Monetary and fiscal stability was thus achieved despite the resource drain imposed by the Korean War. Moreover, a land redistribution program with significant appeal not only internally but externally was carried out during the same period.

This image was greatly reinforced by what at the time appeared to be a gradual and successful program of agrarian transformation based on an increasing degree of producer cooperation. As a result, strong sentiment in favor of learning from the Chinese experience and emulating at least some aspects of it began to develop in India in the mid-fifties. Two official Indian delegations visited China. One was concerned primarily with problems of agricultural production, and the other with problems of agricultural organization.

Rapid industrial growth coupled with the aforementioned agrarian transformation caused many to believe that the Chinese Communists had succeeded in adapting the Soviet growth model to the conditions of an underdeveloped, densely populated economy. Since 1958, however, this image seems to have been tarnished. The extreme regimentation of the communes and the mass labor mobilization projects of the Great Leap seem to have had a negative external impact. More importantly, the profound economic crisis of 1960–62 dramatized the fact that the Chinese Communist regime had paid relatively little attention to agricultural development. At the same time, it again drove home the lesson that agricultural development is a necessary condition for economic development in densely populated, low-income countries.

The appeal of the Chinese Communist development model has no doubt been undermined by the economic setbacks on the mainland. Yet the force of the initial successes lingers on— partly because of an information lag, partly because of a statistical blackout since early 1960 which has helped to conceal the extent of the economic difficulties, and partly because of agricultural stagnation and difficulties of food supply in other underdeveloped countries (particularly India).

China's Vulnerability
to External Economic Pressure

The preceding brief review would tend to suggest that Communist China's capacity to use economic instruments for the attainment of its foreign policy goals is quite limited. At best, they could serve only as secondary tools in support of policies based on other kinds of inducements or pressures. In large part, this situation is due to the smallness of the foreign trade sector, a smallness which is in turn a function of the country's economic backwardness and of its vast size. The same combination of factors reduces mainland China's vulnerability to external economic pressure.

In a vast country such as China, there are few absolute resource barriers to initiating and expanding production of any one item or group of items even at the country's present stage of relative backwardness. There are, however, serious economic and technical limitations to such expansion. In a command economy of this size, the planners can, if they so desire, concentrate scarce technical, scientific, and other resources upon the development and large-scale production of items of a high degree of complexity. But this type of production tends to be costly and therefore to entail a reduction in the rate of expansion of output in other sectors. Nevertheless, if the Chinese Communist leaders were to choose a path of virtual autarky or if the world were to impose a total embargo on trade with China, the economy and the system as a whole could probably survive. However, such circumstances would reduce the possibilities for her economic growth, curtail the modernization of her economy and defense establishment, and increase her vulnerability to sharp fluctuations in food supply.

THE ROLE OF IMPORTS IN THE CHINESE ECONOMY. As was shown in Chapter 4, China's imports were crucial for the expansion of her plant, the relief of her acute shortages of food after 1960, and the modernization of her defense establishment. During the period of the First Five Year Plan as a whole, about 20–40 per cent (depending at what exchange rate the dollar figures for imports are converted to yuan) of the equipment component of investment was imported. In the absence of these imports, Communist China's economic growth might possibly have fallen from an average annual rate of 6–7 per cent to 3–5 per cent (about 3 per cent if we use the former equipment import share and

5 per cent if we adopt the latter). Moreover, a cessation of imports would have greatly retarded technological progress and the modernization of the economy, particularly of industry. It would almost certainly have stifled the development of the iron and steel, electric-power, chemicals, and other technically complex industrial branches.

Since 1960 this type of import has greatly diminished in importance, for the construction of new plants has been drastically curtailed. Because most industries are operating well below capacity, imports of equipment are confined to those branches which have continued to expand throughout the depression, *i.e.*, chemicals and petroleum extraction and refining. As long as this condition prevails, trade controls and embargoes curbing shipment of industrial machinery and equipment to China are not likely to have a significant impact on industrial expansion. In a few years, when industry returns to operation at full capacity, this situation may be expected to change.

As capital goods imports diminished, food (particularly grain) imports gained greatly in importance. Although such imports have only increased China's total grain supply by 3-4 per cent, they have been of considerable importance in marginal terms. They have greatly eased the distribution burden, reduced the collection pressures in the countryside, relieved the transport system of a heavy load, and provided the cities with a guaranteed food supply. As late as 1965 indications were that Chinese Communist policy makers and planners intended to continue importing grain for at least the next two to three years. Whether such imports will become a longer-term feature of Chinese Communist trade policy is impossible to forecast at the time this study is written. In the meantime, a total non-Communist world embargo on food exports to China would undoubtedly increase strains in the Chinese economy, particularly if the exports were cut off suddenly. Such an embargo would once more introduce difficulties of food supply, particularly in the cities, and would force the regime to step up its pressure on the peasantry.

There is no doubt that imports played a crucial role in the modernization of the Chinese Communist military establishment. While there are no data on the quantity or value of Chinese military imports, some crude guesses about the relative importance of these purchases from abroad can be made on the basis of certain assumptions. Were one to assume that all "other" (*i.e.*, unitemized) exports from the Communist countries to China comprised military equipment and matériel, these might have constituted 20–40 per cent of total defense expenditures exclusive of outlays for subsistence of the armed forces between 1955 and 1960.[6] In all probability, this "other" category includes nonmilitary items as well. However, military imports may also be hidden under "machinery" and some other items. The officially published figures on the defense budget are undoubtedly understated because some military outlays are concealed under other budget categories. For these reasons, the ratio of "other" imports to non-subsistence military outlays in the budget probably overstates the importance of imports. If the non-subsistence outlays contain a sizable component for military construction, however, then the ratio of 20–40 per cent would greatly understate the importance of imported matériel.

It is quite apparent that the import component of defense was sizable enough to be of considerable significance regardless of what the precise figure may have been. The scanty information available would suggest that the planes and some other types of equipment of the Chinese Communist armed forces have deteriorated in recent years—partly because of the decline in imports and partly because of the general economic decline on the mainland. The development of a nuclear device probably did not affect this trend too much. According to one estimate, the Chinese nuclear program may have entailed an annual investment of about U.S.$100 million and an annual allowance of about $30 million for operating costs and fuel.[7]

The development of a modest nuclear strike capability will naturally be much more expensive but not necessarily beyond China's capabilities even at her present stage of development. One might hypothesize that the development of a French-type nuclear *force de frappe* may cost China around U.S.$1 billion a year or more.[8] Depending upon the rate of exchange at which this figure is converted to yuan, such outlays would absorb at least half of the present defense budget.[9] As we noted earlier, however, the official budget figures certainly understate military outlays, which could actually be twice as high. At this higher figure, a nuclear-strike program of modest proportions might absorb about 25 per cent of the military budget.

Under these assumptions, the development of a French-type nuclear program would require an allocation of 2–3 per cent of GNP. Such an allocation would represent a quite sizable diversion of resources for an underdeveloped country with scarce technical manpower and a modest industrial base. As a matter of fact, a diversion of this magnitude could not help but interfere with the growth, development, and modernization of conventional military capabilities and/or with investments in agriculture and industry. Therefore, the development of a modest nuclear strike capability is really a problem in planning priorities and of planners' choices.

It is perfectly possible, of course, that the Chinese Communist leadership has made a conscious choice to sacrifice its conventional capabilities in order to develop a nuclear force, a choice which in many ways would resemble that made by the Eisenhower administration some years ago. Such a choice, conditioned by economic limitations, would necessarily have major implications for foreign policy. It could mean that China would increasingly expect to rely on nuclear deterrence for her defense against the United States and for the pursuit of her foreign policy goals on her periphery. China's neighbors would necessarily perceive her possession of even a modest nuclear capability as a threat. This threat, coupled with other instruments of foreign policy, might suffice to achieve Communist China's objectives through political means without the use of ground and/or air forces.

THE COST OF TRADE CONTROLS. As was noted in Chapter 5, it is difficult to determine whether trade controls applied by other countries imposed any resource costs on mainland China's economy. From one point of view, it would seem that at least some "losses" must have been incurred because a large share of China's imports had to be transported by rail from the Soviet Union over great land distances. Moreover, the lack of free access to all sources of supply necessarily circumscribed her choice as to quality, models, types, and price much more than would otherwise have been the case. Furthermore, it greatly increased her dependence on a limited number of suppliers and weakened her economic bargaining power.

For all these reasons, it would be fair to postulate that the Chinese had to obtain their imports at unfavorable prices and that they may have been forced into suboptimal factor combinations and patterns of resource allocation. These combinations and patterns, in other words, were in part a function of the types of goods available rather than the kinds best suited to China's factor endowments. It would be difficult to quantify and measure the "losses" resulting from possible distortions in resource allocation. In contrast, no serious conceptual difficulties stand in the way of measuring price differentials for imports. However, there are numerous statistical difficulties, as was pointed out in Chapter 5. If we overlook these difficulties, the studies cited in that chapter suggest that China incurred a loss of about $940 million between 1955 and 1959 because of an "overpricing" of her imports. That is, if she had been able to buy the same goods from Western Europe (on the assumed conditions spelled out in Chapter 5), she would have saved that much. Because of serious gaps in the available information, it is difficult to determine whether this figure is subject to an upward or downward bias.

With an estimated total "overpricing" of $940 million, the loss in national product for the 1955–59 period as a whole would be about 0.5–1.0 per cent (depending on what exchange rate is used to convert the dollar figure to yuan). In reality, the "loss" is likely to have been less, for the sample of commodities on which Mah's findings are based is more likely to overstate, than understate, the differential.[10]

From another point of view, one could argue that there may have been no "losses" at all, even on the import side. It is far from a foregone conclusion that even in the absence of Western trade controls the Chinese could have purchased the machinery and equipment imported from the Soviet Union in the world market at lower prices than those paid to the Soviets. Doubts as to possible trade "losses" are reinforced if one examines imports and exports simultaneously. Even if there were "losses" on the import side, "gains" on the export side may have compensated for them. China may have sold her exports—particularly coarse, low-quality textiles—at higher prices in Soviet markets than she could have sold them for elsewhere.

Of course, there is one area in which trade controls have undoubtedly had an effect—the military field. Partly as a result of the controls, Communist China has been exclusively dependent on the Soviet bloc for its military imports. Because of the lack of data, we have no way of ascertaining what China paid for these supplies and whether the prices at which they were obtained were "excessive," "reasonable," or "subsidized" in world market terms. Since China could not obtain these from its non-Communist trading partners at any price, the issue of a "China differential" in this field is academic. What is not academic is the differential cost of providing the wherewithal for defense from domestic production as opposed to imports. This issue has assumed particular significance since 1960 because of the marked curtailment of military imports from the Soviet Union. The curtailment had a threefold effect: (a) it led to a marked deterioration in the equipment of the Chinese Communist armed forces, (b) it postponed the acquisition of nuclear capability by at least two years,[11] and (c) it undoubtedly must have raised the cost of nuclear development (although the extent of this increase in costs cannot be determined on the basis of presently available data).

Another area in which trade controls may have imposed certain costs on the Chinese economy is credit. Present understandings between countries participating in the system of trade controls impose a five-year limit on credits to all Communist countries. Thus far, this limitation has been adhered to in trade with China, but there have been breaches of it vis-à-vis the Soviet Union. The United Kingdom, France, and Japan have extended longer-term credits to Russia. Japan in particular may be under increasing pressure to extend seven- or eight-year credits to China as well.

One of the most remarkable facts about Communist China today is that it is among the few underdeveloped countries free of any long-term debt. In one sense, this fact can be interpreted as an element of strength, an indication of the country's ability to be self-reliant and to stand alone. From the point of view of economic development, though, it represents a serious handicap. It means that the country must depend exclusively on its own savings to finance capital formation. Therefore, either investment must be reduced, or the pressures to raise domestic saving must be increased. The issue in its current form has not been faced and up to now has not needed to be, for the economy has been operating in comparatively low gear. If and when another major industrialization drive is launched, however, the absence of long-term credits may be expected to impose new strains on the economy. We can carry the same reasoning one step further. There is no doubt that sizable long-term credits could accelerate economic recovery in Communist China and facilitate the early start of another major industrialization drive.

If such credits were to be of decisive importance, they would have to be larger than those which the Soviets extended in the early 1950s. These contributed a maximum of 1–2 per cent of China's gross national product and provided roughly 30 per cent of the financing for imports. Partly because the economy has since expanded, a much larger absolute volume of credit—perhaps $400–500 million a year—would be required to make the same relative contribution to GNP.

In the meantime, some of the gap has been filled by medium-term credits. These have been extended by Western Europe and Japan as part and parcel of their complete plant sales to China. If the 1963–64 rate of such sales were to continue, China would obtain an average of $40 million a year in five-year credits. By way of comparison, the Soviets between 1950 and 1955 extended an average of about $220 million a year in the form of 10-year loans. Moreover, the Soviet loans carried a 1–2 per cent rate of interest, while the Japanese and West European credits involve an interest rate of 5–6 per cent. Thus, even if due allowance is made for the availability of short-term commercial credit, the Chinese Communists have a long way to go to fill the credit gap left by the cessation of long-term Soviet lending in 1957.

This analysis would tend to suggest that in the 1960s trade

controls have imposed costs on the Chinese economy in at least two ways: by reducing the quality of the defense establishment and by denying the economy long-term credits. The effect of the latter really depends on what size credits might have been available rather than simply on the terms on which they might have been extended. It does not make much difference, for example, whether a small, one-time loan of $40 million has to be repaid over 5 years or 20 years. In the case of a loan of $400 million, however, the terms assume considerable importance. If such a loan had to be repaid over a 5-year period, for example, about 5 per cent of China's exports at the 1962–63 level would have to go to meet the repayment obligation. With a 20-year period of repayment, on the other hand, the figure would be only about 1.3 per cent. Let us assume for a moment, then, that in the early 1960s China could somehow have obtained annual credits of $500 million for 5 years. In relative terms, the total amount involved would have been roughly equivalent to the Soviet contribution of the early fifties. Such large credits could not have been serviced on a medium-term basis, for repayment over a 5-year period would have imposed a heavy balance-of-payments burden on the economy.

Implications for U.S. Trade Policy

Since 1950, U.S. policy on trade with China has involved a virtually total embargo on all economic contacts between ourselves and the mainland and the maintenance of as stringent controls as possible on trade between our allies and the mainland.[12] This policy was initiated as an emergency measure during the Korean War and was conceived within the context of economic warfare. It has been maintained since on the technical ground that the Korean War has never been formally terminated but ended only in an armistice.

To be more precise, U.S. policy and regulations concerning trade with China have remained unchanged since 1950, while those of our allies have gradually and progressively been liberalized, more or less to our displeasure and in a number of cases despite our resistance. As a result, essentially all that is left of the elaborate structure of COCOM controls constructed in the early fifties is a continuing ban on the shipment of arms, weapons, military matériel of all kinds, fissionable materials, and some other clearly strategic goods. In addition, there is an agreement to limit credits to a term of five years.

Apart from its technical and legal basis rooted in the Korean War, what is the rationale of this trade policy vis-à-vis Communist China? U.S. policy toward China in effect is designed to isolate it and to contain it within its present boundaries, and trade controls are intended to support both these objectives. If adhered to by all major trading countries, such controls would, of course, limit intercourse with China and therefore isolate her not only commercially but politically as well. At the same time, they would deprive her of modern weapons and other defense materials and thus tend to weaken her militarily. Finally, to the extent that they could deny China the wherewithal for modern industrial development, they would at least retard the country's economic growth and postpone the day when it would acquire a large enough industrial base to support a strong and more or less modern military posture. U.S. trade policy, thus, is designed to reduce Communist China's military potential in both the short and the long run.

Let us examine the logic of the rationale for this policy and then appraise the policy's practical effects.

THE RATIONALE OF U.S. TRADE POLICY. With respect to the logic of the policy's rationale, two questions may be posed: Is it in the national interest of the United States to isolate China, and is it in the national interest of the United States to weaken China economically? In examining the question of isolation, we must remember that we are dealing with a regime which rules over a country of more than 700 million people—that is, the largest national entity in the world. On the basis of all available evidence, moreover, it seems to be a regime which is here to stay for some time to come. While one can never rule out the possibility of a collapse under some hypothetical combination of circumstances, its *probability* may be rated as low.

Thus, we find ourselves in the same world and on the same planet with a country which has vowed unalterable hostility to us and one which we consider as actually or potentially a dangerous, threatening, and disequilibrating influence in the world international system. Yet the Chinese must somehow learn to live with us, and we must learn to live with them. Such "coexistence" requires increasing communication and contact between Communist China and the United States. Continuing efforts to isolate China are bound to reinforce the regime's implacable hostility to the United States and its determination to wage an unrelenting campaign to isolate the United States in Asia and in the world at large. At least to some extent, Communist China's strategy of revolution, her propagation of national wars of liberation, and her push for militancy in various parts of the world are related to this effort or countereffort to isolate the United States. Because we have a stake in growth (national, political, and economic) under more or less stable conditions while the Chinese Communists have a vested interest in disturbance, some form of coexistence is of much greater importance to the United States.

Of course, the United States and Communist China have in one sense been in more or less continuous contact—but within a war or quasi-war context, such as that which prevails in Korea, in Vietnam and Laos, and in the Taiwan Straits. Such contacts undoubtedly involve one form of communication. There have also been limited diplomatic contacts at the Warsaw talks and at occasional international conferences such as the Geneva Conference on Laos. This kind of contact, however, does not amount to a departure by either country from a policy of isolating the other.

In approaching the problem of whether we should try to weaken mainland China's economy—that is, to retard or throttle its growth—we may find it useful to distinguish between *capacity* and *propensity* for aggression. Other things being equal, a viable and growing economy is undeniably in a much better position to provide a growing military potential than a stagnating one. Nevertheless, the share of economic growth which a country will actually divert to the military establishment is clearly a matter of choice. Furthermore, a country may face economic difficulties but still choose to divert a significant or possibly even growing portion of its national product to defense, at least for a certain period of time. Therefore, no direct or automatic relationship between economic and military growth can be assumed. All that one can postulate *a priori* is that economic development increases and broadens a country's opportunities to step up military allocations.

In the case of Communist China, the size and character of the military establishment will be determined not only by the country's economic capabilities but by the nature of her foreign policy objectives, the type of power configuration which confronts her (or the opportunities for expansion or subversion which exist), and the kind of military instruments best suited to exploit these opportunities. By way of illustration, one may cite the Sino-Indian border war. The Chinese did not need a vast, modern military machine to give the Indians a bloody nose in the Himalayas. It is also important to note that Communist China may expect to attain a whole host of foreign policy objectives through political rather than military means.

In light of the tremendous power gap between China on the one hand and the United States and the Soviet Union on the other, it would take a long time to narrow this gap appreciably, even with fairly rapid economic growth in China. One could therefore argue, particularly since she is now apparently on the way to acquiring a nuclear-strike capability, that Communist China has enough of an economic base at present to maintain the type of military posture she can use or may be expected to need in Asia short of an all-out war with the United States and/or the Soviet Union. Not even with rapid economic growth, furthermore, could she hope to alter significantly the economic and strictly military balance between herself and the two superpowers.

In effect, then, China's *propensity* for aggression may be said to be a function not only of her *capacity* but of the opportunities for aggression and subversion confronting her, of her fear of invasion and attack—direct and indirect, and of her assessment of the intentions and policies pursued by her adversaries, *i.e.*, primarily the United States. Ultimately, what this analysis points to is that the United States in formulating its China policy (including its trade policies) cannot afford to look only at the *capacity* side of the problem. It must also take into account the variables bearing on *propensity*, including most particularly the impact of its own policy on Chinese Communist behavior.

IMPACT OF U.S. TRADE POLICY ON COMMUNIST CHINA'S ECONOMY. Regardless of the merits of a policy designed to isolate China, are trade controls suitable and effective as one of the instruments for the implementation of this policy? As was shown above and in the preceding chapters, a cutting off of all exports to China would undoubtedly have damaged her economy in several ways. It would have significantly reduced the country's economic growth, would have rendered difficult if not impossible the expansion of her heavy industry, and in the early 1960s would have greatly complicated her problem of food supply. The Chinese economy, however, did not suffer these consequences because (a) no other major trading nation followed the U.S. policy of total embargo and (b) up to 1960 China could obtain from other Communist countries virtually any commodities which allied trade controls denied her. During the period of intimate Sino-Soviet economic relations (1950–60), therefore, the practical consequences of the U.S. embargo and allied trade controls were negligible. The Sino-Soviet trade relationships may possibly have increased the cost of China's imports, but the evidence on this matter is far from conclusive. Even if some costs did result, they were probably minimal.

The situation, however, changed after 1960. Sino-Soviet economic relations deteriorated markedly. As a result, China has had great difficulty in obtaining imports of armaments and military goods, and she has been unable to obtain long-term credits. For the first time, it could be argued, enforcement of the whole system of trade controls became theoretically possible. From the mid-1950s on, however, allied trade controls have gradually been eased. Therefore, Western countries were prepared and in a position to move into the breach left by the Soviets. While U.S. trade policy was formerly ineffective because China could obtain controlled and embargoed goods from the Communist countries, it is now ineffective because these same goods (except for military matériel) can be obtained from practically every country which exports them except the United States and, to some extent, the Soviet Union.

The only practical economic impediment to which China is still exposed under the controls lies in the field of credit. This fact raises two questions: how much damage do credit controls impose on the Chinese economy, and, conversely, to what extent could credits be used to induce modifications of Chinese Communist policies?

The Chinese Communists do not seem to have any difficulties in obtaining all the short- and medium-term credits they can use at present. Their international credit rating is good, and they have met their financial obligations without delay. In a practical sense, therefore, access to long-term credits would simply mean that China could either lighten her current annual debt burden by converting her present obligations or that she could service, at the current rate of yearly debt payments, a much larger credit.

Whether China could obtain sufficient economic benefits from this access to induce her to pay a political price for it is difficult to forecast. On the basis of experience, it would seem rather doubtful unless, perhaps, the economic gain to be derived were indeed of major proportions. The history of Sino-Soviet relations, for example, would suggest that the Chinese were not prepared to sacrifice what they considered to be vital political objectives even if they had to suffer the economic consequences of a break. In her relations with the West, therefore, China probably cannot be expected to give up or modify seriously any of her important foreign policy objectives even though such decisions might benefit her economy. This judgment, however, does not necessarily mean that there may be no chance to obtain concessions in a mutual bargaining situation—at least concessions as to timing, relative priorities, and direction. For several years, for instance, the Chinese Communists maintained that they would not carry on trade with Japan unless the latter accorded them *de facto* recognition. Yet since 1962 trade relations, partly because of the Sino-Soviet split, have been reactivated and broadened essentially on Japanese terms.

POSSIBLE U.S. POLICY MOVES. As I have indicated, the U.S. embargo is practically of no economic significance, for China has been and is currently able to obtain virtually all the goods she needs from other countries at no significant additional cost. Therefore, the embargo has only a symbolic meaning. It stands as a symbol of our determination to isolate China, to treat her as an outlaw, and to refuse to have any dealings with her.

The embargo also serves, however, to maintain the illusion at home that we are somehow inflicting serious damage upon the Chinese Communists through it. Moreover, the embargo and our general policy on trade with China have three other consequences. They separate us from our allies, who do not see the point of our policy on either theoretical or practical grounds. They contribute to frictions between ourselves and our allies whenever we attempt to press our allies to bring their policies into line with ours. Finally, they deprive our businessmen of their potential share, however modest, of the China trade now carried on by other countries.

This analysis really indicates that a trade control policy inflicts costs not only on China but on other countries as well. The more important trade with China may be to the country concerned, the greater these costs tend to be. Actually, as we have noted earlier, the costs imposed are likely to be minimal in most cases, just as the costs imposed on China appear to be small. Nevertheless, to the extent that embargoes and controls reduce the gains in international trade it is far from clear which side incurs greater losses, Communist China or its potential trading partners.

Should the time arrive when a *détente* with China becomes a feasible policy alternative, removal of the embargo may be peculiarly well suited to serve as the first step on the road to normalization between the United States and China. It can be initiated unilaterally without resort to negotiation, and it can be implemented without any economic cost. If the move is made, it should be carried out as a low-key measure and as a signal that other overtures might possibly follow if the Chinese respond to it.

Just as the embargo now stands as a symbol of our determination to isolate Communist China, its removal could symbolize a new policy posture on the part of the United States. At the maximum, such a move, possibly coupled with other similar measures, might widen our channels of communication with China and maybe even improve the general atmosphere of U.S.-China relations. At the minimum, a complete rebuff to our overtures would place the onus for implacable hostility at the door of Communist China.

In the same general vein, it may be worth considering some experimentation in the field of credit policy. A rigid policy of credit limitation ties the hands of our allies and deprives them of any bargaining power. On the other hand, a policy which would leave credit terms vague and unpublished would make it much easier to obtain a *quid pro quo* not only in economic terms but perhaps in political terms as well.

Ultimately the crux of the problem is: What should be the overall character of our policy toward China? Should we assume a new posture and take new initiatives, or should we permit ourselves to remain preoccupied with the difficulties of change rather than with the penalties attendant upon holding a fixed position. These problems, of course, range well beyond the economic realm and carry us well beyond the scope of this study; they encompass the totality of our policy in Asia. In this realm, economic considerations and economic instruments can and should play only a subsidiary and supporting role.

APPENDIX A

A Brief Note on the Quality and Reliability
of Chinese Communist Statistics

The problems of statistical reliability have been examined in a number of specialized studies such as C. M. Li, *The Statistical System of Communist China* (Berkeley, University of California Press, 1962); T. C. Liu and K. C. Yeh, *The Economy of the Chinese Mainland: National Income and Economic Development, 1933–1959* (Princeton University Press, 1965); Alexander Eckstein, *The National Income of Communist China* (New York: Free Press of Glencoe, 1961); Chao Kang, *The Rate and Pattern of Industrial Production in Communist China* (Ann Arbor: University of Michigan Press, 1965), and others. Therefore, it will suffice for present purposes to summarize the findings which emerge from these studies.

In appraising the quality and reliability of mainland China's statistics, we must remember that a State Statistical Bureau (SSB) of genuinely national, rather than local or regional, scope was founded only in late 1952. Before then, there was at no time a statistical network or organization which really encompassed the whole country. Moreover, qualified technical personnel were scarce.

Despite these handicaps and despite the vastness of the country and its population, significant strides in building a reasonably good statistical apparatus were made during the period of the First Five Year Plan (1953–57). A number of statisticians were trained in the Soviet Union and in Eastern Europe, and a number of Russians came to advise the statistical organs in China. As a result, the network was gradually extended, and its capacity to collect and process data was improved. This trend was sharply reversed in 1958, however, because of the Great Leap. The local statistical organs were subordinated to local party control, and their professional integrity and independence were thus destroyed. They degenerated into instruments for self-delusion and exhortation. There are a number of indications that this process of disintegration was halted in 1961–62 and that the painful process of rebuilding the statistical system has begun.

As a result of these trends, the quality and reliability of Chinese Communist statistics varies from period to period. One might perhaps distinguish five periods: 1949–51, 1952–54, 1955–57, 1958–59, and 1960 to the present. During the first of these, the new regime was still consolidating its hold over the country and organizing its system of administration and control. Therefore, statistics for this period are fragmentary and in many cases not comparable from year to year. With the organization of the SSB in 1952, one sees a gradual improvement in the quality of the data. However, this improvement introduced an element of incomparability, for increases in the output of some products—notably agricultural products—were due to better accounting rather than rising production. By 1955 the building of statistical institutions was essentially completed, so the territorial and accounting scope of the data remained fairly stable between 1955 and 1957. The best Chinese Communist statistics, thus, are those for these three years. The process of deterioration set in in 1958, and most of the published data for that year and for 1959 are of a low order of reliability. In early 1960 the regime imposed a nearly total blackout on statistics—probably in part to conceal the extent of the economic downturn in the country and in part because of the breakdown of the statistical apparatus. If this hypothesis has any validity, one could reasonably hope that as the economic situation improves and as the process of statistical reconstruction is completed, the Chinese Communists will resume the publication of statistics.

Just as the quality of Chinese Communist statistics differs by period, it also differs by economic sector. These differences are largely a function of the ease with which basic economic data can be collected. Thus, it is generally easier to collect more or less reliable economic information for large-scale as compared to small-scale enterprises and for state as compared to private establishments. The data for modern industry and modern transport, therefore, tend to be much better than those for agriculture, handicrafts, and native transport.

Beyond the question of basic quality and reliability is another question. How faithfully do the Chinese Communist authorities convey their statistical findings to the outside world? Do they deliberately falsify the data they present? Do they, in effect, keep two sets of books?

There is no evidence to support the hypothesis that they keep two sets of books, one for internal administrative use and another for external propaganda. Even if we assumed that the regime is committed to such a policy, it would be difficult to implement without producing administrative confusion and chaos. Economic statistics serve an important function in planning and in measuring performance. Publication of falsified statistics might mislead not only the people at large but the planners as well. Theoretically, the job of double bookkeeping could be done so well that this difficulty would be avoided. In practice, however, double bookkeeping would be most difficult to implement and would require considerable inputs of personnel highly skilled in statistics and accounting. Such skills are quite scarce in China.

Furthermore, there is some direct evidence to suggest the absence of two sets of books. When the statistical system disintegrated under the impact of the Greap Leap, fantastic production claims for agriculture and industry were advanced. These were then drastically revised downward in 1959. If published claims have only a propaganda function, why should they be revised downward? Such revisions would not make sense unless these statistics have some functional meaning in planning and administration.

Finally, the double-bookkeeping hypothesis appears implausible because the propaganda objectives it might be designed to achieve can be effectively accomplished by other means which are less expensive and administratively less disruptive. For example, the Chinese Communists can and do publish statistics in a camouflaged and misleading light. They may provide fairly complete data for those sectors which are performing well but suppress or present in a camouflaged form (*e.g.*, as percentage increases from an unknown base) information concerning other branches of the economy. Certain of their measures and indicators of performance may be methodologically faulty and may contain a strong upward bias. They may change the scope, comprehensiveness, and definition of certain series in ways which yield an upward bias without explicitly indicating that such a change has been made. In light of these circumstances, Chinese Communist statistics cannot be taken at face value, but neither can they be rejected as worthless—except for some sectors in 1958–59. One of the most important and continuing tasks is to penetrate the maze of statistical camouflage, to explore the derivation of Chinese figures, to test the plausibility and mutual consistency of their data, and thus to attempt to eliminate or reduce the biases built into the data.

APPENDIX B

The Foreign Trade Statistics

As the text of this study points out, all data on the foreign trade of mainland China were compiled from the trading partners' side. Some of the problems such a compilation presents have already been noted in Chapters 3, 4, and 5. In this appendix, the basic data for each country's trade with China will be presented, and some additional complications involved in aggregation will be pointed up.

The Non-Communist Countries. Table B-1 gives the exports and imports of virtually all non-Communist countries trading with mainland China. These data were compiled by the U.S. Department of Commerce from the foreign trade statistics of each individual country. The original data were then converted into dollars by the Department of Commerce and published in the annual reports of the Administrator of the Mutual Defense Assistance Control Act of 1951.

The table excludes countries with only minor trade with China. In addition, for some years it necessarily omits countries which did not report their trade with China. In all these cases, however, exports and imports were small.

As was noted in Chapter 4, non-Communist countries report their exports f.o.b., but most of them report their imports c.i.f. In this study, the latter were adjusted to an f.o.b basis for two reasons. First, the imports of the Soviet Union and Eastern Europe are accounted for on an f.o.b. basis. Second, it is important to separate the commodity components from the service components of foreign trade in order to make balance-of-payment calculations. If a trading partner's imports are accounted for on a c.i.f. basis, China may show a surplus in its trade with that country, and this fact will suggest that she earned some foreign exchange from the trade. An adjustment to an f.o.b. basis, however, may show a deficit in China's trade with that country. If the services, the charges for which are incorporated in the c.i.f. accounts, are all performed by the Chinese, then the net foreign exchange earnings will be the same regardless of how the trade is accounted for. If goods are shipped in foreign vessels and insured by foreign companies, on the other hand, there may in fact be a foreign exchange deficit, which the c.i.f. accounts will hide.

TABLE B-1. Trade of Non-Communist Countries with Communist China, 1952–63

(in millions of U.S. dollars)

Country (By Region)	1952 Ex	1952 Im	1953 Ex	1953 Im	1954 Ex	1954 Im	1955 Ex	1955 Im	1956 Ex	1956 Im
EAST, SOUTHEAST, AND SOUTH ASIA										
Burma	0.1	2.3	1.4	1.4	0.1	0.5	17.5	2.2	14.4	20.9
Cambodia	—	—	—	—	—	—	n.a.	n.a.	n.a.	n.a.
Ceylon	26.0	6.5	50.9	41.3	46.5	30.1	25.5	15.8	38.3	26.4
Hong Kong										
(1) Including re-exports	91.0	145.3	94.6	150.0	68.4	121.1	31.8	157.1	23.8	181.7
(2) Net of re-exports	(2.4)	(87.2)	(2.4)	(90.0)	(2.4)	(72.7)	(2.4)	(105.3)	(2.4)	(121.7)
India	10.2	32.0	7.3	3.3	8.6	4.5	19.1	7.6	13.8	20.2
Indochina	0.1	7.0	n.a.	5.6	0.2	8.4	—	—	—	—
Indonesia	—	1.8	—	2.0	2.3	3.3	6.2	9.3	11.7	28.4
Japan	0.6	14.0	4.5	27.9	19.1	38.4	28.5	76.0	67.3	78.7
Malaya and Singapore	—	37.1	1.9	32.3	6.4	26.8	4.2	35.5	7.8	40.5
Pakistan	83.9	3.5	7.3	5.8	26.1	3.5	31.7	0.4	15.9	8.3
Sarawak	—	—	—	—	—	—	—	—	—	—
Taiwan	—	9.1	—	5.5	—	3.2	—	1.8	—	1.4
Thailand	—	—	—	—	—	—	—	—	—	—
Vietnam	—	—	—	—	—	—	—	8.6	—	—
TOTAL										
(1) Including re-exports	211.9	258.6	167.9	275.1	177.7	239.8	164.5	314.3	193.0	406.5
(2) Net of re-exports	123.3	200.5	75.7	215.1	111.7	191.4	135.1	262.5	171.6	346.5
EUROPE										
Austria	0.3	n.a.	n.a.	0.9	1.3	0.8	1.8	1.1	7.4	2.0
Belgium and Luxembourg	0.6	4.4	1.4	6.9	0.5	2.1	7.0	1.8	21.4	4.7
Denmark	0.2	n.a.	0.3	2.0	0.4	0.3	0.1	0.2	3.1	1.3
Finland	6.6	0.3	5.4	1.5	6.6	2.6	12.5	3.9	7.5	2.4
France	3.2	5.3	12.4	10.3	8.7	8.8	7.2	11.1	22.8	13.9
Germany, Federal Republic	2.8	16.5	25.0	31.2	21.5	33.9	26.2	43.1	37.1	50.0
Greece	—	—	—	—	—	—	—	0.1	0.2	0.1
Ireland	—	—	—	—	—	—	—	—	—	—
Italy	3.7	2.1	4.7	7.0	6.2	2.0	5.7	3.9	10.4	10.7
Netherlands	n.a.	4.6	4.0	14.2	1.0	5.8	2.9	7.6	6.0	10.7
Norway	1.7	3.0	0.9	3.4	n.a.	2.3	n.a.	1.8	2.3	2.4
Portugal	—	0.1	—	0.2	—	0.2	—	0.1	0.3	0.2
Spain	—	—	—	—	—	—	—	—	—	—
Sweden	0.6	0.8	2.7	1.5	0.7	1.5	1.9	2.4	6.1	2.4
Switzerland	18.0	9.3	26.5	15.1	23.2	10.3	23.7	14.9	35.3	18.0
Turkey	0.1	—	—	—	—	—	—	—	—	—
United Kingdom	12.8	7.9	17.5	27.1	19.4	23.7	22.2	32.5	30.2	33.1
Yugoslavia	n.a.	n.a.	n.a.	n.a.	n.a.	n.a.	n.a.	n.a.	4.4	3.8
TOTAL	50.6	54.3	100.8	121.3	89.5	94.3	111.2	124.5	194.5	155.7

a January-March only

	1957		1958		1959		1960		1961		1962		1963	
	Ex	Im	Ex	Im	Ex	Im	Ex	Im	Ex	Im	Ex	Im	Ex	Im
	10.2	11.8	3.0	15.6	0.4	15.4	7.9	23.2	38.0	19.4	18.9	26.9	12.3	24.8
	n.a.	2.3	—	4.4	1.4	4.2	1.3	7.6	0.7	5.7	3.5	7.8	1.5	9.2
	35.2	16.5	16.3	30.0	16.4	29.6	25.3	26.1	17.4	6.9	28.0	8.1	21.1	27.3
	21.6	197.9	27.3	244.5	20.0	181.0	21.0	207.5	17.3	180.0	14.9	212.3	12.3	260.2
	(2.2)	(136.6)	(2.7)	(160.6)	1.5	(148.6)	2.3	(173.5)	1.4	(153.0)	1.5	(183.2)	1.4	(219.4)
	13.8	11.6	10.6	13.5	17.7	11.0	11.8	6.4	0.4	3.4	0.4	2.4	—	0.3
	—	—	—	—	—	—	—	—	—	—	—	—	—	—
	26.3	25.4	43.4	39.3	53.1	57.5	35.4	53.6	36.4	37.5	34.4	(42.0)	7.3[n]	n.a.
	60.5	75.7	50.6	51.1	3.6	17.8	2.7	19.5	16.6	29.0	38.5	43.2	62.4	70.1
	24.2	49.1	38.0	60.1	39.7	48.0	28.4	53.7	3.8	52.9	0.8	61.9	5.4	88.3
	9.5	7.3	7.6	9.7	0.7	3.9	14.8	3.8	10.0	3.4	1.6	3.9	12.9	5.5
	—	2.1	0.1	3.1	0.1	3.9	—	4.7	—	6.0	—	7.4	—	—
	—	1.5	—	1.3	—	1.5	—	2.1	—	1.0	—	1.0	—	1.0
	3.3	—	3.0	—	—	—	—	—	—	—	—	—	0.4	—
	—	—	—	—	—	—	—	—	—	—	—	—	—	—
	204.6	401.2	199.9	472.6	153.1	373.8	148.6	408.2	140.6	345.2	141.0	416.9	135.6	486.7
	185.2	339.9	175.3	388.7	134.6	341.4	129.9	374.2	124.7	318.2	127.6	387.8	124.7	445.9
	7.8	2.2	14.3	2.4	14.4	3.0	12.9	3.5	2.1	3.3	1.1	3.4	1.1	3.1
	22.2	3.8	52.1	5.7	33.5	8.2	44.6	9.3	10.2	3.2	8.0	4.5	9.5	7.7
	0.7	0.5	3.9	3.8	3.6	15.8	2.1	16.0	4.2	12.7	3.7	8.8	0.6	6.3
	6.3	5.7	8.4	3.7	16.5	4.4	6.6	4.2	6.0	2.4	5.1	2.0	5.7	2.8
	20.5	13.2	44.4	10.7	39.8	15.2	52.8	21.3	36.4	14.9	43.3	15.9	58.4	19.8
	47.6	38.7	162.3	55.0	128.7	62.3	95.4	65.2	30.5	37.3	31.2	36.9	15.4	38.4
	—	—	0.1	0.1	—	0.9	—	0.1	—	0.1	—	0.1	—	0.1
	—	0.4	—	0.7	—	0.3	—	1.3	—	0.8	—	0.6	0.1	0.9
	15.0	6.6	32.7	12.9	36.4	12.5	39.7	22.7	29.7	11.6	19.2	13.3	19.3	17.8
	5.5	9.2	11.9	16.1	20.8	11.2	6.9	20.1	4.1	14.3	3.6	13.1	12.9	14.8
	1.8	1.4	4.8	2.5	7.6	2.4	4.1	2.9	4.9	1.7	0.9	1.4	3.3	1.8
	0.3	0.3	0.2	0.2	0.6	0.2	0.3	0.3	0.1	0.3	0.1	0.1	0.2	0.2
	—	0.1	0.2	0.3	1.1	0.4	0.6	0.2	—	—	—	0.2	—	1.4
	27.0	2.9	17.6	3.6	14.4	5.1	13.3	5.5	7.6	4.0	4.8	4.9	4.7	7.2
	43.4	11.8	31.5	10.3	35.0	10.9	8.1	8.3	5.5	8.8	3.6	9.3	3.9	9.8
	—	—	—	—	—	—	—	—	—	—	—	—	—	—
	34.1	37.4	76.3	48.8	69.4	51.9	89.8	65.0	36.6	81.2	24.1	61.0	37.4	48.8
	4.1	6.8	4.6	1.3	1.4	2.4	1.1	0.5	n.a.	n.a.	n.a.	n.a.	n.a.	0.1
	236.3	141.0	465.3	178.1	413.6	216.7	378.3	248.4	177.9	196.6	148.7	175.5	172.5	181.0

TABLE B-1. (*Continued*)

	1952		1953		1954		1955		1956	
Country (By Region)	Ex	Im	Ex	Im	Ex	Im	Ex	Im	Ex	Im
OCEANIA										
Australia	0.6	3.3	5.3	3.9	3.2	3.8	6.3	4.1	10.1	4.2
New Zealand	—	0.7	—	0.6	—	0.6	0.4	0.8	0.4	0.9
TOTAL	0.6	4.0	5.3	4.5	3.2	4.4	6.7	4.9	10.5	5.1
NORTH AMERICA										
Canada	—	1.2	—	1.0	0.1	1.6	1.0	3.0	2.5	5.5
United States	—	23.1	—	0.6	—	0.2	—	0.2	—	0.2
TOTAL	—	24.3	—	1.6	0.1	1.8	1.0	3.2	2.5	5.7
NEAR EAST AND NORTH AFRICA										
Aden	—	—	—	—	—	—	—	—	—	—
Algeria	—	—	—	—	—	—	—	—	—	—
Cyprus	—	—	—	—	—	—	—	—	—	—
Egypt	8.9	0.7	10.4	0.7	11.4	0.8	24.5	0.8	24.2	10.4
Iran	—.	0.1	—	1.8	—	—	—	—	—	—
Iraq	—	—	—	—	—	—	—	—	—	—
Israel	—	0.1	—	—	—	—	—	—	—	—
Jordan	—	—	—	—	—	—	—	—	—	—
Kuwait	—	—	—	—	—	—	—	—	—	—
Lebanon	—	0.5	0.1	0.2	—	0.1	—	0.2	0.5	0.5
Libya	—	—	—	—	—	—	—	—	—	—
Malta	—	—	—	—	—	—	—	—	—	—
Morocco	—	5.2	—	6.8	—	10.4	—	17.9	—	18.6
Syria	—	0.1	—	1.0	0.6	0.2	0.2	0.2	1.6	0.3
Tangier	—	—	—	—	—	—	—	—	—	—
Tunisia	—	—	—	—	—	—	—	—	—	—
TOTAL	8.9	6.7	10.5	10.5	12.0	11.5	24.7	19.1	26.3	29.8
SUB-SAHARAN AFRICA										
Angola	—	—	—	—	—	—	—	—	—	—
Belgian Congo	—	—	—	—	—	—	—	—	—	—
Cameroon	—	—	—	—	—	—	—	—	—	—
Ethiopia	—	—	—	—	—	—	—	—	—	—
French West Africa	—	—	—	—	—	—	—	—	—	—
Ghana	—	—	—	—	—	—	—	0.1	—	0.1
Guinea	—	—	—	—	—	—	—	—	—	—
Ivory Coast	—	—	—	—	—	—	—	—	—	—
Kenya and Tanganyika	—	—	—	—	—	—	—	—	—	—
Mali	—	—	—	—	—	—	—	—	—	—
Nigeria	—	0.1	—	—	—	—	—	0.6	—	1.2
Rhodesia and Nyasaland, Federation of	—	—	—	—	—	—	—	—	—	—
Senegal, Soudan, and Mauritania	—	—	—	—	—	—	—	—.	—	—
Sierra Leone	—	—	—	—	—	—	—	—	—	—
Sudan	—	—	—	—	—	—	—	—	—	—
Uganda	—	—	—	—	—	—	—	—	—	—
Union of South Africa	—	0.1	0.1	0.5	0.7	0.8	1.2	0.9	1.2	0.9
TOTAL	—	0.2	0.1	0.5	0.7	0.8	1.2	1.6	1.2	2.2

1957		1958		1959		1960		1961		1962		1963	
Ex	Im	Ex	Im	Ex	Im	Ex	Im	Ex	Im	Ex	Im	Ex	Im
20.5	5.4	27.2	7.6	30.1	7.8	23.5	9.7	161.5	6.5	97.8	10.4	207.8	13.6
1.7	0.9	2.7	1.2	7.0	1.1	6.5	1.1	3.7	1.1	3.3	1.1	4.9	1.8
22.2	6.3	29.9	8.8	37.1	8.9	30.0	10.8	165.2	7.6	101.1	11.5	212.7	15.4
1.5	5.2	8.1	5.2	1.8	4.7	8.9	5.5	120.9	3.0	137.0	4.0	96.9	4.5
—	0.1	—	0.1	—	0.2	—	0.3	—	0.4	—	0.2	—	0.3
1.5	5.3	8.1	5.3	1.8	4.9	8.9	5.8	120.9	3.4	137.0	4.2	96.9	4.8
0.3	0.4	0.1	0.1	0.2	0.1	0.1	0.2	—	0.1	—	0.1	—	0.1
—	2.4	—	2.3	—	1.9	—	1.7	—	0.8	—	—	—	—
—	—	—	—	—	—	—	—	—	—	—	—	—	—
42.1	19.4	34.9	23.6	33.8	22.3	44.5	18.3	14.6	17.8	19.1	18.1	16.4	18.7
—	—	—	0.2	2.3	3.3	1.6	6.8	1.5	5.9	4.0	8.7	4.5	11.8
—	—	—	—	—	—	—	—	—	—	—	—	—	—
—	0.1	—	0.4	—	—	—	1.0	—	0.8	—	1.2	—	1.9
—	0.4	—	1.0	—	2.0	—	1.1	—	1.5	—	2.1	—	—
—	0.5	—	0.6	—	—	—	1.3	—	1.0	0.2	2.0	—	—
—	—	—	0.1	—	0.1	—	0.3	—	—	—	—	—	0.3
—	—	—	—	—	—	—	0.1	—	0.1	—	0.1	—	0.1
—	11.8	3.1	15.0	6.5	7.5	6.6	6.7	3.7	8.1	4.2	8.4	6.2	6.4
10.0	0.5	6.7	1.1	0.1	1.6	2.3	1.2	12.1	1.0	4.4	3.5	19.9	2.8
—	0.1	—	0.1	—	0.2	—	—	—	—	—	—	—	—
—	0.6	—	0.5	0.8	1.3	—	0.8	0.5	1.2	0.2	0.6	—	0.9
52.4	36.2	44.8	45.0	43.7	40.3	55.1	39.5	32.4	38.3	32.1	44.8	47.0	43.0
—	—	—	—	—	—	0.4	—	—	—	—	—	—	—
—	—	—	—	—	—	—	—	—	—	—	0.1	0.6	—
—	—	—	0.1	—	0.1	—	—	—	—	—	0.1	—	0.2
—	—	—	—	—	0.1	0.1	0.2	—	0.3	—	1.0	—	—
—	1.8	—	3.7	—	—	—	—	—	—	—	—	—	—
—	0.8	—	0.7	—	2.1	1.4	2.8	0.2	2.3	1.2	3.6	0.5	2.0
—	—	—	—	—	—	—	0.6	2.1	4.3	0.6	0.5	0.9	3.9
—	—	—	—	—	1.2	—	—	—	1.2	—	1.6	—	—
—	—	—	—	—	—	1.0	0.1	0.2	—	0.5	0.1	11.4	0.5
—	—	—	—	—	—	—	—	—	0.1	—	0.8	—	1.1
—	2.7	—	3.9	0.1	4.9	1.2	4.7	3.8	6.0	—	4.1	1.0	4.1
—	—	1.0	0.1	1.0	0.1	0.5	0.1	—	0.2	2.5	0.3	0.8	—
—	—	—	—	—	6.1	—	6.0	—	3.1	—	4.9	—	2.1
—	—	—	—	—	—	—	0.3	—	0.4	—	0.5	—	0.3
1.7	0.7	2.1	1.4	2.9	2.4	9.4	2.1	4.0	4.4	9.6	3.6	9.0	3.6
2.3	—	—	—	—	—	—	5.1	—	9.4	—	—	11.2	0.8
2.8	1.3	7.0	3.8	11.9	1.9	9.3	2.2	—	0.8	1.3	1.2	6.0	2.4
6.8	7.3	10.1	13.7	15.9	18.9	28.4	19.1	19.7	23.1	15.7	22.4	41.4	21.0

TABLE B-1. (*Continued*)

Country (By Region)	1952		1953		1954		1955		1956	
	Ex	Im	Ex	Im	Ex	Im	Ex	Im	Ex	Im
LATIN AMERICA										
Argentina	—	0.3	—	—	—	—	1.0	—	0.8	1.0
Brazil	—	—	0.9	—	2.6	—	4.6	—	0.7	—
Chile	—	—	—	—	—	—	—	—	—	—
Colombia	—	—	—	—	—	—	—	—	—	—
Ecuador	—	—	—	—	—	—⁄	—	—	—	—
Haiti	—	—	—	—	—	+—	—	—	—	—
Mexico	—	—	—	—	—	—	—	—	—	—
Peru	—	—	—	—	—	—	—	—	—	—
Uruguay	—	—	—	—	—	—	—	—	0.1	—
Venezuela	—	—	—	—	—	—	—	—	—	—
TOTAL	—	0.3	0.9	—	2.6	—	5.6	—	1.6	1.0
TOTAL—ALL COUNTRIES										
(1) Including re-exports	272.0	348.4	285.5	413.5	285.8	352.6	314.9	467.6	429.6	606.0
(2) Net of re-exports	183.4	290.3	193.3	353.5	219.8	304.2	285.5	415.8	408.2	546.0

Notes: Figures in parentheses are the author's estimates.
n.a. stands for "not available."

The total trade figures in Table B-1 are subject to additional margins of error arising from some double counting. This double counting stems chiefly from the fact that a certain share of Hong Kong's imports from the non-Communist world is re-exported to China and a certain portion of the colony's imports from China is re-exported to the non-Communist world. To the extent that countries report their exports by country of destination and imports by country of origin, goods to and from China will be counted twice if they are shipped through Hong Kong: once in the trade statistics of the exporting or importing country and a second time in Hong Kong's foreign trade accounts. The problem has been taken care of as far as exports to mainland China for the period since 1959 are concerned. In 1959, the Hong Kong government began separate publication of data on domestically produced exports and on re-exports by country of destination (Hong Kong Department of Commerce and Industry, *Hong Kong Trade Statistics, Exports*). Similarly, since 1960 the reports of the Administrator of the U.S. Mutual Defense Assistance Control Act of 1951 have shown only domestic exports from Hong Kong.

While such data eliminate double counting on the export side, they introduce a discontinuity and incomparability into the series. Therefore, both the export and re-export figures are shown in Table B-2. The table also includes my estimates of domestic exports for the earlier years. For 1959–62, domestic exports to China amounted to around 10 per cent of the total, and the remaining 90 per cent were re-exports. I assumed that this percentage would also hold for 1956–58,

1957		1958		1959		1960		1961		1962		1963	
Ex	Im	Ex	Im	Ex	Im	Ex	Im	Ex	Im	Ex	Im	Ex	Im
0.7	0.1	0.1	—	0.4	—	1.4	—	4.2	0.2	26.4	0.2	3.1	0.1
—	—	7.5	—	—	0.1	0.5	—	—	0.1	—	0.4	0.2	0.8
—	0.6	—	1.3	—	—	—	—	—	—	—	—	—	—
—	—	—	—	—	0.1	—	0.1	—	—	—	—	—	0.05
—	—	—	—	—	—	—	—	—	—	—	—	—	—
0.6	0.5	0.3	0.3	1.5	0.5	—	—	—	—	—	—	. —	—
—	—	—	—	—	—	—	—	—	—	—	—	—	—
2.6	—	1.0	—	2.8	—	4.3	—	2.4	—	0.7	—	0.1	—
—	0.1	—	0.2	—	0.2	—	0.5	—	0.5	—	0.3	—	0.2
3.9	1.3	8.9	1.8	4.7	0.9	6.2	0.6	6.6	0.8	27.1	0.9	3.4	1.2
527.7	598.6	767.0	725.3	669.9	664.4	655.5	732.4	663.3	615.0	602.7	676.2	709.5	753.1
508.3	537.3	742.4	641.4	651.4	632.0	636.8	698.4	647.4	588.0	589.3	647.1	698.6	712.3

— stands for "none" or "not entered under that political entity."
Sources: U. S. Mutual Defense Assistance Control Act Administrator, *Report to Congress* for various years.

when total exports were relatively stable. Total exports, of course, were much higher in the early fifties than later. Nevertheless, a significantly larger portion of the exports of non-Communist countries to China went through Hong Kong, and manufacturing was not yet as important in the colony's economy as it became during the latter part of the decade. Therefore, it is most unlikely that domestic exports to China during the early fifties could have exceeded the 1956 level.

Unfortunately, the Hong Kong government has not changed its procedure for reporting imports. Imports for domestic consumption and processing are still lumped together with those for re-export. Theoretically, one could make three alternative assumptions about the composition of the colony's imports from China: namely, that (a) none are retained, (b) none are re-exported, and (c) some, but not all, are re-exported. The first two possibilities can be ruled out since they are contrary to all the available evidence. Therefore, the problem is to estimate the re-export share.

The import adjustment in Table B-2 is based on the assumption that the re-export share of Hong Kong's imports from China was roughly the same as that for total imports into the colony. Proceeding from this assumption, I first estimated the share net of re-exports to China for 1959–62 on the basis of the published figures cited above. For 1957 and 1958, there are data for total imports and total re-exports, but the latter are not broken down by destination. I therefore estimated the net re-export share for these years by assuming that

TABLE B-2. Hong Kong's Trade with Communist China, 1952–63

Year	Exports to China	Re-exports	Net Exports (1)-(2)	Imports from China	Estimated Re-export Share	Estimated Re-exports	Net Imports (4)-(6)
	(in millions of U.S. dollars)			(in millions of U.S. dollars)	(in per cent)	(in millions of U.S. dollars)	
	(1)	(2)	(3)	(4)	(5)	(6)	(7)
1952	91.1	(88.6)	(2.4)	145.3	(40.0)	(58.1)	(87.2)
1953	94.6	(92.2)	(2.4)	150.0	(40.0)	(60.0)	(90.0)
1954	68.4	(66.0)	(2.4)	121.1	(40.0)	(48.4)	(72.7)
1955	31.8	(29.4)	(2.4)	157.1	(33.0)	(51.8)	(105.3)
1956	23.8	(21.4)	(2.4)	181.7	(33.0)	(60.0)	(121.7)
1957	21.6	(19.4)	(2.2)	197.9	(31.0)	(61.3)	(136.6)
1958	27.3	(24.6)	(2.7)	244.5	(34.3)	(83.9)	(160.6)
1959	20.0	18.5	1.5	181.0	(17.9)	(32.4)	(148.6)
1960	21.0	18.7	2.3	207.5	(16.4)	(34.0)	(173.5)
1961	17.3	15.9	1.4	180.0	(15.0)	(27.0)	(153.0)
1962	14.9	13.5	1.5	212.3	(13.9)	(29.1)	(183.2)
1963	12.3	10.9	1.4	260.2	(15.7)	(40.8)	(219.4)

Note: The figures in parentheses are the author's estimates.

Sources: Hong Kong, Department of Commerce and Industry, *Hong Kong Trade Bulletin* and *Hong Kong Trade Statistics, Exports.*

re-exports to China would comprise the same proportion of total re-exports as they did during 1959–62. For 1955–56, I assumed that the share was about the same as for 1957–58. In the earlier years, however, it must have been higher. As we have already noted, manufactures were not so highly developed in Hong Kong in the early fifties; moreover, the population was much smaller. It is therefore reasonable to assume that the share of Chinese imports retained in the colony was smaller at that time. The net import series thus estimated is probably subject to a considerable margin of error. This error is probably significantly larger for the earlier than for the later years, and it is more likely to involve an understatement rather than an overstatement of the re-export share.

The double-counting problem is not confined to Hong Kong. For example, a sizable share of West Germany's trade with China was transshipped through third countries. The same applies to several other European countries. To eliminate this source of error would be a formidable statistical task which we did not attempt here. As a result, the data in Table 4-1 overstate China's exports and imports.

The trade data presented in Table B-1 also contain some less important sources of error. For instance, certain countries include Outer Mongolia and Macao in their definition of the Chinese mainland. For details of these errors and qualifications, the reader is referred to the appendices of the annual reports of the Administrator of the U.S. Mutual Defense Assistance Control Act of 1951.

The adjustments for double counting and for the c.i.f. factor described above could not be applied to the data on commodity composition. My adjustment factors are averages based on the trade data for one or two years. We would need detailed breakdowns of freight charges commodity by commodity to make the necessary c.i.f. adjustments in the tables on commodity composition. Similarly, we would require transshipment data for the different commodities. This type of information would be difficult, if not impossible, to obtain and even then would be time-consuming and laborious to compile. Therefore, the attempt was not made in this study. For this reason, the total values given for imports and exports in the commodity composition tables differ from those given in all the other tables.

Soviet Union. Soviet export and import data for 1955–63 were taken from the foreign trade handbooks published annually by the Ministry of Foreign Trade. The specific volumes actually used are cited in Tables 4-5, 5-3, and 5-5. Trade figures for 1950–54 were obtained from M. I. Sladkovskii, "The Development of the Soviet Union's Trade with the Chinese People's Republic," *Vneshniaia Torgovlia*

[*Foreign Trade*], v. 29, no. 10, October 1959, pp. 2–10. The foreign trade data thus compiled are perfectly straightforward with one exception. Prior to 1957 and most particularly prior to 1955, as was noted earlier, some exports from Western Europe to China were shipped through the Soviet Union. These goods were on the Chinese but not the Soviet control list. Similarly, there were certain commodities which the Soviets purchased from China but then resold in West European markets. To the extent that such trade took place, West European exports to and imports from China are understated, and those for the Soviet Union are correspondingly overstated. Furthermore, this trade probably led, depending upon how it was accounted for, to some double counting. Unfortunately, there are no detailed data on transshipments and resales, so it is impossible to adjust for this source of error.

Eastern Europe. For many years, data concerning the trade of the East European countries with mainland China could be obtained from the United Nations *Yearbook of International Trade Statistics.* These data are in national currency units and were converted to dollars at the official exchange rates. For several countries, trade figures for some of the earlier years were obtained from national statistical sources. When data could not be obtained from one of these two kinds of primary sources, the secondary sources cited in Table B-3 were used. In some of these secondary sources, the trade values are expressed in rubles. These values were converted to dollars at the official exchange rate. The economic rationale for converting trade values to dollars at official exchange rates is explored in Appendix C.

For Rumania, no trade data could be obtained for 1952–54 and for 1957. The trade totals given for these years in Table B-3 are based on the assumption that annual changes in Rumania's exports to and imports from China moved in the same direction and at the same rate as those of the other East European countries combined.

The 1963 figures for Albania, Bulgaria, and Hungary also had to be estimated. For Albania, only total export and import figures were available. I derived exports to and imports from China by assuming that the mainland share in Albania's trade remained constant between 1962 and 1963. In the case of Bulgaria, I could find no 1963 trade data. In estimating exports to and imports from China, I assumed that they increased at the same rate as did those of all the other East European countries combined. For Hungary, only total turnover data on trade with China were available. From these, I estimated exports and imports by assuming that the ratio of these to each other remained unchanged between 1962 and 1963.

Asian Communist Countries. As was indicated in Chapter 4, there are virtually no data for mainland China's trade with North Korea, North Vietnam, and Outer Mongolia. Some scattered data for some years can be found in secondary sources, and these served as the basis for the estimates in the present study. After the completion of this manuscript, estimates for China's exports to and imports from the Asian Communist countries were published in *A Background Study on East-West Trade*, Prepared for the Senate Committee on Foreign Relations by the Legislative Reference Service of the Library of Congress, April 1964, Committee Print, 89th Cong., 1st sess. (Washington, D.C.: GPO, 1965). By the time these came to my attention, however, it was no longer possible to take account of them in this study. My estimates are based on the following data:

(a) Dollar figures for China's exports to and imports from this group of countries in 1953–56 (as estimated by the Research and Planning Division of the Economic Commission for Europe and published in the *Economic Survey of Europe, 1957* [Geneva: Author, 1958], Chapter 6, p. 5).

(b) Total turnover figures, expressed in dollar values, for China's trade with these countries in 1957–59 (obtained from some unpublished studies and from trade sources in the Far East).

(c) Total Chinese exports to and imports from the Communist world for 1960 and 1961 (obtained from the same sources noted in b).

(d) China's total trade turnover and her trade with the Soviet Union, Eastern Europe, and the non-Communist world for 1963 (obtained from the same sources noted in b).

China's trade with the Soviet Union and Eastern Europe for 1960–61 could be derived on the basis of the data and methods outlined above and in Chapters 4 and 5. By deducting the values for Soviet and East European exports and imports given in Table 4-3 and B-3 from the Communist world totals cited above, I obtained the 1960 and 1961 export and import figures for China's trade with the Asian Communist countries as a residual. As a result, I now had dollar figures for these countries' exports to and imports from China during 1953–56 and 1960–61. Combining these data with those for the Soviet Union, Eastern Europe, and the non-Communist world, I computed China's total exports and imports for these years. On this basis, it seemed that

TABLE B-3. Trade of East European Countries with Communist China, 1952–63

(in thousands of U.S. dollars)

Country	1952 Ex	1952 Im	1953 Ex	1953 Im	1954 Ex	1954 Im	1955 Ex	1955 Im	1956 Ex	1956 Im	1957 Ex	1957 Im
Albania	—	—	—	—	—	—	—	1,268	724	4,094	676	5,904
Bulgaria	575	1,910	4,500	5,250	4,012	3,797	4,559	4,265	5,147	5,147	3,971	4,559
Czechoslovakia	(48,000)	(47,000)	60,695	55,695	64,445	55,000	57,639	60,695	64,723	66,389	81,251	66,945
East Germany	41,025	30,010	60,386	53,035	97,768	67,387	97,418	86,666	94,942	85,915	105,770	88,566
Hungary	20,625	27,275	29,522	33,543	30,859	27,077	36,500	29,011	30,868	29,496	29,445	31,345
Poland	23,750	33,750	31,000	27,250	37,000	29,500	34,950	35,400	50,300	35,225	44,800	37,325
Rumania	n.a.	n.a.	n.a.	n.a.	n.a.	n.a.	6,000	14,000	17,000	11,000	n.a.	n.a.
Total a	143,205	146,777	198,926	182,268	250,214	191,645	237,066	231,305	263,704	237,266	283,913	248,707

a The totals include an allowance for Rumania for those years for which there are no data.

Notes: Data in parentheses are the author's estimates.
  — stands for "none."
  n.a. stands for "not available."

Country	1958		1959		1960		1961		1962		1963	
	Ex	Im	Ex	Im	Ex	Im	Ex	Im	Ex	Im	Ex	Im
Albania	810	1,684	846	2,412	2,082	6,972	2,770	18,940	11,700	42,100	(13,700)	(45,300)
Bulgaria	11,029	7,059	6,324	10,588	7,500	9,559	7,500	4,523	3,324	3,243	(3,700)	(3,400)
Czechoslovakia	109,170	90,973	99,584	95,556	109,310	93,334	34,028	41,945	11,900	25,600	24,100	30,700
East Germany	133,270	107,450	106,470	115,010	97,119	100,230	55,116	40,115	21,780	31,890	10,400	24,700
Hungary	57,578	33,543	39,618	44,295	40,214	36,295	28,798	17,253	11,888	11,000	12,000	11,300
Poland	72,150	36,250	42,875	56,050	49,950	46,375	26,700	20,675	15,050	22,750	11,200	24,800
Rumania	25,851	16,600	29,451	29,934	33,334	23,600	9,284	19,734	2,183	10,534	13,800	14,100
Total[a]	409,858	293,559	325,168	353,845	339,509	316,365	164,196	163,185	77,825	147,117	88,900	154,300

Sources: United Nations, Yearbook of International Trade Statistics for 1956, 1957, 1958, 1960, 1961, and 1962; Albania, Annuari Statistikor, 1961 (Tirana, 1962); Hungary, Statisztikai Evkönyv, 1961 (Budapest, 1962); Statisztikai Havi Közlemenyèk (Budapest), September and December 1957; Poland, Rocznik Statystyczny, 1961 (Warsaw, 1962); Biuletyn Statystyczny (Warsaw), June 1963; Handelj Zagranicbnii (Warsaw), no. 11, 1956, and no. 4, 1957; Tribuna Ludu (Warsaw), February 15, 1958; U.S. Department of Agriculture, Trends and Developments in Communist China's World Trade in Farm Products, 1955–1960, Foreign Agricultural Economic Report, no. 6 (Washington, D.C.: Author, September 1962), Table 5, p. 16; Oleg Hoeffding, "Sino-Soviet Economic Relations in Recent Years," in Kurt London, ed., Unity and Contradiction: Major Aspects of Sino-Soviet Relations (New York: Praeger, 1962), pp. 295–311; Heinz Köhler, East Germany's Economic Integration into the Communist Bloc (Ann Arbor, unpublished doctoral dissertation), pp. 84–88 and 398–400; United Nations, Economic Commission for Europe, Economic Survey of Europe, 1957 (Geneva: Author, 1958), chapter 6, pp. 35–36; U.S. Central Intelligence Agency, Foreign Trade of the European Satellites, 1963, Intelligence Report (Washington, D.C.: Author, December 1964).

mainland China had obtained about 4.1 per cent of her total imports from these countries in 1956 and 4.4 per cent in 1960. It thus appeared reasonable to assume that in the intervening years—that is, between 1957 and 1959—the ratio of China's imports from these countries had remained more or less constant. With China's imports from other countries given for these years, it was then possible to estimate the values of her purchases from her Asian Communist neighbors. On the basis of the total trade turnover data cited under (b) above, it was then possible to derive exports as a residual.

From the 1963 data at my disposal, total turnover values for the Asian Communist countries could be derived as residuals. They show that China's total trade with these countries increased by 7 per cent between 1961 and 1963. I assumed that imports and exports rose at the same rate and then computed the 1963 sales and purchase values. Finally, with the 1961 and 1963 import and export figures given, I could derive the 1962 data by interpolation.

Since the original country figures for these Asian Communist countries are not available and since the method of converting the original currencies into dollars is not given in my sources, all these figures are subject to sizable margins of error. However, even large errors in the Asian bloc totals would not greatly affect Communist China's aggregate trade values, for trade with the Asian Communist countries constitutes a comparatively small share of Communist China's total trade.

Cuba. In the tables in Chapter 4, Cuba appears in a category by itself—under neither the Communist nor the non-Communist countries. The reason is that it would have to be included in the non-Communist total prior to 1960 but would have to be shifted to the Communist column after that. Under such circumstances, neither the Communist nor the non-Communist series would be comparable from year to year. The export and import figures for Cuba's trade with China were obtained from the annual reports of the Administrator of the U.S. Mutual Defense Assistance Control Act of 1951.

APPENDIX C

Foreign Exchange Rates *

In China, as in all Communist countries, foreign trade is nationalized. Thus, it is carried on by various state enterprises enjoying complete export or import monopoly in their special fields. These enterprises, in turn, buy their products for export from or sell their imports to state companies engaged in domestic trade. The performance of the foreign trade enterprises may be evaluated according to criteria other than profits—such as total turnover or earnings of foreign exchange. The measurement of performance according to these criteria is facilitated by the fact that the profits of foreign trade enterprises are paid into the state treasury and entered on the revenue side of the government budget, while their losses are subsidized and carried on the expenditure side of the budget. This situation does not necessarily mean that an enterprise has no profit (or maximum-loss) plan but merely that profits may be subordinated to other considerations.

Under such circumstances, foreign-trade pricing can easily be divorced from domestic pricing, as it indeed is in China and other Communist countries. Similarly, foreign exchange rates can be set at arbitrary levels, and multiple rates can be introduced. Such rates may involve differentiation either between countries and/or between types of transactions.

Since 1950, Communist China's international transactions have apparently been based on multiple and disequilibrium rates. For example, it was officially admitted in 1957 that, on the basis of the prevailing exchange rate, the yuan was overvalued in relation to the dollar and to other Western currencies.[1] On the other hand, it was undervalued in relation to the "trade ruble." [2] Until 1960 there were at least two ruble-yuan rates on record, one for commercial exchanges (the "trade ruble") and the other for noncommercial transactions. These different rates can be summarized as follows:

* I am indebted to Professor Chao Kang for his most useful insights on a number of points relating to this subject.

Yuan-dollar rates [3]

1950–December 1952	2.2–4.2 yuan to the dollar
December 1952–1953	2.46 yuan to the dollar
1954–mid-1957	2.36 yuan to the dollar
Mid-1957–present	2.617 yuan to the dollar

Ruble-yuan rates [4]

1950–60

(a) official rate	1.00 ruble to the yuan
(b) special rate for non-commercial payments	6.00 rubles to the yuan
1961–present	0.45 rubles to the yuan

Ruble-dollar rates [5]

1950–59

(a) official rate	4.00 rubles to the dollar
(b) special rate for non-commercial payments	10.00 rubles to the dollar
1961–present	0.90 rubles to the dollar

Occasional references can also be found to another rate of two old rubles to the yuan.[6] The significance of this rate and the types of payments it would be used for could not be ascertained.

For purposes of this study, the exchange rates are of prime importance in three contexts: the valuation of foreign trade, the valuation of capital flows and of noncommercial items in the balance of payments, and the valuation of international transactions as a whole in the national income accounts.

Foreign Trade Values and the Exchange Rates. The above figures clearly show that the yuan-dollar and ruble-dollar rates were inconsistent with the official ruble-yuan rate before 1961. On the basis of the former rates, the ruble-yuan rate should have been 1.63:1 up to 1953, 1.70:1 up to mid-1957, and 1.53:1 up to 1960 instead of the actual rate of 1:1. As a result, the yuan was undervalued in relation to the ruble, and the ruble was correspondingly overvalued in relation to the yuan. As was shown in Chapter 4, these mutually inconsistent exchange rates overstate the total value of China's foreign trade at any one time, and they exaggerate the yuan share of her trade with the Soviet Union and Eastern Europe in the total. The larger this share is in fact, the more the percentages for both total trade and trade with the European Communist countries are overstated. Moreover, shifts in the share of her trade with the European bloc can affect value totals even in the absence of any changes in volume. This fact may be illustrated by the following hypothetical example:

Total Trade Turnover in Year 1

Region	in original currencies (1)	in yuan at official exchange rates (2)	in dollars at official exchange rates (3)
Soviet Union and Eastern Europe	60 rubles	60	15
Non-Communist world	40 dollars	95	40
		155	55

Total Trade Turnover in Year 2

Region	in original currencies (1)	in yuan at official exchange rates (2)	in dollars at official exchange rates (3)
Soviet Union and Eastern Europe	160 rubles	160	40
Non-Communist world	25 dollars	59	25
		219	65

For both years the original currency values were converted to yuan and dollars respectively at the official exchange rates. The dollar values here increased by about *18 per cent,* but as a result of the simultaneous reorientation of trade in favor of the Soviet Union and Eastern Europe, the yuan value of trade rose by more than *40 per cent.* Because of these distortions, the yuan values of trade were not used in this study. Instead, trading partner data were converted to dollars, and the whole analysis is based on these dollar values.

How valid are the dollar values, and what are the appropriate rates of exchange to use to convert the trade figures? The figures for Communist China's trade with the non-Communist world are compiled annually in dollar terms by the U.S. Department of Commerce, and these figures are shown in Appendix B. The Chinese Minister of Foreign Trade has indicated that the non-Communist world's trade with China is conducted on the basis of world prices. These price quotations may be stated in dollars or in other currencies converted to dollars at the prevailing rates of exchange. In recent years, during which the currencies of most non-Communist countries have become freely convertible, these exchange rates may be considered more or less near the equilibrium levels. For the early 1950s, when a number of currencies were not yet fully convertible to the dollar, the same may not be equally true.

The situation is different and much more complicated with respect to trade with the European Communist countries. Figures for this trade were obtained from Soviet and East European statistics, and the ruble values were converted to dollars at the 4:1 rate. How valid is this rate? To what extent does it reflect the actual dollar value of goods traded?

We know that the trade of the Soviet Union and Eastern Europe with China is accounted for in rubles. That is, the ruble serves as the unit of account. In principle, the prices of the goods exported or imported are based on *world market prices* quoted in dollars, sterling, French francs, etc.[7] These quotations are then translated into rubles at the 4:1 rate in case of the dollar or at corresponding rates for other currencies, all of which are reducible to the dollar. This procedure permits trade values quoted in rubles to be converted back to the original dollar values.

If we assume, therefore, that all ruble values of the European Communist countries' exports to and imports from China are based on world market quotations, it does not matter what the ruble-dollar rate is and how closely it approximates or how far it departs from the standard of purchasing power parity. For our particular purposes, it also does not matter what the relationship between world market prices—at which goods are traded—and domestic prices is. Within the context of Soviet-type economic institutions, as was pointed out earlier, the pricing of foreign trade can be divorced from domestic pricing, so the two markets can, at least in theory, be completely separated and need not mutually interact.

The situation would, of course, be vastly different if foreign trade prices were based on domestic price quotations. In that case, it would be crucial to establish what the purchasing power parity of the foreign trade commodity basket is. On the basis of available studies, it is likely to have been closer to 10 (old) rubles to the dollar than 4 to 1.[8] Therefore, the validity of the 4:1 rate used in this study rests on the assumption that China's trade with the Soviet Union and Eastern Europe was based on world market prices.

What is the actual evidence on the pricing of foreign trade? F. H. Mah, in the study cited in Chapter 5, found that for the sample of commodities he studied, the unit values of Soviet exports to China, in 1955–59 were on the average 35.3, 31.2, 26.9, 5.7, and 30.0 per cent above the corresponding values of Soviet exports to non-Communist Europe. For the same sample, on the other hand, the unit values of Soviet imports from China were on the average 3.7 and 4.4 per cent above those of imports from non-Communist Europe in 1955 and 1956 respectively, and 2.5, 6.6, and 5.6 per cent below in 1957, 1958, and 1959 respectively. These findings would suggest a "China differential" in the pricing of Soviet exports but virtually none in the pricing of imports. However, as I noted in the text of Chapter 5, the bulk of the differential in Soviet exports was due to the high cost of transporting goods overland from factories in European Russia to the Russian-Chinese border in Asia.

Other evidence would also tend to support the general conclusion that while prices in trade with the European Communist countries do often depart from world market prices, these departures tend to be of modest proportions. Moreover, even if these prices deviate from world market prices, they are much closer to the latter than to domestic prices.[9]

Exchange Rates for Sino-Soviet Credits.   Throughout this study, it was assumed that Soviet credits to China and Chinese repayments should be accounted for at the official ruble-yuan rate of 1:1 and that, correspondingly, both the yuan and ruble values should be converted into dollars at the 4:1 rate. This assumption is based on the fact that the bulk of credits is embodied in Soviet exports and the largest share of loan amortization payments is embodied in Chinese exports. Therefore, the application of the commercial 1:1 rate would seem reasonable.

The noncommercial rate of 6:1 (prior to 1961) seems to have applied only to tourist, diplomatic, student, and some other special categories of exchange. However, Professor Chao Kang in a recent paper presents some evidence which suggests that the flows of Sino-Soviet credit and repayment and exports and imports financed by these were carried in a special dollar account and converted to rubles and yuan at their respective exchange rates of 4:1 and 2.36–2.62:1.[10]

If so, the actual ruble-yuan rates would have been 1.63:1 up to 1953, 1.69:1 from 1954 to mid-1957, 1.53:1 from mid-1957 to January 1, 1961, and 0.34:1 since.

Chou En-lai in his "Report on the Government's Work" at the December 1964 session of the National People's Congress stated that "in this period foreign debts outstanding plus interest charges due totaled 1,406 million new rubles. . . ." [11] This would amount to about $1,560 million (at the official exchange rate of $1.111 to the new ruble). On the other hand, as was noted in Chapter 5, the Chinese Minister of Finance in 1957 indicated that total Soviet credits extended to the mainland were about 5,300 million yuan, which at a 1:1 ruble-yuan rate and a 4:1 ruble-dollar rate would amount to $1,325 million.

It is not clear from the context of Chou En-lai's speech what precise period his figures refer to and whether they include both long-term and short-term loans. If one hypothesized that Chou's figures covered only long-term borrowing, the $1,560 million inclusive of interest charges could then be considered equivalent to the $1,325 million figure, which excludes interest. Chou's loan figures could therefore be regarded as a confirmation of the hypothesis that Soviet loans should be converted into yuan at the same trade-ruble rate as the export and import values.

This interpretation is open to question, however. Chou's figures may refer to a shorter period such as 1960–64, in which case cumulative Chinese indebtedness for the 1949–64 period would have been larger. This assumption would seem to be confirmed by Mikhail Suslov's speech to the Central Committee of the Soviet party on February 14, 1964.[12] In it, he states that the Soviet Union extended to China long-term credits totaling 1,816 million new rubles. This would be equivalent to about $2,020 million—that is, a significantly larger loan total than that cited earlier. There could be two reasons for such a discrepancy. Either the Soviets actually extended credits over and above the 5,300 million yuan mentioned by Li Hsien-nien, or the 1:1 ruble-yuan rate is not applicable to the Russian credits.

Ultimately, what all this analysis suggests is that on the basis of present information we cannot be certain at what exchange rates Sino-Soviet capital movements were accounted for or what the Soviet credit totals or the Chinese repayments actually were.

National Income Accounts and the Valuation of Foreign Trade. For purposes of national income accounting, exports should be valued at their domestic yuan costs or market prices (depending on which con-

cept of national income is used), while imports should be valued at
the yuan price of these goods in China. In this way, foreign trade
values would be fully comparable with those for the domestically
produced portion of GNP.

Unfortunately, conceptual and data complications prevent the
derivation of reliable GNP/foreign trade ratios for China. First of all,
the price structure is distorted; prices do not adequately reflect
relative scarcities in the economy. To the extent that the distortion
varies in different commodity markets, the GNP foreign trade ratios
might be misleading even if we had adequate yuan figures for foreign
trade.

Second, the available yuan figures on foreign trade had to be
rejected for reasons spelled out in Chapter 4 and in the first section
of this appendix. Therefore, it became necessary to estimate the dollar
figures of China's foreign trade from the trading partners' side. To
calculate the percentages of exports and imports in the GNP, however, one must translate these dollar values into yuan. But at what
conversion rates? Theoretically, the appropriate dollar-yuan ratios
should be derived by valuing the goods exported and imported at
their respective yuan and dollar prices. An alternative would be to
convert the gross domestic product to dollars by estimating China's
output of goods and services both in dollar and yuan prices. To
attempt either of these tasks here would carry us well beyond the
scope of our study.

There are two studies which have derived dollar-yuan ratios for
a limited range of output. I estimated the dollar and yuan values of
mainland China's agricultural output in 1952 and thus obtained a yuan-
dollar ratio of about 1:1.[13] This ratio, of course, cannot be applied
either to GNP or to foreign trade as a whole. Another study by Chao
compared the dollar and yuan values of China's output of 186 commodities in late 1951 and early 1952.[14] The 63 commodities primarily
related to consumption had a yuan-dollar ratio of 1.79:1, and the 115
commodities primarily related to production had a 5.91:1 ratio. While
this sample is more representative than mine, it is not adequately
representative of either foreign trade or the total domestic product
basket. Moreover, both refer to price ratios based on relationships
which held more than 10 years ago but may no longer be valid.

In addition, in mid-1957 after Yeh Chi-chuang's statement indicating that the official rate of foreign exchange overvalued the yuan in
relation to capitalist currencies, the Chinese Communist authorities
adjusted the rate to 2.62 to the dollar.

Putting these disparate pieces of information together, I derived three alternatives for the ratios of exports and imports to GNP—one based on the adjusted exchange rate of 2.62:1, another applying Chao's ratio for consumer goods, and a third using his ratio for producer goods. All these must be considered hypothetical and must be viewed as ranges for, rather than precise estimates of, the actual trade shares in GNP. The rate for consumer goods is perhaps more applicable to exports, and that for producer goods is more relevant to imports up to 1960.

APPENDIX D

Estimates of National Income and Capital Formation

For the purposes of this study, estimates of national income and capital formation are of relevance in several contexts: for deriving capital-output ratios, for estimating the rate of saving, and for estimating the effects of a total trade embargo on economic growth.

National Income Estimates. The national income estimates used in this study (see Table 4-9 particularly) are slightly modified versions of the national product estimates in T. C. Liu and K. C. Yeh, *The Economy of the Chinese Mainland: National Income and Economic Development, 1933–1959* (Princeton University Press, 1965). For 1952–54, I used the Liu-Yeh derivations in their original form. For 1955, however, I revised their estimate of agricultural product upward. All available indicators point to a significant improvement in agricultural output between 1954 and 1955, but such an improvement is not reflected in the Liu-Yeh figures. In making this adjustment, I applied an improvement factor based on the rate of growth in agricultural output for 1955 as estimated by W. W. Hollister in *China's Gross National Product and Social Accounts, 1950–1957* (Glencoe, Ill.: Free Press, 1958). For later years, then, I used the Liu-Yeh growth rates for agriculture but applied them to the revised 1955 figure. This adjustment is spelled out in Table D-1.

Capital Formation. My estimates of total gross investment in Table D-2 were taken from the Liu-Yeh study cited above. Their figures, in turn, were based on official Chinese Communist estimates adjusted to definitions of investment most generally used outside the Communist countries. My estimates for fixed-capital formation, however, were taken from Hollister's study (also cited above), for the official figures for "basic" or "capital construction" considerably underestimate private investment, which was still of appreciable importance prior to 1955–56. For a detailed discussion of this problem, see Alexander Eckstein, *The National Income of Communist China* (New York: Free Press of Glencoe, 1961), pp. 43–44 and 51–55.

Since Hollister's series are in current prices and the Liu-Yeh estimates of total gross investment are in 1952 prices, the former had to be converted to 1952 prices. A Liu-Yeh index of investment costs (Table 74) was used for this purpose.

Derivation of Capital-Output Ratios. The capital-output ratio used in this study is based on an assumed output lag of one year. Therefore, the investment totals relate to 1952–56, while the national income aggregates are for 1953–57—all expressed in 1952 prices.

(a) Gross fixed-capital investment for 1952–56   Y65.71 billion
(b) Depreciation for 1952–56   Y20.42 billion
(c) Net fixed-capital investment for 1952–56   Y45.29 billion
(d) Increment in net national product
     during 1953–57   Y26.78 billion
(e) Capital-output ratio   1.69:1

I took the depreciation allowances from Liu and Yeh's Table 8, and I estimated the NNP increment by applying the percentage increase derived from the GNP figures in Table D-1 to Liu and Yeh's NNP figure for 1952.

T A B L E   D - 1 . Agricultural and National
Product Estimates, 1952–62

(in billions of yuan at 1952 prices)

Year	Agricultural Product		Non-farm Product	Gross National Product
	Liu-Yeh	adjusted		adjusted
1952	34.19	34.19	40.48	74.67
1953	34.82	34.82	44.17	78.99
1954	35.50	35.50	47.81	83.31
1955	35.84	37.70	50.73	88.43
1956	36.97	38.90	60.31	99.21
1957	37.16	39.10	63.66	102.67
1958	40.00	45.00 [a]	74.00	119.00
1959	42.00	35.60 [a]	91.00	126.60
1960	n.a.	33.60 [a]	n.a.	n.a.
1961	n.a.	35.20 [a]	n.a.	n.a.
1962	n.a.	38.30 [a]	n.a.	n.a.

[a] Based on index in Table 3-8.

Note: n.a. stands for "not available."

Sources: T. C. Liu and K. C. Yeh, *The Economy of the Chinese Mainland: National Income and Economic Development, 1933–1959* (Princeton University Press, 1965), Table 8; W. W. Hollister, *China's Gross National Product and Social Accounts, 1950–1957* (Glencoe, Ill.: Free Press, 1958), Table 9.

T A B L E   D - 2 . Gross Investment in
Communist China, 1952–57

Year	Gross Investment			Rate of Investment		
	Total	In Fixed Capital Only		Total	In Fixed Capital Only	
	in 1952 prices	in current prices	in 1952 prices	in 1952 prices	in current prices	in 1952 prices
	(in billions of yuan)			(in per cent)		
1952	14.52	7.68	7.68	19.4	10.3	10.3
1953	19.11	11.15	10.47	24.9	14.1	13.2
1954	20.77	13.66	13.39	24.9	16.4	16.1
1955	23.31	12.65	13.08	26.3	14.3	14.8
1956	25.59	19.07	21.09	25.8	20.1	21.2
1957	28.14	15.00	16.59	27.4	14.6	16.1

Sources: T. C. Liu and K. C. Yeh, *The Economy of the Chinese Mainland:
National Income and Economic Development, 1933–1959* (Prince-
ton University Press, 1965), Tables 72 and 74; W. W. Hollister,
China's Gross National Product and Social Accounts, 1950–1957
(Glencoe, Ill.: Free Press, 1958), Table 6.

APPENDIX E

Communist China's Economic Aid

Communist China's aid commitments to other Communist countries are shown in Table E-1. In arriving at my estimates for China's yearly aid expenditures to these countries (see Table 5-6), I assumed that annual installments were the same over the life of the loans or grants. In reality, however, aid outlays must have fluctuated considerably from year to year. Therefore, the figures in Table 5-6 are undoubtedly subject to sizable margins of error.

The periods over which the loans or grants were to be extended are given in the published sources, so my estimates in Table 5-6 are relatively straightforward. Perhaps I should make special note of two things, though. First, the aid China extended to Albania prior to 1961 was primarily for short-term budget assistance and for covering trade deficits, and I have dealt with it on the basis of annual grants. Second, the aid outlay to North Korea in 1953 represents the last installment of free grants China made during the Korean War.

Cuba should really be added to the countries listed in Tables E-1 and 5-6. In 1960, it received a $60 million loan from China. Communist China's total aid commitments to other Communist countries through 1964, therefore, amount to $1,183.5 million. If to this sum one adds total aid commitments of $786.5 million to non-Communist countries (see Table E-2), China's economic assistance program would seem to be nearly a $2 billion operation. However, as is indicated in Chapter 6 and Table E-2, actual outlays to the non-Communist countries through 1963 fell considerably short of commitments. One cannot even rule out the possibility that some of the credits or grants may never be used.

TABLE E-1. Communist China's Aid Commitments to Other Communist Countries, 1953–64 [a]

(in millions of U.S. dollars)

Year	Albania	Hungary	North Korea	North Vietnam	Outer Mongolia	Total
1953	—	—	200	—	—	200.0
1954	—	—	—	—	—	—
1955	4	—	—	200	—	204.0
1956	2	7.5	—	—	40	49.5
1957	4	50.0	—	—	—	54.0
1958	5	—	25	—	25	55.0
1959	19	—	—	100	—	119.0
1960	5	—	105	—	50	160.0
1961	125	—	—	157	—	282.0
1962	—	—	—	—	—	—
1963	—	—	—	—	—	—
1964	—	—	—	—	— b	—
Total	164	57.5	330	457	115	1,123.5

[a] Excluding Cuba.

[b] In 1964, Communist China provided Outer Mongolia with a 200,000-yuan grant ($80,000 at the official exchange rate of 2.62:1). Since this was a negligible amount, I chose to disregard it.

Note: — stands for "none."

Sources: U.S. Department of State, Communist China's Economic Aid to Other Countries, Intelligence Information Brief, no. 357 (Washington, D.C.: Author, February 2, 1961), Table 1, pp. 4–5; Pauline Lewin, The Foreign Trade of Communist China (New York: Praeger, 1964), Appendix V, pp. 113–123; Survey of the China Mainland Press for various years.

TABLE E-2. Communist China's Aid to Non-Communist Countries, 1956-64

(in millions of U.S. dollars)

	1956	1957	1958	1959	1960	1961	1962	1963	1964	Total	Drawn Through 1963
Sub-Saharan Africa											
Central African Republic	—	—	—	—	—	—	—	—	4.0	4.0	0.0
Congo (Brazzaville)	—	—	—	—	—	—	—	—	25.2	25.2	0.0
Ghana	—	—	—	—	—	19.6	—	—	22.4	42.0	0.0
Guinea	—	—	—	.5	26.0	—	—	—	—	26.5	5.5
Kenya	—	—	—	—	—	—	—	—	18.0	18.0	0.0
Mali	—	—	—	—	—	19.6	—	—	—	19.6	0.3
Somali Republic	—	—	—	—	—	—	—	21.6	—	21.6	0.4
Tanzania	—	—	—	—	—	—	—	—	45.5	45.5	0.0
Asia											
Burma	—	—	—	—	—	84.0	—	—	—	84.0	4.5
Ceylon	—	15.8	10.5	—	—	—	10.5	—	4.2	41.0	10.7
Cambodia	22.9	—	—	—	26.5	—	—	—	—	49.4	34.9
Indonesia	16.2	—	11.2	—	—	30.0	—	—	50.0	107.4	27.4
Laos	—	—	—	—	—	—	4.0	—	—	4.0	0.0
Nepal	12.6	—	—	—	21.0	9.8	—	—	—	43.4	6.3
Pakistan	—	—	—	—	—	—	—	—	60.0	60.0	0.0
Near East and North Africa											
Algeria	—	—	—	—	—	—	1.8	50.0	—	51.8	1.8
Syria	—	—	—	—	—	—	—	16.3	—	16.3	0.0
U.A.R.	4.7	—	—	—	—	—	—	—	80.0	84.7	4.7
Yemen	—	—	12.7	.7	—	—	—	.2	28.5	42.1	12.5
Total	56.4	15.8	34.4	1.2	73.5	163.0	16.3	88.1	337.8	786.5	109.0

Note: — stands for "none."

Sources: U.S. Department of State, *Communist China's Economic Aid to Other Countries*, Intelligence Information Brief, no. 375 (Washington, D.C.: Author, February 20, 1961), Table 1, pp. 4-5; U.S. Department of State, *The Sino-Soviet Economic Offensive Through June 30, 1962*, Research Memorandum, RSB-145 (Washington, D.C.: Author, September 18, 1962); U.S. Department of State, *The Communist Offensive Through 1963*, Research Memorandum, RSB-43 (Washington, D.C.: Author, June 18, 1964). The data in the preceding sources have been updated on the basis of newspaper and periodical clippings and a variety of other sources, some of which are unpublished.

NOTES

Chapter Two

1. The power orientation of Communist China's development program permeates most major policy statements. See, for instance, Li Fu-ch'un's *Report on the First Five-Year Plan for Development of the National Economy of the People's Republic of China in 1953–57* (Peking: Foreign Languages Press, October 1955).

2. In reality, this process was in most cases more complex than it is presented here, and the relationships described do not apply equally to all parts of China. The picture sketched above, for example, is more representative of areas in which tenancy and population pressure were especially high than of areas where they were relatively low. Moreover, these particular aspects of rural stagnation have been quite widespread in many other underdeveloped countries besides China.

3. Mainland China (excluding Outer Mongolia and Tibet), with an area roughly the same as the United States', had a railroad network which was not much more than one-twentieth of the latter's.

4. E. B. Schumpeter and others, *The Industrialization of Japan and Manchukuo, 1930–1940* (New York: Macmillan, 1940), Table 103, p. 388; Alexander Eckstein, "Conditions and Prospects for Economic Growth in Communist China," *World Politics*, v. 7, no. 1, October 1954, Table 1, p. 9.

5. Officially, the Plan was launched in January 1953; however, it was not fully elaborated until the spring of 1955 and not formally accepted by the People's Congress until July 1955.

6. For fuller documentation of these statements, see Alexander Eckstein, "Conditions and Prospects for Economic Growth in Communist China," *World Politics*, v. 7, no. 2, January 1955, Table 7, p. 258. Japan, India, and the Soviet Union are used as yardsticks for comparison for differing reasons. Japan serves as an example of a country which started the process of industrialization from roughly the same base as Communist China and is by now well on the way to development. India, on the other hand, started from roughly the same base and at the same time as China but seems to be falling behind. The Soviet Union, using a more or less similar development model as China, started from a more advanced base and is by now much more advanced than China.

7. State Statistical Bureau, *Ten Great Years, Statistics of the Economic and Cultural Achievements of the People's Republic of China* (Peking: Foreign Languages Press, 1960).

8. "Population Statistics of Our Country, 1949–56," *T'ung-chi Kung-tso* [*Statistical Work*], no. 11, June 14, 1957, pp. 24–25, and M. B. Ullman, *Cities of Mainland China, 1953 and 1958*, International Population Reports, series P-95, no. 59 (Washington, D.C.: U.S. Bureau of the Census, August 1961), p. 7.

9. Y. L. Wu, *The Economic Potential of Communist China* (Stanford Research Institute, 1963), pp. 63–64, 70.

10. Same, p. 113. All the data concerning reserves must be considered as highly tentative and subject to sizable margins of error. Unlike production statistics, which can be checked against information on producing capacity, labor force, etc., data on reserves lend themselves much more easily to manipulation for propaganda and other purposes. Quite apart from these political considerations, there are many technical problems in measuring reserves, and there are of course wide variations in the quality of these. Nevertheless, the basic conclusion that mineral and energy resources are adequate to support a high level of industrialization in China would not be affected by these qualifications, for even the most conservative estimates sustain such a judgment. On strictly *a priori* grounds, moreover, it would be surprising indeed if a country of this territorial size does not have within its boundaries mineral resources in sufficient quantities to mount a full-fledged industrialization program. As the experience of other large countries has shown, initially low estimates of reserves tend to be due more to inadequate geological exploration than to the absence of reserves.

11. Same, p. 118.

12. Russian grain exports hovered around 10 million tons on the eve of World War I and constituted about 15 per cent of the harvest. They dropped drastically in the twenties, both in volume and as a percentage of the harvest. However, under the impact of an export drive accompanying the launching of the First Five Year Plan, they rose to a peak of about 4.8 million tons in 1930 and 5.1 million tons in 1931 and made up 5.7 per cent and 7.7 per cent respectively of the grain harvest. Thus, interwar grain exports even at their peak never reached more than half the prewar level, either in volume or as a share of output. This reduction in exports provided Russia's food supply with a cushion that was not available to Communist China. For further details concerning Russia's grain position, see Naum Jasny, *The Socialized Agriculture of the USSR* (Stanford University Press, 1949), pp. 67, 86, 751, 776, and 792.

13. According to D. R. Hodgman's adjusted index of industrial production, the output of large-scale industry in the Soviet Union increased by about 50 per cent between 1928 and 1932. See his *Soviet Industrial Production, 1928–1951* (Cambridge: Harvard University Press, 1954), p. 73. Raymond P. Powell in a more recent study found that the final industrial product grew at an average annual rate of 7.1 per cent during 1928–32 when valued at 1937 and 1950 prices and at a rate of 18.1 per cent when valued at 1928 prices. During the 1932–37 period, this rate increased to 12.6 per cent in terms of 1937 prices and to 10.9

per cent in terms of 1950 prices, but it declined somewhat to 17.7 per cent in terms of 1928 prices. These findings, however, need to be qualified if one looks at the year-to-year rates of growth rather than at the periods as a whole. Industrial output seems to have declined in 1932 and 1933 (except when valued at 1928 prices), while it grew rapidly in the preceding and subsequent years. This fact would suggest that in the Soviet Union, too, the drastic decline in agricultural production occasioned by collectivization affected industrial production, but the industrial decline seems to have been less severe and of shorter duration than in China. For the detailed data, see R. P. Powell, "Industrial Production" in Abram Bergson and Simon Kuznets, eds., *Economic Trends in the Soviet Union* (Cambridge: Harvard University Press, 1963), chapter 4, Tables 1, 9, and 10.

14. In 1926, the U.S.S.R. had 207,000 engineers, architects, and intermediate technical personnel, while in 1952 Communist China's engineers and technical personnel numbered 164,000. See Nicholas DeWitt, *Soviet Professional Manpower: Its Education, Training and Supply* (Washington, D.C.: The National Science Foundation, 1955), p. 246, and Leo Orleans, *Professional Manpower and Education in Communist China* (Washington, D.C.: GPO, 1960), p. 165.

15. One evidence of this fact is that total enrollment in higher educational institutions was 247,000 in Russia in 1929 (DeWitt, cited, p. 160) and only 153,000 in China in 1951/52 (Orleans, cited, p. 66).

16. For this concept's full implications for economic development, see Alexander Gerschenkron, *Economic Backwardness in Historical Perspective, A Book of Essays* (Cambridge: Harvard University Press, 1962).

17. Quoted in E. H. Carr, *A History of Soviet Russia: The Bolshevik Revolution, 1917–1923*, v. 2 (London: Macmillan, 1952), p. 365.

18. Same, p. 261.

19. For a detailed chronology of these events, see Conrad Brandt, Benjamin Schwartz, and John K. Fairbank, *A Documentary History of Chinese Communism* (Cambridge: Harvard University Press, 1952), pp. 34–39.

20. See his report at the June 6, 1950, session of the National Committee of the Chinese People's Political Consultative Conference in *New China's Economic Achievements, 1949–1952* (Peking: Foreign Languages Press, 1952), p. 6.

21. Edwin W. Pauley, *Report on Japanese Assets in Manchuria to the President of the United States* (Washington, D.C.: GPO, July 1946), p. 37.

22. This figure is based on the official index compiled by the Central Committee on Financial and Economic Affairs. See "Economic Development in Mainland China, 1949–1953," in U.N. Economic Commission for Asia and the Far East, *Economic Bulletin for Asia and the Far East*, v. 4, no. 3, November 1953, pp. 17–31.

23. See Li Shu-cheng, "New China's Achievements in Agricultural Production during the Past Three Years," in *New China's Economic Achievements*, cited, p. 188.

24. Chen Yun, "The Financial and Food Situation," in same, pp. 53–54.

25. The victory bond unit, known as the *fen*, was quoted nationally every 10 days and was based on the wholesale value of 6 catties of rice

(millet in Tientsin), 1.5 catties of flour, 4 feet of white shirting, and 16 catties of coal in Shanghai, Tientsin, Hankow, Canton, Chungking, and Sian. The commodity basket values in these cities had the following weights in the computation: Shanghai—45; Tientsin—20; Hankow, Canton, and Chungking—10 each; and Sian—5.

Unlike the *fen*, the parity deposit and wage units were quoted separately for all large cities. The exact bases for these varied from city to city, but the commodity basket always included some grain staple, cloth, vegetable oil, and coal.

26. Chung Kan-en, "The Success of the State Bank's Policy on Interest Rate," *Ching-chi Chou-pao* [*Economic Weekly*] (Shanghai), July 3, 1952, as summarized in K. C. Chao, ed., *Source Materials from Communist China*, v. 3 (Cambridge: Harvard University Press, October 1952), p. 62.
27. *Ta Kung Pao* [*Impartial Daily*] (Shanghai), June 10, 1949.
28. Hsueh Mu-ch'iao, director of the State Statistical Bureau, "Report Before the Third National Conference on Statistical Work," *Hsin-hua Yueh-pao (HHYP)* [*New China Monthly*], no. 5, May 1954, pp. 103–107.
29. Chou En-lai, "Report About the Second Five-Year Plan," *Hsin-hua Pan-yueh-k'an (HHPYK)* [*New China Semimonthly*], no. 20, October 23, 1956, and *Jen-min Jih-pao (JMJP)* [*People's Daily*], September 29, 1956.
30. Alexander Erlich, "Stalin's Views on Soviet Economic Development" in E. J. Simmons, ed., *Continuity and Change in Russian and Soviet Thought* (Cambridge: Harvard University Press, 1955), pp. 81–99.
31. For an analysis of population trends, see Ullman, cited, Table B, p. 7; Ernest Ni, *Distribution of the Urban and Rural Population of Mainland China, 1953 and 1958*, International Population Reports, series P-95, no. 56 (Washington, D.C.: U.S. Bureau of the Census, 1960), Table B, p. 4; "Population Statistics of Our Country, 1949–56," cited; and "How to Organize Agricultural Labor," *Chi-hua Ching-chi* [*Planned Economy*], no. 8, August 1957, pp. 6–9. For data on agricultural collections, consult K. C. Chao, *Agrarian Policies of Mainland China: A Documentary Study (1949–1956)* (Cambridge: Harvard University Press, 1957), Table VII, p. 150; K. C. Chao, *Economic Planning and Organization in Mainland China: A Documentary Study (1949–1957)*, v. 2 (Cambridge: Harvard University Press, 1960), p. 5; *Ten Great Years*, cited, p. 167.

For illustrative purposes the following data (in millions of tons) may be illuminating:

	1954/55	*1955/56*	*1956/57*
Total grain output (including soybeans)	169.5	183.9	192.7
Total collections and purchases	53.9	52.0	49.9
Resales to rural areas	24.7	20.2	24.5
Available for urban consumption, exports, and government stockpiles	29.2	31.8	25.2

Source: Chou Po-ping, "The Policy of Unified Purchase and Sale of Grain Shall Not be Frustrated," *Liang Shih* [*Food-Grain*], no. 7, July 1957.

32. If one compares annual rates of change in agricultural and industrial production in mainland China between 1949 and 1957, it is clear that the latter tends to follow the former with a one-year lag.

33. This fact is quite evident in the major policy pronouncements made in the latter part of the year, *e.g.*, Teng Hsiao-p'ing's "Report on the Rectification Campaign," rendered to the Third Enlarged Plenum of the Eighth Central Committee of the Chinese Communist party on September 23, 1957 (*Current Background [CB]*, no. 477, October 25, 1957), or Li Fu-ch'un's "The Achievements of China's First Five-Year Plan and the Tasks and Policy for Future Socialist Construction," a speech made at the Eighth All China Trade Union Congress on December 7, 1957 (*CB*, no. 483, December 16, 1957).

34. See Liu Shao-ch'i's "Report on the Work of the Central Committee of the Communist Party of China to the Second Session of the Eighth National Congress," the official English text of which is available in *Second Session of the Eighth National Congress of the Communist Party of China* (Peking: Foreign Languages Press, 1958), pp. 16–66.

35. Total fixed-capital investment rose by 59 per cent and within-plan investment by 62 per cent between 1955 and 1956. At the same time, the percentage of peasant households in agricultural producers co-operatives rose from 14 to 96 per cent. See *Ten Great Years*, cited, pp. 35, 55–56.

36. This aspect of the new strategy was officially enunciated in the "Communique of the Sixth Plenary Session of the Eighth Central Committee of the Chinese Communist Party" on December 17, 1958 (*Peking Review*, v. 1, no. 43, December 23, 1958, pp. 6–9).

37. The data on the number and size of the collectives and the communes were obtained from K. C. Chao, *Agrarian Policies of Mainland China: A Documentary Study (1949–56)*, cited, Table II, p. 56; and *Ten Great Years*, cited, pp. 31 and 43.

38. This note is pronounced in Teng Hsiao-p'ing's "Report on the Rectification Campaign," cited, and is explicit in Liu Shao-ch'i's "Report on the Work of the Central Committee of the Communist Party of China to the Second Session of the Eighth National Congress," cited.

39. See Mao Tse-tung's report of July 31, 1955, on "The Question of Agricultural Cooperation" (*HHYP*, no. 11, November 1955, pp. 1–8) and the "Resolution on Agricultural Cooperation" adopted by the Sixth Enlarged Plenum of the Central Committee of the Chinese Communist party on October 11, 1955 (same, pp. 9–13).

40. It is of course true that this spirit was dampened by the economic strains, shortages in consumer goods, and bottlenecks in the supply of raw materials in 1957. However, these were viewed as no more than temporary dislocations produced by overinvestment and overcentralization in 1956. The latter was engendered in part by the all-out drive to complete the collectivization of agriculture and socialization of private enterprise that year.

41. See "Regulations on Improving the Industrial Management System" and "Regulations on Improving the Commercial Management System," both of which were promulgated on November 15, 1957 (*HHPYK*, no. 24, December 25, 1957, pp. 57–60).

42. See Li Fu-ch'un's report to that plenary session, *JMJP*, January 21, 1961.

43. See the "Press Communique of the Third Session of the Second National People's Congress" (New China News Agency—English, April 16, 1962, in *CB*, no. 681, April 18, 1962, p. 2).
44. *JMJP*, editorial, December 4, 1963. Britain was chosen as a target for a combination of reasons. First, the leaders must clearly have felt that if they could overtake Britain, the oldest industrial nation, they could much more convincingly project an image of China as an industrially advanced country. Second, although Britain had a large industrial product per capita, its total output of manufacturing and mining was, by virtue of its small size (at least relative to the Chinese mainland), much more within China's reach than that of the United States or the U.S.S.R.
45. This idea was first advanced by Li Fu-ch'un in his report on the draft economic plan for 1960, *JMJP*, March 31, 1960; however, it did not acquire major programmatic significance until a year later. It was reaffirmed and elaborated upon by Liu Shao-ch'i on June 30, 1961, in his speech celebrating the 40th anniversary of the Chinese Communist party (*CB*, no. 655, July 12, 1961, p. 6).
46. These details of the new policy were set forth on a number of occasions in many different publications. For a good explicit statement, see Feng Chung, "An Economic Policy That Wins, A Survey of the Policy of Readjustment, Consolidation, Filling Out, and Raising Standards," *Peking Review*, v. 7, no. 11, March 13, 1964, p. 6.

Chapter Three

1. It must be emphasized that the estimates in Table 3–1 are necessarily tentative. Much more detailed and painstaking studies of growth trends in individual sectors are needed before we can make careful and well-founded national income comparisons for a number of years. As a matter of fact, it is for this reason that Table 3–1 contains no data for the more recent years, for which the quantitative information available is particularly unreliable.
2. It is interesting to note that in terms of current rubles the Soviet Union allocated only 3 per cent of GNP to defense in 1928 and 7 per cent in 1937, as compared to China's 6 and 7 per cent in 1952 and 1955 respectively. See Abram Bergson, *The Real National Income of Soviet Russia Since 1928* (Cambridge: Harvard University Press, 1961), Table 3, p. 46.
3. See T. C. Liu and K. C. Yeh, *The Economy of the Chinese Mainland: National Income and Economic Development, 1933–1959* (Princeton University Press, 1965), Table 37, p. 141.
4. State Statistical Bureau, *Ten Great Years, Statistics of the Economic and Cultural Achievements of the People's Republic of China* (Peking: Foreign Languages Press, 1960), pp. 148–149.
5. The nonagricultural component of these GNP estimates for all years except 1962 is based on Liu and Yeh, cited. The agricultural estimates for 1952 to 1959 are also based on the same source. However, the improvement factor which Liu and Yeh employed in estimating the farm product for 1955 does not seem to be borne out by a number of

indicators pointing to a much better weather year in 1955 than in 1954 and to a bumper crop. Therefore, for 1955 I adopted the growth rate for farm product in W. W. Hollister's *China's Gross National Product and Social Accounts, 1950–1957* (Glencoe, Ill.: Free Press, 1958) and applied it to the Liu-Yeh estimate of agricultural output in 1954. For 1956 and 1957, I used the Liu-Yeh agricultural growth factors but applied them to the revised estimate for farm product in 1955. The estimate of the agricultural product for 1958 and 1959, on the other hand, is based on the index of food crop production in Table 3–8. This procedure is unavoidably crude, for industrial crops and livestock products did not necessarily behave the same way as food crops. Yet it should provide a fairly good indicator since the latter constitute about 60 per cent of the total farm product. Of course, another possible source of error lies in the assumption, implicit in this procedure, that the input-output ratio remained unchanged between 1957 and 1959.

6. Chao Kang, *The Rate and Pattern of Industrial Growth in Communist China* (Ann Arbor: University of Michigan Press, 1965), Table 26, p. 101.

7. Same.

8. See Liu Shao-ch'i's "Report on the Work of the Central Committee of the Communist Party of China to the Second Session of the Eighth National Congress," in *Second Session of the Eighth National Congress of the Communist Party of China* (Peking: Foreign Languages Press, 1958), pp. 16–66.

9. *Ten Great Years*, cited, p. 96.

10. See Y. L. Wu, *The Economic Potential of Communist China* (Stanford Research Institute, 1963), Tables 41 and 86, pp. 206 and 362, and *Far Eastern Economic Review*, v. 43, no. 7, February 13, 1964, p. 341, and v. 44, no. 3, April 16, 1964, p. 160.

11. See Table 3–9 in this chapter and *Far Eastern Economic Review*, v. 43, no. 1, January 2, 1964, p. 5.

12. Symptomatic of these efforts are the agreements for the delivery of two complete synthetic fiber plants by Japan.

13. Alexander Eckstein, *The National Income of Communist China* (New York: The Free Press of Glencoe, 1961), Table 1, p. 35, and Table 8, p. 68.

14. *Ten Great Years*, cited, pp. 11, 119, and 124; Helen Yin and Y. C. Yin, *Economic Statistics of Mainland China, 1949–1957* (Cambridge: Harvard University Press, 1960), pp. 3 and 30.

15. See *Chi-hua Ching-chi* (*CHCC*) [*Planned Economy*], no. 2, February 1958, pp. 21–24. For a more detailed appraisal of Chinese Communist agricultural statistics, see India, Ministry of Food and Agriculture, *Report of the Indian Delegation to China on Agricultural Planning Techniques, July–August, 1956* (New Delhi: Author, 1956), pp. 86–87; C. M. Li, *Economic Development of Communist China* (Berkeley: University of California Press, 1959), pp. 59, 61–65; Eckstein, cited, p. 32.

16. State Statistical Bureau, "The Basic Situation of Planned Purchase and Planned Supply of Food Grains in China," *T'ung-chi Kung-tso* [*Statistical Work*], no. 19, October 14, 1957, pp. 28, 31–32.

17. These conclusions, of course, hinge critically upon the reliability of the official procurement statistics. While it is perfectly possible that total

government collections of grain, through taxation and purchases combined, did not increase perceptibly between 1952 and 1957, this is far from certain. As is noted in the text, farm production probably increased, although less than the official figures would suggest. It is therefore difficult to believe that tighter controls over agriculture would not have been reflected in higher farm procurements. Ultimately, there are three possibilities: namely, that the official data are more or less correct and indicate the government's inability to raise the compulsory grain purchase quotas, that grain collections are systematically and deliberately understated to counter the image that the peasantry was being squeezed, or that the government consciously chose to restrict collections to encourage increases in farm production.

18. See Yin and Yin, cited, p. 33.
19. See Liao Chi-li, "About the Two-Account System," *CHCC*, no. 5, May 1958, pp. 8–9; Wei I, "Revolution in the Method of Planning," *Hsueh-hsi* [*Study*], no. 8, April 28, 1958, pp. 10–12; and C. M. Li, *The Statistical System of Communist China* (Berkeley: University of California Press, 1962), pp. 69–73.
20. See Chou En-lai's "Report on Government Work" at the First Session of the Second National People's Congress on April 18, 1959 (*Hsin-hua Pan-yueh-k'an* [*New China Semimonthly*], no. 9, May 6, 1959, p. 2).
21. The draft program was adopted by the Supreme State Conference on January 25, 1956, and its English language text was published by the Foreign Languages Press in Peking that same year.
22. *Jen-min Jih-pao* (*JMJP*) [*People's Daily*], December 18, 1958; Wang Hsiang-shu, "The Myth of Diminishing Returns," *Peking Review*, v. 1, no. 35, October 28, 1958, pp. 10–12.
23. "Communique of the Eighth Plenary Session of the Eighth Central Committee of the Chinese Communist Party," *JMJP*, August 27, 1959, and the State Statistical Bureau's "Communique Concerning Adjustments in the Agricultural Production for 1958," same.
24. *JMJP*, April 16, 1960, reported a speech by Chang Nai-ch'i in which he stated that "even an annual increase of 10–12 per cent in production may be regarded as a leap forward."
25. For a good summary of agricultural production trends in mainland China during these years, see U.S. Department of Agriculture, "Food Shortages in Communist China," *Foreign Agriculture Circular*, FATP 5–61 (Washington, D.C.: Author, March 1961).
26. *Peking Review*, v. 4, no. 40, October 6, 1961, pp. 6–9.
27. I am indebted to Ed Jones for calling my attention to the significance of this decline in seed requirements and milling rates.
28. *Ta Kung Pao* [*Impartial Daily*] (Tientsin), September 7, 1956, and *JMJP*, November 27, 1958.
29. This information can be gleaned from the top secret *Chung-kuo Jen-min Chieh-fang-chün Tsung-ch'eng-chih-pu Kung-tso T'ung hsün* [*Bulletin of Activities of the General Political Department of the Chinese People's Liberation Army*] for January 1–August 26, 1961, copies of which are now available in American libraries.
30. See India, Planning Commission, *The New India: Progress through Democracy* (New York: Macmillan, 1958), pp. 82–83.
31. Bruce F. Johnston, "Agricultural Productivity and Economic Develop-

ment in Japan," *Journal of Political Economy,* v. 59, no. 6, December 1951, pp. 498–513.

32. E. B. Schumpeter and others, *The Industrialization of Japan and Man-chukuo, 1930–1940* (New York: Macmillan, 1940), p. 251; T. H. Shen, *Agricultural Resources of China* (Ithaca, N.Y.: Cornell University Press, 1951), p. 38.

33. See *Peking Review,* v. 6, no. 19, May 10, 1963, p. 13, and no. 29, July 19, 1963, p. 26, and the *Far Eastern Economic Review,* v. 40, no. 6, May 9, 1963, p. 319.

34. U.S. Joint Publications Research Service, *Reports* (JPRS), no. 6526, January 9, 1961, p. 33.

35. *Hung-ch'i* [*Red Flag*], no. 24, December 16, 1960, and JPRS, no. 8009, March 30, 1961, p. 50.

36. *Chung-kuo Shui-li* [*Chinese Water Conservation*], no. 5, May 14, 1957.

37. JPRS, no. 8015, March 31, 1961, p. 12.

38. Same, no. 922 D, September 18, 1959, p. 16.

39. New China News Agency, January 18, 1960, and *Shui-li Hsueh-pao* [*Journal of the Hydraulic Engineering Society*], no. 4, December 29, 1957.

40. JPRS, no. 1026 D, November 19, 1959, pp. 6 and 26; *JMJP,* January 11, 1959.

41. A Chinese Communist source stated this position quite candidly: "If, after distribution of the land, the individual economy of a single house-hold as the unit of production were allowed to continue for a long period of time, this would simply be creating favorable conditions for the growth of capitalism." *Peking Review,* v. 4, no. 21, May 26, 1961, p. 13.

42. For further details concerning changes in agricultural organization, see T. J. Hughes and D. E. T. Luard, *The Economic Development of Communist China, 1949–1960,* (2d ed.; London: Oxford University Press, 1961), chapters 12 and 13; K. C. Chao, *Agrarian Policies of Mainland China: A Documentary Study (1949–1956)* (Cambridge: Harvard University Press, 1957), chapters 2 and 3; K. C. Chao, *Economic Planning and Organization in Mainland China, A Documentary Study* (1949–1957), v. 1 (Cambridge: Harvard University Press, 1960), section 3, document no. 18; and K. R. Walker, *Planning in Chinese Agriculture, Socialization and the Private Sector, 1956–1962* (London: Frank Cass and Company, Ltd., 1965).

43. These provisions are spelled out in the "Provisional Regulations of Weihsing People's Commune," published in the *JMJP,* September 4, 1958.

44. Proposed by Khrushchev in the spring of 1951.

45. "Communique of the Sixth Plenary Session of the Eighth Central Committee of the Chinese Communist Party" and "Resolution on Some Questions Concerning the People's Communes," *Peking Review,* v. 1, no. 43, pp. 6–9, 10–19.

46. As of August 1959, there were on the average 240 households in a production brigade. See "People's Communes Become Sound and Con-solidated in China," *JMJP,* September 4, 1958.

47. "Appropriately Use Labor, Raise Labor Productivity," *JMJP,* December 18, 1960; Chin Ming, "How People's Communes' Financial Work Serves

Distribution," *Selections from China Mainland Magazines*, no. 238, December 5, 1960, pp. 22–30; Hui Chih, "Three Figures," *JMJP*, February 2, 1961.

48. For good treatments of the evolution of the communes, see Geoffrey Hudson, ed., *The Chinese Commune* (London: Issued under the Auspices of *Soviet Survey*, 1960); Philip P. Jones and Thomas T. Poleman, "Communes and the Agricultural Crisis in Communist China," *Food Research Institute Studies*, v. 3, no. 1, February 1962, pp. 3–22; H. F. Schurmann, "Peking's Recognition of Crisis," *Problems of Communism*, v. 10, no. 5, September/October, 1961, pp. 5–14.

49. In a commune in Honan, for instance, the total income in 1958 was 9.3 million yuan, of which 5.4 million yuan were placed in the capital reserve fund and 2.7 million distributed among the members. (JPRS, no. 1337, March 12, 1959, pp. 28–34.)

50. Chin Ming, cited.

51. "Report on the Tax in Kind, March 15, 1921," *Sochineniya* [*Collected Works*] (2d ed., 30 v.; Moscow: Gosizdat, 1926–32), v. 26, p. 246.

52. For a detailed documentation of Chinese Communist land reform policies between 1949 and 1952, see K. C. Chao, *Agrarian Policies of Mainland China: A Documentary Study (1949–1956)*, cited, pp. 38–53.

53. See, for instance, Teng Tsu-hui's "Report to the Rural Work Conference of the Central Committee of the New Democratic Youth League," *Hsin-hua Yueh-pao* [*New China Monthly*], no. 12, December 1954, pp. 144–150.

54. This position is spelled out explicitly in a number of policy pronouncements, statements, and articles. As an example, see "The Peasant Question in the Socialist Revolution," *Peking Review*, v. 4, no. 21, May 26, 1961, pp. 13–15.

55. The new order of priorities was officially promulgated in Chou En-lai's report to the National People's Congress in April 1962. Unfortunately, neither the full text of this report nor the proceedings of the Congress have been published. A summary of Chou's recommendations was, however, released and published in a number of sources. See for example, *Peking Review*, v. 5, no. 16, April 20, 1962, pp. 5–7.

Chapter Four

1. This trade was carried on within a framework of tributary relations. See J. K. Fairbank, *Trade and Diplomacy on the China Coast: The Opening of the Treaty Ports, 1842–1854*, (Cambridge: Harvard University Press, 1953), v. 1. There are no satisfactory or reliable data on either the value of foreign trade or the value of goods and services produced domestically. Therefore, any conclusions concerning the past relationship of these two must necessarily be based on qualitative rather than quantitative evidence.

2. See P. T. Ho, *Studies on the Population of China, 1368–1953* (Cambridge: Harvard University Press, 1959).

3. See A. O. Hirschman, *The Strategy of Economic Development* (New Haven: Yale University Press, 1958), pp. 173–175.

4. C. P. Kindleberger, *Foreign Trade and the National Economy* (New Haven: Yale University Press, 1962), chapter 12.

5. See, for instance, a statement by Yeh Chi-chuang, Minister of Foreign Trade, that to "export is to import, and imports are for the socialist industrialization of our country," *Hsin-hua Pan-yueh-k'an* [*New China Semimonthly*], no. 16, August 25, 1957, p. 92.

6. For a fuller discussion of the exchange-rate problem, see Appendix C.

7. Dollar data for mainland China's foreign trade in 1929 were obtained from U.S. Department of Commerce, *Foreign Commerce Yearbook, 1933* (Washington, D.C.: GPO, 1934), p. 250. On the basis of the quantum indices of China's exports and imports for 1913–36 which were compiled by the Nankai Institute of Economics, it is clear that 1928 and 1929 were the peak trade years. See Nankai University, Institute of Economics, *Nankai Index Numbers 1936* (Tientsin: Author, 1937), pp. 37–38. For 1932–36, the indices exclude the foreign trade of Manchuria; however, dollar figures for this trade were obtained from Y. K. Cheng, *Foreign Trade and Industrial Development of China, A Historical and Integrated Analysis Through 1948* (Washington, D.C.: University Press of Washington, 1956), p. 269. These combined with the *Foreign Commerce Yearbook's* dollar figures for China proper confirm that the volume of exports and imports was largest in 1928 and 1929. The dollar values for 1929 and 1952–62 were converted to values at 1958 prices by the application of the Asian export and import price indices given in various volumes of the United Nation's *Statistical Yearbook* and the International Monetary Fund's *International Financial Statistics*.

8. Ten per cent of the value has often been used as a rule-of-thumb adjustment factor to convert imports from a c.i.f. to an f.o.b. basis; however, a number of recent studies have shown that such an average is subject to sizable margins of error because the freight costs of commodities vary widely. In an attempt to obviate this difficulty, we applied distinctive freight cost percentages to each commodity or commodity group imported by European countries from Communist China in 1955 and 1958. We used as freight "deflators" the freight costs of identical or similar imports by Germany in 1951. These were obtained from Carmellah Moneta, "The Estimation of Transportation Costs in International Trade," *Journal of Political Economy*, v. 67, no. 1, February 1959, pp. 57–58. The resulting freight factors for the imports of Europe as a whole were 5.8 per cent in 1955 and 6.0 per cent in 1958. We then applied the 6 per cent as an average "deflator" for all imports of the non-Communist world (exclusive of Hong Kong) from China for all years.

This procedure is naturally subject to certain margins of error; nevertheless, in our view they are likely to be significantly less than would be the case with the application of a 10 per cent allowance. Ideally, there should be a separate freight factor for each commodity, for each year, for each country. The realization of this ideal was precluded by the absence of sufficiently detailed information. Since the commodity composition of China's exports to different parts of the world does not vary a great deal and since shipments to points more distant than Western Europe compensate for shorter hauls to the Far

East, the freight factor for Western Europe may be taken as representative of freight costs for all non-Communist world imports. To test for year-to-year variation, we made the calculation for two years and found no significant difference in the results.

9. Y. K. Cheng, cited, Tables 5, 6, and 16, pp. 20, 22, and 45.

10. The findings presented in Tables 4–5 and 4–7 need to be qualified further. As has already been noted, all trade data relating to direction were adjusted to an f.o.b. basis. A similar adjustment for commodity composition was not possible. It would have required extensive research into freight factors for each commodity category. Such an added expenditure of time did not seem warranted for our purposes, for the effect on the results would have been minor in any case. Thus, the export data in Table 4–7 represent a composite of Soviet and non-Communist world imports from China accounted for on an f.o.b. and c.i.f. basis respectively. The effect is to overstate the relative importance of those bulky commodities of which the non-Communist world imported a large share.

11. The latest and most direct evidence to support this conclusion is contained in a letter from the Chinese Communist party to the Communist party of the Soviet Union. The letter states: "As for Soviet loans to China, it must be pointed out that China used them mostly for the purchase of war material from the Soviet Union, the greater part of which was used up in the war to resist United States aggression and to aid Korea." (*The New York Times*, May 9, 1964.)

12. It should be noted that Soviet import statistics contain a category of "metal ores and concentrates." For 1955–59 only three items are listed under it: zinc concentrates, lead concentrate, and aluminum oxide. These are all small items; therefore, there is a large unspecified gap. In 1960 and 1961 tungsten, which is now specifically listed, fills the bulk of this gap. The Soviets undoubtedly imported tungsten in earlier years as well, but for some reason they apparently wished to hide the quantity and value of such imports. Even with the listing of tungsten, however, close to 40 per cent of the category remains unspecified in 1960, and more than 20 per cent in 1961. This situation strongly suggests that certain strategic materials, the importation of which the Russians may want to conceal, must be included here.

13. See U.S. Department of Agriculture, *Trends and Developments in Communist China's World Trade in Farm Products, 1955–1960*, Foreign Agricultural Economic Report, no. 6 (Washington, D.C.: GPO, September 1962), Table 8, p. 20.

14. Since these figures are based on Table 4–5, they refer only to imports from the Soviet Union and the non-Communist world; therefore, China's total food imports were undoubtedly higher. Nevertheless, Eastern Europe was not an important source of supply of such goods.

15. For the details of this transaction, see Chapter 5.

16. See Karl W. Deutsch and Alexander Eckstein, "National Industrialization and the Declining Share of the International Economic Sector, 1890–1959," *World Politics*, v. 13, no. 2, January 1961, pp. 267–299.

17. See, for instance, G. M. Meier and R. E. Baldwin, *Economic Development* (New York: Wiley, 1957).

18. Simon Kuznets, "Quantitative Aspects of the Economic Growth of Nations: IX. Level and Structure of Foreign Trade: Comparisons for Recent Years," *Economic Development and Cultural Change*, v. 13, no. 1, October 1964, pt. 2, pp. 15–16.
19. The bases of these estimates are summarized in the following table:

Year	Estimated Imports of Machinery and Equipment			Gross Investment in Fixed Capital	Equipment Component of This Investment	Import Shares of Equipment Component	
	in millions of U.S. dollars	in millions of yuan		in millions of yuan		(2)/(5)	(3)/(5)
						in per cent	
		at Y2.62:$1	at Y5.91:$1				
	(1)	(2)	(3)	(4)	(5)	(6)	(7)
1952	220	576	1,300	7,680	3,072	18.7	42.3
1953	250	655	1,477	11,150	4,460	14.6	33.1
1954	325	851	1,920	13,660	5,464	15.5	35.1
1955	340	890	2,010	12,650	5,060	17.5	39.7
1956	450	1,180	2,660	19,070	7,628	15.4	34.8
1957	495	1,310	2,925	15,000	6,000	21.8	48.7

Sources: Column 1—For 1952–54, we obtained figures on Soviet exports of machinery and equipment to China from M. I. Sladkovskii, "The Development of the Soviet Union's Trade with the Chinese People's Republic," *Vneshniaia Torgovlia [Foreign Trade]*, v. 29, no. 10, October 1959, pp. 2–10, and similar figures for the non-Communist world from data compiled by the U.S. Department of Commerce. Combining these, we arrived at the totals listed. For 1955–57, we assumed that the percentages for machinery and equipment imports in Table 4–5 would be the same for total imports and then applied these percentages to the sum of Soviet and non-Communist world exports to China to derive the figures listed.

Column 4—These estimates are taken from W. W. Hollister, *China's Gross National Product and Social Accounts, 1950–1957* (Glencoe, Ill.: Free Press, 1958).

Column 5—The text of the First Five Year Plan published in 1955 gives 38 per cent as the equipment component of fixed-capital investment. We rounded this figure to 40 per cent and applied it to the estimates of fixed-capital investment.

Some sources suggest that the equipment component of fixed-capital investment was around 33 rather than 38 per cent. (See "The Scope and Development of China's Basic Construction Investment," *T'ung-chi Kung-tso T'ung-hsun [Statistical Work Bulletin]*, no. 18, September 24,

1956, pp. 4–6.) Were we to use this 33 per cent rather than 40 per cent, the import share in the equipment component would be raised to 18–27 and 40–59 per cent respectively.

20. If one uses 33 per cent instead of 40 per cent as the equipment component of investment (see note 19), the reduction in investment would have been 18–27 and 40–59 per cent respectively.

21. Proceeding on the basis of the capital-output ratio derived in Appendix D, we estimated the impact of import cessation on investment and growth as follows:

    a. Import effects
        (1) Equipment component of gross fixed-capital investment for 1952–56 (See column 5, note 19)   Y25,684 million
        (2) Capital goods imports for 1952–56
            (a) Converted at the 2.62:1 rate (column 2, note 19)   Y 4,152 million
            (b) Converted at the 5.91:1 rate (column 3, note 19)   Y 9,367 million

    b. Investment effects
        (1) Equipment component net of imports
            (a) 25,684–4,152   Y21,532 million
            (b) 25,684–9,367   Y16,317 million
        (2) Gross fixed-capital investment net of imports
            (a) 21,532:40 per cent   Y53,830 million
            (b) 16,317:40 per cent   Y40,790 million

If we assume that this reduction in investment would not significantly affect depreciation allowances, most of which the Chinese set aside for the replacement of old capital, the depreciation totals in T. C. Liu and K. C. Yeh, *The Economy of the Chinese Mainland: National Income and Economic Development, 1933–1956* (Princeton University Press, 1965) must be deducted from these gross investment figures.

        (3) Net fixed-capital investment would then be
            (a)   Y33,410 million
            (b)   Y20,370 million

    c. Growth effects.
        Applying the estimated capital-output ratio to these reduced net investments yields net national product increments for 1953–57 of
            (a)   Y19,770 million
            (b)   Y12,050 million
        As compared to the actually estimated increment of   Y26,780 million

22. Total consumer goods imports were estimated by applying the share of these in Table 4–5 to the import totals of Table 4–1 and then adding to the resulting figure the imports of miscellaneous (unspecified, "other") manufactured goods from the non-Communist world on the assumption that these goods would be mostly consumer manufactures. This total was then related to the Hollister (cited, Table 1, pp. 12–13) and Liu-Yeh (cited, Table 94, pp. 417–419) estimates of personal con-

sumption for 1955, 1956, and 1957. The 0.5 per cent given in the text was arrived at by averaging the Hollister three-year average of 0.46 per cent and the Liu-Yeh three-year average of 0.55 per cent.

23. See Table 6–8.

24. To obtain 2 per cent, we assumed that all agricultural raw materials and "other" exports were destined for consumption. If we include only those exports which can definitely be identified as consumer goods, the percentage would be no more than 1.5. We calculated the ratio by the same method we used to relate imports to personal consumption (see note 22 of this chapter).

25. *Trends and Developments in Communist China's World Trade in Farm Products, 1955–1960*, cited, Table 17, p. 32.

Chapter Five

1. See, for instance, F. H. Mah, "The First Five-Year Plan and its International Aspects" in C. F. Remer, ed., *Three Essays on the International Economics of Communist China* (Ann Arbor: University of Michigan Press, 1959), pp. 31–117, and C. M. Li, *Economic Development of Communist China* (Berkeley: University of California Press, 1959), chapters 5 and 6.

2. Walter Galenson, "Economic Relations Between the Soviet Union and Communist China," in Nicholas Spulber, ed., *Study of the Soviet Economy* (Indiana University Publications, Russian and East European Series, v. 25; Bloomington: Indiana University, 1961).

3. In an earlier study I advanced a similar view, although my conclusions were more tentative and qualified because of the absence of foreign trade data at the time. See "Moscow-Peking Axis: The Economic Pattern" in Howard Boorman and others, *Moscow–Peking Axis: Strengths and Strains* (New York: Harper and Brothers for the Council on Foreign Relations, 1957), pp. 75–109.

4. *Chung-hua Jen-min Kung-ho-kuo T'iao-yueh Chi* [*Collection of Treaties of the People's Republic of China*], v. 1 (Peking: Fa-lu Ch'u-pan-she, 1957), p. 250.

5. Same.

6. "Text of the Soviet-Chinese Communist Communique on 7 Accords," *The New York Times*, October 12, 1954.

7. Li Hsien-nien's "Report on 1954 Final Accounts and the 1955 Budget," *Jen-min Jih-pao* (*JMJP*) [*People's Daily*], July 10, 1955.

8. *Chung-hua Jen-min Kung-ho-kuo T'iao-yueh Chi*, cited, p. 250.

9. This provision appears in the 1950 trade agreements with the Soviet Union and Czechoslovakia respectively. In the Soviet case, it was confirmed by an exchange of notes between the Soviet Minister of Foreign Trade and the Chinese Vice-Minister of Foreign Trade on April 11, 1957. *Chung-hua Jen-min Kung-ho-kuo T'iao-yueh Chi*, v. 6 (Peking: Fa-lu Ch'u-pan-she, 1958), pp. 92–93, and C. F. Remer, *The Trade Agreements of Communist China*, RAND P-2208 (Santa Monica: RAND Corporation, February 1, 1961), p. 38.

10. For a detailed discussion of payment provisions governing commercial agreements within the Communist world, see A. M. Smirnov, *Interna-*

tional Currency and Credit Relations of the USSR, U.S. Joint Publications Research Service, no. 4147 (Washington, D.C.: U.S. Joint Publications Research Service, October 31, 1960).

11. For an interesting account of Soviet efforts and Chinese rebuffs in these negotiations, see Oleg Hoeffding, "Sino-Soviet Economic Relations in Recent Years" in Kurt London, ed., *Unity and Contradiction: Major Aspects of Sino-Soviet Relations* (New York: Praeger, 1962), pp. 295–312.

12. The evidence is twofold. On the one hand, official Chinese sources indicate that Soviet credits during 1950–52 totaled 2,007 million yuan, which at a yuan-ruble commercial exchange rate of 1:1 would amount to about U.S. $500 million. This figure is well in excess of the $180 million that was provided for in the 1950 loan. This discrepancy suggests that the Soviet Union extended additional credits of about $320 million during the Korean War for some unspecified purpose. A 1956 speech by Lung Yun (a former Kuomintang warlord who was given various honorary positions by the Chinese Communists) further suggests that these were probably military credits. In the speech, Lung complained about the fact that Korean War deliveries were financed by Soviet credits which had to be repaid under rather onerous conditions. On the other hand, there are some indications that the Russians provided military hardware for the Korean front free and demanded compensation only for goods that were in the pipeline at the time of the 1953 armistice.

13. That the commitment for the 91 projects was made in May 1953 is explicitly spelled out in Li Fu-ch'un's report on the First Five Year Plan at the National People's Congress on July 5, 1955. See *Hsin-hua Yueh-pao (HHYP)* [*New China Monthly*], no. 8, August 1955, pp. 1–22. The text of Mao's letter to the Soviet government was published in *JMJP* on September 16, 1953, without reference to the fact that the agreement was concluded in May. Li Fu-ch'un's report also indicates that the earlier agreement for the rehabilitation of 50 enterprises was concluded in 1950.

14. *HHYP*, no. 11, November 1954.

15. *Hsin-hua Pan-yueh-k'an (HHPYK)* [*New China Semimonthly*], no. 9, May 6, 1956.

16. *JMJP*, August 12, 1958 and April 22, 1959.

17. *China Weekly* (Hong Kong), June 6, 1960; September 19, 1960; March 6, 1961.

18. Same, June 6, 1960.

19. "Text of the Soviet-Chinese Communist Communique on 7 Accords," cited.

20. Speech delivered on February 14, 1964. An English translation of the text may be found in *The Current Digest of the Soviet Press*, v. 16, no. 13, April 22, 1964, pp. 5–16, and no. 14, April 29, 1964, pp. 3–17.

21. In 1952, the Soviet government agreed to pay a monthly stipend to Chinese students being trained in the U.S.S.R. The Chinese government had to repay half the amount, but the other half represented a Soviet gift.

22. See Table 4–1, the national statistical yearbooks of East European countries, and U.S. Central Intelligence Agency, *Foreign Trade of the*

European Satellites, 1963, Intelligence Report (Washington, D.C.: Author, December 1964).
23. This fact was explicitly recognized in Soviet writings on China trade, *e.g.,* M. I. Sladkovskii, "The Development of the Soviet Union's Trade with the Chinese People's Republic," *Vneshniaia Torgovlia [Foreign Trade],* v. 29, no. 10, October 1959, pp. 2–10.
24. B. Gordeev and A. Galanov, "The Growth of Exports of Machine-building Goods," same, v. 28, no. 11, November 1958, p. 32.
25. A. Smirnov, "The Soviet Union's Technical Assistance in the Construction of Enterprises Abroad," same, v. 29, no. 9, September 1959, p. 11.
26. "According to the Sino-Soviet credit agreement of February 14, 1950, all goods bought in the U.S.S.R. as well as *technical aid received is to be paid for* by exports of Chinese products to the U.S.S.R., except for the equipment and materials which were to be financed by the credits granted in the agreement." M. I. Sladkovskii, *Ocherki Ekonomicheskikh Otnoshenii SSSR s Kitaem [Essays on the Economic Relations of the USSR with China]* (Moscow: Vneshtorgizdat, 1957), p. 314.
27. Li Hsien-nien: "Report on the 1956 Final Accounts and the 1957 State Budget," *HHPYK,* no. 14, July 25, 1957, pp. 16–28.
28. M. I. Sladkovskii, "Indestructible Soviet-Chinese Friendship," *Vneshniaia Torgovlia,* v. 27. no. 2, February 1957, p. 2, and "Sino-Soviet Treaty and Agreements," *Current Background,* no. 62, March 5, 1957, p. 8.
29. For texts of these agreements, see the Supplement to *People's China,* no. 21, November 1, 1954, p. 4, and *The New York Times,* October 12, 1954.
30. C. M. Li, *Economic Development of Communist China,* cited, chapter 8.
31. F. H. Mah, "The First Five-Year Plan and its International Aspects," cited, Table 20, p. 86.
32. In a speech to the National People's Congress on June 29, 1957, Li Hsien-nien, Minister of Finance, stated: "During the reconstruction period and during the early period of our new development, *the Soviet Union helped us on several occasions with loans.*" (New China News Agency, Peking, June 29, 1957.)
33. According to *Pravda [Truth],* February 15, 1956, Soviet credits to Communist countries in Asia amounted to about 8 billion rubles. If one deducts from this amount Soviet loans to North Korea (1,200 million rubles exclusive of military aid during the Korean War and a gift of 1 billion rubles), to Mongolia (1,100 million rubles), and to North Vietnam (400 million rubles), the residual is about 5,300 million rubles for China. For more detailed evidence, see Institut für Asienkunde (Hamburg), *Die Wirtschaftliche Verflechtung der Volksrepublik China mit der Sowjetunion [The Economic Links of the People's Republic of China with the Soviet Union]* (Frankfurt am Main: Alfred Metzner Verlag, 1959), pp. 43–44.
34. For a detailed discussion of the exchange-rate problem, see Appendix C.
35. For an alternative approach and interpretation of the same data, see C. Y. Cheng, *Economic Relations Between Peking and Moscow: 1949–1963* (New York: Praeger, 1964), pp. 76–82. On the basis of different assumptions and reasoning, Cheng arrives at quite different results for the values of the military stockpiles and the Soviet shares in the joint-stock companies. As is noted in the text of the present chapter, official

Chinese sources cannot be used as an authority for such estimates, for these sources give only annual Soviet credits and do not indicate how much of this total was used for various purposes.

36. See *Vneshniaia Torgovlia*, v. 41, no. 5, May 1961, p. 18.

37. Same.

38. Chou En-lai, "Report on Government Work," *JMJP*, December 31, 1964.

39. See Kurt Müller, *Entwicklungshilfe innerhalb des Ostblocks* [*Development Assistance within the Eastern Bloc*] (Frankfurt am Main: Alfred Metzner Verlag, 1960), pp. 66–71, and U.S. Department of State, *Communist China's Economic Aid to Other Countries*, Intelligence Information Brief, no. 375, February 20, 1961, p. 4.

40. United Nations, Economic Commission for Europe, *Economic Survey of Europe 1956* (Geneva: Author, 1957), Table 20, pp. 18–19, and "The Hungarian Economy in the Spring of 1957," *Economic Bulletin for Europe*, v. 9, no. 1, May 1957, Table 19 and note 44, p. 81.

41. *China Reconstructs*, v. 7, no. 12, December 1958, p. 11.

42. Müller, cited, p. 87.

43. William E. Griffith, *Albania and the Sino-Soviet Rift* (Cambridge: M.I.T. Press, 1963); P. H. M. Jones, "Albania, Asia in Europe," *Far Eastern Economic Review*, v. 42, no. 2, October 10, 1963, p. 64.

44. Sladkovskii, *Ocherki Ekonomicheskikh Otnoshenii SSSR s Kitaem*, cited, p. 314.

45. Chou En-lai, *A Great Decade* (Peking: Foreign Languages Press, 1959).

46. I am indebted to Professor Cheng Chu-yuan for making available to me, prior to publication, a paper on "The Role of the Soviet Union in Developing Technical Manpower in Communist China," which will be a chapter in his forthcoming book on technical and scientific manpower in Communist China. The specific examples of scientific collaboration between China and the Soviet Union were culled from p. 2 of the paper.

47. M. I. Sladkovskii, "Chinese Economic Cooperation," *Problemi Vostokovedeniia* [*Problems of Oriental Studies*], July 1960, pp. 108–117.

48. V. Skripnik, "Scientific-Technical Cooperation of the USSR with Socialist Countries," *Vneshniaia Torgovlia*, v. 30, no. 2, February 1960, p. 10.

49. C. Y. Cheng, "The Role of the Soviet Union in Developing Technical Manpower in Communist China," cited, p. 2.

50. Editorial in *JMJP*, February 27, 1963.

51. F. H. Mah, *Communist China's Foreign Trade, Price Structure and Behavior, 1955–1959*, RAND Research Memorandum, 3825-RC (Santa Monica: RAND Corporation, October 1963).

52. F. D. Holzman, "Soviet Foreign Trade Pricing and the Question of Discrimination, A 'Customs Union' Approach," *The Review of Economics and Statistics*, v. 44, no. 2, May 1962, pp. 134–147.

53. All these percentages are based on the Soviet credit figures given in Table 5–5 and on Oleg Hoeffding and Nancy Nimitz, *Soviet National Income and Product, 1949–1955*, RAND Research Memorandum, RM 2101 (Santa Monica: RAND Corporation, April 6, 1959), Table 4, p. 9.

54. United Nations, Economic Commission for Europe, "Foreign Trade and

Economic Development in Eastern Europe and the Soviet Union," *Economic Bulletin for Europe*, v. 2, no. 1, June 1959, pp. 39–76.

55. Same, p. 54.

56. I am endebted to Professor Gregory Grossman for calling this point to my attention and for alerting me to the fact that certain branches of the engineering industry were at times operating well below capacity.

57. J. S. Berliner, *Soviet Economic Aid* (New York: Praeger for the Council on Foreign Relations, 1958), Table 5, pp. 52–53, and Table A, pp. 198–202; George S. Carnett and Morris H. Crawford, "The Scope and Distribution of Soviet Economic Aid" in *Dimensions of Soviet Economic Power*, Hearings together with Compilation of Studies Prepared for the Joint Economic Committee, U.S. Congress, 87th Cong., 2d sess. (Washington, D.C.: GPO, 1962), Tables 1 and 2, p. 474; United Nations Conference on Trade and Development, *Past Trade Flows and Future Prospects for Trade between the Centrally-planned Economies and Developing Countries*, E/Conf.46/35, (New York: Author, February 13, 1964), Appendix Table V.

Chapter Six

1. U.S. Mutual Defense Assistance Control Act Administrator, *The Strategic Trade Control System, 1948–1956*, 9th Report to Congress (Washington, D.C.: GPO, 1957), pp. 12–18.

2. Same and U.S. Mutual Defense Assistance Control Act Administrator, *A Survey of the Strategic Trade Control Program, 1957–1960*, 14th Report to Congress (Washington, D.C.: GPO, December 1960), p. 2.

3. This estimate is based on the assumption that shipping and related costs amounted to 6 per cent of import value and that all imports were carried in foreign ships. In fact, some imports—but an unknown portion—were transported in Chinese ships. Therefore, the figure cited in the text is probably conservative, for it involves an overestimate of the foreign-exchange costs incurred for shipping. It should be noted, in addition, that the estimate is also based on the assumption that China did not use the foreign exchange she earned in her trade with the non-Communist world to meet her obligations vis-à-vis other Communist countries.

4. Unless other sources are specifically noted, all discussions of the commodity composition of Communist China's trade with non-Communist countries are based upon data derived from United Nations, *Commodity Trade Statistics* and *Yearbook of International Trade Statistics* for various years.

5. All references to world trade and to the total trade of non-Communist countries or areas are based upon data in United Nations, *Yearbook of International Trade Statistics* for various years.

6. Derek Davies, "China Earns from Hongkong," *Far Eastern Economic Review (FEER)*, v. 40, no. 12, June 20, 1963, pp. 689–695.

7. See *FEER*, v. 20, no. 19, May 10, 1956, p. 590.

8. Needless to say, these estimates are quite crude and are subject to large margins of error. They are based on a systematic analysis of the notes and news items in the back of the weekly issues of the *FEER*.

9. Same, v. 28, no. 12, March 25, 1960, p. 667; and v. 36, no. 13, June 21, 1962, p. 591.

10. See Edwin O. Reischauer, *Ennin's Travels in T'ang China* (New York: Ronald Press Company, 1955).

11. In these figures, Japan's trade with Taiwan and Korea is treated as foreign trade, while trade between Manchuria and China is treated as domestic trade. (See the sources in Table 6-5.) If Japan, Taiwan, and Korea are treated as one trading unit and if China's trade with Manchuria is excluded from China's foreign trade, as is done in League of Nations statistics, then about 14 per cent of Japan's imports came from China and 24 per cent of its exports went there, while Japan's share of China's foreign trade came to about 15-17 per cent, whether measured by exports or imports. League of Nations, *International Trade Statistics* for 1935, 1936, and 1937, II.A. (Geneva: Author, 1936, 1937, and 1938).

12. See A. Doak Barnett, *Communist China and Asia* (New York: Harper and Row for the Council on Foreign Relations, 1960), pp. 235-238, and C. Martin Wilbur, "Japan and the Rise of Communist China" in Hugh Borton, ed., *Japan Between East and West* (New York: Harper and Brothers, 1957), pp. 199-239.

13. *The New York Times*, August 21, 1963.

14. For the 1934-36, 1950, and 1964 rankings, see Bank of Japan, *Economic Statistics of Japan, 1964* (Tokyo: Author, 1965), pp. 265-268. For the 1960, 1962, and 1963 rankings, see United Nations, *Yearbook of International Trade Statistics, 1963* (New York: Author, 1964), p. 385.

15. On this point, see Warren Hunsberger, *Japan and the United States in World Trade* (New York: Harper and Row for the Council on Foreign Relations, 1964), pp. 204-206.

16. See Japan, Ministry of Finance, *Annual Return of the Foreign Trade of Japan* for various years.

17. See Hunsberger, cited, Table 8-1, pp. 244-245.

18. *Annual Return of the Foreign Trade of Japan* for various years.

19. Japan, Economic Planning Agency, *New Long-Range Economic Plan of Japan (1961-1970)* (Tokyo: The Japan Times, 1961), Tables 16 and 17, pp. 75-81.

20. Norman Sun, "Prospects and Problems of Trade Between Japan and Mainland China" in E. F. Szczepanik, ed., *Symposium on Economic and Social Problems of the Far East: Proceedings of a Meeting Held in September 1961 as Part of the Golden Jubilee Congress of the University of Hong Kong* (Hong Kong University Press, 1962), Table 4, p. 148.

21. This discussion of the commodity composition of Communist China's trade with the countries of South and Southeast Asia is based upon information gleaned from various issues of the *FEER*.

22. See various issues of the *Rubber Statistical Bulletin* (London), published by the International Rubber Study Group.

23. See Organization for Economic Cooperation and Development, *The Flow of Financial Resources to Less-developed Countries, 1956-1963* (Paris: Author, 1964); U.S. Agency for International Development, *U.S. Overseas Loans and Grants and Assistance from International Organizations: Obligations and Loan Authorizations, July 1, 1945-June 30, 1964*, Special Report Prepared for the House Affairs Committee

(Washington, D.C.: Author, March 3, 1965) and earlier volumes in this series; United Nations Conference on Trade and Development, *Past Trade Flows and Future Prospects for Trade between the Centrally-planned Economies and Developing Countries*, E/Conf.46/35 (New York: Author, February 13, 1964), Appendix Table V.

24. See United Nations, Economic Commission for Asia and the Far East, *Economic Survey of Asia and the Far East, 1961*, 1962.II.F.1 (Bangkok: Author, 1962), p. 197, and *Economic Survey of Asia and the Far East, 1963*, 1964.II.F.1 (New York: Author, 1964), pp. 221–222; United Nations, *Economic Bulletin for Asia and the Far East*, v. 25, no. 3, December 1964, pp. 111–112.

25. If Chinese shipments of silver—mostly for monetary purposes—are excluded, the small surpluses in 1961 and 1962 become deficits.

26. These sales were reported at the time in various newspapers and journals. See, for instance, *The Economist* (London), June 30, 1962, p. 1368, and January 19, 1963, p. 241.

27. See Colina MacDougall, "Eight Plants for Peking," *FEER*, v. 43, no. 4, January 23, 1964, pp. 156–157; and *Survey of the China Mainland Press (SCMP)*, no. 3202, April 20, 1964, p. 26; no. 3234, June 9, 1964, pp. 22–23; no. 3296, September 11, 1964, pp. 30–31; and no. 3332, November 5, 1964, pp. 24–25.

28. See MacDougall, cited, pp. 155–156.

29. Actually, there is no information on the total value of the complete plants Eastern Europe delivered to Communist China. If these plants constituted the same percentage of Eastern Europe's exports to China as complete plants did of the Soviet exports to China, they would have amounted to about $610 million in 1959. However, if the percentage was higher for Eastern Europe than for the Soviet Union, as is possible for the reasons outlined in Chapter 4, they might have totaled as much as $650 million.

30. See Chapter 4, pp. 126–127.

31. See "China 1963," *FEER*, v. 41, no. 13, September 26, 1963, p. 805.

32. *China Trade Report* (Hong Kong), March 1964, p. 4. This report is published monthly by the *FEER*.

33. See various volumes of Food and Agriculture Organization of the United Nations, *World Grain Trade Statistics*; U.S. Department of Agriculture, *Foreign Agriculture*, April 13, 1964, p. 10.

34. Same, March 16, 1964, p. 11.

35. *FEER*, v. 42, no. 1, October 3, 1963, pp. 6–7.

36. *The New York Times*, May 3, 1961, and August 3, 1963.

37. *FEER*, v. 43, no. 12, March 20, 1964, pp. 637–638.

38. On these motivations, see Richard Lowenthal, "China" in Zbigniew Brzezinski, ed., *Africa and the Communist World* (Stanford University Press, 1963), pp. 142–203, and Howard L. Boorman, "Peking in World Politics," *Pacific Affairs*, v. 34, no. 3, Fall 1961, pp. 227–241.

39. U.S. Department of State, *The Sino-Soviet Economic Offensive Through June 30, 1962*, Research Memorandum, RSB-145 (Washington, D.C.: Author, September 18, 1962); *Past Trade Flows and Future Prospects for Trade between the Centrally-planned Economies and Developing Countries*, cited, Appendix Table V.

40. Daniel Wolfstone, "Sino-African Economies," *FEER*, v. 42, no. 7, February 13, 1964, pp. 349-351.
41. Same.
42. Same.
43. See United Nations, *Commodity Trade Statistics;* and Federation of Nigeria, *Digest of Statistics*, v. 11, no. 2, April 1962.
44. Wolfstone, cited.
45. *FEER*, v. 43, no. 9, February 27, 1964, p. 450.
46. U.S. Department of State, *The Sino-Soviet Economic Offensive Through June 30, 1962*, cited; U.S. Department of State, *The Communist Economic Offensive Through 1963*, Research Memorandum, RSB-43 (Washington, D.C.: Author, June 18, 1964); Wolfstone, cited.
47. See National Bank of Egypt, *Economic Bulletin*, no. 2, for 1959, 1960, 1961, and 1963; United Nations, *Yearbook of International Trade* for 1958 and 1961.
48. Wolfstone, cited.
49. Arslan Hambaraci, "Chou's Mediterranean Tour," *FEER*, v. 43, no. 4, January 23, 1964, p. 154.
50. The information on the commodity composition of trade comes from U.S. Department of Commerce sources.
51. Same.
52. *Survey of the China Mainland Press*, no. 2653, January 8, 1962, p. 38.
53. Hambaraci, cited, pp. 153-154.
54. *FEER*, v. 43, no. 7, February 6, 1964, p. 293.
55. U.S. Department of State, *The Communist Economic Offensive Through 1963*, cited.
56. Daniel Tretiak, "China's Latin American Trade," *FEER*, v. 41, no. 4, July 25, 1963, pp. 221-224.
57. See *SCMP*, no. 2307, July 29, 1960, pp. 30-31, and no. 2391, December 6, 1960, pp. 29-35.
58. U.S. Department of State, *The Communist Economic Offensive Through 1963*, cited.
59. Communist aid commitments to the non-Communist world through December 1963 totaled $4,899 million. See U.S. Department of State, *The Communist Economic Offensive Through 1963*, cited. New commitments in 1964 amounted to about $1,340 million. See *Foreign Assistance, 1965*, Hearings before the Committee on Foreign Relations, U.S. Senate, 89th Cong., 1st sess. (Washington, D.C.: GPO, 1965), p. 87.
60. U.S. Department of State, *The Sino-Soviet Economic Offensive Through June 30, 1962*, cited.
61. For a most interesting analysis of Sino-Soviet aid competition in the African arena, see Robert A. Scalapino, "Sino-Soviet Competition in Africa," *Foreign Affairs*, v. 42, no. 4, July 1964, pp. 640-654.

Chapter Seven

1. These and subsequent rankings are based upon a comparison of my figures for Communist China's foreign trade with those of the foreign trade of other countries as reported in United Nations, *Yearbook of International Trade Statistics, 1963* (New York: Author, 1965), Table A, pp. 12-17.

2. *The New York Times*, November 20, 1964.
3. I am indebted to Professor J. M. Montias of Yale for calling this point to my attention.
4. See various issues of the *Rubber Statistical Bulletin* (London), published by the International Rubber Study Group, and the *Yearbook of International Trade Statistics, 1963*, cited. All subsequent references to the total exports of any country except Communist China are based upon data in the latter source.
5. See United Nations, *Commodity Trade Statistics*. Most subsequent references to the commodity composition of the trade of any country except Communist China are based upon data in this source.
6. The percentages cited in the text are based on column 7 of the following table (with some allowance for understatement) on the assumption that the 5.91:1 yuan-dollar rate is a more realistic converter for military hardware than the official rate is. They are subject to large margins of error and should in no sense be viewed as highly reliable estimates.

Year	Chinese Communist Defense Expenditures [a]	Estimated Outlays for Military Subsistence [b]	Other Outlays (1)–(2)	"Other" Imports [c]		Ratio of Military Imports to Total Other Outlays	
				converted to yuan at the rate of		(4)/(3)	(5)/(3)
				2.62:1	5.91:1		
	(1)	(2)	(3)	(4)	(5)	(6)	(7)
	(in millions of yuan)					(in per cent)	
1955	6,500	1,500	5,000	700	1,550	14	31
1956	6,120	1,425	4,695	590	1,350	13	28
1957	5,510	1,225	4,285	270	600	6	14
1958	5,000	1,170	3,830	295	650	8	17
1959	5,800	1,350	4,450	410	950	9	21
1960	5,800	1,225	4,450	330	770	7	17

a These are official budget figures taken from State Statistical Bureau, *Ten Great Years, Statistics of the Economic and Cultural Achievements of the People's Republic of China* (Peking: Foreign Languages Press, 1960), pp. 23–24, and *Second Session of the Second National People's Congress of the People's Republic of China* (Peking: Foreign Languages Press, 1960), pp. 50, 58, and 60.

b In my study of *The National Income of Communist China* (New York: Free Press of Glencoe, 1961), Table 3, p. 391, I estimated the cost of subsistence of the armed forces as $1,000 million for 1952. In arriving at the figures in the present table, I assumed that the share of subsistence outlays in total military expenditures remained more or less stable between 1952 and 1960. Actually, this share probably declined during the period.

c As is indicated in the text, I have assumed that "other" (unitemized) Soviet and East European exports to China consisted solely of military goods. Thus, there is probably an overstatement involved here. It is probably offset, however, by the fact that other military exports might be hidden under the unitemized portions of several commodity categories.

7. Dwight Perkins, *The Economics of Chinese Communist Foreign Policy* (mimeographed, July 1964), p. 18.

8. Same.

9. The share of the defense budget which would be absorbed depends not only on the dollar estimate but also on what exchange rate one uses to convert these cost figures into yuan.

10. Mah's sample perforce excludes many types of machinery and equipment because of the difficulties of cross-country comparability. However, the transport factor is likely to be less important in the case of machinery and equipment than it is in the case of bulk commodities. To the extent that the "overpricing" can be ascribed to transport costs, therefore, one would expect the differential to be reduced significantly if machinery and equipment were fully represented in the sample.

11. It is generally assumed that the withdrawal of Soviet technicians in 1960 may have postponed the detonation of China's first nuclear device by about two years, *i.e.*, from 1962 to 1964.

12. It is labeled a "virtually total embargo" because limited imports of a highly specialized character (such as books, periodicals, newspapers, etc., for university libraries) are permitted under conditions of carefully controlled Treasury licensing.

Appendix C

1. In his report on foreign trade at the Fourth Session of the First National People's Congress on July 11, 1957, Yeh Chi-chuang, Minister of Foreign Trade, stated:

> In our trade with capitalist nations we have been working out prices of our import and export commodities on the basis of market prices in capitalist countries. Since *we have segregated out domestic prices from the foreign market, prices prevailing* for our import and export commodities, if converted into our currency at the foreign exchange rate, will generally show discrepancies which indicate that *we lose in export and gain in import.*

See *Hsin-hua Pan-yueh-k'an* [*New China Semimonthly*], no. 16, August 22, 1957, pp. 90–94.

2. Undervaluation certainly seems evident if we compare the official ruble-yuan rate with the dollar-yuan and dollar-ruble rates. The application of a noncommercial rate of 6 rubles to the yuan for tourist and related ex-

penditures indicates that the yuan is also undervalued in terms of purchasing power parity.

3. Chao Kang, "Pitfalls in the Use of China's Foreign Trade Statistics," *The China Quarterly*, no. 19, July/September 1964, p. 49.

I. P. Aizenberg, *Valutnaia Sistema SSSR* [*The Currency System of the USSR*] (Moscow: Izd-vo Social'no-ekon. Lit-ri, 1962), pp. 149–151. Same.

For instance, *Chi-hsieh Kung-yeh* [*Machine Industry*], no. 10, May 24, 1957, p. 5, states that "the cost of design performed in the Soviet Union required 4,000 rubles per person per month. This amount is equal to 2,000 yuan." This comment would suggest a 2:1 ruble-yuan rate. Similarly, in *Soviet Scientist in Red China* (New York: Praeger, 1964), p. 57, M. A. Klochko indicates that "at the official exchange rate, one yuan was worth two old rubles, but in purchasing power it was worth more. In reports on the Chinese national economy, Soviet economists placed the purchasing power of one yuan at about six old rubles."

7. I do not mean to imply that commodities entering Chinese-European Communist trade are valued precisely at world market prices. These prices are used as a reference, but actual prices are set by bargaining and take into account a variety of factors like transport costs, quantity discounts, and domestic costs of production. Such an approach to price-setting is indicated in general terms in Yeh Chi-chuang's speech cited above. It is confirmed by other information on price-setting practices within the bloc. For further details, see Horst Mendershausen, "Terms of Trade Between the Soviet Union and Smaller Communist Countries, 1955–1957," *Review of Economics and Statistics*, v. 41, no. 2, May 1959, pp. 106–118, and "The Terms of Soviet-Satellite Trade: A Broadened Analysis," *Review of Economics and Statistics*, v. 42, no. 2, May 1960, pp. 152–163; F. D. Holzman, "Soviet Foreign Trade Pricing and the Question of Discrimination, A 'Customs Union' Approach," *Review of Economics and Statistics*, v. 44, no. 2, May 1962, pp. 134–147; and Frederic L. Pryor, *The Communist Foreign Trade System* (Cambridge: M.I.T. Press, 1963), chapter 5.

8. See F. D. Holzman, "Some Financial Aspects of Foreign Trade" in *Comparisons of the United States and Soviet Economies*, pt. 2, Papers Submitted by Panelists Appearing before the Subcommittee on Economic Statistics, Joint Economic Committee, 86th Cong., 1st sess. (Washington: GPO, 1959), p. 432; Norman M. Kaplan and William L. White, *A Comparison of 1950 Wholesale Prices in Soviet and American Industry*, RAND Research Memorandum, RM-1443 (Santa Monica: RAND Corporation, May 1, 1955); Norman M. Kaplan and Eleanor S. Weinstein, "A Comparison of Soviet and American Retail Prices in 1950," *Journal of Political Economy*, v. 44, no. 6, December 1956, pp. 470–491, and "A Note on Ruble-Dollar Comparisons," *Journal of Political Economy*, v. 45, no. 6, December 1957, p. 543; U.S. Central Intelligence Agency, *1955 Ruble-Dollar Price Ratios for Intermediate Products and Services in the U.S.S.R. and the U.S.* (Washington, D.C.: Author, June 1960).

9. See Mendershausen, cited; Holzman, cited; and Pryor, cited.

10. Chao, cited, pp. 54–58.
11. *Jen-min Jih-pao* [*People's Daily*], December 31, 1964.
12. An English translation of this speech may be found in *Current Digest of the Soviet Press*, v. 16, no. 13, April 22, 1964, pp. 5–16, and no. 14, April 29, 1964, pp. 3–17.
13. Alexander Eckstein, *The National Income of Communist China* (New York: Free Press of Glencoe, 1961), Table F–5, p. 186.
14. Chao Kang, "Yuan-Dollar Price Ratios in Communist China and the United States," *Occasional Papers* of the Center for Chinese Studies, University of Michigan, no. 2, July 1963.

A SELECTED BIBLIOGRAPHY

Chinese Communist Sources

I. Documents, Official Policy Statements, Statistical Series.

Central Committee of the Communist Party of China. "Resolution on Agricultural Cooperation," *Hsin-hua Yueh-pao* [*New China Monthly*], no. 11, November 1955, pp. 9–13.

Chen Yun. "The Financial and Food Situation" in *New China's Economic Achievements, 1949–1952.* Peking: Foreign Languages Press, 1952. Pp. 47–60.

Chin Ming. "How People's Communes' Finance Work Serves Distribution," *Selections from China Mainland Magazines,* no. 238, December 5, 1960, pp. 22–30.

Chou En-lai. "Report on the Draft Second Five-Year Plan," *Hsin-hua Pan-yueh-k'an* [*New China Semimonthly*], no. 20, October 23, 1956, pp. 35–49.

——. *A Great Decade.* Peking: Foreign Languages Press, 1959.

——. "Report on Government Work," *Hsin-hua Pan-yueh-k'an,* no. 9, May 6, 1959, pp. 2–15.

——. "Report on Government Work," *Jen-min Jih-pao* [*People's Daily*], December 31, 1964.

Chou Po-ping. "The Policy of Unified Purchase and Sale of Grain Shall Not Be Frustrated," *Liang Shih* [*Food Grain*], no. 7, July 1957.

Chung-hua Jen-min Kung-ho-kuo T'iao-yueh Chi [*Collection of Treaties of the People's Republic of China*]. Peking: Fa-lu Ch'u-pan-she, 1957– .

Chung-kuo Jen-min Chieh-fang-chün Tsung-ch'eng-chih-pu Kung-tso T'ung-hsün [*Bulletin of Activities of the General Political Department of the Chinese People's Liberation Army*], January 1–August 26, 1961.

Feng Chung. "An Economic Policy That Wins, A Survey of the Policy of Readjustment, Consolidation, Filling Out, and Raising Standards," *Peking Review,* v. 7, no. 11, March 13, 1964, pp. 6–9.

Hsueh Mu-ch'iao. "Report before the Third National Conference on Statistical Work," *Hsin-hua Yueh-pao*, no. 5, May 1954, pp. 103–107.

Li Fu-ch'un. *Report on the First Five-Year Plan for Development of the National Economy of the People's Republic of China in 1953–57.* Peking: Foreign Languages Press, October 1955.

——. "The Achievements of China's First Five-Year Plan and the Tasks and Policy for Future Socialist Construction," *Current Background*, no. 483, December 16, 1957.

——. "Report on the Draft Plan for the National Economy for 1960," *Jen-min Jih-pao*, March 31, 1960.

——. "Report to the Ninth Plenary Session of the Eighth Central Committee," *Jen-min Jih-pao*, January 21, 1961.

Li Hsien-nien. "Report on 1954 Final Accounts and the 1955 Budget," *Jen-min Jih-pao*, July 10, 1955.

——. "Report on the 1956 Final Accounts and the 1957 State Budget," *Hsin-hua Pan-yueh-k'an*, no. 14, July 25, 1957, pp. 16–28.

——. "Report on the 1957 Final Accounts and the 1958 State Budget," *Hsin-hua Pan-yueh-k'an*, no. 5, March 10, 1958, pp. 3–12.

Li Shu-cheng. "New China's Achievements in Agricultural Production during the Past Three Years" in *New China's Economic Achievements, 1949–1952.* Peking: Foreign Languages Press, 1952. Pp. 187–194.

Liao Chi-li. "About the Two-Account System," *Chi-hua Ching-chi [Planned Economy]*, no. 5, May 1958, pp. 8–9.

Liu Shao-ch'i. "Report on the Work of the Central Committee of the Communist Party of China to the Second Session of the Eighth National Congress" in *Second Session of the Eighth National Congress of the Communist Party of China.* Peking: Foreign Languages Press, 1958. Pp. 16–60.

Mao Tse-tung. "The Question of Agricultural Cooperation," *Hsin-hua Yueh-pao*, no. 11, November 1955, pp. 1–8.

Nankai University. Economic Research Institute. *I Chiu I San Nien–I Chiu Wu Erh Nien Nan-k'ai Chi-shu Tzu-hao Hui-pien [Compilation of Nankai Index Number Data and Materials for 1913–1952].* Peking: T'ung-chi Ch'u-pan-she, 1958.

Second Session of the Second National People's Congress of the People's Republic of China. Peking: Foreign Languages Press, 1960.

State Statistical Bureau. "The Basic Situation of Planned Purchase and Planned Supply of Food Grains in China," *T'ung-chi Kung-tso [Statistical Work]*, no. 19, October 14, 1957, pp. 28, 31–32.

——. "Communique Concerning Adjustments in the Agricultural Production Statistics of 1958," *Jen-min Jih-pao*, August 27, 1959.

——. *Ten Great Years, Statistics of the Economic and Cultural Achievements of the People's Republic of China.* Peking: Foreign Languages Press, 1960.

Teng Hsiao-p'ing. "Report on the Rectification Campaign," *Current Background*, no. 477, October 25, 1957.

Teng Tsu-hui. "Report to the Rural Work Conference of the Central Committee of the New Democratic Youth League," *Hsin-hua Yueh-pao*, no. 12, December 1954, pp. 144–150.

Wang Hsiang-shu. "The Myth of Diminishing Returns," *Peking Review*, v. 1, no. 35, October 28, 1958, pp. 10–12.

Wei I. "Revolution in the Method of Planning," *Hsueh-hsi* [*Study*], no. 8, April 28, 1958, pp. 10–12.

II. Newspapers and Periodicals

Chi-hsieh Kung-yeh [*Machine Industry*], Peking. (Superseded by *Chi-hsieh Kung-yeh Chou-pao* in 1959.)
Chi-hua Ching-chi [*Planned Economy*], Peking. (Merged with *T'ung-chi Kung-tso* to become *Chi-hua Yu T'ung-chi* in January 1959.)
China Reconstructs, Peking.
Ching-chi Chou-pao [*Economic Weekly*], Shanghai.
Chung-kuo Nung-pao [*Agricultural Journal of China*], Peking.
Chung-kuo Shui-li [*Chinese Water Conservation*], Peking. (Merged with *Shui-li Fa-tien* to become *Shui-tien Chien-she* in November 1958.)
Hsin-hua Pan-yueh-k'an [*New China Semimonthly*], Peking. (January 1956–December 1962.)
Hsin-hua Yueh-pao [*New China Monthly*], Peking. (November 1949–December 1955 and January 1963–   .)
Hsueh-hsi [*Study*], Peking. (Discontinued in 1958.)
Hung Ch'i [*Red Flag*], Peking.
Jen-min Jih-pao [*People's Daily*], Peking.
Liang Shih [*Food Grain*], Peking. (January 1957–December 1957.)
Peking Review, Peking. (Superseded *People's China* in March 1958.)
Shui-li Hsueh-pao [*Journal of the Hydraulic Engineering Society*], Peking.
Ta Kung Pao [*Impartial Daily*], Tientsin and Peking.
T'ung-chi Kung-tso [*Statistical Work*], Peking. (Superseded *T'ung-chi Kung-tso T'ung-hsun* in 1957 and then merged with *Chi-hua Ching-chi* to become *Chi-hua Yu T'ung-chi* in January 1959.)
T'ung-chi Kung-tso T'ung-hsun [*Statistical Work Bulletin*], Peking. (Superseded by *T'ung-chi Kung-tso* in 1957.)
T'ung-chi Yen-chiu [*Statistical Research*], Peking.

Other Sources

I. Official Government and International Agency Publications

Bank of Japan. *Economic Statistics of Japan, 1964.* Tokyo: Author, 1965.
Food and Agriculture Organization of the United Nations. *Trade Yearbook.* Rome: Author, annual.
——. *World Grain Trade Statistics.* Rome: Author, annual.
India. Ministry of Food and Agriculture. *Report of the Indian Delegation to China on Agricultural Planning Techniques, July–August, 1956.* New Delhi: Author, 1956.
International Monetary Fund. *Balance of Payments Yearbook.* Washington, D.C.: Author, annual.
Japan. Economic Planning Agency. *New Long-Range Economic Plan of Japan (1961–1970).* Tokyo: The Japan Times, 1961.
Japan. Ministry of Finance. *Annual Return of the Foreign Trade of Japan.* Tokyo: Japan Tariff Association, annual.

League of Nations. *International Trade Statistics.* Geneva: Author, annual.
Organization for Economic Cooperation and Development. *The Flow of Financial Resources to Less-developed Countries, 1956–1963.* Paris: Author, 1964.
U.S.S.R. Ministry of Foreign Trade. *Vneshniaia Torgovlia SSSR za 1955–1959 Godi: Statisticheskii Sbornik* [*The Foreign Trade of the USSR for 1955–1959: A Statistical Compilation*]. Moscow: Vneshtorgizdat, 1961.
———. ———. *Vneshniaia Torgovlia SSSR: Statisticheskii Obzor* [*Foreign Trade of the USSR: Statistical Handbook*]. Moscow: Vneshtorgizdat, annual.
United Nations. *Commodity Trade Statistics.* New York: Author, annual.
———. *Statistical Yearbook.* New York: Author, annual.
———. *Yearbook of International Trade Statistics.* New York: Author, annual.
———. Economic Commission for Asia and the Far East. *Economic Survey of Asia and the Far East.* Bangkok: Author, annual.
———. Economic Commission for Europe. *Economic Survey of Europe.* Geneva: Author, annual.
United Nations Conference on Trade and Development. *Past Trade Flows and Future Prospects for Trade between the Centrally-planned Economies and Developing Countries.* E/Conf.46/35. New York: Author, February 13, 1964.
U.S. Central Intelligence Agency. *A Comparison of Capital Investment in the U.S. and the U.S.S.R., 1950–1959.* Washington, D.C.: Author, February 1961.
———. *Foreign Trade of the European Satellites, 1963.* Intelligence Report. Washington, D.C.: Author, December 1964.
———. *1955 Ruble-Dollar Price Ratios for Intermediate Products and Services in the U.S.S.R. and the U.S.* Washington, D.C.: Author, June 1960.
U.S. Congress. Joint Economic Committee. *Annual Economic Indicators for the U.S.S.R.* 88th Cong., 2d sess. Washington, D.C.: GPO, 1964.
U.S. Department of Agriculture. "Food Shortages in Communist China," *Foreign Agriculture Circular.* FATP 5–61. Washington, D.C.: Author, March 1961.
———. *Trends and Developments in Communist China's World Trade in Farm Products, 1955–1960.* Foreign Agricultural Economic Report, no. 6. Washington, D.C.: Author, September 1962.
U.S. Department of Commerce. *Foreign Commerce Yearbook 1933.* Washington, D.C.: GPO, 1934.
U.S. Department of State. *Communist China's Economic Aid to Other Countries.* Intelligence Information Brief, no. 375. Washington, D.C.: Author, February 20, 1961.
———. *The Communist Economic Offensive Through 1963.* Research Memorandum, RSB–43. Washington, D.C.: Author, June 18, 1964.
———. *Soviet Aid to Less-Developed Countries Through Mid-1962.* Research Memorandum. Washington, D.C.: Author, November 14, 1962.
———. *The Sino-Soviet Economic Offensive Through June 30, 1962.* Research Memorandum, RSB–145. Washington, D.C.: Author, September 18, 1962.
U.S. Mutual Defense Assistance Control Act Administrator. *Report to Congress.* Washington, D.C.: GPO, annual.

II. Books and Articles

Aizenberg, I. P. *Valutnaia Sistema SSSR* [*The Currency System of the USSR*]. Moscow: Izd-vo Social'no-ekon. Lit-ri, 1962.

Asian Political Economy Association. *Chugoku seiji keizai soran* [*Abstract of China's Political Economy*]. Tokyo: Author, 1964.

Barnett, A. Doak. *Communist China and Asia*. New York: Harper and Brothers for the Council on Foreign Relations, 1960.

Bergson, Abram and Simon Kuznets, eds. *Economic Trends in the Soviet Union*. Cambridge: Harvard University Press, 1961.

Bergson, Abram. *The Real National Income of Soviet Russia Since 1928*. Cambridge: Harvard University Press, 1963.

Berliner, Joseph S. *Soviet Economic Aid*. New York: Praeger for the Council on Foreign Relations, 1958.

Boorman, Howard and others. *Moscow-Peking Axis: Strengths and Strains*. New York: Harper and Brothers for the Council on Foreign Relations, 1957.

Boorman, Howard. "Peking in World Politics," *Pacific Affairs*, v. 34, no. 3, Fall 1961, pp. 227–241.

Brandt, Conrad, Benjamin Schwartz, and John K. Fairbank. *A Documentary History of Chinese Communism*. Cambridge: Harvard University Press, 1952.

Brzezinski, Zbigniew, ed. *Africa and the Communist World*. Stanford University Press, 1963.

Carnett, George S. and Morris H. Crawford. "The Scope and Distribution of Soviet Economic Aid" in *Dimensions of Soviet Economic Power*. Hearings together with Compilation of Studies Prepared for the Joint Economic Committee, U.S. Congress, 87th Cong., 2d sess. Washington, D.C.: GPO, 1962. Pp. 457–474.

Chao, Kang. *The Rate and Pattern of Industrial Growth in Communist China*. Ann Arbor: University of Michigan Press, 1965.

——. "Pitfalls in the Use of China's Foreign Trade Statistics," *The China Quarterly*, no. 19, July/September 1964, pp. 47–65.

——. "Yuan-Dollar Price Ratios in Communist China and the United States," *Occasional Papers* of the Center for Chinese Studies, University of Michigan, no. 2, July 1963.

Chao, K. C. *Agrarian Policies of Mainland China: A Documentary Study (1949–1956)*. Cambridge: Harvard University Press, 1957.

——. *Economic Planning and Organization in Mainland China, A Documentary Study (1949–1957)*, v. 1 and 2. Cambridge: Harvard University Press, 1960.

Chao, K.C., ed. *Source Materials from Communist China*, v. 3. Cambridge: Harvard University Press, October 1952.

Cheng, C. Y. *Economic Relations Between Peking and Moscow: 1949–1963*. New York: Praeger, 1964.

Cheng, Y. K. *Foreign Trade and Industrial Development of China, A Historical and Integrated Analysis through 1948*. Washington, D.C.: University Press of Washington, 1956.

Davies, Derek. "China Earns from Hongkong," *Far Eastern Economic Review*, v. 40, no. 12, June 20, 1963, pp. 689–695.

Deutsch, Karl W. and Alexander Eckstein. "National Industrialization and the Declining Share of the International Economic Sector, 1890–1959," *World Politics*, v. 13, no. 2, January 1961, pp. 267–299.

DeWitt, Nicholas. *Soviet Professional Manpower: Its Education, Training and Supply*. Washington, D.C.: National Science Foundation, 1955.

Eckstein, Alexander. "Conditions and Prospects for Economic Growth in Communist China," *World Politics*, v. 7, no. 1, October 1954, pp. 1–37, and no. 2, January 1955, pp. 255–283.

——. *The National Income of Communist China*. New York: Free Press of Glencoe, 1961.

Erlich, Alexander. "Stalin's Views on Soviet Economic Development" in E. J. Simmons, ed., *Continuity and Change in Russian and Soviet Thought*. Cambridge: Harvard University Press, 1955. Pp. 81–99.

Fairbank, J. K. *Trade and Diplomacy on the China Coast: The Opening of the Treaty Ports, 1842–1854*, v. 1. Cambridge: Harvard University Press, 1953.

Galenson, Walter. "Economic Relations Between the Soviet Union and Communist China" in Nicholas Spulber, ed., *Study of the Soviet Economy*. Indiana University Publications, Russian and East European series, v. 25. Bloomington: Indiana University, 1961. Pp. 32–56.

Garratt, Colin. "China as a Foreign Aid Donor," *Far Eastern Economic Review*, v. 31, no. 3, January 19, 1961, pp. 81–87.

Gerschenkron, Alexander. *Economic Backwardness in Historical Perspective, A Book of Essays*. Cambridge: Harvard University Press, 1962.

Gordeev, B. and A. Galanov. "The Growth of Exports of Machine-building Goods," *Vneshniaia Torgovlia [Foreign Trade]*, v. 28, no. 11, November 1958, pp. 30–41.

Griffith, William E. *Albania and the Sino-Soviet Rift*. Cambridge: M.I.T. Press, 1963.

Hambaraci, Arslan. "Chou's Mediterranean Tour," *Far Eastern Economic Review*, v. 43, no. 4, January 23, 1964, pp. 153–155.

Hirschman, A. O. *The Strategy of Economic Development*. New Haven: Yale University Press, 1958.

Ho, P. T. *Studies on the Population of China, 1368–1953*. Cambridge: Harvard University Press, 1959.

Hodgman, D. R. *Soviet Industrial Production, 1928–1951*. Cambridge: Harvard University Press, 1954.

Hoeffding, Oleg. "Sino-Soviet Economic Relations in Recent Years" in Kurt London, ed., *Unity and Contradiction: Major Aspects of Sino-Soviet Relations*. New York: Praeger, 1962. Pp. 295–312.

Hoeffding, Oleg, and Nancy Nimitz. *Soviet National Income and Product, 1949–1955*. RAND Research Memorandum, RM 2101. Santa Monica: RAND Corporation, April 6, 1959.

Hollister, W. W. *China's Gross National Product and Social Accounts, 1950–1957*. Glencoe, Ill.: Free Press, 1958.

Holzman, F. D. "Soviet Foreign Trade Pricing and the Question of Discrimination, A 'Customs Union' Approach," *The Review of Economics and Statistics*, v. 44, no. 2, May 1962, pp. 134–147.

——. "Some Financial Aspects of Soviet Foreign Trade" in *Comparisons of the United States and Soviet Economies,* pt. 2. Papers Submitted by Panelists Appearing before the Subcommittee on Economic Statistics, Joint Economic Committee, U.S. Congress, 86th Cong., 1st sess. Washington: GPO, 1959. Pp. 427–443.

Hudson, Geoffrey, ed. *The Chinese Communes.* London: Issued under the Auspices of *Soviet Survey,* 1960.

Hughes, T. J. and D. E. T. Luard. *The Economic Development of Communist China, 1949–1960.* 2nd ed.; London: Oxford University Press, 1961.

Hunsberger, Warren. *Japan and the United States in World Trade.* New York: Harper and Row for the Council on Foreign Relations, 1964.

Institut für Asienkunde (Hamburg). *Die Wirtschaftliche Verflechtung der Volksrepublik China mit der Sowjetunion* [*The Economic Links of the People's Republic of China with the Soviet Union*]. Frankfurt am Main: Alfred Metzner Verlag, 1959.

Jasny, Naum. *The Socialized Agriculture of the USSR.* Stanford University Press, 1949.

Johnston, Bruce F. "Agricultural Productivity and Economic Development in Japan," *Journal of Political Economy,* v. 59, no. 6, December 1961, pp. 498–513.

Jones, P. H. M. "Albania, Asia in Europe," *Far Eastern Economic Review,* v. 42, no. 2, October 10, 1963, pp. 63–65.

Jones, Philip P. and Thomas T. Poleman. "Communes and the Agricultural Crisis in Communist China," *Food Research Institute Studies* (Stanford), v. 3, no. 1, February 1962, pp. 3–22.

Kapelinski, Yu. and others. *Razvitie Ekonomiki i Vneshneekonomicheskikh Sviazei Kitaiskoi Narodnoi Respublike* [*The Development of the Economy and Foreign Economic Relations of the Chinese People's Republic*]. Moscow: Vneshtorgizdat, 1961.

Kaplan, N. M. and E. S. Weinstein. "A Comparison of Soviet and American Retail Prices in 1950," *Journal of Political Economy,* v. 46, no. 6, December 1956, pp. 470–491.

Kaplan, N. M. and W. L. White. *A Comparison of 1950 Wholesale Prices in Soviet and American Industry.* RAND Research Memorandum, RM-1443. Santa Monica: RAND Corporation, May 1, 1955.

Kindleberger, C. P. *Foreign Trade and the National Economy.* New Haven: Yale University Press, 1962.

Klochko, M. A. *Soviet Scientist in Red China.* New York: Praeger, 1964.

Kuznets, Simon. "Quantitative Aspects of the Economic Growth of Nations: IX. Level and Structure of Foreign Trade: Comparisons for Recent Years," *Economic Development and Cultural Change,* v. 13, no. 1, October 1964, pt. 2, pp. 1–106.

Li, C. M. *The Statistical System of Communist China.* Berkeley: University of California Press, 1962.

Liu, T. C. and K. C. Yeh. *The Economy of the Chinese Mainland: National Income and Economic Development, 1933–1959.* Princeton University Press, 1965.

MacDougall, Colina. "Eight Plants for Peking," *Far Eastern Economic Review,* v. 43, no. 4, January 23, 1964, pp. 155–158.

Mah, F. H. "The First Five-Year Plan and its International Aspects" in C. F. Remer, ed., *International Economics of Communist China.* Ann Arbor: University of Michigan Press, 1959. Pp. 31–117.

——. *Communist China's Foreign Trade, Price Structure and Behavior, 1955–1959.* RAND Research Memorandum, 3825-RC. Santa Monica: RAND Corporation, October 1963.

Meier, G. M. and R. E. Baldwin. *Economic Development.* New York: Wiley, 1957.

Mendershausen, Horst. "Terms of Trade Between the Soviet Union and Smaller Communist Countries, 1955–1957," *Review of Economics and Statistics,* v. 41, no. 2, May 1959, pp. 106–118.

——. "The Terms of Soviet-Satellite Trade: A Broadened Analysis," *Review of Economics and Statistics,* v. 42, no. 2, May 1960, pp. 152–163.

Moneta, Carmellah. "The Estimation of Transportation Costs in International Trade," *Journal of Political Economy,* v. 67, no. 1, February 1959, pp. 41–58.

Moorsteen, Richard. *Prices and Production of Machinery in the Soviet Union, 1928–1958.* Cambridge: Harvard University Press for the RAND Corporation, 1962.

Müller, Kurt. *Entwicklungshilfe innerhalb des Ostblocks [Development Assistance within the Eastern Bloc].* Frankfurt am Main: Alfred Metzner Verlag, 1960.

Nelson, R. R. "A Theory of the Low-level Equilibrium Trap," *American Economic Review,* v. 46, no. 5, December 1956, pp. 894–908.

Ni, Ernest. *Distribution of the Urban and Rural Population of Mainland China, 1953 and 1958.* International Population Reports, series P-95, no. 56. Washington, D.C.: U.S. Bureau of the Census, 1960.

Orleans, Leo. *Professional Manpower and Education in Communist China.* Washington, D.C.: GPO, 1961.

Pauley, Edwin W. *Report on Japanese Assets in Manchuria to the President of the United States.* Washington, D.C.: GPO, July 1946.

Pryor, F. L. *The Communist Foreign Trade System.* Cambridge: M.I.T. Press, 1963.

Reischauer, Edwin O. *Ennin's Travels in T'ang China.* New York: Ronald Press Company, 1955.

Remer, C. F. *The Trade Agreements of Communist China.* RAND P-2208. Santa Monica: RAND Corporation, February 1, 1961.

Scalapino, Robert A. "Sino-Soviet Competition in Africa," *Foreign Affairs,* v. 42, no. 4, July 1964, pp. 640–654.

Schumpeter, E. B. and others. *The Industrialization of Japan and Manchukuo, 1930–1940.* New York: Macmillan, 1940.

Schurmann, H. F. "Peking's Recognition of Crisis," *Problems of Communism,* v. 10, no. 5, September/October 1961, pp. 5–14.

Shen, T. H. *Agricultural Resources of China.* Ithaca, N.Y.: Cornell University Press, 1951.

Skripnik, V. "Scientific-Technical Cooperation of the USSR with Socialist Countries," *Vneshniaia Torgovlia,* v. 30, no. 2, February 1960, pp. 9–14.

Sladkovskii, M. I. "Chinese Economic Cooperation," *Problemi Vostokovedeniia [Problems of Oriental Studies],* July 1960, pp. 108–117.

——. "The Development of the Soviet Union's Trade with the Chinese People's Republic," *Vneshniaia Torgovlia,* v. 29, no. 10, October 1959, pp. 2–10.

——. "Indestructible Soviet-Chinese Friendship," *Vneshniaia Torgovlia,* v. 27, no. 2, February 1957, pp. 2–4.

——. *Ocherki Ekonomicheskikh Otnoshenii SSSR s Kitaem* [*Essays on the Economic Relations of the USSR with China*]. Moscow: Vneshtorgizdat, 1957.

Smirnov, A. *International Currency and Credit Relations of the USSR*. U.S. Joint Publication Research Service, no. 4147. Washington, D.C.: U.S. Joint Publication Research Service, October 31, 1960.

——. "The Soviet Union's Technical Assistance in the Construction of Enterprises Abroad," *Vneshniaia Torgovlia*, v. 29, no. 9, September 1959, pp. 8–15.

Sun, Norman. "Prospects and Problems of Trade Between Japan and Mainland China" in E. F. Szczepanik, ed., *Symposium on Economic and Social Problems of the Far East: Proceedings of a Meeting Held in September 1961 as Part of the Golden Jubilee Congress of the University of Hong Kong*. Hong Kong University Press, 1962. Pp. 142–152.

Tretiak, Daniel. "China's Latin American Trade," *Far Eastern Economic Review*, v. 41, no. 4, July 25, 1963, pp. 221–224.

Ullman, M. B. *Cities of Mainland China, 1953 and 1958*. International Population Reports, series P-95, no. 59. Washington, D.C.: U.S. Bureau of the Census, August 1961.

Walker, K. R. *Planning in Chinese Agriculture, Socialization and the Private Sector, 1956–1962*. London: Frank Cass and Company, Ltd., 1965.

Wilbur, C. Martin. "Japan and the Rise of Communist China" in Hugh Borton, ed., *Japan Between East and West*. New York: Harper and Brothers, 1957. Pp. 199–239.

Wolfstone, Daniel. "Sino-African Economics," *Far Eastern Economic Review*, v. 43, no. 7, February 13, 1964, pp. 349–351.

Wu, Y. L. *The Economic Potential of Communist China*. Stanford Research Institute, 1963.

Yin, Helen and Y. C. Yin. *Economic Statistics of Mainland China, 1949–1957*. Cambridge: Harvard University Press, 1960.

III. Newspapers and Periodicals

American Economic Review, Evanston, Illinois.

The China Quarterly, London.

Current Background (American Consulate General, Hong Kong), Hong Kong.

Current Digest of the Soviet Press, Ann Arbor, Michigan.

Current Scene, Hong Kong.

Economic Bulletin for Asia and the Far East (United Nations, Economic Commission for Asia and the Far East), Bangkok.

Economic Bulletin for Europe (United Nations, Economic Commission for Europe), Geneva.

Economic Development and Cultural Change, Chicago.

The Economist, London.

Far Eastern Economic Review, Hong Kong.

Foreign Affairs, New York.

Foreign Agriculture (U.S. Department of Agriculture), Washington, D.C.

Hong Kong Trade Bulletin (Hong Kong, Department of Commerce and Industry), Hong Kong.

344

Hong Kong Trade Statistics, Exports (Hong Kong, Department of Commerce and Industry), Hong Kong.
International Financial Statistics (International Monetary Fund), Washington, D.C.
The Japan Times, Tokyo.
Journal of Political Economy, Chicago.
The New York Times, New York.
Pacific Affairs, Vancouver.
Pravda [*Truth*], Moscow.
Problemi Vostokovedeniia [*Problems of Oriental Studies*], Moscow.
Problems of Communism, Washington, D.C.
Reports (U.S. Joint Publications Research Service), Washington, D.C.
Review of Economics and Statistics, Cambridge, Mass.
Rubber Statistical Bulletin, London.
Survey of the China Mainland Press (American Consulate General, Hong Kong), Hong Kong.
Vneshniaia Torgovlia [*Foreign Trade*], Moscow.
World Politics, Princeton.

Index of Names

Index

Note: The words "China" and "Chinese" have in most instances been omitted from the index, and it should be understood that "Political organization," for example, means "Chinese political organization" unless otherwise described. Data in the tables have not been indexed; for their contents, see the list of tables in the front matter.

PUBLICATIONS

FOREIGN AFFAIRS (quarterly), edited by Hamilton Fish Armstrong.

THE UNITED STATES IN WORLD AFFAIRS (annual). Volumes for 1931, 1932 and 1933, by Walter Lippmann and William O. Scroggs; for 1934–1935, 1936, 1937, 1938, 1939 and 1940, by Whitney H. Shepardson and William O. Scroggs; for 1945–1947, 1947–1948 and 1948–1949, by John C. Campbell; for 1949, 1950, 1951, 1952, 1953 and 1954, by Richard P. Stebbins; for 1955, by Hollis W. Barber; for 1956, 1957, 1958, 1959, 1960, 1961, 1962 and 1963, by Richard P. Stebbins, for 1964, by Jules Davids.

DOCUMENTS ON AMERICAN FOREIGN RELATIONS (annual). Volume for 1952 edited by Clarence W. Baier and Richard P. Stebbins; for 1953 and 1954, edited by Peter V. Curl; for 1955, 1956, 1957, 1958 and 1959, edited by Paul E. Zinner; for 1960, 1961, 1962 and 1963, edited by Richard P. Stebbins, for 1964, by Jules Davids.

POLITICAL HANDBOOK AND ATLAS OF THE WORLD (annual), edited by Walter H. Mallory.

INTERNATIONAL POLITICAL COMMUNICATION, by W. Phillips Davison (1965).

MONETARY REFORM FOR THE WORLD ECONOMY, by Robert V. Roosa (1965).

AFRICAN BATTLELINE: American Policy Choices in Southern Africa, by Waldemar A. Nielsen (1965).

NATO IN TRANSITION: The Future of the Atlantic Alliance, by Timothy W. Stanley (1965).

ALTERNATIVE TO PARTITION: For a Broader Conception of America's Role in Europe, by Zbigniew Brzezinski (1965).

THE TROUBLED PARTNERSHIP: A Re-Appraisal of the Atlantic Alliance, by Henry A. Kissinger (1965).

REMNANTS OF EMPIRE: The United Nations and the End of Colonialism, by David W. Wainhouse (1965).

THE EUROPEAN COMMUNITY AND AMERICAN TRADE: A Study in Atlantic Economics and Policy, by Randall Hinshaw (1964).

THE FOURTH DIMENSION OF FOREIGN POLICY: Educational and Cultural Affairs, by Philip H. Coombs (1964).

AMERICAN AGENCIES INTERESTED IN INTERNATIONAL AFFAIRS (Fifth Edition), compiled by Donald Wasson (1964).

JAPAN AND THE UNITED STATES IN WORLD TRADE, by Warren S. Hunsberger (1964).

FOREIGN AFFAIRS BIBLIOGRAPHY, 1952–1962, by Henry L. Roberts (1964).

THE DOLLAR IN WORLD AFFAIRS: An Essay in International Financial Policy, by Henry G. Aubrey (1964).

ON DEALING WITH THE COMMUNIST WORLD, by George F. Kennan (1964).

FOREIGN AID AND FOREIGN POLICY, by Edward S. Mason (1964).

THE SCIENTIFIC REVOLUTION AND WORLD POLITICS, by Caryl P. Haskins (1964).

AFRICA: A Foreign Affairs Reader, edited by Philip W. Quigg (1964).

THE PHILIPPINES AND THE UNITED STATES: Problems of Partnership, by George E. Taylor (1964).

SOUTHEAST ASIA IN UNITED STATES POLICY, by Russell H. Fifield (1963).

UNESCO: ASSESSMENT AND PROMISE, by George N. Shuster (1963).

THE PEACEFUL ATOM IN FOREIGN POLICY, by Arnold Kramish (1963).

THE ARABS AND THE WORLD: Nasser's Arab Nationalist Policy, by Charles D. Cremeans (1963).

TOWARD AN ATLANTIC COMMUNITY, by Christian A. Herter (1963).

THE SOVIET UNION, 1922–1962: A Foreign Affairs Reader, edited by Philip E. Mosely (1963).

THE POLITICS OF FOREIGN AID: American Experience in Southeast Asia, by John D. Montgomery (1962).

SPEARHEADS OF DEMOCRACY: Labor in the Developing Countries, by George C. Lodge (1962).

LATIN AMERICA: Diplomacy and Reality, by Adolf A. Berle (1962).

THE ORGANIZATION OF AMERICAN STATES AND THE HEMISPHERE CRISIS, by John C. Dreier (1962).

THE UNITED NATIONS: Structure for Peace, by Ernest A. Gross (1962).

THE LONG POLAR WATCH: Canada and the Defense of North America, by Melvin Conant (1962).

ARMS AND POLITICS IN LATIN AMERICA (Revised Edition), by Edwin Lieuwen (1961).

THE FUTURE OF UNDERDEVELOPED COUNTRIES: Political Implications of Economic Development (Revised Edition), by Eugene Staley (1961).

SPAIN AND DEFENSE OF THE WEST: Ally and Liability, by Arthur P. Whitaker (1961).

SOCIAL CHANGE IN LATIN AMERICA TODAY: Its Implications for United States Policy, by Richard N. Adams, John P. Gillin, Allan R. Holmberg, Oscar Lewis, Richard W. Patch, and Charles W. Wagley (1961).

FOREIGN POLICY: THE NEXT PHASE: The 1960s (Revised Edition), by Thomas K. Finletter (1960).

DEFENSE OF THE MIDDLE EAST: Problems of American Policy (Revised Edition), by John C. Campbell (1960).

COMMUNIST CHINA AND ASIA: Challenge to American Policy, by A. Doak Barnett (1960).

FRANCE, TROUBLED ALLY: De Gaulle's Heritage and Prospects, by Edgar S. Furniss, Jr. (1960).

THE SCHUMAN PLAN: A Study in Economic Cooperation, 1950–1959, by William Diebold, Jr. (1959).

SOVIET ECONOMIC AID: The New Aid and Trade Policy in Underdeveloped Countries, by Joseph S. Berliner. (1958).

RAW MATERIALS: A Study of American Policy, by Percy W. Bidwell (1958).

NATO AND THE FUTURE OF EUROPE, by Ben T. Moore (1958).

AFRICAN ECONOMIC DEVELOPMENT, by William Hance (1958).

INDIA AND AMERICA: A Study of Their Relations, by Phillips Talbot and S. L. Poplai (1958).

NUCLEAR WEAPONS AND FOREIGN POLICY, by Henry A. Kissinger (1957).

MOSCOW-PEKING AXIS: Strength and Strains, by Howard L. Boorman, Alexander Eckstein, Philip E. Mosely and Benjamin Schwartz (1957).

RUSSIA AND AMERICA: Dangers and Prospects, by Henry L. Roberts (1956).